East Asia's New Democrac

MW00683069

This collection brings us up to date on the contemporary situations in the new democracies of East Asia, and debates the prospect of introducing liberal democracy to this part of the world. The chapters cover a wide range of cases, including in-depth examinations of China, Korea, Taiwan, the Philippines, Thailand, and broad comparisons of Malaysia, Singapore, Indonesia, Vietnam, and other countries.

The contributors, who are foremost experts in their fields, examine the roles performed by civil society, social classes, and strategic groups, as well as the intertwining of values and interests in the transition to, consolidation of, and reversal from democracy. They also evaluate the extent to which these new democracies have facilitated regional peace, helped extend social welfare benefits, bolstered poverty alleviation, and upheld the rule of law and human rights. Grounding their analyses in the historical development of these societies, and/or examining them through the comparative strategy, they also explore the desirability of liberal democracy, whether in the subjective assessment of the Asian people or in relation to the social-political challenges faced by these Asian countries.

East Asia's New Democracies will be of interest to students and scholars of comparative politics, political science, political sociology, East and Southeast Asian studies.

Yin-wah Chu is Associate Professor at the Department of Sociology, Hong Kong Baptist University.

Siu-lun Wong is Professor and Director of the Centre of Asian Studies, University of Hong Kong.

Politics in Asia series

Formerly edited by Michael Leifer
London School of Economics

Islam in Malaysian Foreign Policy
Shanti Nair

Political Change in Thailand
Democracy and participation
Kevin Hewison

The Politics of NGOs in Southeast Asia
Participation and protest in the Philippines
Gerard Clarke

Malaysian Politics Under Mahathir
R. S. Milne and Diane K. Mauzy

Indonesia and China
The politics of a troubled relationship
Rizal Sukma

Arming the Two Koreas
State, capital and military power
Taik-young Hamm

Engaging China
The management of an emerging power
Edited by Alastair Iain Johnston and Robert S. Ross

Singapore's Foreign Policy
Coping with vulnerability
Michael Leifer

Philippine Politics and Society in the Twentieth Century
Colonial legacies, post-colonial trajectories
Eva-Lotta E. Hedman and John T. Sidel

Constructing a Security Community in Southeast Asia
ASEAN and the problem of regional order
Amitav Acharya

Monarchy in South East Asia
The faces of tradition in transition
Roger Kershaw

Korea After the Crash
The politics of economic recovery
Brian Bridges

The Future of North Korea
Edited by Tsuneo Akaha

The International Relations of Japan and South East Asia
Forging a new regionalism
Sueo Sudo

Power and Change in Central Asia
Edited by Sally N. Cummings

The Politics of Human Rights in Southeast Asia
Philip Eldridge

Political Business in East Asia
Edited by Edmund Terence Gomez

Singapore Politics under the People's Action Party
Diane K. Mauzy and R. S. Milne

Media and Politics in Pacific Asia
Duncan McCargo

Japanese Governance
Beyond Japan inc
Edited by Jennifer Amyx and Peter Drysdale

China and the Internet
Politics of the digital leap forward
Edited by Christopher R. Hughes and Gudrun Wacker

Challenging Authoritarianism in Southeast Asia
Comparing Indonesia and Malaysia
Edited by Ariel Heryanto and Sumit K. Mandal

East Asia's New Democracies

Deepening, reversal, non-liberal alternatives

Edited by Yin-wah Chu and Siu-lun Wong

LONDON AND NEW YORK

First published 2010
by Routledge
2 Park Square, Milton Park, Abingdon, Oxon OX14 4RN

Simultaneously published in the USA and Canada
by Routledge
270 Madison Avenue, New York, NY 10016

*Routledge is an imprint of the Taylor & Francis Group,
an informa business*

Typeset in Times by
RefineCatch Limited, Bungay, Suffolk
Printed and bound in Great Britain by
CPI Antony Rowe, Chippenham, Wiltshire

British Library Cataloguing in Publication Data
A catalogue record for this book is available
from the British Library

Library of Congress Cataloging-in-Publication Data
East Asia's new democracies : deepening, reversal, non-liberal
alternatives / edited by Yin-wah Chu and Siu-lun Wong.
    p. cm.
  1. Democracy—East Asia.   2. East Asia—Politics and
government.   I. Chu, Yin-wah.   II. Wong, Siu-lun.
JQ1499.A91E23 2010
320.95—dc22   2009040594

ISBN 10: 0–415–49930–5 (hbk)
ISBN 10: 0–415–49931–3 (pbk)
ISBN 10: 0–203–85451–9 (ebk)

ISBN 13: 978–0–415–49930–9 (hbk)
ISBN 13: 978–0–415–49931–6 (pbk)
ISBN 13: 978–0–203–85451–8 (ebk)

Contents

Figures

Tables

Contributors

Amitav Acharya is Professor of International Relations at the School of International Service, American University, Washington, DC. His recent publications include: *Constructing a Security Community in Southeast Asia*, 2nd edition (Routledge, 2009) and *Whose Ideas Matter: Agency and Power in Asian Regionalism* (Cornell, 2009). E-mail: aacharya@american.edu.

Ledivina V. Cariño (1942–2009) was Professor of Public Administration at the National College of Public Administration and Governance of the University of the Philippines, Diliman. She was also a founding Board Member and first alternate chair of the Community Policy Research South (CPRsouth). In addition to her academic commitments, she was the vice president of the Executive Council, National Academy of Science and Technology and the chair of the Technical Panel for Public Administration, Commission on Higher Education, Philippines from 2005.

Yin-wah Chu is Associate Professor at the Department of Sociology, Hong Kong Baptist University. She researches aspects of East Asian development, paying particular attention to changing state–business relationships, labor movements, and environmental movements. Her articles have been published in *Asian Survey*, *Economy and Society*, *International Journal of Urban and Regional Research*, *Journal of Contemporary Asia*, and *Urban Studies*. In addition to the present book, she is editing a collection entitled *Chinese Capitalisms* to be published by Palgrave Macmillan in 2010. E-mail: ywchu@hkbu.edu.hk; yinw.chu@gmail.com.

Chua Beng Huat, Provost's Professor, Faculty of Arts and Social Science, is concurrently Head, Department of Sociology and Leader, Cultural Studies in Asia Research Cluster, Asia Research Institute, National University of Singapore. He has published widely in urban planning and public housing, comparative politics in Southeast Asia and the emerging consumerism across Asia. His books include among others, *Communitarian Ideology and Democracy in Singapore* (Routledge, 1995), *Political*

Legitimacy and Housing: Stakeholding in Singapore (Routledge, 1997), and *Life is Not Complete without Shopping* (Singapore University Press, 2003). He is founding coeditor of the journal, *Inter-Asia Cultural Studies*. E-mail: soccbh@nus.edu.sg.

Bruce Cumings teaches international history, modern Korean history and East Asian political economy at the University of Chicago. He is the author of the two-volume study, *The Origins of the Korean War* (Princeton University Press, 1981, 1990), *War and Television* (Visal-Routledge, 1992), *Korea's Place in the Sun: A Modern History* (W. W. Norton, 1997; updated edn., 2006), *Parallax Visions: Making Sense of American–East Asian Relations* (Duke University Press, 1999; paperback 2002), *North Korea: Another Country* (New Press, 2003), coauthored *Inventing the Axis of Evil* (New Press, 2004), and his new book, *Dominion from Sea to Sea: Pacific Ascendancy and American Power*, has been published by Yale University Press in October 2009. E-mail: rufus88@uchicago.edu.

Kevin Hewison completed his Ph.D. in 1984 at Murdoch University. He is currently Director of the Carolina Asia Center at the University of North Carolina at Chapel Hill. He is an adjunct professor at Murdoch University and the University of New England. His current research interests include: globalization and social change in Southeast Asia, especially Thailand; democratization; and labor issues. He is the author of more than 150 publications on Southeast Asia, democratization and globalization. E-mail: khewison@unc.edu.

Ming-sho Ho is Associate Professor in the Department of Sociology, National Taiwan University. He researches Taiwan's labor movement, environmental movement, and education reform, and his works are published in *China Quarterly, China Journal, Journal of Political and Military Sociology*, and *Environment and Planning A*. E-mail: mingshoho@gmail .com.

Jude Howell is Professor and Director of the Centre for Civil Society, The London School of Economics and Political Science, and is also Director of the Economic and Social Research Council (ESRC)'s Non-Governmental Public Action Research Program. Her main research interests include civil society and governance, politics of international development policy and practice, gender, and political participation. Her recent publications include *Governance in China* (Rowman and Littlefield, 2003), *Gender and Civil Society* (Routledge, 2004), and coauthored with Jeremy Lind *Counter-terrorism, Aid and Civil Society: Before and After the War on Terror* (Palgrave Macmillan, 2009). E-mail: J.A.Howell@lse.ac.uk.

Hsin-Huang Michael Hsiao is currently Executive Director of the Center for Asia-Pacific Area Studies and Research Fellow of Sociology, both in Academia Sinica, and Professor of Sociology, National Taiwan University. His research areas include civil society and new democracy, middle classes, sustainable development of island societies. Prof. Hsiao's most recent books are: *Non-Profit Sector: Organization and Practice* (coauthor, 2009), *Rise of China: Beijing's Strategies and Implications for the Asia-Pacific* (coeditor, 2009), *Asia-Pacific Peace Watch* (coeditor, 2008), and *Deepening Local Sustainable Development in Taiwan* (coeditor, 2008), among others. E-mail: michael@gate.sinica.edu.tw.

Hyug-Baeg Im, Ph.D. in politics, University of Chicago, is Professor at the Department of Political Science and International Relations, Korea University, Seoul, South Korea. He is a member of IPSA Executive Committee. He was Visiting Professor at Georgetown University, Duke University, and Stanford University. His publications include "The Rise of Bureaucratic Authoritarianism in South Korea," *World Politics*, Vol. 34, No. 2 (1987), "Faltering Democratic Consolidation in South Korea: Democracy at the End of Three Kims Era," *Democratization*, Vol. 11, No. 5 (2004), and "The US Role in Korean Democracy and Security since the Cold War Era," *International Relations of the Asia Pacific*, Vol. 6, No. 2 (2006). E-mail: hyugim@paran.com.

Takashi Inoguchi, Ph.D. (M.I.T.), President of the University of Niigata Prefecture, is a political scientist who has published 80 books and numerous articles among which the latest include *Globalization, Public Opinion and the State* (Routledge, 2008), *Political Cultures in Asia and Europe* (Routledge, 2006), *Citizens and the State* (Routledge, 2008), *Federalism in Asia* (Edward Elgar, 2007), *Governance and Democracy in Asia* (Trans Pacific Press, 2006). He has directed the AsiaBarometer Survey project since 2004 and is the founding editor of two journals, *Japanese Journal of Political Science* (Cambridge University Press) and *International Relations of the Asia-Pacific* (Oxford University Press). He is also a member of the Science Council and the Legislative Council of the Japanese Government. E-mail: inoguchi@ioc.u-tokyo.ac.jp.

Satoru Mikami is Assistant Professor in the Faculty of Political Science and Economics at Waseda University. He received his Ph.D. in political science from Waseda University in 2006. His research focuses on macro-political change such as revolution, coup d'état, and democratization. E-mail: mikamisatoru@gmail.com.

Randall Peerenboom is Professor of Law at La Trobe University and Associate Fellow in the Socio-Legal Studies Centre at Oxford University. His recent books include *China Modernizes: Threat to the West or Model for the Rest?* (Oxford University Press, 2007) and *China's Long March toward Rule of Law* (Cambridge University Press, 2002). He has been a consultant to numerous international organizations on legal reforms and rule of law in China and Asia, and is the Co-Editor in Chief of *The Hague Journal of Rule of Law*. E-mail: rpeerenboom@gmail.com.

Mark R. Thompson is Professor of Politics at the University of Erlangen-Nuremberg and 2008–2009 Lee Kong Chian NUS-Stanford distinguished fellow for Southeast Asian studies. He is the author of *The Anti-Marcos Struggle* (1995) and *Democratic Revolutions* (2004). He is currently completing a manuscript about "late democratization" in Pacific Asia. E-mail: mark_euro@web.de.

Joseph Wong is Associate Professor of Political Science at the University of Toronto, where he holds a Canada Research Chair and is the Director of the Asian Institute. His books include *Healthy Democracies: Welfare Politics in Taiwan and South Korea* (Cornell University Press, 2004), and (with Edward Friedman) *Political Transitions in Dominant Party Systems: Learning to Lose* (Routledge, 2008). Wong is currently completing a book manuscript on the knowledge economy in Asia. E-mail: joe.wong@utoronto.ca.

Siu-lun Wong is Professor and Director of the Centre of Asian Studies at the University of Hong Kong. His research interests include the study of entrepreneurship, business networks, migration, social indicators, and the development of sociology in China. His books include, among others, *Sociology and Socialism in Contemporary China* (Routledge and K. Paul, 1979), *Emigrant Entrepreneurs: Shanghai Industrialists in Hong Kong* (Oxford University Press, 1988), *Hong Kong's Transition: A Decade after the Deal* (Oxford University Press, 1995), and *Hong Kong in the Asia-Pacific Region: Rising to the New Challenges* (Centre of Asian Studies, The University of Hong Kong 1997). E-mail: slwong@hkucc.hku.hk.

Acknowledgments

This collection is an outgrowth of an international conference, "The Experiments with Democracy in East and Southeast Asia: two decades after," organized by the Centre of Asian Studies (CAS) at the University of Hong Kong, and held between May 2 and 3, 2008. It was in 2006 that we began to consider the value and possibility of organizing such a conference. The reasoning was straightforward: the Philippines, Korea, Taiwan, and other East Asian societies have undergone democratic transitions about two decades ago; the two-decade interim is a good time to reexamine the processes of democratic transitions in and recent developments of these new democracies.

The organization of the conference has benefited much from the support of the research and clerical staff at the CAS. Gan Yan, Nick Thomas, Tsaiman Ho, and Chin Kong have given excellent advice on possible themes and prospective speakers, whereas Becky Fung, Cathy Wong, Teresa Tsai, and others have provided very competent assistance in the day-to-day organization of the meeting. On the financial front, we have received generous support from the Hang Seng Bank Golden Jubilee Education Fund for Research, and above all, the Chiang Ching-kuo Foundation for International Scholarly Exchange, without which the conference would never have taken place. However, it is to the conference participants that we owe the greatest debt. Their keen interest has kept the discussion lively and rendered the event valuable.

Most conference participants have continued to render support by consenting to contribute to this edited collection. The chapters have been written expressly for this volume, though parts of Randall Peerenboom's chapter have been taken from his book *China Modernizes: threat to the West or model for the rest?* (Oxford University Press, 2007), and for this we are thankful to the publisher. We are grateful that the authors have taken the trouble to revise their chapters in response to comments made by the anonymous reviewers solicited by the publisher and ourselves. Their efforts to address the issues raised by other contributing authors have, in addition, enhanced the coherence of the collection. One of the contributors, Professor Ledivina V. Cariño, died after a courageous battle with cancer. She made the effort to revise her chapter even as she was undergoing chemotherapy. We are most grateful to her for this. We consider her death a tremendous loss to the academic community, and are deeply sorry about this.

In planning the book and preparing the manuscript, we have benefited very much from the guidance rendered by Sonja van Leeuwen, Stephanie Rogers, and Leanne Hinves at Routledge. We also benefit from the suggestions made by the three anonymous reviewers, though we may not have addressed all the issues raised by them. Finally, Mike Poole and Tszming Or have provided very capable assistance in copy-editing, and relieved us from much of the burden in finalizing the manuscript. We are thankful to all of them.

Yin-wah Chu
Sociology, Hong Kong Baptist University
Siu-lun Wong
Centre of Asian Studies, University of Hong Kong

1 East Asia's new democracies

An introduction

Yin-wah Chu and Siu-lun Wong

Introduction

The third wave of democratization, begun in Portugal in 1974, has ignited a sequence of democratization and liberalization in Latin America, Africa, Asia, and more recently East-Central Europe. Within East and Southeast Asia, the process commenced with the 1986 People's Power Revolution in the Philippines and was succeeded by Korea's eight-point reform in 1987, the repeal of martial law in Taiwan in the same year, the introduction of two-party electoral competition in Mongolia during 1990, Thailand's return to civilian rule in 1992, and the downfall of the Suharto regime in the aftermath of the financial crisis. Malaysia, Singapore, and Hong Kong have also witnessed a certain measure of liberalization.[1]

For some observers, the third wave appears to be so powerful that they even talk of the triumph of democracy as if it marks the "end of history" (Fukuyama 1992). Yet, just like earlier democratization efforts, both the processes and outcomes have been problematic. Democratization has not taken place in cases where favorable conditions are present. Some of the new democracies have reverted to authoritarian rule, while the seemingly "consolidated" cases have continued to be afflicted by corruption, infringement of checks and balances, violation of human rights, political gridlock, ineffective administration, and failure to promote distributive justice. Wary of some of these problems, Huntington (1997) lamented two decades after the emergence of the third wave that most of the newly democratized countries were no more than electoral democracies where leaders acted arbitrarily, individual rights were suppressed and parochialism reinforced. Collier and Levitsky (1997) also suggest that "democracy with an adjective" such as hybrid-democracy, semi-democracy, illiberal democracy, elite democracy and the like has turned into a "growth industry" as more and more of the young democracies become mired in such situations (Zakaria 1997).

The contributors to this book have concentrated on the East and Southeast Asian societies that have undergone transitions to democracy in the last two decades, though one has examined the case of China. The questions addressed in these thirteen chapters include: What forces and processes are involved in these countries' quest for democracy? How well are East Asia's new democracies faring after about two decades of experimentation with the system? Why have some become consolidated, while a few have experienced reversals? Are they no more than electoral democracies that fail to address other substantive goals? Do East Asian societies face specific challenges that limit the applicability of liberal democracy? In addressing these issues, the authors necessarily enter into a dialogue with some of the emerging and long-standing theoretical debates on democracy and democratization.

This introductory chapter does not try to provide a comprehensive discussion and evaluation of the ongoing debates on democracy and democratization; the literature is too voluminous and complex to be tackled here. Instead, it highlights the major lines of inquiry as a backdrop, introduces the main arguments proposed in the twelve remaining chapters, and in the course of doing so, examines their opinions on specific controversies and the ways in which they help to advance the research agenda.

Democracy and democratization: East Asia and the ongoing debates

The third wave of democratization has inspired scholarly research from a multiplicity of academic disciplines, including history, international relations, law, philosophy, political science, and sociology, among others. Over the years, a most robust and divergent literature has emerged, both responding to the ongoing challenges to the new democracies and in relation to theories of democracy and democratization that predate the third wave. The literature is immense and it has been habitual to organize studies according to their explanatory concerns (transition, consolidation, quality) and levels of analysis (macro, meso, micro).

As the late Charles Tilly (2007) has argued eloquently, to analyze democracies according to their transition, consolidation, and quality implies a *procedural* conception of democracy. The popular election of top government officials and legislators is singled out as an important turning point, and the remaining tasks would be to identify the conditions that make possible the transition and the system's furtherance (see also Munck 2004). The procedural definition not only downplays the substantive aspects of democratization and other qualities of good governments, but its limitations also become obvious when applied to pre-third wave cases where the definition of democracy was a subject of much political and cultural contest, and suffrage was *extended* after a lengthy period of political contention (Buchanan and Conway 2002; Berg-Schlosser 2004; Held 2006; Tilly 2007). However, the possibility of directly electing top officials and legislators does denote a major transformation for the third wave cases and, just as important, contributors to this book have in one way or another geared their analyses to the prevalent literature. This collection accordingly organizes the chapters into two parts, with the first examining actors involved in the transition, consolidation, and reversal, and the second focusing on the achievements of and enduring challenges for these East Asian democracies. The issues addressed in the second part are relevant to the discussion on the quality of democracy and also touch on the debates on the applicability of liberal democracy to East Asia. As the following discussion shows, a few of the chapters actually address issues raised in both parts.

Transition, consolidation, reversal: actors then and now

Researchers seeking to explain the transition to democracy have examined factors at the macro, meso, and micro levels, with some of them analyzing the interaction of factors at more than one level. The macro-level analysis refers to a tradition of pre-third wave research that highlights the impacts of structural transformation on democratization. A most prolific line of inquiry has been proposed by Seymour Lipset (1959, 1994) and other students espousing the modernization perspective.[2] In their view, high levels of socioeconomic development, urbanization, and literacy are the necessary preconditions for the emergence of democracy. Criticizing the gradualist vision of the modernization approach, a second line of macro-level analysis has been advanced by neo-Marxists, who draw our attention to changes in class structure and the dynamic interaction among different classes. In his ground breaking comparative research, Barrington Moore (1966) has identified three routes to modernity and proclaims boldly "no bourgeois, no democracy." Extending this line of analysis to the late-developing countries, Rueschemeyer *et al.* (1992) argue that an alliance between the working and middle classes is more important (Koo 1991; Collier 1999).

Related to the analysis of class interaction are studies that focus on the meso-level of civil society and social movements (Keane 1988; Collier and Collier 1991; Hall 1995; Tarrow 1995; Cheng and Brown 2006). Civil society, defined broadly to encompass labor unions, social movements, religious groups, student organizations and so forth, has often sought social and political goals that may not relate immediately to political democracy. However, in wrestling for greater influence in the public sphere, they help to undermine authoritarian rule on both the political and cultural levels.

The most prevalent line of research on democratic transition in the third wave is, however, geared at the micro-level. Proponents, referred to as transitionists, usually examine the agency of a political elite, arguing that strategic choice and tactical interaction among the hardliners and softliners within both the regime and the opposition are more important than structural constellations of a society (Rustow 1970; O'Donnell and Schmitter 1986). Reviewing the literature, Huntington (1991) identifies four possible modes of transition: transformation, transplacement, replacement, and foreign intervention. Foreign intervention refers to situations in which countries democratize under the auspices of powerful foreign governments and, in some cases, foreign donors. The other three modes vary from an instance where the elite takes the initiative to democratize without facing any pressure, to one where

the political elite and opposition are more or less caught in a stalemate and
have to negotiate, and finally a case where the elite is practically overthrown
by the general public in the aftermath of an unresolved political or economic
crisis. Given the focus on the drama of transition, democracy is sought
explicitly by actors studied in this type of research, which is quite different
from studies at the macro or meso level.

In the present collection, the chapters by Jude Howell, Hsin-Huang Michael
Hsiao and Ming-sho Ho, Bruce Cumings, and Mark R. Thompson have all
devoted much attention to the actors facilitating the transition. However,
regardless of their position on "transitology," none focus on the strategic
interaction of the political elite. Similarly, despite the high level of economic
development in the cases they examine, no author subscribes to the modernization theory. Instead, they concur on the rather brute and simple fact that
democratization is a process of contention between regime power holders
and those being excluded. In this connection, these authors have expended
their efforts to examine civil society, social classes, and "strategic groups,"
and came up with rather divergent observations.

In Chapter 2, Jude Howell examines the case of China, which has yet to
undergo democratic transition, and puts forth an argument concerning the
rise of civil society, state response, and democratization. In her view, China's
economic reform is in a way similar to the liberalization of authoritarian
regimes. The structural changes so induced have posed serious governance
challenges, including the rise in social inequality, the limits of rapid growth as
the basis of legitimacy, the increasing number of social protests, and escalating demands for political reform. Civil society, in addition to being shielded
by the country's more liberal political and economic environments, has
also been reorganized as networks and projects of welfare provision in the
aftermath of the Tiananmen incident, rendering its containment by the
party-state's outmoded Leninist "mass organizations" difficult. In the midst
of these gathering domestic forces, Howell identifies an important role to be
played by international ones. Not only has China found it difficult to control
the flow of information through the internet and civil society's efforts at
international networking, but the country's growing gravity in global matters
has placed it under the international spotlight. As a result, there has emerged
a constant ebb and flow between the party-state and society in contesting for
an increase in the public sphere. However, it is Howell's contention that
China is unlikely to introduce Western liberal democracy in the foreseeable
future. Given the party-state's astuteness in making ideological and political
shifts and its concern for maintaining social stability, it might undertake
selective political liberalization by introducing what might be called reformed
authoritarianism.

Focusing on the case of Taiwan in Chapter 3, Hsin-Huang Michael Hsiao
and Ming-sho Ho also explore the relationships between civil society and
democratization.[3] Seeking to make a meaningful contribution to the literature,
which in their view has been mired by a rather non-specific usage of the civil

society concept and a failure to examine civil society in the political institutional context, the authors seek to undertake a "comprehensive historical
analysis of the link between civil society and democracy-making in one particular new democracy" (p. 45). In six stages, they trace the development of
Taiwan from a situation where civil society was practically non-existent in the
1960s to the first decade of the twenty-first century when social movements
and protest activities became a normal aspect of life. In general, Hsiao and
Ho concur with the transitionists that liberalization and democratization
prove to be critical turning points after which many more civil society organizations emerge and some become politicized. They also agree with the
optimists that civil society was vital in preventing the Kuomintang (KMT)
from pursuing a conservative backlash in the late 1990s and that, despite
its tension-ridden relationships with both the KMT and the Democratic
Progressive Party (DPP), it has managed to help deepen Taiwan's democracy
at a later stage. Furthermore, despite the surfacing of conservative mobilization in the early 2000s, this materialized in only sporadic instances.

Although Howell, Hsiao and Ho focus on civil society, it is notable
that while Howell makes no distinction between the state-sponsored All
China Women's Federation and networks that provide services to migrant
workers, save for the party-state's greater difficulty in maintaining surveillance
over the latter, Hsiao and Ho come up with a more differentiated view of civil
society. They consider it possible to differentiate civil society in terms of its
social class dispositions: middle class, grassroots, and "conservative," and
contend that not only have the middle-class and grassroots civil society gone
their own ways, but the conservative segment has even mobilized against
further democratization.

Like Howell, Hsiao and Ho, Bruce Cumings also draws our attention in
Chapter 4 to social forces that have attended Korea's democratization. Leading readers through a tour of historical documents and personal observations, Cumings provides a moving account of how peasants staged popular
resistance as early as the 1890s and how indiscriminate suppression of
"communists" on the part of the American military government fueled
the resentment of peasants toward both the Americans and the landlords/
capitalists they supported. Students and workers came gradually onto the
scene, protesting against harsh authoritarian domination, economic exploit-
ation, and the Americans who benefited from and provided staunch support
to the regimes. Although Cumings does not use the term civil society, he
would certainly side with Hsiao and Ho, rather than Howell, in preferring a
more differentiated treatment of civil society. Furthermore, in arguing that
Korea's democratization has deep historical roots, and that peasants, workers,
and students have spearheaded the resistance, Cumings treads a rather narrow
theoretical path. On the one hand, although he introduces a distinct geopolitical angle, he argues against the transitionists who have placed too much
weight on the American government's last-minute support and the authoritarian regime's liberalization in the 1980s, while on the other, he disagrees

with the argument of Rueschemeyer *et al.* (1992) and other structuralists that the middle class plays a most crucial role in the democratization of late-developing countries.

Moving on to Chapter 5, Mark R. Thompson undertakes an ambitious paired comparison of actors in the democratic transition and consolidation of ten Pacific Asian cases. In his view, although these cases appear to support the modernization theory, a closer examination reveals that while some countries democratize at too low a level of economic development, others are too wealthy not to democratize. Taking inspiration from Barrington Moore and seeking to bridge the gap with the actor-centered approach, he analyzes the political contention between regime power holders, student activists, religious authorities, and other actors who constitute what the German Bielefeld School has called "strategic groups." Democratic transition, in this analysis, is a function of the unity and adroitness of the political elite on the one hand, and the unity and social origins of the opposition on the other hand. Early democratization in the Philippines and Thailand is made possible by an opposition led/backed by the business elite and religious groups. Lacking such leadership, the middle class-based opposition in Korea and Taiwan can only achieve democratization at a later stage. In turn, whereas Indonesia's split elite has found it difficult to withstand challenges posed by the less strategically threatening student-led opposition, the juxtaposition of divided oppositions with the unified state elite in Singapore, Hong Kong, and Malaysia have much delayed their democratization.[4] As for China and Vietnam, Thompson believes the state elite have tried to imitate Singapore's authoritarianism, which if successful would support Przeworski and Limongi's (1997) arguments on authoritarian stability. Thompson also uses the same approach at the end of the chapter to outline a path-dependent analysis of the countries' democratic consolidation. Taken together, although not everyone would agree with his analysis,[5] Thompson's effort to introduce the idea of "strategic groups" and analyze their political contention represents an admirable attempt on two fronts. First, the concept presents a way to overcome the oft-noted difficulty in the structural analysis of democratization that not all players are class actors and, conversely, not all class actors have sought political democracy (Rokkan 1996). Second, Thompson's analysis also represents a first step at integrating a general analysis. The latter, according to Tilly (2007), is a long-standing difficulty in the historical-comparative study of democratization, which has an abundant supply of excellent studies that delineate the political orientations of particular social classes or communal groups in concrete situations.[6]

Consolidation and reversal

The issue of democratic consolidation and reversal, implied by Hsiao and Ho and explored in passing by Thompson, is formally taken up by Hyug-Baeg Im and Kevin Hewison. Indeed, given the pervasiveness of breakdown and reversal among the new democracies, students of the third wave have devoted much attention to these phenomena. Unfortunately, the meaning of consolidation has been much contested (Munck 2004). Whereas Huntington (1991) considers a democracy to be consolidated when it has passed the "two turn-over test," Linz and Stepan (1996) contend that:

> democratic transition is complete when sufficient agreement has been reached about political procedures to produce an elected government, when a government comes to power that is the direct result of a free and popular vote, and when this government *de facto* has the authority to generate new policies, and when the executive, legislative, and judicial power generated by the new democracy does not have to share power with other bodies *de jure*.
>
> (Linz and Stepan 1996: 3)

Linz and Stepan's definition, in the view of some observers, implies the institutionalization of procedures for open political competition, multi-party contest, and legally guaranteed civil and political rights—all of which are manifested at the constitutional, behavioral, and attitudinal levels (Haynes 2001; see also Sørensen 1998). Given the divergent usages, countries considered to be consolidated by one definition would be considered otherwise by another.[7] Not only do these divergent definitions threaten to confound the concept of democratic consolidation with democratic stability and the quality of democracy, but they also make it difficult to compare and evaluate research findings.

Like the research on democratic transition, studies of democratic consolidation have also proceeded at the macro, meso, and micro levels. Examining the phenomenon's unique features, Tilly (2007) inadvertently puts forth a micro-level analysis when he notes that while democratization involves the promotion of social inclusion and sharing of political power for the general public, which tends to be a lengthy process, democratic breakdown hinges on dissents among the elite, which tend to occur rapidly. Concurring on the significance of elite dissent, Karl (1990) pays particular attention to the mode of transition, arguing that a transition that allows the traditional elite to retain at least part of their power is more conducive to democratic stability (see also Higley and Gunther 1992; Mainwaring *et al.* 1992). Apart from examining the political elite, scholars have also paid much attention to the institutional setup and prospects for political crafting. There has been much debate on the merits of different electoral systems (Di Palma 1990; Reilly 2007), the pros and cons of presidential versus parliamentary governments (Linz and Valenzuela 1994; Stepan and Linz 2001, and Stepan and Skach 2001), and the stabilizing impact of the presence of a small number of programmatic, rather than personalistic, political parties (Schmitter 1992; Mainwaring and Scully 1995; Lijphart 1999).

Finally, observers have also looked to structural factors and collective

action for explanation. For instance, Przeworski (1991) suggests that democratic consolidation is more likely for countries that succeed in generating a
reasonable level of economic growth and in allowing most citizens to share in
the benefits. However, demands for redistribution have in some cases jeopard-
ized democratic consolidation,[8] though their significance is said to have
declined relative to social divisions along the lines of culture, language, and
ethnicity since the 1980s[9] (Huber and Stephens 1999; Linz 2004). In turn,
the impact of civil society is said to depend on the latter's make-up and the
nature of the party system (Schmitter 1997).

It is notable in the present collection of works that even though Kevin
Hewison makes reference to the political elite and both he and Hyug-Baeg Im
comment on political institutions such as the party system and the judiciary,
the explanations put forth by them and indeed by Thompson, and Hsiao
and Ho, center on macro socio-cultural forces. In Chapter 6, Hyug-Baeg Im
contends that Korea's telescopic industrialization and democratization have
given an ambivalent character to the country's democratic consolidation. In
particular, the project of political modernization has proceeded amid social
relations typical not only of the modern age, but also of both the pre-modern
era and the post-industrial information society. Consequently, just as civilian-
ization, electoral competition, and alternation of power have been instituted
under the Three Kims, the lingering influence of Confucian patrimonialism
has contributed to the persistence of regionalism, delegative presidency,
personalized political parties, and ideological orthodoxy. However, Im also
believes that these pre-modern features will be obliterated and the quality
of democracy enhanced as Korea moves closer to becoming an information
society, which will not only increase the extent of internet-based political
participation, but will also contribute to the fluidity of residence, occupation,
and social class.

Turning to Chapter 7, Kevin Hewison brings us up to date on what might
be called democratic reversal since the launch of the progressive 1997 constitution in Thailand and explains why, despite numerous "democratic transitions" in the country, few have lived up to the benchmark set by Linz and
Stepan (1996). In his view, struggles over democratic practices in Thailand
are effectively struggles over the control of the political regime. The 1997
constitution was an outcome of a liberal–conservative compromise that
allowed electoral progress without touching on the military and monarchy.
Unfortunately, the political assertiveness of the voting public and Thaksin's
pursuit of personal goals have exposed the "inadequacy" of the 1997 constitution, which eventually led to the coup in 2006 and attempts by the
conservative–middle class alliance to purge pro-Thaksin governments. In out-
lining the above, Hewison devotes the bulk of his chapter to examining how
the constitution, judiciary, and monarchy have become arenas and/or actors
in the process of political contention.

For Im, the factor accounting for the lack of horizontal accountability and
transparency, and the persistence of delegative presidency and regionalism in

Korea is cultural, namely, the lingering influence of Confucian patrimonialism. For Hewison, however, values and interests are tightly intertwined in the degeneration of Thailand's constitution and judiciary into arenas of political contention. In his words, the coup and subsequent events aimed:

> to re-establish a regime that included elections and political parties but where the interests of the conservatives were predominant . . . [where] the poor, the dispossessed, the working class, and rural people held to be unimportant for a conservative semi-democratic regime that emphasizes royalism, traditionalism, nationalism and paternalism.
>
> (p. 137)

From this perspective, the road to democratic consolidation in societies characterized by sharp structural inequality and a rigid system of social privileges is destined to be a tortuous one. In highlighting the influence of social structural factors, these authors also question the widely held idea that factors that make democratic transition possible are different from those facilitating democratic stability (Rustow 1970; see also Rodan and Jayasuriya 2009).

This emphasis on cultural and structural factors, however, has not prevented these scholars from shedding light on studies of democratic consolidation that focus on the political elite and political institutions. Importantly, while Hsiao and Ho's argument on Taiwan seems to support the observation that moderation on the part of civil society and the opposition regime help to maintain democratic stability (Schmitter 1997; see also Karl 1990; Tilly 2007), Hewison's study reveals a complex and indeed perplexing situation. At one level, the political assertiveness of the voting public in Thailand can be considered the mirror image of the case of Taiwan and supports the "moderation" thesis. At another level, however, as the 1997 constitution was already an outcome of a liberal–conservative compromise, it would be hard to come to terms with Karl's (1990: 9) assertion that stable democracy is more likely to emerge in situations [of transition] where "traditional rulers remain in control, even if pressured from below, and successfully use strategies of either compromise or force—or some mix of the two—to retain at least part of their power." Clearly, despite the 1997 compromise, which accords much control to the military and monarchy, it is still considered too threatening by the Thai elite. The difficulty of defining "moderation" apparently questions the value of such a thesis (cf. Bermeo 1999).

Above all, Thompson and Im together point to ambiguities in the concept of democratic consolidation and its possible overlap with the ideas of democratic stability and quality of democracy. By most standards, the democratic governments in Korea and Indonesia are stable. Depending on the criteria used, both can also be considered consolidated. However, while in the opinion of Im patrimonialism has continued to undermine accountability and transparency, thus rendering its quality of democracy deficient, it is Thompson's contention that traditional cultural identities have gone on to divide

Indonesia's rural poor and, in depriving the bourgeoisie of a potential ally, make possible the country's democratic stability. Their chapters show rather clearly that the stalemate in Indonesia can be deemed equivalent to the stability in Korea. Although it is Przeworski's (1985) contention that there can be different equilibriums for attaining democratic stability, the equation of "stalemate" with "stability" still amounts to the obliteration of two rather different phenomena. To regard stability as *de facto* consolidation, and to relegate the inadequacies of Indonesia and Korea as shortfalls in the quality of democracy, is to introduce further confusion (Zakaria 1997; Munck 2004; Linz 2004).

Democracy in East Asia: achievements and enduring challenges

Part Two is devoted to the analysis of what we call "achievements and enduring challenges" to East Asia's new democracies. The authors evaluate the extent to which democratization has helped to generate regional peace, provide social welfare, strengthen local governance, enhance human rights, improve ethnic harmony, and alter Asian opinions of desirable government. In so doing, they engage in a dialogue with the literature on the quality of democracy and shed light on the desirability and applicability of liberal democracy to East Asia. A few points on the literature on the quality of democracy are accordingly highlighted as a backdrop.

As more of the third wave democracies become stabilized, observers have begun to notice that the holding of regular elections has not always been accompanied by support for the rule of law or protection of human rights. O'Donnell (1999) draws our attention to the quality of democracy by delineating new concepts such as "delegative democracy" and "informally institutionalized polyarchy." Similar efforts have also been made by other scholars (Collier and Levitsky 1997).

A main challenge in this field of study has been to specify "the standards [of democracy] . . . weighting of different dimensions and ranges of tolerance of imperfection" (Linz 2004: 127). Lijphart (1999), for instance, considers the values of representation, equality, participation, proximity, satisfaction, accountability, and majority rule in a comparative study of 36 countries (see also Inglehart 1997; Altman and Perez-Linan 2002). Recently, Linz (2004) highlights as benchmarks civil peace, basic civil liberties, temporal limits to power, the possibility of accountability, and a margin of tolerance for government failure. Morlino (2004) also makes a most systematic effort by underlining the importance of procedure, content, and result in the evaluation of democracy and delineates the rule of law, vertical and horizontal accountability, responsiveness, freedom, and equality as the pertinent dimensions (see also Diamond and Morlino 2005).

Related to these strategies for measuring the quality of democracy are attempts to account for their variations. At the meso level are efforts to examine party systems (Mainwaring 1999), state institutions (Morlino 1998), institutional reforms that facilitate direct participation in policy-making (Harbers 2007), civil society (Feinberg *et al.* 2006), and social capital (Fishman 2004). However, a more prevalent line of investigation is to tap citizens' subjective evaluation, as has been done through various rounds of barometer surveys in Latin America, Africa, and Asia (Lagos 2001; Chu 2008). In addition to assessing the people's opinions on the quality of democracy thus instituted in their countries, these surveys have also followed Almond and Verba's (1963) pioneering study and sought to understand if their attitudes (or culture if measured at the societal level) might account for variations in quality.[10]

Before moving on, it is notable that many scholars have also made admirable attempts to evaluate the domestic and international consequences of democratization without using the term "quality of democracy." Among other issues, they have examined the new democracies' performance in the areas of civil liberty, rule of law, due process, corruption, distributive justice, ethnic relations, and trilateral cooperation (e.g. Case 2001; Choi 2005; Ferdinand 2003; Bertrand 2004; Croissant 2004; Hahm 2004; Wong 2004; Yoshihide 2004).

The six chapters in Part II mostly refrain from using the term "quality of democracy" and none examine the role of political institutions. However, they in their own ways contribute to the debate through their critical evaluation of the new democracies' substantive achievements. In Chapter 8, Amitav Acharya appraises the implications of democracy for regional peace and security in East Asia by focusing on dyadic inter-state relationships. Beginning with a discussion of democratization's potential threat to regional stability, Acharya goes on to explain why, despite his disagreement with the democratic peace theory, he believes that democratization can mitigate such threats. At a general level, he highlights the priority given by democratized regimes to democratic consolidation, transparency in political processes that facilitate regional understanding and trust, the quest for rule-based interactions on regional matters, and enhanced regional socialization by addressing the concerns of and drawing upon transnational linkages of civil society. Examining empirical cases in Northeast (Korea and Taiwan) and Southeast (Thailand, Cambodia, and Indonesia) Asia, Acharya also points to the powerful mechanisms of the transnational moral obligation of the new democratic regimes, positive nationalism, and the cooperative security effect of democratization.[11]

Chapters 9 and 10 examine the extent to which social equality has been enhanced with the introduction of democracy. Compared with Amitav Acharya, the views presented are less sanguine. In Chapter 9, Joseph Wong reviews the introduction of the universal National Health Insurance Program and the National Pension Program in post-transition Taiwan and Korea, respectively. In his view, although democracy is not a prerequisite for the formation of a welfare state, the political dynamics emitted by the transition to democracy exert definitive impacts. In part because political parties in East

Asia tend to be less programmatic than those in Europe, electoral competition, societal mobilization, and policy path dependency, all of which are associated with the transition to democracy, have compelled the Taiwanese and Korean governments to extend the aforementioned social welfare programs. The same democratic politics, however, have also prevented the emergence of a rational discussion of policy options, and have restricted existing debates on the long-term sustainability of these programs to the matter of finance alone.

Turning to Chapter 10, the late Ledivina V. Cariño assesses the performance (in terms of legislation, implementation, and conflict resolution) of the Philippines' local governments in the area of community-based coastal resource management for poverty alleviation. In her opinion, the transition to democracy has produced mixed results. On the one hand, devolution as one of the best legacies of the 1986 People Power Revolution has prompted stronger government and citizen action for public interests. Local communities, non-government organizations, academic institutions, and funding agencies have taken initiatives to work with government offices to manage coastal resources. On the other hand, at the same time that local officials might ally with elite interests and make existing law a tool to suppress people's initiative, deficiencies in the administrative capacity of some officials have prevented them from undertaking consultation, implementing agreed programs, establishing mechanisms for conflict resolution, and coordinating effectively with other local or regional governments. In other words, Cariño is not unlike Wong in underlining democratization-related political dynamics and institutional capacity as the explanatory factors.

Randall Peerenboom deals with the yardsticks of the quality of the new democracies in Chapter 11, which in his opinion include economic growth, political stability, institutional development, human rights protection, and other indicators of human well-being. In the first part of the chapter, he questions the alleged relationships between democracy and the rule of law, and also suggests that countries seeking to introduce elections at a low level of wealth have mostly continued to perform badly in economic development, confronting pressing social problems, and facing the threat of democratic breakdown. With this understanding, Peerenboom moves on to examine the rather disappointing implementation of democracy in Asia. In his view, elections have been messy and have failed to hold governments responsible, with the countries concerned performing poorly in wealth generation, political stability, good governance, corruption, and the protection of human rights. Reflecting on the modern history of the Asian people, Peerenboom seeks to explain why they value collective interests and strong leaders more than individual liberty and, consequently, argue that not only have existing Asian "democracies" failed to impress the Chinese, but the country will most likely introduce some form of elitist democracy, if at all. Furthermore, he argues that the deficient qualities of democracy are perhaps expected to surface when elections are introduced amid entrenched social divisions, poorly developed political institutions, and weak administrative capacity, thus endorsing a reexamination of theories on the "preconditions" for democratization (cf. Hadenius and Teorell 2005).

Democratization, according to these studies, presents invaluable opportunities for the pursuit of civil peace, distributive justice, the rule of law, human rights, and related social and political goals. However, other than Acharya, who believes democracy to possess properties that assure the realization of such goals, the other scholars fear that the latter might be deterred by factors that are related directly or indirectly to democracy as such. One factor emphasized in particular by Peerenboom is the level of wealth. In his view, the introduction of elections at a low level of wealth is not conducive to the rule of law, good governance, protection of human rights, etc. Unfortunately, the precise mechanisms by which wealth exerts its impact are not spelled out.[12]

A second factor that is examined quite extensively by these authors concerns social divisions of both modern and pre-modern origin. Divergent interests that crosscut small employers and workers in Taiwan and Korea, as well as patron–client relationships in the Philippines, are cases in point. Similar to Im and Hewison, who argue for the difficulties of consolidating democratic systems in societies characterized by sharp structural inequality and a rigid system of social privileges, Wong, Cariño, and Peerenboom also argue for the negative impact exerted by social divisions on the extension of social welfare, the introduction of a poverty alleviation program, and upholding the rule of law and human rights.

A third factor considered by these authors is political institutions, but not in the sense of a party system or constitutional arrangements as emphasized by Mainwaring (1999) and Morlino (1998). On the one hand, these studies suggest that the aforementioned social divisions have obstructed the deepening of democracy in part because the political elite were unable to disentangle themselves from the web of patron–client relationships and overcome the fear of offending their electorates, whereas state institutions were unable to rise above competing sectarian demands and propose policies that were economically viable and best addressed national goals. To do this implies the emergence of an inclusionary state–citizen relationship, which in the opinion of Mazzuca (2007) presupposes the rise of a new (perhaps rational–legal) authority relationship that permeates all areas of social life. This requires far-reaching social-structural and cultural transformations that imply not only regime change, but also a fortification of the state's political capacity (Linz and Stepan 1996; Suleiman 1999; Tilly 2007). On the other hand, the studies also point to incompetence on the part of financial institutions in assessing and collecting tax from the self-employed in Taiwan and Korea, as well as confusion over administrative boundaries in the Philippines. Again, both these challenges are to be tackled by the building of an effective civil bureaucracy that has little to do with democratization as such (Tilly 2007).

Authoritarian resilience and the uniqueness of East Asia

Much of the above discussion and indeed most studies of the third wave have proceeded as if the problems of democratic consolidation and deepening are but temporary, that liberal democracy is the ultimate destiny, and it is indeed a goal sought by the people of East Asia. Despite the apparent prevalence of these suppositions, they have not gone uncontested. Observers increasingly find that signs of authoritarian rule persist and have accordingly shifted their attention from research on democratic consolidation and deepening to the resilience of authoritarianism. Rodan and Jayasuriya (2009), for instance, have reexamined the experiences of capitalist development in Singapore, Malaysia, Thailand, and the Philippines in analyzing how the associated processes have undermined the bases of support for liberal democracy in those countries (see also Diskin *et al.* 2005). Other scholars, however, focus on authoritarian regimes that have withstood democratization. Gandhi and Przeworski (2007), for instance, contend that autocrats successful in building the institutions necessary to co-opt outside interests tend to survive longer (see also Nathan 2003). Pushing the point further, Dimitrov (2008) suggests that China's success in amassing institutional power has tempted the country to present its form of regime as a viable alternative to liberal democracy.

The latter point in a way echoes a body of research that emerged in the 1990s, which suggests that, for cultural or political-economic reasons, East Asia is distinct from the West and therefore may not find liberal democracy suitable. The most well-known argument has been put forth by Lee Kuan Yew and other venerable Asian leaders, though a more serious body of philosophical research also emerged at about the same time (Kausikan 1997; Tatsuo 1999; Bell and Hahm 2003). Daniel A. Bell (2006), for instance, argues quite convincingly that the cultural specificity of East Asia (which he defines as civilizations influenced by Confucianism) might affect the prioritization of rights in the face of taxing circumstances, lead the people to endorse a set of fundamental human goods that are not recognized by the human rights regime of the West (e.g. the duty of adult children to care for elderly parents), and guide them to pay greater respect to a ruling educated elite. With these and related arguments, he argues for greater caution in pronouncing the universal applicability of liberal democracy.

Howell, Thompson, and Peerenboom's comments on China, Vietnam, and Singapore are reminiscent of the structural arguments on the resilience of authoritarianism. However, it is in the chapters written by Beng Huat Chua and by Satoru Mikami and Takashi Inoguchi that the issues of liberal democracy's suitability for and appeal to East Asians are explored more systematically. In Chapter 12, Beng Huat Chua highlights the complexity of ethnic relations in Asia and explains why non-liberal forms of democracy might serve the group rights of ethnic and religious minorities better. In his view, a democratizing state necessarily seeks to "centralize power and authority over the national territory," which unavoidably conflicts with minorities' quest for autonomy through the formation of an independent state. At the same time, minority group formation, which emphasizes collective membership and group-oriented cultural differences, is at odds with the logic of citizenship formation, which celebrates individual rights and cultural choices. In the West, governments have been able to accommodate sub-ethnic identities with a liberal democratic ideology in part because such minorities no longer pose security threats. In Asia, a liberal democratic "solution" is not only impracticable, but might even be harmful to minorities given the region's shallow roots of liberalism and a history of colonial domination that results in persistent disputes over national boundaries. Examining the cases of Singapore, Malaysia, and Aceh in Indonesia, Chua demonstrates how some forms of recognition of ethnic minorities have evolved or have been devised by Asian states even as they avoid the promotion of Western liberalism and multiculturalism.

Turning to Chapter 13, Satoru Mikami and Takashi Inoguchi seek to evaluate Asian people's support for democracy after their countries have experimented with the system. Analyzing the AsiaBarometer surveys[13] (2003–2008), which cover 24 Asian and three Pacific Rim countries, the authors find that even though most people consider democracy to be desirable, many do not find the rule of powerful leaders too objectionable, and a majority of people in all Asian democratic countries actually accept technocracy. In accounting for this pattern, they find that while education and income exert consistently positive impacts on the preference for democracy, the impacts of religious affiliation and employment status are ambiguous. Most important, not only have they found democratic attitudes to be dampened by the sense of political inefficacy, but they also find, contrary to their hypothesis, that perceived untrustworthiness of incumbent leaders actually exerts both *positive* and negative impacts on the preference for democracy. Citing Lucian Pye's argument concerning the tendency for Asians to find in the acceptance of authority a key to personal security, they seek to explain why the cultivation of trustworthiness "does not necessarily reinforce democratic attitudes" and why Asians are so ready to delegate authority to technocrats, and in some cases, powerful leaders.[14]

Like some of the scholars who argue for the resilience of authoritarianism in and the inapplicability of liberal democracy to Asia, Chua, Mikami and Inoguchi, and in a more rudimentary way, Howell, Thompson, and Peerenboom, have also couched their arguments in terms of the distinctiveness of East Asia. Two dimensions of East Asia's uniqueness have been identified. The first is cultural. At the same time that Chua has noted the weakness of liberal tradition in Asia, Mikami and Inoguchi have contended for Asians' willingness to submit to authority. These observations are similar to Bell's (2006) argument on the prevalence of communitarian-based human rights in East Asia and the long tradition of respect for the ruling educated elite. The second aspect of East Asia's uniqueness moves away from culture as such to interweave with the region's modern history. Chua and Peerenboom's arguments concerning the experiences of war devastation, colonial domination, their agitating impacts on ethnic problems, as well as the Asian tendency to value collective interests even at the expense of individual liberty, are cases in point.

We do not intend to evaluate at this juncture the claim concerning East Asia's cultural and historical specificity. However, the challenges highlighted by Chua, Mikami and Inoguchi, and Peerenboom could be quite revealing if we were to follow these authors in adopting the historical approach and place their observations in a broader context. On one hand, as noted earlier, divergent meanings have been attached to the term democracy and it is through a lengthy process of political and ideological contention that liberal democracy has emerged as the predominant model in the West (Buchanan and Conway 2002; Held 2006). Furthermore, one only needs to consider the contrast between Sweden and the United States in terms of private property rights to note that so-called Western democracy is far from a unitary affair (Zakaria 1997). Not unlike the East–West distinction outlined by Bell (2006), individual Western countries have attached different priorities to divergent aspects of human rights despite their shared cultural legacies.

On the other hand, the challenges that confront East Asia because of its modern historical experiences, and indeed its effort at democratization, can be considered issues relating to state formation, nation-building, and the formation of a modern citizenry, which are linked to but not synonymous with democratization; and though they might appear to be more acute in Asia, are not atypical of other late-developing or newly emerging states. The issue of accommodating minority ethnic interests is an issue of nation-building, just as the collective interest of upholding state sovereignty and the importance of building an effective civil bureaucracy are challenges in state formation. In turn, the need to maintain a healthy balance between institutional trust and distrust (and hence non-acceptance of authority) can be considered a challenge in the formation of a modern citizenry that is by no means confined to Asians. Arguing against Robert Putnam, Tilly (2007: 93) contends that democratization also implies a certain distrust or unwillingness to offer rulers a "blank check" without the potential threat of voice or exit. As pointed out by a number of observers, so long as democracy implies the rule of the people, state-formation and nation-building logically constitute an integral part of the explanation for democratization. More often than not, however, they have made up no more than what Robert Dahl has called a "shadow theory" in the study of democracy (Berg-Schlosser 2004; Tilly 2007). The omission is particularly appalling for many late-developing countries and states emerging from political turbulence, which have to tackle at once all three objectives, the dynamics of which often conflict with each other (Linz 2004; see also Zakaria 1997; Mann 2005).

In placing the alleged cultural and historical specificity of East Asia in a broader historical context, the above has far from argued against the uniqueness of Asia. However, the historical perspective, in showing the multitude of political and cultural choices involved in the emergence of liberal democracy in the West, would perhaps endorse a greater openness to the prospect of addressing the moral and practical concerns of Asians when devising democratic systems for the region. In delineating more clearly challenges relating to democratization vis-à-vis state-formation and nation-building, the historical perspective also facilitates a more accurate assessment of the possibilities and challenges associated with democratization. With this, it will hopefully prevent the dual tendencies of either assuming that democracy "guarantees a comprehensive catalog of social, political, economic, and religious rights" and therefore adopt it as the only yardstick to judge the quality of governance (Zakaria 1997); or conversely, blaming democracy for all the difficulties confronted by the late-developing or newly emerging states and arguing against its pursuit, as has been done by apologists of authoritarian domination. On that note, we conclude this introductory chapter. We encourage readers to examine for themselves the contributing authors' arguments, which are more complex and profound than summarized here, concerning the multitude of actors involved in the democratization of East Asia, and the achievements of and enduring challenges faced by these new democracies.

Notes

1 Although we have not attempted to define democracy in this chapter, we would not disagree with Charles Tilly's (2007: 13–14) definition that: "a regime is democratic to the degree that political relations between the state and its citizens feature broad, equal, protected and mutually binding consultation."

2 Another line of research within the modernization perspective is the study of political culture pioneered by Almond and Verba (1963).

3 Hsiao and Ho's chapter actually also covers the development of civil society after the democratic transition.

4 In the view of Thompson, while state maneuver was the reason behind the split of the middle class in Singapore, ethnicity was the cause in Malaysia.

5 In this collection, Cumings would clearly disagree with Thompson's analysis of Korea.

6 The literature on democratic transition and consolidation also confronts the challenge of integrating different levels of analysis, which is not addressed by Thompson in his chapter.

7 Japan is a good case to illustrate the implications of the two definitions. While Linz and Stepan would consider the country to have been a consolidated democracy since the 1960s, it was only in 1993 that it passed Huntington's two turnover test.

8 While the elite in Western Europe have accepted such demands in exchange for political moderation among workers (Przeworski 1985), they have led to democratic breakdowns in Latin America in the 1950s and 1970s (O'Donnell 1973).

9 According to this line of reasoning, labor demands have been dampened by the rise of neo-liberalism since the 1980s.

10 In the Asian Barometer Survey, for instance, people are asked if they would accept a breach of the rule of law, tolerate the suppression of political freedom and minority rights, or endure the subordination of the judiciary to the executive branch of the government (Chu 2008). This attempt to measure the extent to which citizens are willing to "respond to, accept or freely condone bad leadership"

is seldom found in studies of political culture that originate from Western democratic countries (Linz 2004: 132).

11 Other than these, Acharya also points to relative prosperity and economic interdependence in Northeast Asia, and to regionalism and regional institutions in
Southeast Asia, as important stabilizing factors.

12 The ways in which wealth affects democracy are complex. While Przeworski (1991)
contends that democratic consolidation is more likely for countries that generate
a reasonable level of economic growth, Przeworksi *et al.* (1996) argue that given
other favorable conditions, democracy can survive at a lower level of economic
development.

13 This AsiaBarometer Survey is different from the Asia Barometer Survey led by
Yun-han Chu of Taiwan.

14 It is difficult to compare Mikami and Inoguchi's study with the Asian Barometer
Survey mentioned in the introductory passages to this subsection. However, the
Asia Barometer Survey has found that while Asians are in general not very
demanding citizens, they are similar to those in Eastern Europe and Latin America
in that economic performance as such does not affect the subjective evaluation
of the legitimacy of democratic institutions (Linz and Stepan 1996; Lagos 2001),
which appears to differ from the findings of Mikami and Inoguchi.

Bibliography

Almond, G. A. and Verba, S. (1963) *The Civic Culture*, Princeton: Princeton University
Press.

Altman, D. and Perez-Linan, A. (2002) "Assessing the quality of democracy,"
Democratization, 9 (Summer), 85–100.

Bell, D. A. (2006) *Beyond Liberal Democracy*, Princeton: Princeton University Press.

Bell, D. A. and Hahm, C. (eds) (2003) *Confucianism for the Modern World*, Cambridge:
Cambridge University Press.

Berg-Schlosser, D. (2004) "Introduction," in D. Berg-Schlosser (ed.) *Democratization:
the state of the art*, VS Verlag: Für Sozialwissenschaften, pp. 13–29.

Bermeo, N. (1999) "Myths of moderation: confrontation and conflict during democratic transitions," in L. Anderson (ed.) *Transitions to Democracy*, New York:
Columbia University Press, pp. 120–40.

Bertrand, J. (2004) "Democratization and religious and nationalist conflict in post-
Suharto Indonesia," in S. J. Henders (ed.) *Democratization and Identity*, Lanham:
Lexington Books, pp. 177–200.

Buchanan, T. and Conway, M. (2002) "The politics of democracy in twentieth century
Europe: introduction," *European History Quarterly*, 32(1): 7–12.

Case, W. (2001) "Malaysia's resilient pseudodemocracy," *Journal of Democracy*,
12(1): 43–57.

Cheng, T. J. and Brown, D. A. (eds) (2006) *Religious Organizations and Democratization*, Armonk: M. E. Sharpe.

Choi, J. J. (2005) *Democracy after Democratization: the Korean experience*, translated
by Kyung-hee Lee, Seoul: Humanitas Press.

Chu, Y. H. (2008) "East Asia's struggling democracies: a view from the citizens," paper
delivered at the International Conference on the Experiments with Democracy
in East and Southeast Asia: two decades after, organized by the Centre of Asian
Studies, University of Hong Kong, 2–3 May 2008.

Collier, D. and Levitsky, S. (1997) "Democracy with adjectives: conceptual innovation
in comparative research," *World Politics*, 49(3): 430–51.

Collier, R. B. (1999) *Paths toward Democracy: the working class and elites in Western Europe and South America*, New York: Cambridge University Press.

Collier, R. B. and Collier, D. (1991) *Shaping the Political Arena: critical junctures, the labor movement, and regime dynamics in Latin America*, Princeton: Princeton University Press.

Croissant, A. (2004) "From transition to defective democracy: mapping Asian democratization," *Democratization*, 11(5): 156–78.

Di Palma, G. (1990) *To Craft Democracies: an essay on democratic transitions*, Berkeley: University of California Press.

Diamond, L. and Morlino, L. (eds) (2005) *Assessing the Quality of Democracy*, Baltimore: Johns Hopkins University Press.

Dimitrov, M. (2008) "The resilient authoritarians," *Current History*, January, 24–9.

Diskin, A., Diskin, H. and Hazan, R. Y. (2005) "Why democracies collapse: the reasons for democratic failure and success," *International Political Science Review*, 26(3): 291–309.

Feinberg, R, Waisman, C. H. And Zamosc, L. (eds) (2006) *Civil Society and Democracy in Latin America*, New York: Palgrave Macmillan.

Ferdinand, P. (2003) "Party funding and political corruption in East Asia," in R. Austin and M. Tjernstrom (eds) *Funding of Political Parties and Election Campaigns*, Stockholm: International IDEA.

Fishman, R. M. (2004) *Democracy's Voices: social ties and the quality of public life in Spain*, Ithaca: Cornell University Press.

Fukuyama, F. (1992) *The End of History and the Last Man*, New York: Free Press.

Gandhi, J. and Przeworski, A. (2007) "Authoritarian institutions and the survival of autocrats," *Comparative Political Studies*, 40(11): 1279–301.

Hadenius, A. and Teorell, J. (2005) "Cultural and economic prerequisites of democracy: reassessing recent evidence," *Studies in Comparative International Development*, 39(4): 87–106.

Hahm, C. (2004) "Rule of law in South Korea: rhetoric and implementation," in R. Peerenboom (ed.) *Asian Discourses of Rule of Law*, London: Routledge, pp. 385–416.

Hall, J. A. (ed.) (1995) *Civil Society*, Cambridge: Polity.

Harbers, I. (2007) "Democratic deepening in third wave democratization: experiments with participation in Mexico City," *Political Studies*, 55(1): 38–58.

Haynes, J. (2001) *Democracy in the Developing World*, Cambridge: Polity.

Held, D. (2006) *Models of Democracy*, Cambridge: Polity.

Higley, J. and Gunther, R. (eds) (1992) *Elites and Democratic Consolidation in Latin America and Southern Europe*, Cambridge: Cambridge University Press.

Huber, E. and Stephens, J. D. (1999) "The bourgeoisie and democracy: historical and contemporary perspectives," *Social Research*, 66(3): 759–88.

Huntington, S. P. (1991) *The Third Wave*, Norman: University of Oklahoma Press.

—— (1997) "After twenty years: the future of the third wave," *Journal of Democracy*, 8(4): 3–12.

Inglehart, R. (1997) *Modernization and Postmodernization: cultural, economic, and political change in 43 societies*, Princeton: Princeton University Press.

Karl, T. L. (1990) "Dilemmas of democratization in Latin America, Southern and Eastern Europe," *Comparative Politics*, 23(1): 1–21.

Kausikan, B. (1997) "Governance that works," *Journal of Democracy*, 8(2): 24–34.

Keane, J. (1988) *Democracy and Civil Society*, London: Verso.

Koo, H. (1991) "Middle classes, democratization, and class formation: the case of South Korea," *Theory and Society*, 20 (August): 485–509.

Lagos, M. (2001) "Between stability and crisis in Latin America," *Journal of Democracy*, 12: 137–45.

Lijphart, A. (1999) *Patterns of Democracy: government forms and performance in thirty-six countries*, New Haven: Yale University Press.

Linz, J. J. (2004) "Some thoughts on the victory and future of democracy," in D. Berg-Schlosser (ed.) *Democratization: the state of the art*, VS Verlag: Für Sozialwissenschaften, pp. 114–33.

Linz, J. J. and Valenzuela, A. (1994) *The Failure of Presidential Democracy*, Baltimore: Johns Hopkins University Press.

Linz, J. J. and Stepan, A. (1996) *Problems of Democratic Transition and Consolidation*, Baltimore: Johns Hopkins University Press.

Lipset, S. M. (1959) "Some social requisites of democracy," *American Political Science Review*, 53: 69–105.

—— (1994) "The social requisites of democracy revisited," *American Sociological Review*, 59(1): 1–22.

Mainwaring, S. (1999) *Rethinking Party Systems in the Third Wave Democratization: the case of Brazil*, Stanford: Stanford University Press.

Mainwaring, S. and Scully, T. R. (1995) *Building Democratic Institutions: party systems in Latin America*, Palo Alto: Stanford University Press.

Mainwaring, S., O'Donnell, G. and Valenzuela, J. S. (eds) (1992) *Issues in Democratic Consolidation*, Notre Dame: University of Notre Dame Press.

Mann, M. (2005) *The Dark Side of Democracy*, New York: Cambridge University Press.

Mazzuca, S. L. (2007) "Reconceptualizing democratization: access to power versus exercise of power," in G. L. Munck (ed.) *Regimes and Democracy in Latin America*, Oxford: Oxford University Press.

Moore, B. Jr. (1966) *Social Origins of Dictatorship and Democracy*, Boston: Beacon Press.

Morlino, L. (1998) *Democracy between Consolidation and Crisis: parties, groups, and citizens in southern Europe*, New York: Oxford University Press.

—— (2004) "What is a 'good' democracy?" *Democratization*, 11(5): 10–32.

Munck, G. L. (2004) "Democracy studies: agendas, findings, challenges," in D. Berg-Schlosser (ed.) *Democratization: the state of the art*, VS Verlag: Für Sozialwissenschaften, pp. 65–97.

Nathan, A. J. (2003) "Authoritarian resilience," *Journal of Democracy*, 14(1): 6–17.

O'Donnell, G. (1973) *Modernization and Bureaucratic-Authoritarianism*. Berkeley: University of California Press.

—— (1999) *Counterpoints*, Notre Dame: University of Notre Dame Press.

O'Donnell, G. and Schmitter, P. C. (1986) *Transitions from Authoritarian Rule: tentative conclusions about uncertain democracies*, Baltimore: Johns Hopkins University Press.

Przeworski, A. (1985) *Capitalism and Social Democracy*, Cambridge: Cambridge University Press.

—— (1991) *Democracy and the Market*, Cambridge: Cambridge University Press.

Przeworski, A. and Limongi, F. (1997) "Modernization: theories and facts," *World Politics*, 49(2): 155–83.

Przeworski, A., Alvarez, M., Cheibub, J. A. and Limongi, F. (1996) "What makes democracy endure?" *Journal of Democracy*, 7(1): 39–55.

Reilly, B. (2007) "Democratization and electoral reform in the Asia-Pacific region—is there an 'Asian model' of democracy?" *Comparative Political Studies*, 40(11): 1350–71.

Rodan, G. and Jayasuriya, K. (2009) "Capitalist development, regime transitions and new forms of authoritarianism in Asia," *Pacific Review*, 22(1): 23–47.

Rokkan, S. (1996) *State Formation, Nation-Building, and Mass Politics in Europe*, Oxford: Oxford University Press.

Rueschemeyer, D., Stephens, E. H. and Stephens, J. D. (1992) *Capitalist Development and Democracy*, Chicago: Chicago University Press.

Rustow, D. (1970) "Transitions to democracy," *Comparative Political Studies*, 2(3): 337–63.

Schmitter, P. C. (1992) "Interest systems and the consolidation of democracies," in G. Marks and L. Diamond (eds) *Reexamining Democracy: essays in honor of Seymour Martin Lipset*, Newbury Park: Sage, pp. 156–81.

—— (1997) "Civil society East and West," in L. Diamond, M. F. Platner, Y. H. Chu and H. M. Tien (eds) *Consolidating the Third Wave Democracies*, Baltimore: Johns Hopkins University Press, pp. 239–62.

Sørensen, G. (1998) *Democracy and Democratization: processes and prospects in a changing world*, Boulder: Westview Press.

Stepan, A. and Linz, J. J. (2001) "Political crafting of democratic consolidation or destruction: European and Southern American comparisons," in A. Stepan, *Arguing Comparative Politics*, Oxford: Oxford University Press.

Stepan, A. and Skach, C. (2001) "Constitutional frameworks and democratic consolidation: parliamentarianism versus presidentialism," in A. Stepan, *Arguing Comparative Politics*, Oxford: Oxford University Press.

Suleiman, E. (1999) "Bureaucracy and democratic consolidation," in L. Anderson (ed.) *Transitions to Democracy*, New York: Columbia University Press.

Tarrow, S. (1995) "Mass mobilization and elite exchange," *Democratization*, 2(3): 221–45.

Tatsuo, I. (1999) "Liberal democracy and Asian orientalism," in J. R. Bauer and D. A. Bell (eds) *The East Asian Challenge for Human Rights*, Cambridge: Cambridge University Press, pp. 27–60.

Tilly, C. (2007) *Democracy*, New York: Cambridge University Press.

Wong, J. (2004) *Healthy Democracies*, Ithaca: Cornell University Press.

Yoshihide, S. (2004) "Democratization in Northeast Asia and trilateral cooperation," in T.-H. Kim and B. Glosserman (eds) *The Future of US-Korea-Japan Relations*, Washington, DC: CSIS Press, pp. 85–96.

Zakaria, F. (1997) "The rise of illiberal democracy," *Foreign Affairs*, 76 (November/December): 22–43.

Part I

Transition, consolidation, reversal

Actors then and now

2 Social and political developments in China

Challenges for democratization

Jude Howell

China's economic growth has proceeded at breakneck speed over the past three decades. This has led to major changes in the socioeconomic fabric of Chinese society. The most outstanding of these include the restructuring and closure of state enterprises, the growth of the private economy, the tidal wave of rural to urban migration, the growth of the middle classes and the concomitant disenfranchisement of the working classes, and finally increasing exposure to external influences through the internet, media, travel, and exchange. While the seeming miracle of China's relentless economic growth has in general raised living standards, it has also both intensified some old social and political cleavages as well as created new sources of inequality, tension, and discontent. These social and political strains call for considerable statecraft and political adroitness. However, it is questionable whether the party/state is well-equipped to address these challenges.

This chapter argues that the internationalization of civil society and the more strident articulation of domestic discontent are putting considerable pressure on the Chinese party/state to reform politically. Though the party/state has made some attempt to become more accountable, transparent, and inclusive, its inherent reluctance to share power and authority positively limits the effectiveness of these efforts. Unless it can develop more effective ways of mediating conflict, of engaging with an increasingly diverse and demanding citizenry, and promoting social justice, it is unlikely that any transition to a more democratic regime will proceed without considerable and probably violent conflict.

Reformed authoritarianism with limited, selective political liberalization will be more favorable to the Chinese Communist Party (CCP) than a Western-style model of liberal democracy. Authoritarianism in other East and Southeast Asian states has proved remarkably resilient to deepening democracy. This is despite the adornment of those states with the skeletal trappings of liberal democracy. This has yielded perverse hybrid political formations of democratic authoritarian states. China, however, is distinct in that the Chinese Communist Party has maintained its ruling position for over six decades. Authoritarianism is much more deeply embedded in China. Moreover, the party has been adept at reinventing itself both ideologically and in terms of economic strategy. Thus, we can expect reformed authoritarianism to persist and to resist pressures for wholesale democratic regime change.

This chapter begins by tracing the contours of social and political change during the reform period. It then highlights some of the governance challenges that these pose for the Chinese party/state. The third section examines the changing nature of state–civil society relations, drawing particular attention to the ebb and flow pattern of governance. It is argued here that this pattern of governance will become increasingly hard to maintain for three reasons: first, because of the internationalization of civil society, which seizes the notion of "a public issue" from the monopoly of the party/state; second, because the simmering discontent emerging out of uneven economic development coupled with rising expectations places constant pressure on the party/state to open up spaces and discourses for the discussion of public issues; and third, because attempts by the party/state to devolve some power and authority through controlled processes of "democratization" collide with an entrenched systemic impulse to retain the monopoly over public affairs. In the concluding section, we consider the implications of this for processes of democratic change in China.

Contours of social and political development

Over the last three decades of reform, China has experienced staggering and constant growth rates averaging around 10 percent per year. Economic reforms have involved gradual processes of marketization and privatization. In the rural areas, the introduction of the household responsibility system has led to increases in agricultural output and incomes, at least in the first decade of reform. The growth of township and village enterprises and the creation of small towns across China have provided employment opportunities for surplus rural labor and spurred a process of labor-intensive industrialization. Crucial to China's rapid growth and industrialization has been the reformers' policy of opening up to global markets through foreign trade and investment. From the 1980s onwards, central reformers have gradually extended the array of policy incentives available to draw in foreign direct investment from coastal regions to inland areas. By mid-2007, over 610,000 foreign-invested enterprises had been established in China, with the amount of foreign direct investment actually used exceeding US$750 billion (Xinhua 2007a). The bulk of these enterprises are located in coastal areas and tend to be small-scale, export-oriented, labor-intensive operations owned by investors of Hong Kong, Macao, Taiwanese, or overseas Chinese origin. By 2005, China ranked third in the world in terms of foreign trade volume and held foreign exchange reserves of over US$800 billion (Xinhua 2006).

This growth in the foreign-invested economy has gradually been matched by the emergence of a substantial domestic private economy. By 2007 there were over 5.5 million private enterprises in China and more than 26.21 million individual industrial and commercial entities employing more than

70 percent of urban employees, according to the All-China Federation of Industry and Commerce (Xinhua 2007b).[1] There has also been an increase in the number of Chinese companies investing overseas, both in manufacturing and in mineral exploration and development. This growth in the private economy has been accompanied by a fundamental overhaul of the state enterprise sector. The process of reform gathered pace from the mid-1990s onwards, leading to the closure, merger, and streamlining of unprofitable state enterprises and the concomitant laying-off of over 60 million workers. By 2005, the number of state-owned enterprises in China had declined by 48 percent in comparison with 2001 (Du 2005).

These fundamental changes in the economy have inevitably led to a socio-economic restructuring of society. The most outstanding features of this restructuring include the breakdown of urban/rural barriers; social diversification and new processes of class formation; rising inequalities; and the collapse of social welfare systems. The relaxation of restrictions over rural–urban movement from the mid-1980s triggered a tidal wave of internal migration. Rural residents headed in their millions towards the coastal provinces of Guangdong, Fujian, and later Shanghai, Zhejiang and elsewhere in search of jobs in newly established factories. It is estimated that there are over 110 million rural migrants working in China's cities as construction workers, factory workers, and housemaids.[2] Often spurned by urban residents as illiterate and uncultured, rural migrants work long hours for relatively low wages in jobs that urban residents are reluctant to do themselves (Pun 2005). Moreover, they lack basic rights of access to welfare, medical care, housing, and schooling that urban residents enjoy (Solinger 1999).

The second-class citizen status of migrant workers is but one dimension of a new prism of inequality which underpins China's growth. China's rapid economic growth has also been a process of uneven development, which, as Deng Xiaoping forecast, allowed some to "get rich quick." From a regional perspective, there is a persistent gap in the GDPs of coastal and inland areas, of the inland and coastal parts of coastal provinces, in the mountain and plains areas, and between rural and urban areas. Recent estimates put China's Gini coefficient at 0.45, hovering close to that of Brazil, which has one of the world's highest income disparities. However, it should also be noted that China has made significant progress in reducing poverty levels, with the number of people living in poverty falling from around 250 million in 1978 to 26 million in 2004 according to official statistics.[3]

Rural–urban migration, the rise of foreign and domestic private investment, and the reform of state enterprises have led to increasing social differentiation and social fracturing along class lines. Opportunities to establish private manufacturing, trade, and commercial businesses have created a new layer of nouveau riche in China. According to a Merrill Lynch report on rich people in the Asia-Pacific region, by the end of 2007 there were more than 414,900 people in China with assets of over US$1 million, putting China in fifth place behind the U.S.A., Japan, Germany, and Britain (Shanghai Daily

2008). Increases in the salaries of state functionaries and university lecturers and the higher wages paid to those in supervisory and managerial positions in foreign companies have fostered a growing middle class with rising expectations.

While private entrepreneurs, managers in foreign enterprises, senior state functionaries, and intellectuals generally constitute a social stratum that has gained considerably under the economic reforms implemented to date, state workers have fallen behind in terms of economic, social, and political status. The reforms have restructured the notion of the working class. In the pre-reform era, state enterprise workers, particularly those in large, successful enterprises, were at the pinnacle of the working class, enjoying an "iron rice bowl"—permanent employment, high political and ideological status as "masters of the country," and considerable housing, welfare, and medical benefits. Workers in collective enterprises were next in line, with temporary and seasonal workers coming last. Thirty years after the reform process was initiated, migrant workers form the backbone of the manufacturing sector in China, whereas state workers have lost many of their privileges and much of their status. Though their wages are often higher than they would earn in rural areas, they are low-paid, working long hours and often in poor and unsafe working conditions. Many state workers have been made redundant and are unable to find further employment or employment that is as well-paid because they are perceived as unskilled, old, and unwilling to work the hours that migrants will. The rise of migrant workers embodies a new process of proletarianization that the existing trade union is struggling to deal with (Howell 2006; 2008). Moreover, the global recession that set in with a vengeance from late 2008 has led to reduced orders, downsizing, factory closures, and mass lay-offs of migrant workers, posing yet more major challenges to the party/state and the official trade union.

The rise in inequalities is also related to the collapse of the communal-and unit-based social welfare systems in urban and rural areas. As communes have given way to townships and collective production to household and individual-based production, so too have collective systems of healthcare, albeit rudimentary and uneven, disintegrated. In urban areas, access to medical care, pensions, housing, and social welfare in the pre-reform period varied according to the city and the resources of the employing enterprise. Those employed in large successful state enterprises fared better on all these fronts than temporary workers in neighborhood factories or workers in small collective enterprises. With the restructuring of state enterprises, work units ceded responsibility for housing, medical care, social welfare, and pensions to the market. Though local governments have put in place medical insurance, social protection, and unemployment benefit systems, access to healthcare has become an increasingly divisive marker in society.

Governance challenges

These far-reaching changes in the socioeconomic fabric of China over the last three decades of reform pose numerous governance challenges relating to social justice, social order and control, representation and participation, regime legitimacy, and the relationship between economic and political reform. The increasing regional and income inequalities now visible in China are testimony to the uneven process of development resulting from the high priority given to economic growth. These inequalities present the party with particular dilemmas. As a party claiming a communist ideology, it has become increasingly difficult for party leaders to marry ideological rhetoric with reality. Though Jiang Zemin introduced the concept of the Three Represents to incorporate new social groups such as private entrepreneurs into the party, thereby endorsing the reform process, this does not resolve the issue of the declining status of both state enterprise workers and farmers. Nor does it adequately deal with issues of participation and representation. Maintaining the legitimacy of the regime by drawing on clumsy adaptations of a communist ideology is hard, if not impossible, to sustain. Instead, the party/state has relied more on its ability to promote living standards and to maintain social stability and unity to justify its rule. Given China's increasing engagement with the world economy and therefore potential vulnerability to fluctuations in world markets, coupled with the environmental limits of growth, basing its legitimacy on high growth rates is risky and unsustainable.

There are also governance challenges relating to social order and stability, representation, and participation. There has been a spiraling number of protests, demonstrations, and sit-ins across China over the past twenty years. These forms of civil action have arisen in response to a range of grievances held by various social groups. Migrant workers have organized protests, sit-ins, strikes about non-payment or late payment of wages, low wages, excessive overtime, and unsafe working conditions, while state enterprise workers have occupied buildings, demonstrated and protested about lay-offs, non-payment of compensation, or pensions, and about corruption in the processes of restructuring state enterprises (Chen 2000; Howell 1997a, 1997b, 2003, 2009; Lee 2007; Pan 2002; Weston 2004; Thireau and Hua 2003). In rural and urban areas, residents have protested about environmental damage caused by polluting industries or the corrupt purchase of farming land by commercial developers. In some villages, corruption in village elections has led to violent clashes between village residents and local party leaders, who have allegedly hired gangs to put down protests. Such protests have underlined the party/state's inability to manage issues of social justice and related conflicts in an effective manner and its too frequent use of repression and force. Moreover, the involvement of local authorities and party leaders in the misuse of land and the violation of village election procedures has raised key issues about whose interests the party represents.

There are also key governance challenges concerning the relationship between political and economic reform. This has long been a thorn in the side of many party leaders. In the run-up to the seventeenth Party Congress, advocates of political reform astutely argued that political reform was a necessary prerequisite for any further economic reform. The new leadership did not embrace this idea with any vigor, and for the immediate future, we can expect little movement on this front. However, it should be noted that there has been some slow but gradual change in the political system over the past three decades that should not be underestimated. This includes the introduction of village elections; experimentation with elections at county level and within the All-China Federation of Trade Unions (ACFTU); moves towards greater "inner party democracy"; a concerted effort to clamp down on corruption, though not very successful; and moves towards more inclusive policy processes through consultation with intellectual and professional elites, and public tribunals.

In addressing these challenges, the party/state faces numerous constraints, the most salient of which include an increasingly outmoded system of engaging with society through mass organizations; a more liberal political and cultural context that has had to evolve to enable market reforms and that includes more room for self-expression and the emergence of a nascent civil society; increasing international exposure; rising expectations; and the systemic problems of corruption and probity. These constraints are important to note, for they frame how the party/state engages with civil society, the focus of the next section. In the pre-reform period, the Chinese Communist Party established a Leninist-style edifice of intermediary institutions designed to link the party to particular social constituencies. These mass organizations (*qunzhong tuanti*) served as transmission belts linking the party with key social groups such as workers, women, and youth. In theory, they operated according to the Leninist principles of democratic centralism, relaying party policy downwards and supposedly the views and opinions of workers, women, and youth upwards to the party nucleus. Apart from these intermediary institutions, the work unit (*danwei*) and the commune and its lower levels were also key nodal points which the party used to control society.

Rapid economic development has unsettled all of these intermediary sites of party control. Though the mass organizations had become inactive during the Cultural Revolution, they have been reinvigorated since 1978. The Fourth World Conference on Women held in Beijing in 1995 gave a boost to the prestige and activities of the All China Women's Federation (Howell 1997b; Du 2004). The All-China Federation of Trade Unions has remained heavily under the shadow of the party, struggling to find a more autonomous route so as to better protect and represent the interests of workers. The Communist Youth League remains an important avenue for recruitment of young people into the party and has astutely gained wider appeal through its appendage organization, the Youth Development Foundation, which spearheaded Project Hope, the popular charitable initiative.

Though these mass organizations have breathed new life in the reform period, they cannot wield the same level of control over their targeted constituencies for various reasons. First, because of the excesses of the Cultural Revolution, it is much harder to use techniques of mass mobilization or mass propaganda to galvanize mass action or persuade people on a mass scale. Second, social diversification and pluralization have complicated these very constituencies. Whereas the term "workers" once referred predominantly to state or collective workers, the nature of the working class has changed significantly over the course of the reform period. Not only are there different types of workers in enterprises under different forms of ownership, who enjoy different working conditions and distinct social and political rights, but they are also more difficult to organize. In particular, until relatively recently the All-China Federation of Trade Unions has not sought to reach out to rural migrant workers or laid-off or unemployed workers. While the party has welcomed capitalists into its fold, it has been much more reluctant to see workers organize beyond the ACFTU, not least for fear that this would jeopardize economic development. Similarly, the All-China Federation of Women has to satisfy a much wider range of different interests. Whereas in the past it thought of women in terms of class divisions and rural/ urban groupings, in the reform period, the needs and interests of women are far more diverse, key distinctions including rural migrant women workers, rural migrant women in the service sector, laid-off female state enterprise workers, unemployed women, housewives, sex workers, women working in the foreign enterprise sector, university-educated women meeting discrimination in gaining employment, and so on.

Third, the work unit and the commune were key bases from which the mass organizations could reach out to their respective constituencies. However, both these institutions have been considerably weakened in the reform period because of the diversification of forms of enterprise ownership and the introduction of the household responsibility system, respectively. This has had serious consequences for social welfare and protection in both urban and rural areas. Though medical care and social welfare provision were basic and fragmentary in rural areas before the reforms began, in the post-reform era, the privatization of healthcare has rendered it unaffordable to most rural residents. In the urban areas, new systems of tripartite medical and social insurance have gone some way to compensating for the loss of social welfare provision under the work-unit model. However, not only are there many migrant workers, retirees, and low-income workers who are effectively excluded from these schemes, but even under such schemes the cost of major medical care remains prohibitive for many. Finally, the emergence of both competing gender ideologies and consumerism have rendered it more difficult to use mass mobilization techniques, "revolutionary" images, and rhetoric to appeal to, persuade, or control people.

The second and related constraint is the more liberal political and cultural environment that the reformers have tolerated and, to some extent, nurtured. To promote science, technological innovation, and learning, the reformers encouraged a more open intellectual environment, international exchange, and the formation of academic and learned associations. Similarly, reformist leaders fostered the development of professional, business, and trade associations both to strengthen learning from international sources and to devolve some of the economic functions carried out by state institutions (Unger 1996; Pei 1998). However, the party has been much slower to allow the development of non-economic social sciences such as sociology, political science, and anthropology, subjects which lead to the questioning of social structures, systems, and meanings. Though there are still limits on the degree of self-expression, particularly as it relates to political issues in China, the more open political and cultural context and the emergence of a nascent civil society in comparison with thirty years earlier does make it more difficult for the Chinese Communist Party to roll back the tide and rely on a combination of repression and ideological manipulation to control society. In the last ten years, Chinese journalists have used investigative journalism to expose the cracks and hypocrisies of the political system, to reveal corruption in elections, business, and politics, and to expose environmental damage. Moreover, intellectuals have used the expanding spaces given to them to criticize government policy, although they are always careful to phrase their views in appropriate language. As will be discussed in the next section, the ebb and flow of restriction and relaxation that the party has used to govern society has become harder to steer.

The third key constraint on governance choices relates to the increasing exposure of China to international pressures, norms, and values.[4] Like the Qing modernizers, the reformist government has tried to control its interaction with outside forces by separating out what it considers good and advantageous to China's growth and modernization from what it deems bad and destructive. The more China opens itself up to the world economically, politically, technologically, and culturally, the more difficult it will be to control that process, to control what its citizens think and believe, and to control how the world views it. The recent events around the global Olympic torch relay demonstrate how little the party had grasped the strength of international perceptions of its human rights record. As will be discussed in greater depth in the next section, the effects of globalization, such as those spurred by the internet and faster communications, make it more difficult for the party to control information and to use repression against dissidents without incurring international rebuke.

Apart from these key constraints of systemic rigidity, a more liberal political and social context, and increasing international exposure, other constraints such as the rising expectations of the growing middle classes, corruption within the party/state, the need to balance growth with redistribution and environmental sustainability, and the weak binding power of communist ideology all shape the possible governance routes. In the next section, we explore in greater detail the challenges of social control by tracing the development of civil society over the past three decades and the party's attempts to "manage" citizens who have sought to organize through a dualistic pattern of "restriction" and "relaxation." We suggest that this pattern of governance will become increasingly hard to maintain because of the internationalization of civil society and the growing appreciation of what constitutes a "public issue" in China, rising demands from below, and the bumbling efforts of the party to cede some power over public affairs as an alternative way of "relaxing" control over society.

The ebb and flow of civil society: when "the public" becomes more public

In this section, we briefly outline the key contours of civil society development over the past decade. We then go on to argue that the familiar pattern of governance by restriction and relaxation, which results in the ebb and flow of civil society, is becoming harder to enforce because of the increasing internationalization of public action in China, the simmering discontent and rising expectations emerging out of uneven economic development, and the clumsy and contradictory efforts of the party/state to both dominate and relinquish control over the sphere of public action.

As discussed earlier, in an effort to promote the process of marketization, modernization, and technological development, the reformers promoted the emergence of more autonomous forms of social organization from the mid-1980s onwards. The 1980s thus witnessed the gradual growth of numerous professional, academic, business, and trade associations. The reformers also used the business and trade associations to devolve certain functions that had previously been carried out by the state as part of a broader strategy to separate the political from the economic and to shift away from micro-management to macro-management of the economy. This was the first "flow" of civil society in the post-reform period. However, growing discontent over inflation and corruption, coupled with demands for democratization, led to the tumultuous democracy movement of 1989. The party/state responded with force, leading to crackdowns on several, but not all, social organizations. While groups perceived as threatening to the party/state such as autonomous student groups or autonomous trades unions, were prohibited, others were allowed to continue their activities provided they registered under the new 1989 regulations.

In the first few years of the 1990s, the growth of social organizations stagnated as bureaucratic processes of investigation and registration got underway. However, the political shift signaled by Deng Xiaoping's tour of the South and the Fourth World Conference on Women held in Beijing in 1995 provided the catalyst for the emergence of a new layer of more independent women's organizations. Indeed, the rise of these new women's organizations pointed to a new phase in the development of civil society characterized by two key features: first, the more rapid growth of associations concerned with providing services on behalf of and/or representing the interests of groups marginalized in the reform process; and second, the flourishing of new forms of association such as networks, centers, user groups, projects, and third- or fourth-level associations, which bypass the need to register as social organizations.[5]

Since the market reforms began, social organizations have operated across a range of domains, such as academia, professional interests, trade, business, culture, arts, services, charitable work, religion, friendship, and recreation. However, in the 1980s and early 1990s, the majority of social organizations were active in the fields of academia, the professions, business, and trade, while charitable-type groups or organizations concerned with public welfare issues or marginalized and vulnerable groups were few in number. Since the early 1990s, a new stratum of associations concerned with societal groups that are marginalized and vulnerable to the process of reform have emerged. These new organizations include women's groups, legal counseling centers for women, children, and workers, prisoners' wives groups, rural development centers and organizations, associations for people living with HIV/AIDS, self-help cancer groups, poverty alleviation associations, disabled groups, and charitable foundations. The exact number of these organizations is difficult to quantify, though available evidence suggests that by the turn of the millennium, they numbered several hundred. Though organizations concerned with marginalized interests developed rapidly in the 1990s, their numbers are still limited, particularly for those concerned with the interests of marginalized groups such as people living with HIV/AIDS or sex workers, who encounter considerable social prejudice, or with interests the party/state perceives as a threat to social stability, such as workers' rights organizations.

The second key feature in the development of civil society since the mid-1990s is the continuing bypassing of the registration process. Though the 1989 and 1998 regulations on social organizations proved to be a powerful mechanism for stunting the growth of registered intermediary forms of association, they did not succeed in hemming in associational activity. Social actors have responded with ingenuity in finding alternative ways of associating, such as through affiliations to established associations, thereby avoiding the need to register; setting up research institutes and centers under the protective umbrella of more liberal university environments; forming networks and thereby circumventing the restrictions on forming branches; establishing salons, clubs, and informal, loose groups; and organizing through projects. In this way, they have recaptured associational space, pushed back the boundaries set by the party/state, and thereby redefined the truces staked out in both 1989 and 1998.

Nevertheless, whether or not a particular group of people can succeed in bypassing the registration process and deflecting the attention of the party/state depends not least on how threatening their activities appear to local and/or central authorities. The boundaries of this space are subject to constant contestation, negotiation, and repression. This is most evident in the case of organizations attempting to address the needs and interests of laid-off workers, where most initiatives are quickly banned and forced underground, or in the case of spiritual groups such as the Falun Gong, whose capacity to penetrate and mobilize society took the Chinese Communist Party by surprise, unleashing a fierce response.

The period of relative tolerance by the state towards civil society from the mid-1990s onwards was bound to experience some reversal as the CCP intensified preparations for both the 17th Party Congress in 2007 and the Olympic Games in 2008. During that decade of unregistered growth, civil society actors pushed the boundaries of public action, not least because some of the new civil society organizations sought to address social issues that were of considerable concern to the party due to their implications for social stability. Though it was somewhat predictable that the party would seek to reinstate tighter controls over civil society actors in the run-up to and during the 17th Party Congress, the level of tension has not since diminished because of the Olympic Games held in Beijing in August 2008, only one year after the Congress.

The creeping imposition of repressive measures against civil society actors was underway as early as late spring 2005. Influenced by the then president of Russia, Vladimir Putin, China also began to conduct quiet investigations into the activities of foreign non-government organizations (NGOs) in China. In the wake of the Color Revolutions in Georgia, Ukraine, and Kyrgyzstan, President Putin and other former Soviet state leaders asserted that foreign governments were behind these political upheavals. In particular, they maintained that foreign governments had deliberately fomented organized dissent through their support for democracy and human rights groups. This led to the Russian Duma passing a bill in January 2006 that promised to severely restrict NGO activity by providing the authorities with greater powers to regulate and monitor the work, expenditures, and financing of NGOs. In the immediate aftermath of this move, the Russian authorities accused British diplomats of spying in Moscow and making clandestine payments to Russian human rights NGOs. Hundreds of Russian NGOs then released a joint statement arguing that such accusations were reminiscent of Soviet-style denunciations. This clampdown on NGOs was repeated across other former Soviet states such as Kazakhstan, Tajikistan, and Kyrgyzstan.

It was against this background of the Russian government's suspicion of NGOs that China too began to investigate foreign NGOs in China and domestic NGOs receiving grants from external sources in late spring 2005. Conferences on topics perceived as sensitive, such as labor issues that involve external sponsorship, were postponed. Plans to draft a new law on social organizations in China were delayed again as the government looked afresh at the activities of NGOs, especially foreign or foreign-funded groups. Hopes that the constraining regulation requiring domestic social organizations to identify a supervisory agency (*guakao danwei*) were dashed as government anxiety about civil society groups mounted. Moreover, a review of NGOs that registered under the Industrial and Commercial Bureau, not least so as to avoid the more stringent requirements for registration with the Ministry of Civil Affairs, led to the closure of several NGOs carrying out activities deemed politically sensitive. Even though the U.S. government, through its development agencies, has not been able to carry out any extensive democracy promotion work in China in comparison with the so-called "transition" states of the former Soviet Union, the Chinese government's concern about rising social instability has prompted an over-reaction to events in Russia and elsewhere.

China's over-reaction to perceptions of foreign agencies' roles in the Color Revolutions led the party to make a significant blunder in 2007, when it came down hard on the bilingual development magazine entitled China Development Brief. Though the reasons for the clampdown remain obscure, and the subsequent expulsion of Nick Young from China even more perplexing, the behavior of the party/state towards this China-friendly publication reflects an acute sense of insecurity around the party's hold over society. The closure of the English language version of the printed and web versions of the publication was part of an accelerating pre-emptive crackdown on dissidents, internet cafés, and journalists as the date of the Party Congress approached and the Olympics came nearer on the horizon.[6] Across China, surveillance of internet sites, internet cafés, and internet users was stepped up. Dissenting intellectuals and activists were detained for no clear reason. Security in Tibet and Xinjiang was tightened as party leaders feared protests and terrorist attacks during the Olympics. As a prelude to this, the Chinese government signed a memorandum of understanding with members of the Shanghai Co-operation Organization and the Commonwealth of Independent States in April 2005 to cooperate among other things on counter-terrorism, the chief target here being the so-called East Kurdistan terrorist forces.

Though many of these tactics, methods of repression, and targets were not new, controlling society now proved considerably harder than it previously had been for domestic and international reasons. At the domestic level, mounting dissatisfaction in rural areas over land issues, environmental pollution, and political corruption was fueling increasingly strident protests, at times involving violent clashes with local authorities.[7] In the urban areas, migrant workers were becoming more conscious of their worth. By the turn of the millennium, prospects of higher wages in other factories and cities in Shanghai, Zhejiang, and elsewhere were already prompting migrant workers to abandon their jobs in parts of Guangdong. Those who did not vote with their feet gained some leverage in negotiating for better working conditions. Nevertheless, the ongoing throb of workers' protests across China continued to prove a vexing concern for China's political leadership. China's middle classes were growing in number and becoming increasingly vocal around material issues such as property rights, and to a more limited extent around civil and political rights such as freedom of expression. In the run-up to the Party Congress, debate about the prospects for political reform intensified, with contributions being made by leading intellectuals in the Party School such as Yu Keping and Wang Guixiu.[8] Furthermore, civil society actors had already gained space and confidence to maneuver since the mid-1990s, which could not now be withdrawn without resistance.

While these domestic factors were not necessarily new in nature, their intensification and increasing diversity made the job of controlling society much harder, calling for more sophisticated and varied methods of control. However, an increasingly important constraining factor was the internationalization of public issues in China. The internationalization process this involves has various facets. First, political leaders across the world were becoming increasingly aware of the rising economic and political power of China. In some Western countries, political leaders framed a debate around China as a potential threat or opportunity. In its search for minerals and resources, China had busied itself investing in Africa, while major Western powers were caught up waging wars in Iraq and Afghanistan. Moreover, the importance of China's role in international institutions such as the Security Council was becoming more evident as international solutions to the Darfur crisis were proving intractable. Hence, the international spotlight fell more than ever on China. Compared with previous Party Congresses, the recent 17th Party Congress attracted considerable international media attention, as Western political leaders realized that the nature of China's leadership mattered significantly for global economic and political affairs.

Second, the Olympics provided a high-profile opportunity for international critics of China to raise issues around human rights, Tibet, religious freedom, and, to a lesser extent, workers' rights. China's hosting of the Olympics was controversial from the start. The success of this event was crucial to the CCP in providing it with an opportunity to display China's prowess as an economic and political leader and strengthen the legitimacy of the party. However, it also was an occasion on which various international groups could publicize the political fault-lines that exist in China. Though the CCP continues to adhere to the principle that sovereignty prevents external interference in its domestic affairs, China's deepening involvement in global economic and political processes makes it more difficult to realize this principle in practice.

Third, global issues such as climate change, international crime, drug-trafficking, and terrorism require international cooperation. Given China's rapid industrial development, growing middle classes, and rising living standards, China's contribution to climate change has become an international concern. Access to the internet has enabled environmental groups in China to increase their sources of information and establish contact with environmental activists elsewhere. Hence, such issues cannot be treated as solely the prerogative of the CCP. In a nutshell, China's domestic affairs are now increasingly a matter of international concern; or, what constitutes a public issue is becoming more internationalized.

Finally, faster and more extensive electronic communications, more rapid travel, and greater exposure to international news, culture, and media have weakened the party's control over information and international contact, despite China having the world's most stringent regime for controlling the internet. Civil society actors organizing around issues such as Tibet, Xinjiang, the Falun Gong, workers' rights, civil and political rights, freedom of expression and so on have, over the past decades of opening up, forged closer links with supportive non-governmental organizations and actors abroad. Any reports of arrests, closures of organizations, or protests quickly filter out to international sources, which can mobilize a response on a global scale. The increasingly international weave of civil society actors has made it more difficult for the party/state to label certain public issues as "domestic" matters and contain them within China's borders. Thus, the CCP has to tread much more carefully than it may have done in the past. Its intransigencies are more visible and open to international criticism, even though the latter may be muted to some extent as Western political leaders guard economic interests.

What does this all mean for the future of civil society and democratic transition in China?

What then does this most recent ebb and flow in the development of civil society tell us about processes of governance in China and the prospects for democratic transition? Has the Chinese Communist Party consolidated its control over society through corporatist regulation, or has the space for autonomous organization become increasingly plural, diverse, and wider? Have societal actors begun to carve out a public sphere that allows for critical debate around issues that were once regarded as matters in the exclusive domain of the party/state? Is governance becoming more plural, more democratic, more negotiated than before? Or, is the party/state able to maintain and tighten its grip over society? To what extent are state–civil society relations increasingly subject to international influences?

    First, the party/state's attempt to regulate society through a corporatist regulatory framework has proven cumbersome and ineffective. The ingenuity of social actors in bypassing restrictive bureaucratic procedures has weakened the potency of the corporatist framework. Even those organizations registered as social organizations have managed to keep at bay any unwanted state intervention. Citizen organizing has become too widespread and too diffused for the party/state to contain or control it completely. The increasingly complex landscape of associational forms that is successfully circumnavigating regulatory restrictions reflects the ongoing seizure of crevices and spaces by societal actors and the continuing diversification of interests in the arena of civil society. Yet the boundaries of this non-governmental public action are tentative and precarious, as seen in the ebb of civil society since mid-2000. Once the party perceives critique to have gone too far and organizing to have become destabilizing, it sets in train mechanisms of repression to claw back some of those spaces. The party/state and society are caught in a constant ebb and flow of contestation around the spaces for organizing and expression.

However, the development of electronic communications, faster travel, the relaxation of travel restrictions on Chinese citizens, and exposure through international media to different cultures, ideas, and perspectives have made the task of controlling information, contacts, and civil society actors much more complicated for the Chinese party/state. Neither regulation nor repression can yield certain control. The deepening internationalization of issues such as human rights, Tibet, and religious freedom, coupled with the increasingly global nature of problems such as the environment, people-trafficking, and international crime, challenge the very notion of public matters and public authority. The CCP thus faces some serious dilemmas which affect the extent to which it is prepared to liberalize.

On the one hand, the party/state seeks to encourage the development of a "non-profit sector" or "third sector" dedicated to service-delivery. In this way it can address some of the burgeoning social welfare issues. On the other hand, it seeks to contain the emergence of a public sphere that might challenge its monopoly over the determination of public issues. Yet service-delivery and engagement in public affairs and advocacy are rarely neatly separated. At the heart of democracy is the right of citizens to deliberate on public issues. On the one hand, the party is trying to forge a more open political route through inner-party democracy, village elections, public tribunals, and a general rhetoric of more participation. In this way, it is trying to expand the terrain of what can be publicly discussed and by whom. On the other hand, this top-down approach is a cautious attempt to choreograph participation so the aspects of public affairs that can be "shared" more widely remain carefully controlled.

This attempt to widen participation and pluralize the arena of public affairs collides with the CCP's desire to confine public issues to its own territorial boundaries. Certain issues are to remain domestic matters requiring domestic solutions. However, greater global communications and links mean that certain issues are continuously given an international profile. Although the party leadership is concerned with the threat to social stability arising out of uneven economic development, it is aware that too much repression strains its legitimacy and risks fuelling protest and further discontent. Furthermore, while it would like to keep such instability and state repression out of public and international view, processes of internationalization make this increasingly hard to achieve. Thus, internal pressures to open up public affairs, to permit greater freedom of speech and association, and to allow public debate about the political system are much harder for the party to contain and control. In conjunction with international pressures, these internal demands will increasingly combine to push forward a process of political liberalization. However, it is unlikely that this will lead to democratic regime change in the short term; rather, it is likely to lead to more open, transparent, and accountable processes of governance. In some respects, this is the compromise that the party is likely to accept. The party will prefer reformed authoritarianism with limited, selective political liberalization to wholesale democratic regime change. While different political parties have come to power in most other East and Southeast Asian states, the Chinese Communist Party has now maintained its hold on power for over six decades. It has demonstrated chameleon-like qualities in astutely shifting its ideological and economic direction without fundamentally compromising its power and authority. Only a crisis situation is likely to bring about any such fundamental regime change.

In brief, the boundaries around public action and the public sphere are increasingly contested, both domestically and internationally. Amid concern over social stability and awareness of the diversification of interests and of the need to find new mechanisms of participation and interest expression, the party/state is trying to let go of its monopoly over public action, but in a controlled and paternalistic way. Its vision of a depoliticized public sphere dedicated to service-delivery is appealing, as it is to many governments, both democratic and authoritarian. However, it is also illusory, as both domestic actors and international players contest the notion of what is in the public domain. On the domestic front, proto-public spheres of rational-critical debate are beginning to emerge. Researchers and activists are pushing open the spaces for critical reflection by tackling complex and sensitive issues in their research, by linking up with sympathetic media workers, and by influencing government officials through training, personal connections, and advisory positions. Furthermore, they are able to make use of international sources of information and learn about alternative perspectives through global communications, contacts, and travel. Though these proto-spheres of debate are limited to an intellectual and technical elite with patronage links to party/state officials, they nevertheless open up the spaces for non-governmental public action.

As China becomes more embedded in the global economy, the impact of international development agencies, social movements, and global civil society on Chinese civil society is likely to increase. This has implications not only for the future trajectory of civil society, but also for the direction of politics and governance. Given the deepening fissures within society, the likelihood of a deepening global recession, and the potential for social discontent and protest, the importance of fashioning robust, predictable, and legitimate arrangements for the articulation and intermediation of diverse and conflicting interests cannot be underestimated. Without these, state–society relations in China are likely to become increasingly fraught.

Notes

1 See Lin and Zhu (2007) for a detailed exposition of private enterprises in China.
2 See Xinhua (2004).
3 These figures are, however, contested. Using the internationally recognized poverty line of an average income of one US dollar per day, there are 90 million people living in poverty in China (Xinhua 2005).

4 For an excellent discussion of the internationalization of China see Zweig (2002).

5 For a more detailed exploration of this phase see Howell 2004: 143–71.

6 For example, several websites linked to Mongolia, such as the discussion forum Mongolian Youth Forum, the Mongolian Landscape Forum, The New Tribe and others, were closed down over the summer in the run-up to the 17th Party Congress (Reporters Sans Frontieres 2007).

7 For example, in Dongzhou town in Shanwei county, Guangdong province, 2,000 villagers and 1,000 armed police clashed in August 2007 when villagers stopped the construction of a power plant nearby. In the same town two years earlier, the police had shot dead demonstrating villagers (Mingpao 2007). Similarly in Chizhou, Anhui province, one day after the start of the 17th Party Congress, 1,000 people stormed a local police station because of the unfair handling of a traffic accident (HKICHRD 2007). Such large-scale and often violent clashes with public authorities have caused increasing alarm among party leaders and concern as to how best to handle such incidents (Jen 2007).

8 As Wang Guixiu argued, "political structural reform's lagging behind has seriously hindered the in-depth development of economic structural reform" (Ma 2007).

Bibliography

Chen, F. (2000) "Subsistence crises, managerial corruption and labour protests in China," *The China Journal*, 44: 41–63.

Du, Jie (2004) "Gender and governance: the rise of new women's organizations," in J. Howell (ed.) *Governance in China*, Boulder: Rowman and Littlefield Publishers, pp. 172–92.

Du, Jing (2005) "Results of national economic census issued," *Xinhua News Agency*, 6 December 2005.

HKICHRD [Hong Kong Information Centre for Human Rights and Democracy] (2007) "In the 17th Party Congress period, an incident of storming the police station occurred again in Chizhou, Anhui, involving some 1,000 people," (25 October 2007). Online. Available HTTP: <http://www.hkhkhk.com/english/areports.html> (accessed 25 October 2007).

Howell, J. (1997a) "Looking beyond incorporation: Chinese trade unions in the reform era," *Mondes en Developpement*, 25: 73–90.

—— (1997b) "Post-Beijing reflections: creating ripples, but not waves in China," *Women's Studies International Forum*, 20(2): 235–52.

—— (2003) "Trade unionism in China: sinking or swimming?" *The Journal of Communist Studies and Transition Politics*, 19(1): 102–22.

—— (2004) "New directions in civil society: organizing around marginalized interests," in J. Howell (ed.) *Governance in China*, Boulder: Rowman and Littlefield, pp. 143–71.

—— (2006) "New democratic trends in China? Reforming the all-China federation of trade unions," IDS Working Paper 263, Institute of Development Studies.

—— (2008) "ACFTU: beyond reform? The slow march of direct elections," *The China Quarterly*, 196: 845–63.

—— (2009) "Civil society and migrants in China," in R. Murphy (ed.) *Labor Migration and Social Development in Contemporary China*, London: Routledge, pp. 171–94.

Jen, H. W. (2007) "Emergency incidents annoy Zhongnanhai," *Hong Kong Economic Journal*, 20 July 2007, reported in BBC Summary of World Broadcasts, 28 August 2007.

Lee, C. K. (2007) *Against the Law: labor protests in China's rustbelt and sunbelt*, Berkeley: University of California Press.

Lin, S. L. and Zhu, X. D. (2007) *Private Enterprises and China's Economic Development*, London: Routledge.

Ma, H. L. (2007) "Political reform faced with inflection point," Da Gongbao website 18 September 2007, reported in BBC Monitoring Global News, 18 September 2007.

Mingpao News (2007) "Three thousand policemen and villagers clash in Shanwei, Guangdong Province: sanguinary suppression in 2005 causes a sensation; and power plant disputes are sparked off once again," (26 August 2007). Online. Available HTTP: <http://www.mpinews.com/> (accessed 26 August 2007).

Pan, P. (2002) "When workers organize, China's party-run unions resist," *Washington Post Foreign Service*, 15 October 2002.

Pei, M. X. (1998) "Chinese civic associations: an empirical analysis," *Modern China*, 24(3): 285–318.

Pun, N. (2005) *Made in China: women factory workers in a global workplace*, Durham: Duke University Press.

Reporters Sans Frontieres (2007) "Press release," Paris (26 July 2007). Online. Available HTTP: <http://www.rsf.org/> (accessed 26 July 2007).

Shanghai Daily (2008) "China now fifth in millionaire race." Online. Available HTTP: <http://www.china.org.cn> (accessed 31 January 2009).

Solinger, D. (1999) *Contesting Citizenship in Urban China: peasant migrants, the state, and the logic of the market*, Berkeley: University of California Press.

Thireau, I. and Hua, L. S. (2003) "The moral universe of aggrieved Chinese workers: workers' appeals to arbitration committees and letters and visits offices," *The China Journal*, 50: 83–106.

Unger, J. (1996) "Bridges in private business, the Chinese government and the rise of new associations," *The China Quarterly*, 147: 795–819.

Weston, T. B. (2004) "The iron man weeps: joblessness and political legitimacy in the Chinese rustbelt," in P. Hays and S. Rosen (eds) *State and Society in 21st-century China: crisis, contention and legitimation*, New York and London: RoutledgeCurzon, pp. 67–86.

Xinhua [Xinhua News Agency] (2004) "Chinese migrant workers from rural areas totaled 113.9 million in 2003," (14 May 2004). Online. Available HTTP: <http://www.chinaview.cn/>.

Xinhua [Xinhua News Agency] (2005) "90 million Chinese under poverty line," Beijing (27 May 2005). Online. Available HTTP: <http://www.chinaview.cn/>.

Xinhua [Xinhua News Agency] (2006) "Report on China's Foreign Trade," Beijing (29 January 2006). Online. Available HTTP: <http://www.chinaview.cn/>.

Xinhua [Xinhua News Agency] (2007a) "Cumulative FDI in China Exceeds US$750 billion," Beijing (28 August 2007). Online. Available HTTP: <http://www.chinaview.cn/>.

Xinhua [Xinhua News Agency] (2007b) "More than 5.5 million private enterprises now operating in China," (20 November 2007). Online. Available HTTP: <http://www.chinadaily.com.cn/china/2007-8/28/content_6062409.htm> (accessed 20 November 2007).

Zweig, D. (2002) *Internationalizing China: domestic interests and global linkages*, New York: Cornell University Press.

3 Civil society and democracy-making in Taiwan

Reexamining the link

Hsin-Huang Michael Hsiao and Ming-sho Ho

Introduction

Two decades ago, democratizing countries all over the world witnessed groundswells of popular organizing against non-democratic incumbents. The global resurgence seen in grassroots activism was remarkable, as the participants seemed to speak the same language in justifying their struggles, despite the vast cultural differences between them. In the 1980s, the term "civil society" became a universal lingua franca that was freely used in the Polish Solidarity movement (Ost 1990: 21), and the Korean opposition movement (Koo 1993), among Chinese dissident intellectuals and by the Taiwanese opposition (Hsiao 1989: 127–33; He 1995). Whether civil society was expressed in Chinese (*shimin shehui*), Korean (*minjung*), or Taiwanese (*minchian shehui*), it denoted an autonomous and oppositional sphere of independent and voluntary associations that resisted state control and prefigured the state of affairs that was to come following the demise of authoritarianism.

Just as Minerva's owl spread its wings only at dusk, most contemporary scholars of democratic transition failed to take the "civil society fever" seriously. In the 1980s, the so-called transition-by-transaction paradigm conceptualized democratic transition as a game between rival elites whose interactions explained the political trajectory away from authoritarianism (O'Donnell and Schmitter 1986; Share 1987; Di Palma 1990). Collective social actors were assigned a secondary role in this scenario. The rise of social protests was usually seen as a consequence of elite disagreement as well as a transient phenomenon that would come to an end once elites reached a new settlement. It was even feared that an overactive civil society might jeopardize the fragile democratic consensus.

There then came a reevaluation of civil society. Political theorists discussed the liberating potential of the civil society ideal (Taylor 1990; Walzer 1992; Cohen and Arato 1994; Hsiao *et al.* 1995: 110–16). In empirical studies, collective action was now seen as an integral component of breaking loose from authoritarian control. Working-class mobilization played a critical role in the path toward democracy (Tarrow 1995; Collier and Mahoney 1997;

Collier 1999). Even when analyzing the less overtly politicized sectors of civil society, scholars discovered that the equal and open style of self-organizing in NGOs, civil associations, or rural cooperatives was a major progress from elite-dominated clientelism (Fox 1996; Schak and Hudson 2003; Hsiao 2005). Summarizing the existing literature, Larry Diamond (1994, 1999: 233–50) provided a thorough list of the democratic functions of civil society, such as monitoring of the state, facilitating public participation, creating cross-cutting cleavages, training leadership, and so on.

Undoubtedly, the most influential scholar who argues for a positive link between civil society and democracy is Robert Putnam (1994, 2000). He contends that the presence of "civic community," i.e. the readiness to cooperate with others in an equal, trustful, and tolerant fashion, enhanced the performance of political institutions. He later uses the term "social capital" to highlight the beneficial consequences of associational capacity. Basically, Putnam conceptualizes civil society as a political culture that lubricates the democratic machinery. Without it, no matter how well an institution is designed, it is not going to work well.

However, the reverse assessment of civil society's role and the attempt to bestow on it the privilege of being the most significant variable has given rise to skepticism since the late 1990s. Was social capital per se an unmitigated good thing? What happened when the bad guys, for example, Nazis, racists, and criminal gangs, got their own associations? Skeptics often pointed to the tragedy of the Weimar Republic as a grim reminder that widespread associationism in a polarized society did not help democracy to take root, but rather hastened its demise (Berman 1997; Tenfelde, 2000; Anheier 2003; Bermeo 2003). In addition, the eulogists of civil society were criticized for neglecting social conflicts and narrowly looking at the consensual and integrating aspect only (Whitehead 1997; Edwards and Foley 1998; Edwards *et al.* 2001; Szreter 2002). Armony (2004) further contends that the supposed link between civic engagement and democracy is dubious at best. Without the rule of law, voluntary associationism is liable to breed antidemocratic organizations. Therefore, it is not true that association is inherently and universally positive for democracy; instead, "what matters was the context in which people associated" (Armony 2004: 2).

Reflecting on this debate, one is likely to gain the impression that optimists and skeptics simply look at different social organizations and quickly generalize from them. Bluntly put, while Putnam takes the parent–teacher associations (PTAs) as his exemplary case, Armony appears to be more concerned with the Aryan Brotherhood. Despite the seemingly intense academic cross-fire, they avoid shooting at each other's territory. Given the fact that civil society is necessarily heterogeneous, one should always be specific when using that term.

Second, for a more fruitful reexamination, we need to pay serious attention to the state–civil society link in a critical way. As stressed by many critics (Levi 1996; Tarrow 1996), the 1990s theorizing of civil society failed to take political institutions into consideration. Take the paradigmatic collapse of the Weimar Republic as an example: polarized patterns of civic associations are certainly not conducive to a sustainable democracy. Notwithstanding this, the insights gained from the earlier studies should not be slighted. Gerschenkron (1989: 92–3) and Moore (1978: 381–91) have demonstrated that the political ascendancy of Nazism was facilitated by the reactionary forces that controlled the military and judicial apparatus of state. It follows that blaming everything on an "overactive" civil society is not a fair call. Consequently, analyzing the behavior of civil society would not be complete without understanding its political context.

What is needed is a comprehensive historical analysis of the link between civil society and democracy-making in one particular new democracy. Taiwan is a suitable case on the ground that it has completed all phases of democratization since the 1980s. The first regime change took place in 2000 as the Democratic Progressive Party (DPP) won the presidential election for the first time, and the second regime change happened in 2008 when the Kuomintang (KMT) made a successful comeback. This chapter will examine civil-society forces and their influences on the making of Taiwan's new democracy in the three decades since the 1970s.

We devote our exclusive attention to social movements as the most critical sector in Taiwan's civil society. As a pattern of contentious claim-making (McAdam *et al.* 1996), social movement is highly sensitive to the political surroundings in which it operates. While other sectors of civil society might be tolerated during a period of high authoritarianism as long as they stay clear of the dangerous realm of politics, due to the oppositional nature of social movement, it is vulnerable to repressive control. As a result, by tracing the evolution of social movements, we can gain a clearer picture of the progressive development of civil society.

In the following sections we will analyze Taiwan's social movements through different stages: authoritarian crisis (1970–1979), soft authoritarianism (1980–1986), liberalization (1987–1992), democratization (1993–1999), and the DPP government (2000–2007). We then conclude with a preliminary diagnosis of the second KMT government (2008–).

The emergence of the public sphere in the authoritarian crisis (1970–1979)

Before Taiwan entered the tumultuous decade of the 1970s, the KMT regime had consolidated its control on the island. In 1947, the Taiwanese call for political reform and autonomy (the 28 February incident) was ruthlessly crushed. Following the military massacre and the white-terror reign, the émigré regime was free of all potential opposition. The KMT was subsequently able to embark on the systematic social engineering of Taiwanese society, first for anti-communist war mobilization, and later for export-led industrialization.

During this period, Taiwan had virtually no bona fide civil society organizations. Furthermore, since the KMT adopted a Leninist control strategy, its penetrating power had been considerably stronger than that of other run-of-the-mill authoritarian regimes. By planting the party-state into every sphere of daily life and preemptively fostering pro-regime organizations, the KMT succeeded in stultifying organizing attempts from below (Dickson 1993; Kung 1998; Ho 2007). Even apparently harmless popular religious activities, arguably the most important vehicle for communal self-organizing before the advent of modernity, were placed under watchful surveillance, with ritual festivals being ordered to be curtailed (Jordan 1994: 150–1; Gates 1996: 231–6).

Prior to the 1970s, Taiwan's civic organizations existed in a highly atrophied pattern. Local charity-oriented associations and foundations were allowed to exist only with the blessing of KMT officials. The international linkage to the United States helped some transplanted social organizations to obtain permission. Middle-class social clubs, such as Junior Chambers of Commerce International, Rotary Clubs, and Lion Clubs, were primarily led by politically connected mainlanders and Taiwanese elites. In addition, some church-related international philanthropic organizations were allowed to operate, such as World Vision, the Christian Children's Fund (CCF), the Young Men's Christian Association (YMCA), and the Young Women's Christian Association (YWCA). All these organizations were "depoliticized" or "nonpolitical" in nature. Their right to exist was conditionally granted so that they were certainly not in a position to promote an independent agenda for social change or to influence the course of state policy (Hsiao, 2005).

In 1971, Taiwan's representative was expelled from the United Nations. Richard Nixon's 1972 visit to China and the subsequent normalization of relations between the People's Republic of China and other major countries further eroded the legitimacy of the KMT government in the international community (Wakabayashi 1994: 174–5). A series of diplomatic setbacks prompted a "soul-searching" process among Taiwanese intellectuals. At that time, a so-called "postwar generation" came of age. This generation was more willing to look at Taiwan's current situation realistically, without nostalgia for the Japanese period or exiled Chinese nationalism (Hsiau 2008). As a result, a new indigenous consciousness began to emerge in the cultural arena, as manifested in the rise of the Cloud Gate Dance Group (1975), the campus folk song movement (1976), indigenous literature (1977), and indigenization of the social sciences (1979).

These four successful cultural indigenization movements together formed the first "voice" of civil society after a prolonged period of forced silence. The KMT's initial response to these cultural initiatives can be characterized as guarded suspicion. The state avoided taking the route of direct repression for many reasons. First, by limiting themselves to the purely cultural sphere, they did not immediately raise political demands. Second, the internationally besieged KMT regime needed social support from Taiwanese society. As a consequence, Chiang Ching-Kuo, who took over the reins in the mid-1970s, proceeded to indigenize the political leadership gradually as a gesture designed to appeal to the alienated Taiwanese majority.

Aside from cultural indigenization, intellectuals began to call for political reforms during the 1970s. As the legal space for voluntary association was highly restricted at that time, magazine publishers turned out to be an easier yet effective channel, though censorship was still ubiquitous. Two magazines, *University* (*tahsüeh*) (1971–1973) and *Formosa* (*meilitao*) (1979), bore witness to the rise and fall of these efforts.

University was founded in 1968, but did not become a political magazine until 1971, when its editorial group began to include a broader array of younger activists from academia and business. *University* advocated a number of reforms, such as the reelection of aging parliamentarians, abolishing the compulsory fertilizer-for-crops program, and freedom of speech. Ideologically, *University* supported the KMT's anti-communism while championing a form of moderate liberalism. In the initial period, its core activists worked *sub rosa* with Chiang Ching-kuo, who was then building up his power base, and was welcomed as a more palatable alternative to other old guards. Nonetheless, once Chiang secured his position, the honeymoon was over. *University's* conservative members were recruited into the government, while its radicals were harassed and persecuted by the KMT. The antagonism culminated in the National Taiwan University Philosophy Department incident (1974). In that event, some liberal faculty staff and students were expelled—a very symbolic move aimed at disciplining dissident intellectuals (Huang 1976).

Five years after the collapse of *University*, the opposition scored a major victory in the 1977 election. Encouraged, the opposition adopted a bolder strategy by staging street demonstrations and organizing *Formosa* in 1979, which was intended as the embryonic form of a political party. Like *University*, opposition intellectuals were concerned with political liberties as well as the social plight of the lower class. The first issue of *Formosa* featured articles on the victims of nuclear energy and exploited cabdrivers. However, unlike its predecessor's more conciliatory approach, *Formosa* demanded immediate democratization from the KMT. On 10 December 1979, a human rights demonstration in Kaohsiung led to a bloody clash with the police force in an event commonly known as the *Formosa* incident. The subsequent round-up and prosecution of *Formosa* activists was a grave, if temporary, setback for the opposition movement.

To conclude, cultural indigenization movements, *University*, and *Formosa* were the precious sprouts of the public sphere in the 1970s. Given the harsh reality of political control, Taiwan's civil society could only manage to survive in the rarified sphere of cultural and intellectual activities. The tragedy of the *Formosa* incident not only concluded a decade of intellectual agitation, but also clearly demonstrated the highly proscribed scope of civil society activities.

The rise of social movements under soft authoritarianism (1980–1986)

Winckler (1984) uses the term "soft authoritarianism" to characterize the period immediately after the 1979 *Formosa* incident. In the early 1980s, the KMT resorted to undisguised repression less frequently, while the anti-KMT forces were also able to secure their status as the opposition. It was during this period that Taiwan's social movements emerged, largely crystallized in the form of middle-class advocacy and grassroots protests.

A group of reform-minded middle-class professionals (lawyers, professors, medical doctors, and journalists) spearheaded the development of civil society with their public engagement (Hsiao and Koo 1997). Their participation was instrumental in facilitating a number of social movement organizations that played pioneering roles. They were the Consumers' Foundation (1980), *Awakening* magazine (1982) (which supported the women's movement), *Mountain Youth* magazine (1983) (which advocated for the aboriginal movement), the Taiwan Association for Human Rights (1984), the Taiwan Labor Legal Support Association (1984), and *New Environment* magazine (1986). It should be noted that establishing a legally registered membership organization was still very difficult at that time. Most of those early efforts took the organizational form of magazine publishers or foundations (*Awakening* and *New Environment* were later reorganized into foundations), while others deliberately chose to operate outside state regulations.

The social profile of the middle-class leadership largely determined the style of the movement. They regarded themselves as altruistic educators whose role was to enlighten the public and governmental officials. Many of these activists went to the United States for advanced education, so they were eager to bring back the new ideas that they acquired overseas. For example, the 1979 Three Mile Island accident converted many university professors into anti-nuclear crusaders. In a sense, these activists worked to shepherd Taiwanese society along the road of modernization. They expected cooperative responses from the more liberal segments of the KMT, rather than challenging them directly.

Middle-class reform advocates were circumspect in their tactics. While many of them sympathized with the political opposition, they were careful to present a non-partisan facade to avoid antagonizing the KMT. In addition, when facing the mounting grassroots discontents, they played the role of advisers and avoided becoming involved in disorderly protests. Victims of consumer problems and industrial pollution were provided with legal advice; however, when they decided to take it to the streets, their middle-class allies simply backed off.

In environmental movements, the simultaneous rise of middle-class advocacy and grassroots protests was most noticeable. The former focused on the "soft issues" of nature conservation (Hsiao 1998: 36–7) or high-level energy policy (Ho 2003a: 688–92). Their early efforts were somewhat successful in that some state-sponsored projects were abandoned due to environmental considerations and the government even decided to halt temporarily the construction of a controversial nuclear power plant. While middle-class environmentalists sought to create a favorable climate of public opinion, grassroots pollution victims could air their grievances only through unruly protests. By organizing vigilante groups, blockading factories, and vandalism, they insisted on immediate compensation and relief from polluters (Ho and Su 2008: 2405–7). By the mid-1980s, anti-pollution protests had converged into a strong stream of locally based environmentalism.

The initial development of the Taiwanese women's movement also reflected these characteristics. A contemporary report on the early *Awakening* activists showed that they tended to be young, highly educated, working professionally, and living in the Taipei metropolitan area (Wang 1988: 103–4). Immediately after *Awakening* was first published, there was a debate over abortion as the Eugenics Law was under review (1982–1984). When Taiwan's feminists campaigned for a liberal version, it was noteworthy that they refrained from using the "rights argument" that might sound too provocative to the conservatives. Instead, they pleaded for the so-called "unfortunate girls" who needed legalized abortion to end their miseries. As a result, women's rights and bodily autonomy were little talked about at that time (Kuan 2008: 145).

Again, the KMT government's response to the nascent social movements was largely suspicious and resistant. When the cost of repression was low, the state managed to stifle the open expression of discontents by expelling college students, taking workers' leaders to court, and harassing anti-pollution demonstrators. In some cases, KMT officials preempted the emergence of social movement organizations by establishing pro-regime groups with a similar purpose. Taiwan's consumer movement and environmental movement encountered this "soft form of control" in 1980 and 1982, respectively.

In sum, amid clamorous grassroots protests and middle-class advocacy, Taiwan's civil society gave rise to bona fide social movements in the early 1980s. Equally evident was the evolution of political opposition, as it succeeded in establishing the first tolerated opposition party, the Democratic Progressive Party (DPP), on 28 September 1986. The resilience of the opposition was in part explained by the strong support it received from middle-class professionals and small-and-medium businesspersons who were alienated by the KMT's pro-big business orientation (Solinger 2006). The fact that the DPP's founding ceremony at Taipei's Grand Hotel was made possible through the arrangements made by its Rotary Club supporters (Roy 2003: 172) bore testimony to the maturation of civil society in Taiwan.

Popular upsurge during liberalization (1987–1992)

When political opposition activists decided to organize the DPP, it was an act of defiance that was expected to be met with a merciless crackdown. Instead, Chiang Ching-kuo signaled his tolerance and further proceeded to end the

38-year martial rule in July 1987. With the onset of political liberalization, the government legalized rallies and demonstrations (1988) and gave greater latitude to civic organizing (1989). Encouraged by this favorable political wind, Taiwan's social movements attracted more broad-based participation, adopted radical strategies, and built political alliances with the DPP. Frustrated by the mounting wave of popular uprising, the KMT had reverted from its initial tolerance to repression by the end of the decade. Civil society and the KMT regime were closing in on a collision course, and the former won the final confrontation as KMT hardliners were forced to take a political bow by the Taiwanese chairman, Lee Teng-hui.

The long overdue end to martial law was a significant stimulus to Taiwan's civil society, as many latent discontents suddenly emerged into the public arena. Social movements began to embrace wider sectors, even among those who were thought to be too "conservative" or "traditional" to join the bandwagon of social protests, such as farmers, the Hakka ethnic group, schoolteachers, and the urban lower middle class. Long regarded as the stable pillars of rural society, Taiwan's peasants erupted in a violent anti-government protest on 20 May 1988, which was triggered by the threat of agricultural imports that would endanger their livelihoods. As Taiwan's farmers' movement took to the stage, its leaders also articulated a number of demands aimed at addressing their economic and social plight, such as the lack of social insurance, overpriced fertilizers, and undemocratic governance in farmers' associations and irrigation associations. The Hakka used to be a socially "invisible" ethnic minority in Taiwan in that they were constantly assimilated into dominant groups and mainstream society. In December 1988, a historic demonstration was staged to demand recognition of their specific culture and mother tongue (Hsiao and Huang 2001: 330).

In the past, schoolteachers were assigned with the mission of "spiritual national defense." As a result, schoolteachers were placed under strict control from their training stage onwards. A month after the lifting of martial law, dissident teachers organized the Taiwanese Teachers' Human Rights Association to demand freedom in teaching and legalization of their labor union. Two teachers' strikes subsequently took place. Finally, the speculative boom of the late 1980s angered the urban salaried class who resented climbing house prices. With their hopes of homeownership dashed, they called themselves "snails without shells" and initiated a series of protests in 1989 (Hsiao and Liu 2001). In addition to these newcomers, the pre-1987 style of more or less moderate reformism persisted. In 1988, the Humanistic Education Foundation was set up with the help of middle-class parents and scholars to promote a more liberal education system.

The newly liberalized atmosphere also encouraged more people to mobilize around sensitive issues involving political taboos. Ex-political prisoners and overseas Taiwanese banned from returning home struggled to have their voices heard, and their efforts were often assisted by the newly formed DPP. The first public commemorative activities for the 28 February incident took place in 1987, forty years after the tragedy, and later even evolved into a fully fledged peace movement demanding that the KMT rectify its historical wrongdoings.

The second characteristic of social movements in this period was their radicalization. Gone was the era of parallel mobilization by middle-class advocates and grassroots activists; now, they joined hands to pressure the reluctant KMT government. During its first year, the *New Environment* witnessed an internal dispute, and some of its radical members left to organize the Taiwan Environmental Protection Union at the end of 1987. The latter vowed to work with localized grassroots anti-pollution protest groups which were emerging everywhere. Similarly, Taiwanese workers staged two waves of spontaneous strikes for annual bonuses in 1988 and 1989. Workers were encouraged to wrest back control of their labor unions, which had been under the sway of the KMT party/state (Ho 2003b).

There was a widespread zeitgeist among movement activists to move toward bolder gestures and claims. The aboriginal movement began to demand the ownership of their ancestral lands, and a contingent of activists bulldozed a statue that glorified a biased and historically disputed figure (the so-called Wu Fong myth). Earlier, university students' activism was largely confined to campuses, where they were involved in skirmishes with conservative administrators. After 1987, students built up inter-campus organizations. They were not only active in the rising workers' and farmers' movements, but also took part in the debate on the revision of the University Law in 1988. The first protest against the unfair burden of tuition fees was staged in 1989. As they mobilized for these activities, students became better organized and more self-conscious. In March 1990, students initiated a week-long protest demanding the immediate abolition of the National Assembly and other steps to hasten the advent of democratization by occupying Chiang Kai-shek Memorial Hall. The 1990 student protest, modeled after the Tiananmen movement that had taken place one year previously, captured national attention, and in the end helped Lee Teng-hui to gain the upper hand over his hardliner rivals within the KMT (Wright 2001: 95–128).

Finally, radicalized social movements tilted toward an alliance with the DPP. In a number of cases, social movement activists had outgrown their psychological fear of being "partisan." DPP politicians were most heavily involved in workers' movement and environmental movement. Its local office-holders offered favorable legal interpretations to support protestors, while some of its activists assumed protest leadership positions directly. In March 1990, student protestors and liberal intellectuals kept at arm's length with the DPP, but two months later, in a protest against the nomination of the military strongman Hau Po-tsun for premier, they closely coordinated their efforts with the DPP (Teng 1992: 318–25).

The gradual opening up of political seats for election also encouraged social movements to try this new avenue. In the 1989, 1990, and 1992 elections, many movement activists joined electoral races. More often than not, they campaigned as DPP candidates, which further helped the opposition and social movements to cooperate in a united front against the KMT.

The widening scope of social movements as well as their radicalization and politicization could be characterized as "popular surge" (O'Donnell and Schmitter, 1986: 53–4). Facing an ever-increasing wave of social protests, the KMT government was initially tolerant, and even sought to incorporate their demands through administrative initiatives. The Environmental Protection Administration, the Council of Labor Affairs, and a Mountain-area Administration Section under the Ministry of the Interior were set up to meet the challenges of environmental, workers', and aboriginese movements within one month of the lifting of martial law. The government was busy in reforming its legal framework so as to channel social contentions peacefully. Even when dealing with radical protests, the KMT government demonstrated its self-restraint. The aboriginal protestors who demolished the Wu Fong statue were later acquitted in court. A violent blockade against a state-owned enterprise in Kaohsiung was tacitly tolerated, allowing it to continue for more than three years.

However, from 1989, the KMT government shifted to a repressive stance against social movements. One year into his presidential tenure, Lee Teng-hui allied himself with KMT hardliners and their shared diagnosis was that the insurgent civil society needed to be curbed. The conservative involution culminated in May 1990, as Lee appointed the archconservative Hau Po-tsun to become Premier. As soon as Hau took office, he vowed to reassert "public authority" against the lawlessness that had emerged. Social protests were framed as a disturbance of social order, and their leaders were characterized as "social movement bullies." Workers' movement, environmental movement, and farmers' movement were most victimized by such state repression, as many activists were indicted and sent to jail. New legal drafts restricting the scope of demonstration rights and removing workers' protections were considered and sent to the Legislature. With its defiant move to raise the Taiwan independence issue, the DPP was even threatened with dissolution by decree.

While many social movements experienced a temporary setback in those mean years, the reinvigorated state repression ultimately failed. There were two main reasons for this. First, despite the high-handed treatment of social movements, opinion surveys showed that public support for social movements had not declined as expected. Instead, a 1992 survey showed a higher level of support than in the previous year, which persuasively demonstrated the futility of state repression (Hsiao 1997: 7). Second, one side effect of the KMT's about-face was to help cement the political alliance between social movements and the DPP. When the DPP scored a major victory in the 1992 legislative election, it was immediately seen as a vindication of social movement activists. The KMT's electoral setback hastened the political demise of the hardliners, as symbolized in Hau Po-tsu's reluctant resignation in early 1993. As Lee Teng-hui shifted again toward a reformist course, social movements were no longer singled out for repression.

In hindsight, the sudden and widespread rise of social movements put positive pressure on the government as Taiwan moved away from authoritarianism. It is important to note that one of the last attempts made by the KMT hardliners was to suppress social movements, and their subsequent failure cleared a major obstacle toward the eventual democratization of Taiwan. In this sense, civil society played an undeniably important role in defeating the conservative backlash, even if in an indirect and unforeseeable way.

Toward a movement society in the democratizing period (1993–1999)

The period between the convocation of the Second Legislative Yuan (1993) and the DPP's rise to power (2000) saw the gradual institutionalization of competitive party politics in Taiwan. With the stepwise opening up of top-level political seats to election, mayoral and provincial governor seats in 1994 and presidential elections being held in 1996, the DPP became an established contestant in the political race and its linkage with social movements began to weaken. Weaned off their political support, social movements embarked on a more independent course. They were capable of devising innovative strategy, making substantial policy impacts, and reaching out to broader society with the help of the more liberal political climate. It was during this period that social movements became a recognized, accepted, and routine phenomenon in Taiwan's new democracy. In this sense, the configuration of this period fitted the description of the so-called "movement society" (Meyer and Tarrow 1998).

Immediately after the KMT reorganized its cabinet in early 1993 came the clear signs that the period of reinforced control over civil society was over. Grassroots blockades against polluting factories were not clamped down on as quickly as they used to be, and the legal maneuvers designed to limit workers' rights were soon abandoned. Official statistics demonstrated a greater degree of government lenience in dealing with social protests (see Table 3.1). Clearly, the government prosecuted and sentenced fewer protestors, and turned down applications for legal demonstrations less frequently.

Taking advantage of the favorable political atmosphere, Taiwan's social movements were able to adopt a wider range of tactics. For example, legal lobbying was not a meaningful option prior to the genuine reelection of the Legislative Yuan in 1992. Feminists sought to have their voices heard during the abortion debate in the mid-1980s and initiated a draft law on gender equality in force as early as 1989. But it was not until the mid-1990s that their legal offensives found their way onto the legislative agenda. Revising civil regulations on marriage (1996) and legislation on sexual offenses (1997) and domestic violence (1998) were their major achievements in this period. Other social movement organizations also found the Legislative Yuan a vital source

Table 3.1 A comparison of policing in 1988–1992 and 1993–1999 (annual average)

	1988–1992	*1993–1999*
Number of indicted persons per million participants	24.1	12.6
Number of persons sentenced to more than one year in prison	1	0
Percentage of application cases rejected	0.32%	0.00%

Sources: ROC. Judicial Yuan (1988–2000) *Taiwan Judiciary Statistics*, Taipei: Judicial Yuan. ROC. Ministry of the Interior, National Policy Agency (1988–2000) *Taiwan Police Statistics*, Taipei: National Police Agency.

Note: All of these figures are based on the Demonstration Law. The reported figures are calculated by the authors.

of leverage for realizing their goals. Education reformers succeeded in liberalizing the system of teacher training that shattered the monopoly of conservative normal colleges in 1994. The labor movement was able to extend the scope of the Labor Standard Law to white-collar workers in 1996. Finally, environmentalists were also able to pass their version of an environmental impact assessment in 1994, even though business and economic affairs officials were united in their opposition (Ho 2004). In 1996, the Alliance for Social Movement Legislation was co-founded by many social movement organizations to coordinate their efforts, showed the degree to which lobbying was used as a productive strategy.

Furthermore, social movements also succeeded in gaining other policy participation avenues. The Wildlife Conservation Advisory Committee (1995), the Gender Equality Education Committee (1997), and the Committee on Women's Rights Promotion (1997) represented tangible progress in this regard. Though these organs were mainly consultative in nature, the fact that movement activists had now been awarded quasi-official status showed that Taiwan's democratizing state had begun to incorporate a broader range of demands from civil society. Needless to say, not all movements were equally successful. The teachers' movement to legalize unionism was frustrated, as a compromised version of the Teachers' Association was instituted in 1995. The labor movement's attempt to break loose from KMT state corporatism was only partially successful prior to 2000. Local federations of industrial unions were legalized, but their national representative was not recognized by the KMT government (Ho 2006).

During this period, social movements tried to explore the potential of these newly opened institutional channels and spaces, while continuing to mobilize their constituencies for street demonstrations. Anti-nuclear demonstrations and labor's Mayday rally became institutionalized as a kind of annual ritual. Staging large-scale street protests was still deemed to be the most important movement strategy to galvanize officials into responsive action.

As social movements were gaining political influence, a contingent of activists turned their attention to their local communities in an effort to deepen the demands for social reform. This "community turn" in Taiwan's social movements first took place in the early 1990s, as some activists began to rediscover their hometown history to promote a new local identity. In so doing, they came to face an inevitable challenge from the clientelistic elites that had dominated Taiwanese local politics (Yang 2007). Later, an increasing number of specific anti-pollution movements evolved into more general locality-based community movement organizations that could better sustain the enthusiasm for local activism. Before the mid-1990s, the aboriginal movement was largely limited to the young elites and urban migrants, with a lack of persistent efforts to mobilize hometown residents. By riding the community-turn wave, aboriginal activists also sought to remake their native society. In 1998, education reform advocates redirected their attention away from state policy and initiated a "community college" movement. Rather than being an auxiliary institution to mainstream education, Taiwan's community colleges were devised to foster a greater scope of civil-society participation by bringing critical knowledge to more people at various localities.

In addition, there was also a noticeable "professional turn." A decade ago, a small group of Taiwan's enlightened liberal professionals had played the role of people's advocates to jump-start social movements; in the mid-1990s, a new generation of professionals carried the momentum of activism into their working sphere. Journalists demanded that their professional autonomy be respected by their bosses. Conscientious medical doctors worked for better protection of patients' rights. Lawyers, judges, and public attorneys joined hands in a movement for judicial reform to protect the judiciary from political interference. The Association for Taiwan Journalists (1995), the Judicial Reform Foundation (1997), the Taiwan Health Care Reform Foundation (1999), and the Taiwan Media Watch (1999) were the main organizational bases used to launch these new reform initiatives.

By the mid-1990s, it was clear that the DPP had matured into a would-be ruling party that was ready to assume national leadership. There was a perceptible "centrist turn" as DPP politicians grew more cautious and reserved in dealing with their social movement allies. The intimate camaraderie that prevailed prior to 1992 was gone, and in some cases activists began to criticize the DPP for "taking political advantage of social movements." In 1996, some environmentalists organized the Taiwan Green Party to dramatize their independence from the DPP. Nevertheless, before the 2000 regime change, the DPP was still widely perceived as much more pro-movement than its main political rivals.

At the same time, when the DPP tried to embrace swinging median voters by shedding its radical past, Lee Teng-hui's reformist leadership made significant overtures to social movements. In 1994–1996, an official Advisory Committee on Education Reform was formed. An education reform based on humanistic and liberal values was subsequently adopted as the official policy, at least nominally. The Judicial Yuan also convened a national conference in response to the rising demands for judicial independence in 1994. Around the same period, the national government started to promote an "integrated community building" initiative. Under this policy, state agencies channeled financial resources to nascent community organizations all over Taiwan.

It cannot be overemphasized that the KMT government's responses were highly selective and based upon carefully crafted calculation. The social movements with more system-threatening potential, such as the labor movement and the environmental movement, continued to be politically excluded throughout the 1990s. Nevertheless, the partial incorporation of social movement demands into the official agenda helped to rebuild the government's legitimacy as the spokesperson of Taiwan's civil society, especially after the bruising and confrontational period of 1989–1992. It was an interesting phenomenon that once the state adopted an inclusive attitude, some social movement organizations found it necessary to add the prefix "non-official" or "civil" (*minchian*) to their titles to avoid confusion. Obviously, when the political environment turned out to be favorable for social movements, their collective identity became even more salient even though their distance from government officials had been considerably narrowed.

Incorporation and its discontents under the DPP government (2000–2008)

The DPP's Chen Shui-bian won the 2000 presidential election on a reform agenda (Hsiao 2002: 238). During Chen's campaign, many social movement activists were recruited to formulate his policy proposals, thus adding movement demands to his platform. However, the DPP's eight-year rule proved a bittersweet experience for these once-hopeful activists. While social movements were further incorporated into the policy-making process, it became increasingly difficult to engineer meaningful and significant changes due to the political weakness of the DPP government and its subsequent "conservative turn."

A number of movement activists were able to occupy administrative positions. Among the five Environment Protection Administration ministers the DPP appointed, for example, two were anti-nuclear activists who were considered too radical for the KMT. Two of the three DPP ministers of education were considered to be allies of the education reform movement. In addition, younger activists also obtained the opportunity of working as aides or assistants in state agencies. These appointments facilitated communication between social movements and government officials.

The procedural incorporation of social movements, which had been tentatively developed in the previous era, was further deepened and institutionalized. The Environmental Impact Assessment Committee and the Committee on Women's Rights Promotion, for instance, were respectively set up in 1995 and 1997; some movement activists were then recruited as members of these committees. The DPP government liberalized its composition rule so that activists could be given more latitude in policy-making (Tu and Peng 2008: 128). The DPP recognized the Taiwan Confederation of Trade Unions as a bona fide national federation of labor in 2000, consequently allowing independent unionists to attend the meetings of the Council of Labor Affairs. Moreover, the DPP set up new official institutions which helped to routinize activists' participation, including the Council for Hakka Affairs, the National Human Rights Commissions, and the Committee for a Nuclear-free Homeland.

In terms of law-making, social movements succeeded in implementing their agendas in this period. The Protection for Workers Incurring Occupational Accidents Act (2001), the Gender Equality in Employment Act (2002), the Employment Insurance Act (2002), and the Protective Act for Mass Redundancy of Employees (2003) were the fruits of labor movement lobbying since the 1990s. Environmentalists were also relieved to see the Basic Environment Act (2002) finally being passed after more than a decade's effort.

However, although social movements gained procedural power and made legislative progress, they continued to find it difficult to translate their growing influence into substantial gains. There were several reasons for this.

First, the DPP was handicapped by being a minority government facing a hostile legislature still controlled by the KMT. From 2006, a series of political scandals centering on Chen Shui-bian's family effectively paralyzed the government. Thus, even when DPP incumbents made efforts to promote changes sought by social movements, their ability to do so was highly constrained. For example, the attempt to terminate the controversial nuclear power plant project (2000–2001) met dogged resistance from opposition parties, and was finally abandoned.

Second, weak government invited counter-mobilizations on the part of those who would be negatively affected by the ascendancy of social movements. In 2002, two large-scale mobilizations by schoolteachers who wanted to protect their privileged exemption from income tax and farmers' association leaders who resisted financial regulation of their corrupt cooperatives derailed the government's reform proposals. In 2003, educational conservatives rose to challenge the humanist policy that had been adopted since the late 1990s. Undoubtedly, the rise of counter-mobilizations complicated the political landscape, forcing social movements to fight an increasingly uphill battle.

Last but not least, during its tenure, the DPP constantly changed its position, often swinging back and forth between reformism and political compromise and expediency. In 2001, Chen Shui-bian vowed to "salvage the economy" by loosening environmental regulations and welfare policies. He later maintained that welfare redistribution should take a back seat to economic development (Ho 2005: 411–13). By the time Chen faced reelection in 2004, the DPP government no longer stressed its reformist credentials during the campaign. The DPP government originally put forth a Green Silicon Island Plan with an emphasis on environmental sustainability and social justice. However, this reformist agenda was largely shelved as the DPP took a conservative turn. It only reemerged during Su Tseng-chang's premiership (2006–2007) as he laid out the Big Warmth Plan to increase welfare and social spending. Nevertheless, this belated return to reformism was too brief. As Chen's government was deeply mired in scandals and challenges from both within and without, nationalistic mobilization became the only way to secure Chen Shui-bian's precarious position. In so doing, social reforms were again put to one side and social movement organizations were mostly alienated and frustrated.

This was a frustrating experience for social movement activists who had gained insider status and yet remained "powerless" to influence the government's course. Nevertheless, it would be wrong to characterize the DPP's incorporation of civil society, limited as it was, as pure-and-simple co-optation, as if movement activists had given up on their agendas. In many instances, the strategic use of their political positions still helped to make a difference. In 2001, two national policy advisors to the president who came from the welfare movement and the labor movement threatened to resign in opposition to a planned individualistic version of the national pension system. In 2006, two members of the Committee on Women's Rights Promotion also protested against the move to require a "cooling-off period" before abortion. Both incidents were resolved in favor of the social movements. These examples showed that though movement activists were not necessarily able to make progressive changes, they were still influential enough to prevent obvious policy regression.

By and large, the KMT did not modify its right-wing stand on environmental protection, labor rights, and human rights during its eight-year period of opposition. With the DPP's reorientation, the ideological differences between the two parties were arguably narrower. Before 2004, the KMT made some symbolic gestures in response to social protests against increases in tuition fees and unemployment to embarrass the DPP government. After its second electoral debacle in 2004, the KMT reverted to its traditional aloofness toward social movements. While Pan-Blue rank-and-file supporters joined the 2006 anti-Chen protest en masse, the KMT continued to avoid any contact with social movement activists before the second regime change.

Conclusion: prospects after the second regime change (2008–)

Following its consecutive victories in the legislative and presidential elections in 2008, the KMT under Ma Ying-jeou formed a strong government. Immediately after Ma's government was installed, it sought to implement a series of conservative policies, such as legalizing casinos, trimming the national pension system by exempting farmers, tightening control over public television, and increasing the number of on-campus military officers. These measures galvanized environmentalists, welfare activists, media reform activists, and education reform advocates into opposition. The fact that the KMT government gave a green light to the business practice of furlough to meet the challenge of global recession sparked a new round of labor protests. Furthermore, the public was shocked by the aggressive and bruising police action taken against protestors in November 2008 to ensure the red carpet was rolled out for China's envoy. The student movement, which had been in abeyance for more than a decade, made a dramatic comeback to protest against human rights violations by Ma's government. Obviously, Taiwan's civil society remained resilient and combative after the eight-year estranged cohabitation with the DPP. Threats embodied in the form of negation of previous movement gains turned out to be a stimulating force (Goldstone and Tilly 2001: 181). Social movements were ready to challenge conservative roll-backs by the returning KMT government.

Two factors were critical to the prospects for Taiwan's social movements. First, because movement activists had lost their insider status within the government, they needed to rebuild their grassroots support bases to induce more participation. In the last few years, some movements seemed to have lost their momentum. The anti-nuclear movement, which failed to make a comeback following the disastrous attempt to bring a halt to the construction of the nuclear power plant in 2001, was an obvious example. The institutional incorporation of the Taiwan Confederation of Trade Unions also unexpectedly had a dampening effect on labor movement, as unionized workers enjoyed better protection, while the majority of non-unionized workers, such as part-timers, migrant workers, and subcontracted workers, were increasingly left out. Movement activists have to remaster the art of association to expand their appeal among civil society.

How the DPP reconnected with social movements was no less critical. While the current DPP leadership was preoccupied with dealing with the aftermath of the 2008 defeat and the Chen Shui-bian scandal, its strategy on social movements gradually emerged. In August and October 2008 and May 2009, the DPP led mass protests against the KMT government for its feeble gestures toward China. In early 2009, the DPP reinstalled its Social Movement Department, which had been abolished in 1996. Clearly, with a limited number of political seats in local executives and the Legislative Yuan, the DPP again focused on civil society to boost its strength. However, whether the DPP can regain the trust of movement activists remains to be seen.

In sum, the KMT's new conservatism and the resurgence of social movements aided by the DPP's new orientation seem to portend a contentious scenario in the years to come. How the evolution of state–civil society relations might affect post-transitional Taiwan is a challenging question, both practically and intellectually.

Finally, according to Joseph Wong (2003), Taiwan has been making strides toward "deepening its democracy," as an increasing number of progressive political issues are absorbed into the mainstream agenda. There are many reasons for this positive development, such as the relative equalitarianism in the economy, the absence of unbridgeable social cleavages, and the frequently recurring election cycle that compels politicians to search for new issues. While largely agreeing with Wong's finding, we argue that Taiwan's vibrant civil society should be given more credit.

This chapter traces the development of Taiwan's social movements from the 1970s to the second regime change in 2008 to reexamine the link between civil society and democracy-making. Overall, it has shown that social movements have had a consistently positive impact on democracy. Before the political transition, intellectuals and middle-class advocates utilized the limited channel of the public sphere to articulate the call for democratic reforms. During the transition, social movements rose to articulate the interests of and identities among the disenfranchised social sectors. The wave of popular uprisings in the late 1980s was critical in pushing forward the democratizing momentum beyond the restrictive parameters set by KMT hardliners. In the post-transitional era, as social movements were incorporated into the democratic regime, they obtained legitimate status as policy consultants. Despite some temporary setbacks, there is a progressive pattern of evolution in how social movements have been instrumental in making and transforming democracy in Taiwan over several years. In short, we concur with Charles Tilly (2003: 248) in that social movements are "partly causes, partly effects and almost invariably concomitants of democratic freedoms to speak, assemble, associate and complain."

In general, Taiwan's story confirms the optimistic theory of the role of civil society in the context of new Asian democracies (Hsiao 2008). When viewed against the historical backdrop of state–society relations, social movements tend to be the self-conscious vanguard among all civil-society sectors. The values that underpin their collective vision are usually equality, autonomy, sustainability, and mutual respect, which are in sync with modern democracy. Skeptics of civil society are certainly right when they warn that the vehicle of civic engagement can equally carry anti-democratic passengers. The rise of counter-movements in 2002 and 2003 may fall into this category, but they are isolated and sporadic cases. To maintain a healthy and sustainable democracy in Taiwan, the persistent advocacy, organizing, monitoring, and advice of social movements remain a necessary tonic.

Bibliography

Anheier, H. (2003) "Movement development and organizing networks: the role of 'single members' in the German Nazi party, 1925–30," in M. Diani and D. McAdam (eds) *Social Movements and Networks: relational approaches to collective action*, Oxford: Oxford University Press, pp. 49–76.
Armony, A. C. (2004) *The Dubious Link: civic engagement and democratization*. Stanford, CA: Stanford University Press.

Berman, S. (1997) "Civil society and the collapse of the Weimar Republic," *World Politics*, 49: 401–29.

Bermeo, N. (2003) *Ordinary People in Extraordinary Times: the citizenry and the breakdown of democracy*, Princeton, NJ: Princeton University Press.

Cohen, J. L. and Arato, A. (1994) *Civil Society and Political Theory*, Cambridge, MA: MIT Press.

Collier, R. B. (1999) *Path toward Democracy: the working class and elites in Western Europe and Latin America*, Cambridge: Cambridge University Press.

Collier, R. B. and Mahoney, J. (1997) "Adding collective actor to collective outcomes: labor and recent democratization in South America and Southern Europe," *Comparative Politics*, 29: 285–303.

Di Palma, G. (1990) *To Craft Democracy: an essay on democratic transitions*, Berkeley: University of California Press.

Diamond, L. (1994) "Rethinking civil society: toward democratic consolidation," *Journal of Democracy*, 5: 4–17.

—— (1999) *Developing Democracy: toward consolidation*, Baltimore: Johns Hopkins University Press.

Dickson, B. J. (1993) "The lessons of defeat: the reorganization of the Kuomintang on Taiwan, 1950–52," *The China Quarterly*, 133: 56–84.

Edwards, B. and Foley, M. W. (1998) "Beyond Tocqueville: civil society and social capital in comparative perspective," *American Behavioral Scientist*, 42: 5–20.

Edwards, B., Foley, M.W. and Diani, M. (eds) (2001) *Beyond Tocqueville: civil society and the social capital debate in comparative perspective*, Hanover, NH: University of New England Press.

Fox, J. (1996) "How does civil society thicken? The political construction of social capital in rural Mexico," *World Development*, 24: 1089–103.

Gates, H. (1996) *China's Motor: a thousand years of petty capitalism*, Ithaca, NY: Cornell University Press.

Gerschenkron, A. (1989) *Bread and Democracy in Germany*, Ithaca, NY: Cornell University Press.

Goldstone, J. A. and Tilly, C. (2001) "Threat (and opportunity): popular action and state response in the dynamics of contentious action," in R. R. Aminzade, J. A. Goldstone, D. McAdam, E. J. Perry, W. H. Sewell Jr., S. Tarrow, and C. Tilly (eds), *Silence and Voice in the Study of Contentious Politics*, Cambridge: Cambridge University Press, pp. 179–94.

He, B. (1995) "The ideas of civil society in mainland China and Taiwan, 1986–92," *Issues and Studies*, 31: 24–65.

Ho, M. (2003a) "The politics of anti-nuclear protest in Taiwan: a case of party-dependent movement (1980–2000)," *Modern Asian Studies*, 37: 683–708.

—— (2003b) "Democratization and autonomous unionism in Taiwan: the case of petrochemical workers," *Issues and Studies*, 39: 105–36.

—— (2004) "Contested governance between politics and professionalism in Taiwan," *Journal of Contemporary Asia*, 34: 238–53.

—— (2005) "Taiwan's state and social movements under the DPP government (2000–2004)," *Journal of East Asian Studies*, 5: 401–25.

—— (2006) "Challenging state corporatism: politics of labor federation movement in Taiwan," *The China Journal*, 56: 107–27.

—— (2007) "The rise and fall of Leninist control of Taiwan's industry," *The China Quarterly*, 89: 162–79.

Ho, M. and Su, F. (2008) "Control by containment: politics of institutionalizing pollution disputes in Taiwan," *Environment and Planning (A)*, 40: 2402–18.

Hsiao, H. M. (1989) *Social Forces: Taiwan looks ahead*, Taipei: Independent News Press (in Chinese).

—— (1997) "Social movements and civil society in Taiwan," *Copenhagen Journal of Asian Studies*, 11: 7–26.

—— (1998) "Taiwan's environmental movements: anti-pollution, nature conservation and anti-nuclear," in Y. Lee and A. So (eds) *Asia's Environment Movement*, Armonk, NY: M. E. Sharpe, pp. 31–55.

—— (2002) *The Paradigm Shift in Taiwan's Society and Culture*, Taipei: Lihsü (in Chinese).

—— (2005) "NGOs, the state and democracy under globalization: the case of Taiwan," in R. Weller (ed.) *Civil Life, Globalization and Political Change in Asia: organizing between family and state*, London: Routledge, pp. 42–58.

Hsiao, H. M. (ed.) (2008) *Asian New Democracies: the Philippines, South Korea and Taiwan compared*, Taipei: Taiwan Foundation for Democracy and Center for Asia-Pacific Studies, Academia Sinica.

Hsiao, H. M. and Huang, S. (2001) *A History of Taiwan's Hakka Ethnic Group*, Nantou: Academia Historica (in Chinese).

Hsiao, H. M. and Koo, H. (1997) "The middle classes and democratization," in L. Diamond, M. F. Plattner, Y. Chu, and T. Mao (eds) *Consolidating the Third Wave Democracies: themes and perspectives*, Baltimore: Johns Hopkins University Press, pp. 312–33.

Hsiao, H. M. and Liu, H. (2001) "Collective action toward a sustainable city: citizens' movements and environmental politics in Taipei," in P. Evans (ed.) *Livable cities? Urban struggles for livelihood and sustainability*, Berkeley: University of California Press, pp. 67–94.

Hsiao, H. M., Huang, S. and Wong, S. (1995) "The rise and fall of social forces in Taiwan, 1895–1995," in Taiwan Research Fund (ed.) *Taiwan in the Past One Hundred Years*, Taipei: Vanguard (in Chinese), pp. 110–49.

Hsiau, A. (2008) *Return to Reality: political and cultural change in 1970s Taiwan and the postwar generation*, Taipei: Institute of Sociology, Academia Sinica (in Chinese).

Huang, M. (1976) *Intellectual Ferment for Political Reform in Taiwan, 1971–1973*, Ann Arbor, MI: Center for Chinese Studies, University of Michigan.

Jordan, D. (1994) "Changes in postwar Taiwan and their impact on the popular practice of religion," in S. Harrell and C. Huang (eds) *Cultural Change in Postwar Taiwan*, New York: Westview, pp. 137–60.

Koo, H. (1993) "The state, *minjung*, and the working class in south Korea," in H. Koo (ed.) *State and Society in Contemporary Korea*, Ithaca, NY: Cornell University Press, pp. 131–62.

Kuan, H. (2008) *Abortion Law and Abortion Discourse in Taiwan: rights, social movements and democratization*, Dissertation at University of Pennsylvania Law School.

Kung, Y. (1998) *Émigré Regime and Native Society: the formation of social bases of reorganized KMT regime*, Taipei: Taohsiang (in Chinese).

Levi, M. (1996) "Social and unsocial capital: a review essay of Robert Putnam's making democracy work," *Politics and Society*, 24: 45–55.

McAdam, D., Tarrow, S. and Tilly, C. (1996) "To map contentious politics," *Mobilization*, 1: 17–34.

Meyer, D. S. and Tarrow, S. (1998) "A social movement society," in D. S. Meyer and S. Tarrow (eds) *The Social Movement Society: contentious politics for a new century*, New York: Rowman and Littlefield, pp. 1–28.

Moore, B. Jr. (1978) *Injustice: the social bases of obedience and revolt*, New York: Pantheon.

O'Donnell, G. and Schmitter, P. C. (1986) *Transition from Authoritarian Rule: tentative conclusions*, Baltimore: Johns Hopkins University Press.

Ost, D. (1990) *Solidarity and the Politics of Anti-Politics*, Philadelphia: Temple University Press.

Putnam, R. D. (1994) *Making Democracy Work: civil traditions in modern Italy*, Princeton, NJ: Princeton University Press.

—— (2000) *Bowling Alone: the collapse and revival of American community*, New York: Simon and Schuster.

Roy, D. (2003) *Taiwan: a new political history*, Ithaca, NY: Cornell University Press.

Schak, D. and Hudson, W. (eds) (2003) *Civil Society in Asia*, Hampshire: Ashgate.

Share, D. (1987) "Transitions to democracy and transition through transaction," *Comparative Political Studies*, 19: 525–48.

Solinger, D. (2006) "The nexus of democratization: guanxi and governance in Taiwan and PRC," working paper at Center for the Study of Democracy, University of California at Irvine.

Szreter, S. (2002) "The state of social capital: bringing back in power, politics and history," *Theory and Society*, 31: 573–621.

Tarrow, S. (1995) "Mass mobilization and regime change: pacts, reform, and popular power in Italy (1918–22) and Spain (1975–78)," in R. Grunther, N. P. Diamandouros, and H. J. Puhle (eds) *The Politics of Democratic Consolidation: South Europe in comparative perspective*, Baltimore: Johns Hopkins University Press, pp. 204–30.

—— (1996) "Making social sciences work across space and time: a critical reflection on Putnam's making democracy work," *American Political Science Review*, 90: 389–97.

Taylor, C. (1990) "Modes of civil society," *Public Culture*, 3: 95–118.

Tenfelde, K. (2000) "Civil society and the middle classes in nineteenth-century Germany," in P. Nord and N. Bermeo (eds) *Civil Society before Democracy: Lessons from Nineteenth-Century Europe*, Lanham, MD: Rowman and Littlefield, pp. 83–110.

Teng, P. (1992) *The History of Taiwanese Student Movement in 1980s*, Taipei: Chienwai (in Chinese).

Tilly, C. (2003) "Afterword: agenda for students of social movements," in J. A. Goldstone (ed.) *States, Parties and Social Movements*, Cambridge: Cambridge University Press, pp. 246–56.

Tu, W. and Peng, Y. (2008) "Social movement groups' participation and influence in the policy making process: experiences from the environmental impact assessment commission and the commission on women's rights promotion," *Taiwan Democracy Quarterly*, 5: 119–48 (in Chinese).

Wakabayashi, M. (1994) *Taiwan: divided nation and democratization*, Taipei: Yuetan (in Chinese).

Walzer, M. (1992) "Civil society argument," in C. Mouffe (ed.) *Dimensions of Radical Democracy: pluralism, citizenship, and community*, London: Verso, pp. 89–107.

Wang, J. (1988) "A new era of Taiwanese women's movement," in Editorial Group (eds) *The 1987 Annual Review of Taiwan*, Taipei: Yuanshen (in Chinese).

Whitehead, L. (1997) "Bowling in the Bronx: the uncivil interstices between civil and political Society," in R. Fine and S. Rai (eds) *Civil Society: democratic perspectives*, London: Frank Cass, pp. 94–114.

Winckler, E. A. (1984) "Institutionalization and participation in Taiwan: from hard to soft authoritarianism," *The China Quarterly*, 99: 481–99.

Wong, J. (2003) "Deepening democracy in Taiwan," *Pacific Affairs*, 76: 235–56.

Wright, T. (2001) *The Perils of Protest: state repression and student activism in China and Taiwan*, Honolulu: University of Hawaii Press.

Yang, H. (2007) *Making Community Work*, Taipei: Tsoan (in Chinese).

4 The bottom-up nature of Korean democratization

Civil society, anti-Americanism and popular protest

Bruce Cumings

It is a bipartisan commonplace in Washington for policy-makers and pundits to acclaim the Republic of Korea a grand success in democratization, with the assumption that two strong forces made it possible: the rise of the middle class and American support for democracy. When a new president, Lee Myong-bak, a leader eager to support the alliance and promote good relations with the United States, visited Washington in April 2008, it was as if nothing untoward had ever intruded on this relationship. Pundits blamed two previous presidents, Kim Dae Jung and Roh Moo Hyun, for "10 lost years" of turmoil and anti-Americanism, as if George W. Bush's policies would have met with universal acclaim in Korea had it not been for two misguided presidents and a handful of anti-American demonstrators.[1] It is also assumed time and again that relations with Korea began with the courageous American defense of South Korea in the Korean War, when in fact a three-year American Military Government had preceded it, an occupation almost forgotten to history. When it is recalled (a rarity), again, the assumption is that Americans nurtured a democracy with few bumps in the road: as former chairman of the Council on Foreign Relations, Leslie Gelb, put it in contrasting the turmoil in Iraq to previous occupations, postwar Japan, Germany, and South Korea were "all free from internal warfare and with a good economic base" (Gelb 2008).

It is hard to imagine judgments that could be further from the truth. I will argue that turmoil and an anti-Americanism borne of poor policy choices in Washington have marked our relations with Koreans from the start, that the middle class—tiny at the beginning in 1945 but ubiquitous today—has mostly been a conservative upholder of the status quo, that popular protests by peasants at the start, and students and workers in the 1980s and 1990s, drove democratization, and that street protest, labor organization, and widespread dissent in print media built one of the stronger civil societies in the world today.

A forgotten occupation

Leslie Gelb was right that our occupation of South Korea from 1945 to 1948 provides a good comparison with Iraq, but not in his sense. Without forethought, due consideration or self-knowledge, the U.S. barged into a political, social, and cultural thicket without knowing what it was doing, and soon found that it could not get out. After the death of President Franklin Delano Roosevelt (and with that, the effective death of his trusteeship plans for the decolonization of a unified Korea), the State Department pushed ahead with a full military occupation of Korea, or a part of it—no matter what happened, they wanted a "preponderant role" on the peninsula because they feared the thousands of guerrillas in Manchuria who might combine with Soviet forces should the Red Army fight the Japanese in Korea. Why were they concerned about Korea in the first place, a country that had never attracted serious American attention? Because Korea was thought to be important to the postwar security of Japan (the enemy that the U.S. was still fighting), Kim Il Sung and his allies (who numbered in the hundreds, not the thousands) were the problem then, and they remain the problem today, 63 years later—with no solution to the problem in sight. In the trite phrases of Washington policy-makers, this would be called "lacking an exit strategy."

A window into a different future—a future that might not end up with a divided Korea and an internecine war two years later—opened for the American occupation in the first year after Japan's defeat. In the southwest and especially South Chŏlla province, Americans worked with local leaders and, at least for a while, did not try to change the political complexion of local organs that reflected the will of the people. As historian Kim Yong-sŏp has shown in his many works, South Chŏlla was the site of the Tonghak peasant war in the early 1890s because it occupied the intersection of great Korean wealth—the lush rice paddy fields of the southwest—and Japanese exporters who sent Korean rice flowing out of its ports to Japan and the world economy (Pang and Shin 2005). In other words, here was a concentrated intersection of modernity and empire: Korean desires for autonomy and self-strengthening that took the form of a proto-nationalist rebellion, and imperial interests (Japanese, American, Russian, British) competing with one another in the world economy and determined to take advantage of Korean wealth (and weakness). Even after the Tonghak and the subsequent Ŭibyŏng or "Righteous Army" forces were put down, Japanese travel guides of the 1920s still warned against going into the interior of South Chŏlla, and of course the provincial capital, Kwangju, was the site of a major student uprising against the Japanese in 1929.

I toured South Chŏlla in 1972 while conducting research for my dissertation, riding on local buses through the countryside. Local people frequently stared at me with uncomplicated, straightforward hatred, something I had rarely experienced elsewhere in Korea. The roads were still mostly hard-packed dirt, sun-darkened peasants bent over ox-driven plows in the rice paddies or shouldered immense burdens like pack animals, thatch-roofed homes were sunk in conspicuous privation, old Japanese-style city halls and railroad stations were unchanged from the colonial era. At unexpected moments along the way, policemen would materialize from nowhere and waylay the bus to check the identification cards of every passenger, amid generalized sullenness and hostility that I had only seen before in America's urban ghettoes. This hatred was the residue of foreign occupation and war.

Things might have been different, however. It is a paradox of the American Military Government that its most successful program in the first year of occupation was in South Chŏlla. After the Japanese defeat, local organs of Yŏ Un-hyŏng's Kŏn'guk chunbi wiwŏnhoe (Committee to Build Korean Independence, founded in August 1945) had established themselves, and quickly came to be known as "people's committees." President Kim Dae Jung joined one in Mokp'o at the time, something that the militarists in Seoul always held against him (and it was part of his indictment for sedition by Chun Doo Hwan in 1980). These committees were patriotic and anti-colonial groupings with a complicated political complexion, but Americans in Seoul quickly placed them all under the rubric of "communists." Indeed, the commander of the Occupation, General John R. Hodge, "declared war" on communism in the southern zone on the very early date of 12 December 1945. In the southwest, however, American civil affairs teams worked with local committees for more than a year.

American military forces did not arrive in Kwangju until 8 October 1945 (a month after they got to Seoul), and civil affairs teams did not show up until 22 October. They soon recognized that the people's committees controlled almost the entire province. The man whom the Americans found in charge in Kwangju was Kim Sŏk, who had spent 11 years as a political prisoner of the Japanese. In Posŏng and Yŏnggwang, however, landlords ran the committees, and police who had served the Japanese remained in control of small towns. In the coal town of Hwasun, miners ran the local committee. Several elections had been held since 15 August in Naju, Changhŭng, and other places, excluding only officials who had served the Japanese in the previous decade. Americans in Kwangju, like those in Seoul, wanted to revive the defunct Japanese framework of government and even retained the former provincial governor, Yaki Nobuo, until December (he provided them with secret lists of cooperative Koreans). Kim Sŏk was arrested on 28 October on trumped-up charges of running an "assassination plot." His trial, according to an American who witnessed it, was a complete travesty. He was soon back in his familiar surroundings of the previous decade: prison.

Other Americans, however, recognized that the people's committees represented "a designation applied to some faction in every town," with its influence and character varying from place to place: "In one county, it represents the 'roughnecks'; in another, it is perhaps the only political party and represents no radical expressions; in others, it may even possibly have the [former] county magistrate as its party leader." Lt. Colonel Frank E. Bartlett ran the 45th Military Government team, one of the only such teams to have been trained specifically for Korea (the vast majority had been trained for occupation duty in Japan), and urged his men to know the tenor of local political opinion. This resulted in attempts to "reorganize" the committees in several counties, but Bartlett's group basically allowed most committees in the province to operate until the fall of 1946. A key reason was that the Americans could find no evidence that the committees were controlled "from a strong central headquarters" (Cumings 1981).

It all ended in bloodshed a year later. I still remember the day that I found in the National Archives a 39-page report entitled "Chŏlla-South Communist Uprising of November 1946" (USSIDH 1946). Uprisings had begun in Taegu almost a month earlier and had followed a classic pattern of peasant rebellion: rebellions in one county would move to another and then another, like billiard balls striking one another. This major uprising was the result of intense Korean frustrations with the first year of American occupation and the suppression of the people's committees in the Kyŏngsang and Chŏlla provinces. It was entirely indigenous to the southernmost part of the peninsula, having nothing to do with North Korea or with communism. This report detailed more than 50 incidents in November 1945 of the following kind (Cumings 1981: 364):

- Mob composed of People's Committees types attacked police box; police fired into mob, killing six;
- 1,000 attacked police station . . . cops fired 100 rounds into mob, killing (unknown);
- Police fired on mob of 3,000, killing 5;
- Police fired into mob of 60 . . . tactical [American] troops called out; captured 6 bamboo spears and 2 sabres;
- 600–800 marched on police; police killed 4.

The report went on like this, listing a myriad of small peasant wars. When the reader finally reaches the end of the report, he realizes that he stares into an abyss containing the bodies of countless Chŏlla peasants. In recent years, a single incident of this type would have attracted national and international attention, but these distant events remain an unknown moment of history along the dusty roads and "parched hills" of Chŏlla-do that Kim Chi Ha commemorated in his poem, "The Road to Seoul," except to those who witnessed them, or those who died.

I still wonder what happened to the families of the dead—how do they commemorate a battle that no one has ever heard of? How can Americans occupy a country and, a year later, find themselves firing on people about whom they know next to nothing, but conveniently label as faceless "communists" or inchoate "mobs"? Are some of these same Americans not still living today with memories of a peasant war in South Chŏlla in the fall of 1946? Were they never able to connect the dots between the indigenous organs of self-government that Koreans fashioned in the aftermath of four decades of brutal colonial rule and the peasants armed with the tools of their trade being cut down like rice shoots by the same treacherous Koreans who had served the Japanese? In any case, this was the worst bloodshed in the province since the Tonghak Rebellion, and continued a long protest tradition.

For decades after the bloodletting of the Korean War, the acceptable political spectrum consisted of the ruling forces and parties of Syngman Rhee, Park, Chun, Roh, and Kim (Young Sam—a member of a rightwing youth group in the 1940s), and a very tepid, urban opposition derived from the Korean Democratic Party founded in September 1945 (with American help). The Republic of Korea (ROK) did not undergo a real transition to the opposition until Kim Dae Jung's election in 1998, and it did not have a president who was not part of the political divide (and political system) going back to the U.S. Occupation until February 2003. (Kim Dae Jung, as we have seen, got his political start in the self-governing committees in Mokp'o; soon he made his peace with the existing system in the late 1940s and was an establishment politician thereafter, however much he was hounded by the militarists.) No event contributed more to the ouster of the militarists than another rebellion in the southwest.

Kwangju, 1980

The Kwangju Rebellion was South Korea's Tiananmen crisis, deeply shaping the broad resistance to the dictatorship in the 1980s and paving the way for democratization in the 1990s, as well as for the conviction on charges of treason and sedition of the perpetrators who massacred innocent citizens in Kwangju. As scholars such as Na Kan-ch'ae of Chŏnnam University in Kwangju have argued, the trials of Chun Doo Hwan and Roh Tae Woo and Kim Dae Jung's election in 1997 represented a distinct victory for the people of Kwangju and South Chŏlla, even if they came more than 15 years later and after great suffering.[2] To me, however, the American response to the Kwangju Rebellion represented the most nauseating display of hypocrisy, opportunism, racism, and betrayal of American democratic ideals since the Korean War. Americans, and especially China experts, are capable of going on forever about the perfidy of Beijing's leaders in crushing the Tiananmen demonstrations in June 1989—where Americans had no responsibility at all for what happened. But where Americans were directly implicated in the suppression of the rebellion in Kwangju, the response is mostly silence.

Weeks after the assassination of Park Chung Hee on the seventieth anniversary of An Chong-gun's murder of Ito Hirobumi at Harbin Station in 1909, Chun Doo Hwan, Park's protégé and head of the Defense Security Command, housing military intelligence, mobilized the Army's Ninth Division (commanded by another protégé, Roh Tae Woo), Seoul's capital garrison and various special forces—all formally under American operational command—to seize power within the Korean military. According to a 1994 Seoul District Prosecutor's Office report, Chun and Roh met on 7 December and decided to make 12 December (the thirty-fourth anniversary of Hodge's "declaration of war") their "D-Day." They mobilized armored units in front of Army headquarters, forcing high-level officers to flee through tunnels to the U.S. Eighth Army Command across the street (*Korea Herald* 30 October 1994). Reporters for the *New York Times* rightly called this "the most shocking breach of Army discipline" in South Korea's history and "a ploy that would have been a hanging offense in any other military command structure," but they found American officials unwilling to comment publicly (while privately depicting themselves as being "at a loss" to do anything about it) (Stokes 1979; Sterba 1980). However, reporters did not point out that President Park *and* his assassin, Kim Chae-gyu, then the head of the Korean Central Intelligence Agency, had been Japanese Army officers whom Americans recruited to serve in the fledgling Korean military, both of them graduating in the second class of the American officers' school (later the Korean Military Academy) in 1946.

Four months later, in a further grab for power, Chun made himself director of the Korean Central Intelligence Agency (KCIA) (in addition to his other positions) and thus detonated the worst crisis since the Korean War. Tens of thousands of protesters soon flooded Korea's cities. Chun declared martial law on 17 May 1980 as citizens' councils, provoked by the indiscriminate brutality of Army paratroopers, took over Kwangju. These councils said that 500 people had already died in Kwangju, with some 960 missing.[3] They appealed to the U.S. to intervene, but the Embassy was silent and it was left to General John A. Wickham to release the Twentieth Division of the ROK Army from its duties along the Demilitarized Zone (DMZ) on 22 May; five days later, Korean troops put a bloody end to the rebellion.

Once again, U.S.-commanded troops had been released for domestic repression, only this time the bloodletting rivaled that of Tiananmen in June 1989. The declassified documents that Tim Shorrock, a reporter for the *Journal of Commerce*, obtained through the Freedom of Information Act make clear that the U.S. as a matter of the highest policy determined to support Chun Doo Hwan and his clique in the interests of "security and stability" on the peninsula, and to do nothing serious to challenge them on behalf of human rights and democracy. Indeed, reading through the materials makes it clear that leading liberals—such as Jimmy Carter and his Ambassador in Seoul William Gleysteen, his National Security advisor Zbigniew Brzezinski, and especially Richard Holbrooke (then Under-Secretary of State for East Asia)—had blood on their hands from 1980: the blood of hundreds of murdered or tortured young people in Kwangju.

At a critical White House meeting on 22 May, Brzezinski summed up the conclusions of a Policy Review Committee: "in the short term support [of the dictators], in the long term pressure for political evolution." The Committee's posture on Kwangju was this: "We have counseled moderation, but we have not ruled out the use of force, should the Koreans need to deploy it to restore order." If the suppression of the Kwangju citizenry "involves large loss of life," the Committee would meet again to discuss what to do. But then, when this very "large loss of life" came to pass (for years independent estimates suggested somewhere between 1,000 and 2,000 people died, but official investigations later ascertained that several hundred died, not one or two thousand),[4] Holbrooke and Brzezinski again counseled patience with the dictators and expressed their concern about North Korea: within days, a naval task force led by the carrier Midway steamed for Korean waters, and Holbrooke told reporters that there was far too much "attention to Kwangjoo [sic]" without proper consideration of the "broader questions" of Korean security (*Associated Press* 11 June 1980; Gwertzman 1980; *New York Times* 22 June 1980).

These documents also show that Americans in the Pentagon were well aware in advance of the deployment of Korean special forces to Kwangju, that these troops had a "special" reputation for brutality (in putting down a miner's strike in April, for example). After the troops had bayoneted students, flayed women's breasts, and used flamethrowers on demonstrators, a Defense Department report of 4 June 1980 stated that "the [special forces] troops seem elated by the Kwangju experience"; although their officers desire to get them out of internal security matters, that "does not mean they will in anyway [sic] shirk their duty when called upon, regardless of that duty."

New research by a Ph.D. student at the University of Chicago using the declassified records of the Carter administration shows that Jimmy Carter was genuinely concerned about the despicable human rights record of the Park regime from the time he came into office through his June 1979 visit to Seoul, when he had a memorable confrontation with General Park. Carter got so angry at Park's arrogance and cold demeanor that he wanted to overrule the reversal of his troop withdrawal policy—which was what he had come to Seoul to announce. The president sat in the presidential limousine outside the U.S. Embassy, arguing for 30 minutes with National Security Advisor Brzezinski and Defense Secretary Harold Brown, their voices rising to the point that reporters knew something was wrong.[5] In his last year in office, however, Carter became resigned to the trade-off between Korean security and human rights that has been the mantra of American national security elites for the last 60 years.

It is important to understand that these elites, not the American people, control Korean policy—and foreign policy in general—and that there is little difference between Republican and Democratic policy-makers. (Leslie Gelb (2008: 21) is so arrogant as to write that the influence of "liberals" on foreign affairs "is by and large limited to Democratic Party presidential primaries.") Operating on a bipartisan basis through one presidential administration after another, they focus almost exclusively on containing North Korea and constraining any difficult people who may come along in South Korea, and do not respect the will of Koreans outside the circle of Korean elites whom they know and work with. Their common mindset and their permanent, year-in, year-out influence in Washington can be seen most clearly in the American response to the North Korean nuclear program in the past 15 years (for example, both Bill Clinton and George W. Bush planned preemptive strikes on North Korea), but it also extended to a particular distaste for the Roh Moo Hyun Government (2002–2007) in Washington. Events after the Kwangju Rebellion was crushed also make this pattern clear.

In August, Chun completed his coup by declaring himself president with official American blessing—indeed, the blessing of human rights paragon Jimmy Carter. About a week after the rebellion ended, Carter sent the U.S. Export-Import Bank chairman to Seoul to assure the junta of American economic support, including a US$600 million loan that Carter had just approved; the president told the *New York Times* that "the Koreans are not ready for democracy . . . according to their own judgment" (Lee 1988: 22–3). Jimmy Carter had plenty of help, however. After Tiananmen, critics of China and the first Bush administration made a big issue of official and unofficial visits to Beijing by Brent Skowcroft, Richard Nixon, Henry Kissinger, and others. After the slaughter in Korea, there were many more such contacts, with everyone intoning the mantra that internal turmoil would only hearten the North Koreans and harm South Korean security (and of course the country's business environment)—and hardly any Americans complained about these visits.

The first private American citizen to enter the Blue House for a chat with the new dictator and assure him of American support after Kwangju was Richard "Dixie" Walker (on 6 June), who also denounced the citizens of Kwangju for their "urban terrorism and insurgency"; the press said he was the probable Ambassador to Korea should Ronald Reagan be elected (a supposition that proved to be accurate). He was followed by T. Jefferson Coolidge, Jr. (10 June), a businessman who negotiated Harvard University's original grant for Korean studies from Seoul in the mid-1970s; rightwing national security pundit Frank N. Trager arrived on 5 August, and, somewhat later, world-class banker David Rockefeller (18 September). Berkeley Professor Robert Scalapino was earlier than any of the others, arriving in April to warn everyone (for the umpteenth time) that the Soviets had "vigorously endorsed" Kim Il Sung's policy of armed reunification, then returning in October to say the same thing.[6] Richard Stilwell, an important former CIA official, lifelong "Korea hand," and all-out advocate of the dictators since 1961, flew into Seoul just before Kwangju to assure Chun of Republican support, whatever the Democrats might think of him.[7] In short, a seamless web of Democratic and Republican elites backed Chun's usurpation of power, beginning with Carter, Holbrooke, and Brzezinski and ending with a newly inaugurated Ronald Reagan fêting Chun at the White House in February 1981 for the "new era" he had created. By that time, at least 15,000 dissidents had been newly detained in "reeducation" camps.

In the years after the Kwangju Rebellion, Chun purged or proscribed the political activities of 800 politicians, 8,000 officials in government and business, and sent some 37,000 journalists, students, teachers, labor organizers, and civil servants to "purification camps" in remote mountain areas where they underwent a harsh "reeducation." The Act for the Protection of Society authorized preventive detention for seven to ten years, yet more than 6,000 people were also given "additional terms" under this Act in 1980–1986. The National Security Law defined as "anti-state" (and therefore treasonable) any association or group "organized for the purpose of assuming a title of the government or disturbing the state," and any group that "operates along with the line of the communists," or praises North Korea; the leader of such an organization could be punished by death or life in prison.

Some of the prominent Americans who supported Chun's rise to power were later handsomely rewarded for their efforts. In 1984, Korean newspapers reported that Mr. Scalapino was an advisor to the Daewoo Corporation in Seoul, with a consulting fee estimated at US$50,000 per year.[8] Others included high-level corporate consultants such as disgraced former Vice President Spiro Agnew, Richard Holbrooke (consultant to the Hyundai conglomerate) and Alexander Haig, Reagan's Secretary of State at the time of Chun's White House visit (*Korea Herald* 16 May 1984). Richard Stilwell signed on as a consultant to the Hanil conglomerate in 1986 for an undisclosed fee (*Korea Herald* 18 November 1986). Meanwhile, Korea's exports were flat from 1979–1982 and foreign debt mounted to US$41 billion, third in the world after Brazil and Mexico (according to 1983 Morgan Guaranty figures). What was the Korean government to do? Chun began harping on South Korea's role as a frontline defense of Japan, something no other ROK president had admitted publicly; in return, he wanted a US$6 billion package of aid and credits. Under strong pressure from the Reagan administration, Japanese Prime Minister Nakasone coughed up a package worth US$4 billion in January 1983, equivalent to 10 percent of the ROK's outstanding debt (*Asian Wall Street Journal* 31 May 1982; *New York Times* 12 January and 13 January 1983).

Anti-Americanism in South Korea

Kwangju convinced a new generation of young people that the democratic movement had developed not with the support of Washington, as an older generation of more conservative Koreans thought, but in the face of daily American support for any dictator who could quell the political aspirations of the Korean people. The result was an anti-American movement in the 1980s that threatened to bring down the whole structure of American support for the ROK. American cultural centers were burned to the ground (more than once in Kwangju), students immolated themselves in protest at Reagan's support for Chun, and the U.S. Embassy, which sits conspicuously adjacent to the seat of government in Seoul, came to look like a legation in Beirut with concrete revetments and blanketed security to keep the madding crowd at bay. Nor did it help that the American presence was often marked by racism toward Koreans—whether on the military bases, among the U.S. multinationals doing business there, or in the Embassy entourage.

The inevitable result of these factors was all too apparent in the mid-1980s: anti-Americanism became so bad that few Americans could walk the streets of Seoul without fear of insult, calumny, or worse.

By this time, Seoul was a complete armed camp. Chun Doo Hwan undertook a vast expansion of paramilitary riot police, numbering around 150,000 by the mid-1980s. They bore the main brunt of demonstrations, wearing a strange protective armor: black helmets, tight screens over the face, leather gorgettes protecting the back of their neck, padded clothing, thick elbow, knee, and shin guards, heavy combat boots, a long metal shield in the left hand and riot baton in the right, and with wire-mesh masks, helmets, body padding, and scabbards to protect their necks. On any given day, they could be seen sitting in buses with grated windows all over downtown Seoul, awaiting the next encounter. These were the Darth Vader-like figures that showed up frequently in photos in the *New York Times*, often with no accompanying article (for none was needed). During this period, Han Yun-jo, the woman who owned Samyang Chemicals and wangled an exclusive contract to supply tear gas to the state, frequently paid the highest annual taxes of any business person in Korea (US$3.4 million tax on a gross income of US$7.3 million in one year).

Kim Dae Jung returned home in February 1985, and I was fortunate to be part of an American delegation that accompanied him back to Seoul from exile in the U.S., in the hope that our presence would prevent another airport murder like that which had cut down Benigno Aquino on the Manila tarmac two years earlier. The Chun regime was smart enough not to do that, but was still stupid enough to cause a huge fracas at Kimp'o Airport; a phalanx of KCIA thugs in brown windbreakers pummeled and threw prominent Americans to the floor (two Congressmen were among the delegation), while roughly manhandling Kim and his wife into a waiting car and subsequent years of "house arrest" (riot police surrounded Kim's neighborhood and occupied the homes of his next-door neighbors, surveilling his every movement and refusing to allow him to speak publicly). When we got to the bus that would take us into Seoul, hundreds of Chôlla people in tattered winter clothing milled around us exclaiming that Kim was their "great leader." On the left side of the road leading into Seoul were thousands of riot police. On the right side of the road were enormous numbers of Seoul's common people—workers in denims, students in black uniform, mothers in long skirts, little children wrapped tightly against the wind, old men and women in traditional dress—with placards hailing Kim's return. It seemed as if the whole population had divided between the riot police and the demonstrators.

The touchstone of protests in the 1980s was, of course, the Kwangju Rebellion. It is not a stretch to say that an entire generation of young people was raised in the shadow of Kwangju, just as students in the 1960s lived with Vietnam and the civil rights movement. American officials often saw the students' protests in a narrow empirical light: the students claimed U.S. involvement in Chun's two coups (in December 1979 and May–June 1980) and especially in supporting Chun's crackdown at Kwangju. The Embassy would respond that there was no such direct involvement, which as a matter of high policy in Washington may have been true, but which could not have been true in the dailiness of American–Korean relations. The U.S. maintained operational control of the ROK Army; Chun was head of the powerful Defense Security Command; he grossly violated the agreements of the joint command twice, in December 1979 and May 1980: why did the U.S. not act against those violations? With his service in the Vietnam War and his positions in military intelligence, Chun had to have a thick network of ties with American counterparts: had they stayed his hand, or did they even try? Above all, why did President Reagan invite this person to the White House and spend the early 1980s providing him with so many visible signs of support? There was no good answer to most of these questions, and especially not the last one. The first of many anti-American acts was the arson of the Kwangju United States Information Service (USIS) office in December 1980, and such acts were commonplace by the mid-1980s, with many young people committing suicide for their beliefs.

In the next decade, the Korean people took matters into their own hands and elected two former dissidents, Kim Dae Jung and Roh Moo Hyun, finally ending the long period of dictatorship and militarism that began in 1945. In August 1998, Kim Dae Jung became the first Korean president to visit and pay his respects at the graves of the victims of the Kwangju massacre, where he met with aggrieved relatives and told reporters that the Kwangju Rebellion "was behind the birth of his democratic government" and a key element of his own courage in resisting the dictators: "I never gave in to their death threats because I was unable to betray Kwangju citizens and the souls of the May 18 victims" (*Korea Herald* 26 August 1998). Acts of witness like this and official investigations into what happened in Kwangju went a long way toward finally closing the chapter on this terrible, but also important and determining, episode in recent Korean history—if only Americans would take upon themselves a similar sense of responsibility for finally revealing the full role of the Carter and Reagan administrations in the unfolding of this tragedy.

Another spate of "anti-Americanism" came in recent years, so it might be useful to make some distinctions regarding the South Korean phenomenon that the media calls anti-Americanism. The first would be, was the ROK different from any other country during the Bush administration? Except for the weeks after 11 September, a continuous distaste for American power and policy in one country after another has marked Bush's term in office. The baselines here are the denunciation of the Kyoto Treaty, the International Court of Justice, and the 1972 Anti-Ballistic Missile Treaty, a general tendency toward bluff and stark threats, an inveterate unilateralism, and of course the invasion of Iraq, which generated unprecedented tensions with European allies. As the buildup for war went on, the *New York Times* reported that relations between the U.S. and "two of its most crucial allies— Germany and France—are at their lowest point since the end of the Cold

War." Other observers would say that this was the lowest point since World War II, because Europeans have a widespread sense that the U.S. is at odds with its traditional allies not just over Iraq, but over the usefulness of the world system that Americans have done so much to build since 1945: whether the emergent strains over American policy are healed or not, a senior European diplomat said in 2003 that the next few weeks "will be the defining moment on whether the United States decides to stay within the international system" (Sanger 2003c).

Another distinction would address the term itself: "anti-American" assumes a uniform opposition to Americans as such, instead of distaste for American policies; it also assumes a uniform America, as if all citizens should equally and patriotically feel abused by foreign criticism. In fact, Americans are as conflicted today as they were back in the 1960s, or perhaps more so, with voters split down the middle in their partisan preferences and in their "Red" and "Blue" states. George W. Bush, after all, only got into office through a split decision, five-to-four, in the Supreme Court, after he lost the popular vote by half a million. I was one of those in the 500,000-plus majority, and did not see the values and interests that this majority represented connected in any way with the policies of the Bush administration. Does that make people like me "anti-American"?

A third distinction is to ask whether Koreans today are more critical of Americans than they were in the 1980s, or whether they are simply more free to express their views in the raucous, bumptious atmosphere of a democracy that also subjects its own leaders to withering criticism. (Kim Dae Jung always seems to be honored more outside his own country than within it; not long after he won the Nobel Peace Prize in 2000, his popularity ratings were at their lowest ebb in his five-year term.) Until the decades of military dictatorship ended, you could go straight to jail for publicly advocating the withdrawal of U.S. troops; but now, all kinds of chickens are coming home to roost from an unfortunate and repressed past. So it might be that, as Americans, we are merely experiencing what Korean presidents, conglomerate leaders, university administrators, and the dictatorial generals themselves have experienced in the past decade.

One thing is clear, though: during the second Bush administration, Koreans did not call for the U.S. to return to an international system of its own making, as do Europeans. In Europe, that system was always multilateral, beginning with the four-power allied occupation of Germany at the end of the war. In East Asia, however, ever since Douglas MacArthur's arrival in Tokyo in September 1945, unilateralism has been the name of the game. MacArthur paid no attention to allied opinion in running the occupations of Japan and (at a distance) South Korea; instead, he was the hero of the expansionist, Asia-first wing of the Republican Party (which was the original, if distant, source of Bush's unilateralism). Furthermore, the onset of the Cold War led the U.S. to revive Japan as a regional engine of the world economy, shorn of its political and military clout, and then to reinvolve it in its former colonial economies; it was in that context that Secretary of State George Marshall and Under-Secretary Dean Acheson moved in early 1947 toward the creation of a separate state in southern Korea, and toward an American security guarantee of that same state.[9] Many Koreans now believe that Japan—the just-defeated enemy—loomed much larger in American policy than did concern for Korea's division, or for the authoritarianism of the successive governments that the U.S. supported in Korea.

Many Korean protesters see American policy as standing in the way of South–North reconciliation; if that is a harsh judgment, it is hard to conclude from recent events that the North is solely to blame for the second big nuclear crisis that now besets the peninsula. The North clearly sought diplomatic engagement with Washington from Bush's inauguration until the October 2002 confrontation with James Kelly for highly enriched uranium, something reciprocated by our allies in Seoul and Tokyo and our partners in Moscow and Beijing—but not by Washington. P'yŏngyang then found itself in the "axis of evil" and under a new threat of preemptive attack (the North was high on the list of countries said to be targets of the September 2002 preemptive doctrine). Any general sitting in P'yŏngyang would thus take careful notice of this new "Bush Doctrine" or be fired for dereliction of duty. By January of 2003, Bush was forced to repeat many times that "we have no intention of invading North Korea" (Sanger 2003a, 2003b). Relations with Seoul also became very rocky, as both Kim Dae Jung and President-elect Roh Moo Hyun clung to a doctrine of engagement. So, it is not clear that the distress is directed at Americans generally any more than it was at the Bush administration's derelict, conflicted, and ham-handed Korea policy.[10]

So it appears that the incessant use in the media of the term "anti-American" to describe the discontent in Seoul is flawed and inappropriate. It would be closer to the truth to say that the Bush administration was as responsible as any other party for the upsurge in protest. Of course, it is possible to find restaurants in Seoul that post signs saying "Americans not welcome," and posters that denounce Americans in general terms. You can find the Korean term *"pan-Mi"* (anti-American) on buttons and posters. When I observed demonstrations in August 2001 and December 2002, I was prepared to tell people I was from New Zealand, if asked. But no one bothered me in the slightest. Many Americans and Westerners participated in the massive, dignified, and impressive candlelight vigils held in Seoul on Saturday nights that preceded Roh Moo Hyun's election in December 2002. Furthermore, the term *"pan-Mi"* is a typically terse protester's usage, and has long been a ubiquitous symbol for any number of causes expressing some sort of dissatisfaction with American policies, but usually not Americans or the United States as such. My first book was banned by the Chun Doo Hwan dictatorship (thus enhancing sales of the pirated translation) and denounced by regime scribes as *pan-Han, pan-Mi*, and *ch'in-Buk* (anti-Korean, anti-American, and pro-North, a rightwinger's trifecta), all at the same time. Considering the source, I was proud to be the target of this terse invective.

A Korea Gallup Poll in 2003 showed an increase in those who "disliked the United States" from 15 percent in 1994 to 53 percent in 2003. News reports on this poll did not give the actual questions posed to respondents, but when asked the opposite question—do you like the U.S.?—the response was 64 percent in 1994, compared to 37 percent in 2003 (Goodman and Cho 2003). Putting these results another way, 36 percent of people surveyed in 1994 said they disliked the U.S.—not a particularly comforting figure. More to the point, there is little to indicate one way or the other whether such poll results stem primarily from the Bush administration's policies or from a growing "anti-Americanism." However, one poll for the *Sisa Journal* in 2002 found that 62 percent of the respondents thought that Bush's policies toward North Korea had not been helpful (French, with Kirk 2002).

Moreover, the entire tenor of the "anti-American" demonstrations differs from that at the actual high point of opposition to U.S. policy in the mid-1980s. On Saturday 14 December, a few days before the presidential election, I witnessed what was probably the largest of the "anti-American" demonstrations—both from a high floor of a downtown hotel, and by mingling with the demonstrators. I participated in massive anti-war demonstrations in New York and Washington in the 1960s, and observed many student demonstrations in Korea from the 1960s forward, but I have never seen such an impressive political statement. Tens of thousands of young people, families with little children, painted protesters festooned with slogans, and a sprinkle of middle-aged and elderly people held candles protected from the wind, moving slowly under billowing white banners calling upon the U.S. to support North–South reconciliation, reform the Status of Forces Agreement (SOFA), move military bases outside Seoul, and bring real justice to the American soldiers who had run over and killed two teenage girls in June 2002. It was serious and yet amiable, moving and dignified, and very well organized (both by the protesters and the forces of order).

American responses to the Korean protests

The recent problems between the U.S. and the ROK have occasioned a petulance that seems surprising, coming from Americans who have long experience in Korea, and who presumably possess eyes that enable them to see the same problems James Wade and many others discerned long ago. Richard Allen, who was often registered as an agent of the ROK by the U.S. Justice Department (Cumings 1996), wrote in 2003 that Roh Moo Hyun's election made for "a troubling shift" in U.S. relations with the ROK. Now here was the first democratic election involving two major candidates in which the winner got near a majority since 1971, when Park Chung Hee barely eked out a victory over Kim Dae Jung's 46 percent of the vote amid monumental regime vote-buying. For Mr. Allen, however, Korean leaders seemed now to have "stepped into the neutral zone" and had even gone so far as to suggest, in the current nuclear standoff, that Washington and

P'yŏngyang should both make concessions: "the cynicism of this act constitutes a serious breach of faith." Maybe American troops should be withdrawn, Allen suggested, "now that the harm can come from two directions —North Korea and violent South Korean protesters" (Allen 2003).

In Allen's opinion, the U.S. "is responsible for much of Seoul's present security and prosperity"; the implication being that Koreans are biting the hand that feeds them. Other Americans wonder how Koreans can criticize the U.S. when "North Korea is rattling a nuclear sword." A Pentagon official argued that "it's like teaching a child to ride a bike. We've been running alongside South Korea, holding on to its handlebars for 50 years. At some point you have to let go" (Dao 2003). Another American military official in Seoul said of Roh's election, "There is a real sense of mourning here" (French 2003). Meanwhile, American business interests stated that troop withdrawals would cause investors to "seriously reconsider [. . .] their plans here."[11] This remarkable combination of petulant irritability and grating condescension somehow seems unremarkable both to the people who say such things, and sometimes to the reporters who quote them.

Mr. Allen also complained that some Koreans "still blame America for the division of Korea" in 1945. An index of the gulf separating American and Korean knowledge of this history is a reporter's article in our paper of record, saying that "Many young South Koreans sincerely believe what North Korea has taught for decades: that American troops arrived here in 1950 and split the nation in two. In reality, the Communist North attacked first" (Brooke 2003). He seemed unaware that American combat divisions landed in early September 1945, a few weeks after John J. McCoy directed Dean Rusk and a colleague to an adjoining room to find a place to divide Korea that would keep Seoul in the American zone. Americans consulted no allies, let alone any Koreans, in coming to this fateful (and unilateral) decision. Hyundai heir Chung Mong Jun, whose presidential candidacy gave way to Roh Moo Hyun's in 2002, remarked that "For Koreans, it is very ironic that we were divided by World War II, and Japan, your defeated enemy, was not" (French, with Kirk 2002). It is a perfectly reasonable and understandable judgment about an errant and unjust division of a country that had well-recognized boundaries and integrity for more than a millennium. But few Americans are even aware of this fact, let alone feel any responsibility or remorse for it. Nor do most Americans understand that U.S. troops have now been based in Korea for more than six decades; but is it unreasonable—or "anti-American"—for some Koreans to ask if they ever plan to go home? How would Americans feel if the situation were reversed and foreign troops had been resident on our soil for more than half a century?

In the 1990s, Roh Moo Hyun called for the withdrawal of American troops from Korea. During his presidential campaign, attacks by his opponents led him to say he had long since repudiated that position. Meanwhile, successive administrations in Washington have treated such demands as heresy, and plan to keep American troops on the peninsula—forever? The "Nye Report" in 1995 projected at least another 15 years for the existing bases and troops, in spite of the end of the Cold War and the collapse of the Soviet Union. Three years later, Secretary of Defense William Cohen stated publicly that the U.S. would keep its troops in Korea "even after unification." A blueprint for the Bush administration's policy toward East Asia, formulated under the leadership of Richard Armitage (who served as Colin Powell's deputy in the State Department), also called for an indefinite retention of troops in Korea and Japan.

Conclusions: Americans in the world, Koreans reconciled

Americans are once again mired in a nightmare of their own making, in another country that they neither understand nor care much about. Everyday, the newspapers are full of stories about some congressman demanding a date to pull American troops out of Iraq and supporters of the effort going on about "security" and the necessity to "support our troops." In fact, this affair is already over; the U.S. cannot defeat its enemies and the only question is whether enough of Iraq can be stabilized to allow the permanent stationing of American troops on the many bases the U.S. has been building since 2003. If that outcome is possible, then Iraq will be another Korea and Americans will be ensconced on their bases forever, lest some form of "instability" results or some "evildoer" arises.

Korea is another country, of course, but the lessons of South Chŏlla in the 1940s and 1980s resonated with those of America in the 1960s: if you want your civil and political rights, you have to fight for them or you will never get them. Another lesson of 1946 and 1980 is this: you cannot trust American leaders to support democracy in Korea (a belief of the older generation in the ROK); instead, you have to build democracy yourself. Through a long-term struggle beginning in 1945 and achieving great force in the late 1980s and 1990s, Koreans created an admirable democracy and a strong civil society, moving from the bottom up rather than from the top down. One can only have a deep admiration for the multitude of courageous but ordinary people who took it upon themselves to resist illegitimate power—like those peasants who fell before rifles in the distant November days of 1946.

Ever since this early and determining point, South Korean politics has had a suppressed "third force" with strong roots in the southwest but a presence all over the country. If we locate these forces on the "Left," we reduce them to the polarized and caricatured constructions of the Cold War, in which any kind of mayhem committed by the Right is insufficient truly to distance them from American support, so long as they remain firmly anti-communist. For decades, these political and social forces resided of necessity in the long memories of participants in the local committees, labor and peasant unions, and rebellions of the late 1940s, harboring many personal and local truths that could not be voiced. Suppressed memory, though, is history's way of preserving and sheltering a past that possesses immanent energy in the present; the minute conditions change, that suppressed history pours forth. Thus, in the past 15 years, Koreans have produced hundreds of investigations, histories, memoirs, oral accounts, documentaries, and novels that trace back to the years immediately after liberation—a cathartic politics where many suppressed and unpalatable truths have come forth with enormous political force.

The key turning point came in 1995–1996, in the "Campaign to Rectify the Authoritarian Past" that brought Chun Doo Hwan and Roh Tae Woo into the dock, where they were successfully prosecuted for high treason and monumental corruption. An admirably thorough and honest investigation of the Kwangju Rebellion began, Chun's foul dictatorship was completely discredited, and he found himself with a death sentence hanging over his head (until President-elect Kim Dae Jung magnanimously pardoned him). These trials were very popular. A sophisticated social science analysis by Professor Doh Shin demonstrated deep and widespread support for the cashiering of Generals Chun and Roh: their arrest and prosecution both for their role in squashing the Kwangju Rebellion and their coup d'état, and for taking nearly US$1 billion in political contributions, merited "strong support" from more than 65 percent of respondents in a scientific poll, and over 15 percent said they "somewhat support" these actions. By contrast, there was much more tepid support for punishing the conglomerate leaders who provided the political slush funds (Shin 1999: 203–8).

With little notice in the U.S., in other words, Koreans have been going through an admirable process of reckoning with their history in a manner analogous to South Africa's Truth and Reconciliation Commission. This Commission defined that vexing term, "truth," in four ways: factual or forensic truth, personal or narrative truth, social or "dialogue" truth, and healing or restorative truth. The Korean tide of suppressed memory and contemporary reckoning with the past has established all those meanings of truth for courageous people who, after the dictatorships ended, have pressed their case against all odds for years. For Americans, these Korean truths establish official lies at all levels, perpetrated for half a century, but also (in the Commission's words) "reduce the number of lies that can be circulated unchallenged in public discourse."

For scholars, the strong democracy and civil society that emerged from the bottom up in the South, in the teeth of astonishing repression and with very little support from agencies of government in the U.S., validates a method of going back to the beginning and taking no received wisdom for granted. It also suggests that the rise of the middle class is not some watershed that ushers in democratization, but rather that a middle class newly represented in the national assembly will offer little help to workers and common people who remain disenfranchised. This finding, based on several Latin American cases, resonates particularly strongly in the Korean case: In *Capitalist Development and Democracy*, Rueschemeyer *et al.* (1992) argue that capitalist development is associated with democracy because as a byproduct of growth it transforms class structures, undermining old ones and creating new ones. The new middle classes, however, will fight to the point of their own democratic representation, but not beyond: after that, they will seek to restrict working-class representation. Unlike most accounts, the authors also emphasize that the geopolitical interests of great powers generate direct interventions and support for repressive states. Their conclusions fit South Korea to a "t," so is it any wonder that from time to time Americans may find themselves taken to task over the history of their relations with Korea?

Notes

1 Various issues of *The Nelson Report* <cnelson@samuelsinternational.com> around the time of Lee Myong-bak's visit to Washington in mid-April 2008 illustrated this Beltway consensus.
2 This section relies in part on my introduction to the English edition of Lee Jai-Eui's classic narrative, *Kwangju Diary* (Cumings 1999).
3 These figures were compiled by Kwangju citizens and sent to the most important watchdog group in the U.S. at the time, the North American Coalition on Human Rights in Korea, led by the Rev. Pharis Harvey.
4 Although dissidents in both China and Korea argue that thousands were massacred, it appears that about 700 protesters were killed in China in 1989. In Korea, the exact number has never been established; the Chun Government claimed that about 200 died, but subsequent National Assembly investigations suggested a figure of no lower than 300.
5 These new documents are cited in a paper prepared for my graduate seminar in 2006–2007, and as such, I cannot cite the paper publicly.
6 Walker said nothing could serve Communist purposes better than "internal instability, urban terrorism and insurgency [a reference to Kwangju], and the disruption of orderly processes" (*Korea Herald* 7 June 1980). Coolidge wanted to assure foreign investors that Korea was still a good environment (*Korea Herald* 11 June 1980), while Trager said "the current purge drive in South Korea is good and fine if it is an anticorruption measure" (*Korea Herald* 5 August 1980); Rockefeller called the ROK "a worthy model" of development (*Korea Herald* 18 September 1980). Scalapino turned up during the turmoil in April (*Korea Herald* 9 April 1980) and then again in October at a conference also attended by Walker, where he once again stated that the Soviets and the North Koreans were exploiting internal instability in the South (*Korea Herald* 7 October 1980).
7 Stilwell's visit in early May 1980 and the commotion it caused in the Seoul Embassy (where diplomatic staff thought Stilwell was undercutting its efforts to restrain Chun) are discussed in the Freedom of Information Act documents in the possession of Tim Shorrock. On Stilwell more generally, see Cumings (1992: 245–8).
8 The US$50,000 figure is not reported in this article, but was given to me by a friend of mine who works for Daewoo.
9 This is well known to diplomatic historians, but rarely seeps into public commentary about Korea policy. Relevant documents include Marshall's note to Acheson that said, "Please have [a] plan drafted of policy to organize a definite government of So. Korea and *connect up* [sic] its economy with that of Japan" (740.0019/Control [Korea] file, box 3827, Marshall to Acheson, 29 January 1947).
10 White House reporters wrote that the Bush administration was deeply split over

policy toward North Korea: " 'You step out of a meeting on this,' a senior foreign policy official said, 'and you realize that you've heard 12 ideas and no consensus' " (Sanger and Preston 2003).
11 Tami Overby, an employee of the American Chamber of Commerce in Seoul, as quoted in Brooke (2003).

Bibliography

Allen, R. V. (2003) "Seoul's choice: the U.S. or the North," *New York Times*, 16 January 2003, Op-Ed page.

Brooke, J. (2003) "G.I.'s in South Korea encounter increased hostility," *New York Times*, 8 January 2003, p. A10.

Cumings, B. (1981) *Origins of the Korean War*, vol. I, Princeton, NJ: Princeton University Press.

—— (1992) *War and Television: Korea, Vietnam and the Gulf War*, London: Verso.

—— (1996) "The Korea lobby," Tokyo: Japan Policy Research Institute.

—— (1999) "Introduction," in J.-E. Lee, *Kwangju Diary: beyond death, beyond the darkness of the age*, translated by K. S. Seol and N. Mamatas, Los Angeles: UCLA Asian Pacific Monograph Series.

Dao, J. (2003) "Why keep U.S. troops?" *New York Times*, 5 January 2003, News of the Week in Review, p. 5.

French, H. W. (2003) "Bush and new Korean leader to take up thorny diplomatic issues," *New York Times*, 21 December 2003, p. A5.

French, H. W., with Kirk, D. (2002) "American policies and presence are under fire in South Korea, straining an alliance," *New York Times*, 8 December 2002, p. A10.

Gelb, L. H. (2008) "Neoconner: a life of Ahmed Chalabi, fabricator of the evidence for the invasion of Iraq," *New York Times Book Review*, 27 April 2008, p. 21.

Goodman, P. S. and Cho, J. (2003) "Anti-U.S. sentiment deepens in South Korea," *The Washington Post*, 9 January 2003, pp. A1, A18.

Gwertzman, B. (1980) "Military rule in South Korea gives White House a major challenge," *New York Times*, 29 May 1980.

Lee, S. (1988) "Kwangju and American perspective," *Asian Perspective*, 12(2): 22–3.

Pang, K.-C. and Shin, M. D. (eds) (2005) *Landlords, Peasants, and Intellectuals in Modern Korea*, Ithaca: East Asian Program, Cornell University.

Rueschemeyer, D., Stephens, E. H. and Stephens, J. D. (1992) *Capitalist Development and Democracy*, Chicago: Chicago University Press.

Sanger, D. (2003a) "Bush welcomes slower approach to North Korea," *New York Times*, 7 January 2003, pp. A1, A10.

—— (2003b) "Nuclear mediators resort to political mind reading," *New York Times*, 12 January 2003, p. A13.

—— (2003c) "To some in Europe, the major problem is Bush the cowboy," *New York Times*, 24 January 2003, pp. A1, A10.

Sanger, D. and Preston, J. (2003) "U.S. assails move by North Koreans to reject treaty," *New York Times*, 11 January 2003, p. A1.

Shin, D. C. (1999) *Mass Politics and Culture in Democratizing Korea*, Cambridge: Cambridge University Press.

Sterba, J. P. (1980) "U.S.-Korean bond becomes a marriage of inconvenience," *New York Times*, 15 June 1980.

Stokes, H. S. (1979) "Korean General filling key posts with his men to bolster power; Americans refuse to comment," *New York Times*, 15 December 1979.

USSIDH (U.S. 6th Infantry Division Headquarters) (1946) "Chŏlla-South Communist Uprising of November 1946," in XXIV Corps Historical File, U.S. National Archives, 31 December 1946.

5 Modernization theory's last redoubt

Democratization in East and Southeast Asia

Mark R. Thompson

The clichéd "endogenous" version of modernization theory—that a country's own economic development leads it to eventually undergo democratic transition—has fallen on bad times recently. A major study based on a quantitative comparison of development and democracy in nearly 135 countries over the last 40 years has even claimed to have falsified it (Przeworski and Limongi 1997; Przeworski *et al.* 2000). But East and Southeast Asia are proving to be the theory's last redoubt. Using a simplified version of postwar modernization theory, it has been suggested that democratic transitions in the Pacific Asia region have been "driven by growth" (Morley 1993; Laothamatas 1997). The result of a successful industrialism drive—according to this well-known narrative—is an economy too complex, a social structure too differentiated, and a (middle-class-dominated) civil society too politically conscious for non-democratic rule to be sustained.

In a major new study that brings the "state back in" to society-centered modernization theory, Suehiro (2008) nonetheless sticks to the premise that once substantial development has been achieved, authoritarian developmentalists will yield (or be forced to leave) power in the face of a strengthened civil society. Fulfilling these theoretical expectations, two of the Asian "tiger" economies, South Korea and Taiwan, democratized only after developmental dictatorships had transformed both into newly industrialized countries. Rapid economic growth in the region thus seemed to hold out the promise of more democratic transitions in the future. The World Bank (1993) spoke of the "East Asian [economic] miracle"—until it had second thoughts after the Asian economic crisis of 1997 that is (Wade 1998). Even with the regional "boom" now largely confined to international media focus on China (and to a lesser extent on its fellow communist convert Vietnam), democratic optimism fueled by rapid economic growth has remained prevalent. As Henry Rowen (1998) has argued: "either China will remain relatively poor and authoritarian, or it will become rich and pluralistic—and it seems to have chosen the latter path."

Yet closer examination of the democratic experience of East and Southeast Asia reveals that the timing of democratization has not always followed modernization theory's rigid timetable. Several new democracies in the region were established "too early" in the developmental process—that is, before their countries had high per capita incomes (Indonesia, the Philippines, and Thailand). Other countries (Malaysia and, particularly, Singapore), on the other hand, have been quite *late* in meeting their modernization theory-based "obligation" to democratize. In fact, Singapore is the richest country in the world (that is not primarily an oil producer) that remains authoritarian (World Bank 2008). Malaysia is the second richest non-oil state not to be fully democratic (although it may now be at the beginning of a democratic transition). Rather than democratization after modernization being the only road taken, the political experience of Pacific Asia supports Barrington Moore's thesis that there are other "paths to the modern world" (Moore 1966).

It will be argued in this chapter that "early" transitions in the Philippines and Thailand were led by big business- and religious-based civil society groups. Indonesia democratized because of the support student-led *reformasi* protests received from religious groups and divisions within the Suharto regime. By contrast, Malaysian civil society was divided by communal tensions and the electoral authoritarian regime was able to overcome an internal split. "Late democratization" in South Korea and Taiwan was spearheaded by middle-class professionals, just as modernization theory suggests. But where professionals have been successfully co-opted by the technocratic state elite, as in Singapore, the result has been stable bureaucratic authoritarianism despite modernization. It is far from certain that China and Vietnam will become "late democratizers," as their power holders appear to be moving successfully toward authoritarian modernization along Singaporean lines. The next section of the chapter offers a general discussion of political change in Pacific Asia.

What is Pacific Asia?

Before examining modernization and democratization in the context of Pacific Asia more closely, it is necessary to ask what defines "Pacific Asia" itself (Drakakis-Smith 1992; Rich 2007; Preston 1998). It is sometimes called "East Asia" (but also including Southeast Asia) or the "Asia-Pacific." As a region, it is geographically arbitrary (hard to distinguish from its regional neighbors), culturally heterogeneous (with all five world religions represented), with only weak historical precedents (the Chinese empire and its tributary states are a distant memory, while the more recent "Great East Asian Co-Prosperity Sphere" of militarist Japan is a major source of regional resentment). Rather, "Pacific Asia" has been defined economically. Meiji-Japan was the first non-Western country to modernize. The Cold War, as well as the Korean and Vietnam wars, spurred economic growth among anti-communist states in the region (Stubbs 2005), beginning with the "tiger" economies of Hong Kong, Singapore, South Korea, and Taiwan, followed by the ASEAN-4 (Indonesia, Malaysia, the Philippines, and Thailand). The communist states of China and Vietnam later "converted" to capitalism.

(North Korea remained more totalitarian/Stalinist than developmentalist while non-communist, but once-socialist Burma merely transformed into a quasi-capitalist authoritarian regime). Pacific Asia is a "flying geese formation" of authoritarian regimes with (largely) successful developmentalist projects.

Parallel to Alexander Gerschenkron's (1962) influential theory of "late industrialization," modernization theory can be reconceptualized as a model of "late democratization." Suehiro (2008) argues that democratization can follow after authoritarian developmentalists have successfully achieved economic development. Ideal typically, "late democratization" involves four phases. Power is seized (or government policy changed) in the name of what can be termed "developmentalism"—the ideological claim that economic development must precede democratization. The new power holders seek an alliance with technocrats who are tasked with implementing a plan of export-oriented industrialization. There is a large literature on the role of technocracy in development (for example, Saiedi 1987; Lübbe 1989). In Pacific Asia, the key question is how much influence technocrats have over power holders. Are they merely instrumentalized by neo-patrimonial rulers, integrated in a bureaucratic-rational manner into economic decision-making, or even fused with power holders (where power holders *are* technocrats)?

Second, to promote export-oriented industrialization through low labor costs, Pacific Asian authoritarians have repressed unions, though particular strategies range from overt coercion to authoritarian corporatism (Deyo 1989). Despite the existence of labor-based opposition groups in several Pacific Asian countries, the general weakness of organized workers there distinguishes them from Western Europe and Latin America, where labor often played a decisive role in democratization (Rueschemeyer *et al.* 1992). Labor repression was also a part of the general destruction of the militant left in Southeast Asia (Hewison and Rodan 1996).

While workers were demobilized, capitalists and traditional religious leaders were made dependent on the developmentalist state. In Southeast Asia, the Chinese capitalist minority could be easily intimidated, with their "pariah" status as ethnic-Chinese entrepreneurs instrumentalized by state actors to insure their political dependence, particularly in Malaysia and Indonesia (Reid 1996). In ethnically homogenous South Korea, complicated incentives and punishments were used by the Park government to keep the owners of the powerful *chaebols* in line (including the death penalty for foreign currency violations!) (Amsden 1989). In addition, traditional religious leaders were often dependent upon state support, usually a legacy of the "divide and conquer" pattern of the colonial era.

Finally, middle-class professionals were co-opted and kept from making liberal demands (Jones 1998). Once substantial economic development has been achieved, coercive and "participatory" measures can be mixed with a "culturalist" justification of continued authoritarianism, such as the "Asian values" discussion in Singapore (Zakaria 1994; Emmerson 1995; Thompson 2001b). Technocratic-led development, labor repression, "bourgeois" and traditional religious organizations' dependence on the state, and middle-class co-optation are the main parts of the authoritarian strategy to delay democratization (at least) until substantial industrialization has been achieved.

Given this vacuum due to regime demobilization of society, students have often been the *only* major group engaged in anti-regime protest against Pacific Asian developmental authoritarians (Thompson 2008). The repression of this student-led opposition—ranging from brutal crackdowns in Thailand (1976), South Korea (1979), Burma (1988), and China (1989) to less violent demobilization in much of the rest of Southeast Asia (Indonesia, Malaysia, the Philippines, and Singapore)—ended the first cycle of revisionist protest against authoritarianism. The goal of student activists at this point was reform, not regime change. In the second cycle (above all in South Korea in the 1980s, Indonesia in the 1980s and 1990s, and Thailand in the 1990s), student activists were better able to challenge aging authoritarian regimes by attacking their basic legitimacy. But aware they were unable to threaten the regime on their own, they strove to build broad coalitions through social movements which appealed to business and religious leaders, as well as to professionals.

Given the importance of key groups such as technocrats or students in the argument thus far, a brief methodological remark is helpful at this point. In recent discussions among "transitologists," structuralism has been on the defensive because it is said to focus on constraints to action, not what actors actually do (Przeworski 1986). But the gap between actor-centered and structuralist perspectives in the democratization literature can be bridged when it is conceded that the former also use group-oriented approaches in studying regime change (e.g. the strategic postures of *duros*/hardliners and *blandos*/ softliners in the regime). Instead of conceptualizing "structures" as static, abstract phenomena, they may be understood as dynamic, strategic *groups*. Here, I draw on the largely German language discussion of the Bielefeld school's concept of "strategic groups" (Evers and Schiel 1988) as criticized by Neelsen (1988) and Berner (1995) and adapted to the study of regime change by Schubert *et al.* (1994). Closer to network than class theory, the concept shares Mancur Olson's insight that smaller groups are advantaged over larger, diffuse ones (1971) and Frank Parkin's (1983) neo-Weberian notion that such groups are based on "social closure," not positions in the production process. In Pacific Asia, the process of political change can be conceptualized as involving "political contention" (McAdam 1982) primarily between the following key strategic groups: regime power holders, state technocrats, student activists, business associations, religious authorities, and professionals.

Bourgeois democratization in the Philippines and Thailand

Political comparisons between "Siam and its twin" are rare because of obvious civilizational differences (Berner and Korff 1991; Sidel 1996). What does the only predominantly Christian country in Asia named after a Spanish king with a long civilian democratic tradition going back to U.S.-imposed "colonial democracy" have in common with a Buddhist Kingdom which escaped Western colonialism and has only democratized during brief intervals regularly interrupted by military coups? Despite the deep-seated divergence in the histories of these two nations, there have been important similarities in the formation of their strategic groups.

Following Barrington Moore's insight (1966) that a "vigorous" and "independent" bourgeoisie is a key factor in democratization, it can be suggested that assimilationist policies towards ethnic Chinese entrepreneurs allowed big business to emerge as a strategic group in the Philippines and Thailand (Sidel 2008). Unlike in most of Southeast Asia, ethnic Chinese were well integrated into the larger society in the Philippines and Thailand from the late nineteenth century, enabling them to escape the political marginalization that comes with a "pariah" status. With the rise of national, capital city-based big business leaders in the postwar period, the political economy took on a distinctive bourgeois tinge with the "Makati crowd" displacing landed "*caciques*" in relative importance in the Philippines (contra Anderson 1988) and business-led corporatism supplanting the military-bureaucratic polity in Thailand described by Riggs (1966).

In contrast with South Korea, "developmentalist states" under Marcos in the Philippines and various military rulers in Thailand were too weak to force the business class into permanent political dependency through a system of incentives and punishments. Economically emergent and politically independent, bourgeois elites were one of the two key strategic groups leading "democratic revolutions"—Philippine "people power" in 1986 and the 1992 "black May events" in Thailand. The other key group was a religious one—the Catholic Church in the Philippines led by the bishops, who worked closely with big business in the Bishops-Businessmen Conference, and the reformist Buddhist grouping around Chamlong in Thailand, which had links to the monarchy as well as to Thaksin and other business leaders.

In South Korea, Park and Chun relied on technocrats who used systemic incentives and punishments to make *chaebol* tycoons dependent on the state. In the Philippines and Thailand, by contrast, the regime was either highly patrimonial—Marcos' "politics of plunder" became notorious (Aquino 1987) —or unable to exert systematic control over the economy, as in Thailand, where changing military governments only sporadically employed technocratic expertise in their economic policy-making, such as under Sarit's rule, although less so after his death in 1963 by his successor Thanom, who was toppled ten years later under a cloud of corruption. Given the government's weakness in controlling and directing the economy, big business leaders in the Philippines and Thailand could more easily defy dictators and support civil society.

Reformasi revisited: why Indonesia democratized, but not Malaysia

Strategic group formation in Malaysia and Indonesia stands in stark contrast to the Philippines and Thailand (the *opus classicus* on Malaysia is Jomo 1986). Given their "alien" status, the ethnic Chinese were "in but not of" what J. S. Furnivall (1948) famously characterized as "plural societies" in which different ethnic groups "mix but do not combine." In Malaysia, this ethnic "pluralism" led to the creation of communal parties. While the UMNO (United Malays National Organization) represented ethnic Malays, sister parties in the *Barisan National* (BN, or National Front) ruling coalition represented the ethnic Chinese (the Malaysian Chinese Association, or MCA) and ethnic Tamils (the Malaysian Indian Congress, or MIC). Primarily because of this institutionalized communal divide, opposition to the regime has long been split into "ethnic maximalist" parties catering to ethnic Malays (the Islamist *Parti Islam SeMalaysia*, or PAS) and the ethnic Chinese and Tamils (the Democratic Action Party, or DAP). The *Keadilan* (Justice) party founded by the imprisoned former Deputy Prime Minister Anwar Ibrahim in 1998 (and headed by his wife until his release from prison in 2004) initially had little success in bridging this ethnic divide. It forged a loose multi-ethnic coalition with the PAS and the DAP to contest elections. Yet Anwar's strength in current Malaysian politics, as shown by his party's strong showing in the March 2008 elections, is based less on this multi-ethnic alliance than the support he draws from "semi-oppositionists" within the dominant UMNO party in which he was once a powerful figure and among ethnic Malay voters upon whom he exercises strong charismatic appeal.

With ethnic Chinese politically marginalized despite their continued dominance of the economy (which years of affirmative action with the New Economic Policy or NEP failed to change significantly), opposition in Malaysia has remained more ethnically oriented than "class-based." The key political strategic group in Malaysia is still ethnic Malay politicians jockeying for position within ruling and opposition Malay parties. The communal nature of politics in Malaysia has prevented it from taking on a "bourgeois" character, as in the Philippines and Thailand. As Eva-Lotta Hedman (2001: 941) has written:

> The crystallization of a classic plural society in colonial Malaya prefigured not only the entrenchment of strong communal identities and political parties, but a bourgeoisie whose ethnic identity and/or dependence on the state impaired its capacity for universalist leadership of a broadly Malaysian civil society.

Indonesian communalism, though not as open as in Malaysia, has also inhibited the development of a big business-led civil society. The predominantly ethnic Chinese capitalist class was subject to overt and covert discrimination both under Dutch colonial rule and after independence. Stigmatized and segregated from the Muslim majority, several large Chinese business groups had a symbiotic relationship with Suharto during his long dictatorship. They were at the mercy of the vagaries of his changing goals and perceived interests. Although the regime claimed to promote the growth of an "indigenous" *pribumi* capitalist class (roughly parallel to pro-Malay affirmative action in Malaysia), Suharto often turned to *cukong* (large Chinese conglomerates) when engaged in the secretive deals that lay behind his rapidly growing "family business" at the core of his increasingly patrimonial rule. A major source of popular resentment, the conspicuous wealth of key figures in the community made the Chinese minority a convenient scapegoat when the regime faced popular opposition. Suharto often instrumentalized anti-Chinese feelings by tolerating periodic pogrom-like attacks on ethnic Chinese (Sidel 2006).

But the *reformasi* opposition movement in Indonesia still succeeded in toppling Suharto from power in 1998 despite its lack of support from big business because of two key factors. These were lacking in Malaysia, where an opposition movement that adopted the name "*reformasi*" from the Indonesian anti-dictatorship movement was unable to remove Mahathir and where the UMNO-dominated ruling coalition still holds onto power (even if its grip seems to be slipping). The first factor is that a religious-based strategic group emerged in Indonesia, playing a role roughly similar to that of the Catholic Church in the anti-Marcos struggle in the Philippines and the role of Buddhist-inspired oppositionists linked to the monarchy in Thailand. In contrast to Malaysia, where traditional Muslim leaders have been dependent on the state, in Indonesia the relative autonomy of major religious organizations—the "traditionalist" Nahdlatul Ulama (NU) and modernist *Muhammadiyah*—created a major strategic group of religious leaders able to support regime change. These "religious virtuosos," to use Max Weber's term (1993[1903/04]), invoked religious symbols to undermine the "moral capital" (Kane 2001) of the regime, thus jeopardizing its legitimacy. They thereby also thwarted Suharto's efforts to co-opt Islamic leaders in the 1990s through the founding of the Indonesian Association of Muslim Intellectuals, *Ikatan Cendekiawan Muslim Indonesia*, or ICMI, in which Suharto's future successor B. J. Habibie played the leading role. In contrast with Malaysia, where the Islamist PAS opposition party had radicalized, key Islamic groups in Indonesia were characterized by their advocacy of "civil Islam" (Uhlin 1997; Hefner 2000). They provided invaluable support to student activists, the key strategic group behind the anti-Suharto protests.

Second, the neo-patrimonial character of Suharto's "New Order" regime made it more vulnerable to *reformasi* protests than the electoral authoritarian Malaysian regime proved to be. During Suharto's long rule, fault-lines developed between the president and his family with the "military as institution," on the one hand, and the civilian politicians in the ruling *Golkar* party, on the other. The increasing patrimonialism of the Suharto clique eventually alienated both groups. This helps explain why *reformasi* protests could succeed, though they were much smaller in number and, given the lack of big business support, less strategically threatening than those led by a coalition of capitalist and religious-inspired reformists in the Philippines and Thailand. Both the military and the Golkar leadership used the protests as a pretext to turn on Suharto and force him to resign (Aspinall 2005).

Malaysia, by contrast, has a more coherent "electoral authoritarian" regime in which major splits (in the mid-1980s and late 1990s) have been *within* the UMNO party and not between Prime Minister Mahathir's family and the party leadership. Although there was resentment of some of his family members' and friends' "unusual wealth," it did not approach the level of disillusionment with Suharto in *Golkar*. In addition, unlike in Indonesia under the "New Order," the military in Malaysia has historically been depoliticized, leaving it out of the political equation. With the dissident Anwar faction of UMNO weakened by the imprisonment of its leader, the ruling party swept the 1999 polls, the first held after the *reformasi* protests. The UMNO was able to play on Chinese fears of Muslim extremism in the opposition Islamist PAS party to divide and electorally conquer the opposition (though various forms of electoral manipulation were also employed). The recent strong opposition showing in the March 2008 election seems to be due to growing disenchantment among ethnic Malays, and not just anger at persistent discrimination by ethnic Chinese and Tamils. If Malaysia democratizes, it seems likely to do so through electoral means rather than through a popular uprising. This suggests that a Mexican-style transition through a governing ruling party's loss of hegemony is more probable than another round of extra-parliamentary *reformasi* protests. Malaysian civil society remains relatively weak, lacking support from a politically timid, "pariah" ethnic Chinese-dominated big business community.

"Late" democratization in South Korea and Taiwan

When labor is demobilized, student groups repressed, and big business and religious groups made dependent on the state, democratization involves "waiting" for the middle class, a very different situation than in the Southeast Asian countries discussed above, which are not predominantly middle-class societies (with the partial exception of Malaysia). The South Korean and Taiwanese cases—seen as paradigmatic by modernization theorists—can thus better be understood as specific examples of "late democratization." Democratic transition did not occur earlier because the first round of protests by students/intellectuals was crushed and big business (Kuomintang [KMT]-dominated in Taiwan and organized into *chaebols* in South Korea) was too dependent on the state to act. Only after professionals and/or small businessmen joined protests initiated by activist groups (the *minjung* and *tangwai* movements in South Korea and Taiwan, respectively) were authoritarian regimes finally forced to yield.

David Kang's (2002) comparison of South Korea and the Philippines shows that the key difference between the two countries was not so much the level of corruption—it was high in both cases—but the way the relationship between the Park- and Marcos-led states and their respective private sector business communities differed. Despite common "cronyism," the more coherent, "technocratic" South Korean regime was able to achieve developmental goals unreachable for the "predatory" rule of Marcos in the Philippines. In South Korea, technocrats used "hard" criteria (particularly export targets) to discipline large business conglomerates (*chaebols*) that it had been instrumental in creating in the first place (Amsden 1989). Businesses that did not meet these targets faced tax disadvantages, fines, and even closure; good performance led to lucrative sources of state finance and new contracts, making big business highly dependent on the goodwill of the powerholders whom they richly rewarded financially. It is thus not surprising that industrialists in South Korea played almost no role in the opposition to the Chun dictatorship in the 1980s, emerging as a political force only *after* democratization began and state industrial controls loosened.

Repeated student protests (major demonstrations occurred in 1963, 1964, 1965, 1967, 1969, 1972, and 1979) in South Korea were successful only when they finally reached out to a now large middle class in the mid-1980s (by then estimated to make up over half of the population) under the *minjung* social movement (Han and Park 1993). Even then, the opposition lacked the support of the giant *chaebol* corporations. This enabled the military regime to compromise with the opposition and to avoid collapse. It managed to pass on power to reformist elements within its ranks (with the election of Roh Tae Woo as president in 1988 and the co-optation of former opposition leader Kim Young Sam, who became president in 1993). Only in 1998 did a consistent oppositionist, Kim Dae Jung, finally win the presidency.

In Taiwan, the relationship between the KMT and the business community differed from South Korea's regime–business relationship in that there was a split between the KMT-run sector of large state-owned corporations and the ethnic Taiwanese *Mittelstand* of small- and medium-sized businesses that grew in importance during the years of economic growth, in which they played the leading role. But Robert Wade's influential study (1990) made a similar point to what has been said about authoritarian South Korea above: the market was "governed" by a technocratic elite with a clear developmentalist program. The oppositionist *tangwai* movement which emerged in the 1970s was more "bourgeois" than the opposition in South Korea in that several small businessmen were among its leaders and major financial supporters. But big business, tightly linked to the KMT, remained firmly in the government camp. Rather than a strong student opposition using themes of foreign domination and economic inequality to rally support in several waves of protest as in South Korea, it was the grievances of ethnic Taiwanese that fueled protest in Taiwan. Similar to the role of Christian organizations in South Korea's democratization, a revival of Daoist and Buddhist beliefs, primarily among middle-class ethnic Taiwanese, also contributed to strengthening civil society opposition to the regime (Madsen 2007).

But as in Indonesia and Malaysia, civil society was too weak in Taiwan to force regime change through revolutionary means, as occurred in the Philippines and Thailand. Rather, it was the gradual internal transformation within the KMT itself, which began promoting ethnic Taiwanese in its leadership ranks to counter concerns of discrimination in favor of mainland Chinese who had previously dominated the ruling party. The contribution of the son and successor of Chiang Kai-shek, Chiang Ching-kuo, should not be underestimated—he liberalized in the face of much hardliner resistance within the KMT. But Taiwan's democratic transition involved a process of gradual negotiation (Schubert 1994; Rigger 1999). Moderate opposition leaders in the Democratic Progressive Party (DPP, founded by members of the *tangwai* movement in 1986) negotiated the terms of democratization with softliners in the KMT regime (later led by the native Taiwanese president Lee Teng-hui). An oppositionist DPP candidate, Chen Shui-bian, first won presidential elections only in 2000 and was narrowly reelected in 2004; the KMT candidate, Ma Ying-jeou, swept the 2008 presidential election. A technocratic-oriented, authoritarian developmentalist regime had transformed itself into a democracy under pressure from the growing middle class represented by the DPP and within the ranks of the KMT itself.

Le petit difference: authoritarian Singapore versus semi-democratic Hong Kong

Besides "early" and "late democratization," the case of Singapore demonstrates there has also been a "late, late democratic" route to the modern world in Pacific Asia. The "Singapore puzzle" has been downplayed by invoking the "size matters" argument to explain why highly successful economic and social modernization has not led to full-scale political democratization there. There is a comparative literature that shows small countries are actually more likely to undergo democratic transition (Dahl and Tufte 1973; Ott 2000). Beyond this, it is enlightening to compare the Singaporean experience to the quasi-state of Hong Kong, with which it shares—besides its geographical petiteness—a largely ethnic Chinese heritage and a British colonial history (Chiu *et al.* 1995; Ortmann 2008).

A convincing explanation of Singapore's non-transition compared to Hong Kong's semi-democracy (within the constraints imposed by the Chinese communist authorities) must show why authoritarian leaders of the former were able to control contentious politics that emerged in the early 1980s while a rise in opposition protests in Hong Kong led to liberalization and partial democratization during the same time period. Opposition "victories" in the

1980s in Singapore led to a strong reaction by the People's Action Party (PAP) regime. Though only a handful of oppositionists had won seats, most were middle class—which the PAP found particularly threatening because the rise of the opposition was linked to a growing professional class that was "patently alienated from the government" (Chan 1993: 234). The regime successfully co-opted a number of oppositionists through the nominated members of parliament (NMP) and non-constituency members of parliament (NCMP) schemes. This gave them a seat in parliament without a real say in the opposition. The PAP government also institutionalized feedback channels between the government and the population. But coercion was also applied. Laws were skewed against opposition candidates and public protests, while a politicized judiciary handed down harsh penalties against those found guilty (most notably, many oppositionists were made to pay high penalties in defamation suits filed against them by the government). The press was also tightly controlled.

In Singapore, the ruling elite is highly cohesive, with no known factional splits, sharing high salaries and status, and bound together with effective communication and a "meritocratic" ideology typical of technocracy (Vennewald 1994). Sharing an elitist and paternalist disposition, they have balanced coercion against "radicals" (beginning with operation "Cold Storage" in the early 1960s up to opposition MPs and activist Catholic nuns in the 1980s) to attempts to co-opt opposition moderates.

In Hong Kong, the colonial government also tried to weaken opposition groups through a mixture of coercion and co-optation. As a reaction to the 1966–1967 riots, the government chose to become more involved in society, focusing on improving social welfare and partially abandoning its previously *laissez faire* economic approach. It also tried to implement feedback channels (such as the City District Officers Scheme) with society. In 1979, the government arrested several dozen boat people and social workers who had joined them in their petition to be resettled in public housing, applying the Public Order Ordinance for the first time since it was passed in 1967.

But a freer press and a more independent judiciary than in Singapore made it more difficult for the Hong Kong government to sustain this policy of coercion. Moreover, the largely middle-class character of the opposition made it more respectable and gave it greater social capital that the protesters of the late 1960s. In addition, colonial officials became increasingly concerned about their legitimation *qua* colonialists. Their tendency to water down their technocratic ideology in favor of greater social welfare programs and to compromise with the opposition in the name of stability often only increased demands for greater liberalization, which ultimately led to a partial democratization through elections.

The Hong Kong Legislative Council became a focal point of democratic activism. This differed from the Singaporean parliament, where even the most vocal opposition member (J. B. Jeyeratnam) has accepted a position of NCMP. Although its impact is hard to measure, the "Asian values" discussion among the Singaporean elite, which attacks the drawbacks of "Western democracy," contributed to the perception that even moderate demands for more democracy were too radical (Thompson 2001b). Compared to Hong Kong, Singapore's ruling technocratic elite has been less willing to compromise and more adept at using a mixture of coercion, participation, and culturalism to control a middle-class professional-based opposition.

A note on the conversion to authoritarian developmentalism in China and Vietnam

In the late 1970s and 1980s, China and Vietnam transformed themselves from post-totalitarian communist to capitalist-oriented "developmentalist" regimes. Chinese communists were able to survive student protests because post-totalitarianism was not as "old" in 1989 as it was in Eastern Europe (which began de-Stalinizing in the mid-1950s). The communist leadership in China still retained some ideological legitimacy and totalitarian controls from the Maoist period (Thompson 2001a). But since then, the Chinese and Vietnamese regimes have lost ideological legitimacy, forcing them to rely on pragmatic acceptance derived from promoting rapid economic growth, warding off political chaos, and guarding national interests. They have become similar to the developmentalist regimes elsewhere in Pacific Asia, industrializing via an export drive. Organized labor has continued to be repressed; "red capitalists" are dependent on the state (Dickson 2003), and a rapidly growing group of professionals has been co-opted in part through nationalism and culturalist arguments.

Yet China and Vietnam exhibit clear signs of social crisis. The number of what the Chinese government terms "public order disturbances (protests against land seizures, corruption, pollution, unpaid wages, etc.) increased tenfold in 13 years, from 8,700 in 1993 to 87,000 in 2005. China's National Bureau of Statistics recently released a survey, which showed that in 2006 public security agencies handled 599,392 cases of "disturbances in social order," "disturbances in public spaces," "trouble-making activities," and "obstruction of public service execution" (Mainland Affairs Council 2007). While less well-documented, social unrest in Vietnam appears to be comparable. China and Vietnam are suffering problems typical of mid-level modernization—in Huntington's terms (1968)—social mobilization without sufficient institutionalization. Grassroots dissatisfaction has increased despite (and partially because of) rapid economic growth. Hu Jintao's call for a "harmonious society" is wishful official thinking in the face of such social disharmony.

But with a mixture of co-optation and repression, the government has succeeded in keeping potential strategic groups—students (since 1989), big business, professionals, intellectuals, or other key strategic groups—outside the opposition orbit. The Chinese and Vietnamese leaderships are clearly trying to follow the Singaporean example of effective crisis management justified with a culturalist argument similar to the "Asian values" discourse against "Western" democratization. Nationalism has also been invoked, though the leadership is wary when it leads to societal mobilization that threatens to elude state control.

As Przeworski and Limongi (1997) have shown, modernized authoritarian systems tend to be stable, and are unlikely to become democracies. While economic growth promotes contentious politics, an authoritarian regime that can survive to a certain threshold sharply increases its chances of survival. The determination of the Chinese Communist Party to hold onto power should not be underestimated (Pei 2007). The Vietnamese party appears to be just as determined. Prediction is an occupational hazard in political science, but short of a major crisis, there is at little indication that China and Vietnam will become "late democratizers" as their leaders push their countries toward authoritarian modernity.

Conclusion

This chapter has raised only a few basic issues concerning modernization and democratization in Pacific Asia. It drew on Barrington Moore's insight that there are alternative ways of becoming modern. If modernization theory is understood as a model of "late democratization" involving the demobilization of labor, the dependence of big business and religious leaders on the state, and the co-optation of middle-class professionals, then other paths to modernity in the region become evident.

The comparison of the Philippines and Thailand illustrated how a strong "bourgeoisie" as strategic group makes democratization possible at a relatively early stage of economic development. Though Indonesia lacked a strong business-based civil society, student protests backed by religious groups were able to prompt the breakup of the unstable Suharto regime and initiate a democratic transition. In contrast, in Malaysia, where there was no united religious-based opposition to a regime which was less hybrid than in Indonesia, a split in the ruling party has (thus far) been contained and a democratic transition avoided.

South Korea and Taiwan "fit" the modernization paradigm so well only because an earlier path to democracy was blocked. Developmentalist regimes there successfully "tamed" big business (either through direct party control in Taiwan or through systematic incentives offered to and punishments threatened against South Korea's *chaebols*, the country's large conglomerates). Lacking a strong big business base, oppositionists had to "wait" for the coming of a large middle class (primarily professionals in South Korea, more concentrated in the *Mittelstand* of small- and medium-sized firms in Taiwan). Only then could protestors successfully pressure regimes to negotiate a democratic transition.

Singapore's non-transition was contrasted with semi-democratization in Hong Kong. In Singapore, democratization has been delayed indefinitely despite a high level of economic development. The regime employed an effective strategy of coercion and co-optation against the predominantly middle-class opposition, as well as a strong meritocratic and culturalist ideology that dominates the country's political agenda. By contrast, a more compromising regime in Hong Kong, which shifted away somewhat from its technocratic roots in favor of social welfare-oriented policies, consented to semi-democratization. In China and Vietnam, repression against and co-optation of strategic groups has left opposition weak, though social unrest is growing. The still officially communist leaders of both countries appear determined to follow Singapore's example of authoritarian modernity.

It can also be argued that regional variation of democratic consolidation can best be explained by the path dependency of the different roads taken to democracy. Where democratic transition was "bourgeois-driven," mobilization in the "name of civil society" has tended to be more insurrectionary and "Gramscian." Bourgeois and moralist-religious groups with an agenda of "good governance" attempted to restore their hegemony against populist electoral challenges. They have broken the democratic rules of the game by supporting popular mobilization that has resulted in what can be dubbed a "people power *putsch*" in the Philippines and Thailand. Where the middle class was at the forefront of democratization, civil society has tended to be "Tocquevillian," as modernization theory would lead us to expect, checking the excesses of the democratic system without challenging it directly. The consolidation of democracy in South Korea and Taiwan has followed this pattern. A third route has been where democracy was established in a society that was still more "traditional" than "bourgeoise" in terms of its major political cleavages, as in Indonesia. Here, "civil society" has been less mobilizable at the grassroots level and populist electoral challenges weaker. This helps clarify why "traditionalist" Indonesian democracy with a more "Burkean" civil society has been more stable than the shaky democracies of the Philippines and Thailand (Burke 1790).

Bibliography

Amsden, A. (1989) *Asia's Next Giant: South Korea and late industrialization*, Oxford: Oxford University Press.

Anderson, B. (1988) "Cacique democracy and the Philippines: origins and dreams," *New Left Review*, 169: 3–33.

Aquino, B. A. (1987) *Politics of Plunder: the Philippines under Marcos*, Quezon City: Great Books Trading.

Aspinall, E. (2005) *Opposing Suharto: compromise, resistance, and regime change in Indonesia*, Palo Alto: Stanford University Press.

Berner, E. (1995) "Power resources and dominance: a critique and reformulation of strategic group analysis," Working Paper No. 218, Sociology of Development Research Centre, University of Bielefeld.

Berner, E. and Korff, R. (1991) "Dynamik der Bürokratie und Konservativismus der Unternehmer: strategische Gruppen in Thailand und den Philippinen," *Internationales Asienforum*, 22: 3–4.

Burke, E. (1790) *Reflections on the Revolution in France and on the Proceedings in Certain Societies in London Relative to that Event in a Letter Intended to Have Been Sent to a Gentleman in Paris.* Harvard Classics, 24, 3. Online. Available HTTP: <http://www.bartleby.com/24/3/> (accessed 22 April 2008).

Chan, H. C. (1993) "Singapore: coping with vulnerability," in J. Morley (ed.) *Driven by Growth*, Armonk, NY: M. E. Sharpe, pp. 219–41.

Chiu, S., Ho, K. C. and Lui, T. L. (1995) "A tale of two cities rekindled: Hong Kong and Singapore's divergent paths to industrialism," *Journal of Developing Societies*, 9(1): 98–122.

Dahl, R. A. and Tufte, E. R. (1973) *Size and Democracy*, Stanford: Stanford University Press.

Deyo, F. C. (1989) *Beneath the Miracle: labor subordination in the new Asian industrialism*, Berkeley: University of California Press.

Dickson, B. (2003) *Red Capitalists in China: the party, private entrepreneurs, and the prospects for political change*, Cambridge: Cambridge University Press.

Drakakis-Smith, D. (1992) *Pacific Asia*, London: Routledge.

Emmerson, D. K. (1995) "Singapore and the 'Asian values' debate," *Journal of Democracy*, 6: 95–105.

Evers, H. D. and Schiel, T. (1988) *Strategische Gruppen: vergleichende Untersuchungen zu Staat, Bürokratie und Klassenbildung in der dritten Welt*, Berlin: Dietrich Reimer Verlag.

Furnivall, J. S. (1948) *Colonial Policy and Practice: a comparative study of Burma and Netherlands India*, Cambridge: Cambridge University Press.

Gerschenkron, A. (1962) *Economic Backwardness in Historical Perspective*, Cambridge, MA: The Belknap Press of Harvard University.

Han, S. and Park, Y. C. (1993) "South Korea: democratization at last," in J. Morley (ed.) *Driven by Growth*, Armonk, NY: M. E. Sharpe, pp. 163–91.

Hedman, E.-L. (2001) "Contesting state and civil society: Southeast Asian trajectories," *Modern Asian Studies*, 35: 921–51.

Hefner, R. W. (2000) *Civil Islam: Muslims and democratization in Indonesia*, Princeton: Princeton University Press.

Hewison, K. and Rodan, G. (1996) "The ebb and flow of civil society and the decline of the left in Southeast Asia," in G. Rodan (ed.) *Political Oppositions in Industrialising Asia*, London: Routledge, pp. 40–71.

Huntington, S. P. (1968) *Political Order in Changing Societies*, New Haven: Yale University Press.

Jomo, K. S. (1986) *A Question of Class: capitalism, the state, and uneven development in Malaysia*, Singapore: Oxford University Press.

Jones, D. M. (1998) "Democratization, civil society, and the illiberal middle class in Pacific Asia," *Comparative Politics*, 32(2): 147–69.

Kane, J. (2001) *The Politics of Moral Capital*, Cambridge: Cambridge University Press.

Kang, D. (2002) *Crony Capitalism: Corruption and Development in South Korea and the Philippines*, Cambridge: Cambridge University Press.

Laothamatas, A. (ed.) (1997) *Democratization in Southeast and East Asia*, Singapore: Institute of Southeast Asian Studies.

Lübbe, H. (1989) "Technocracy: political and economic destinies of a philosophical idea," *WeltTrends*, 18: 39–63.

McAdam, D. (1982) *Political Process and the Development of Black Insurgency 1930–1970*, Chicago: Chicago University Press.

Madsen, R. (2007) *Democracy's Dharma: religious renaissance and political development in Taiwan*, Berkeley: University of California Press.

Mainland Affairs Council (2007) "Background information: the frequent occurrence of mass incidents in China pushes it into becoming a 'risky society'," (28 December 2007). Online. Available HTTP: <http://www.mac.gov.tw/english/english/macpolicy/risk961228.htm> (accessed 2 April 2008).

Moore, B., Jr. (1966) *Social Origins of Dictatorship and Democracy: lord and peasant in the making of the modern world*, Boston: Beacon Press.

Morley, J. W. (1993) *Driven by Growth: political change in the Asia-Pacific Region*, Armonk, NY: M. E. Sharpe.

Neelsen, J. P. (1988) "Strategische Gruppen, Klassenbildung und Staat in der Peripherie. Eine Kritik des Bielefelder Ansatzes," *Kölner Zeitschrift für Soziologie*, 40: 284–315.

Olson, M. (1971) *The Logic of Collective Action: public goods and the theory of goods*, revised edn., Cambridge, MA: Harvard University Press.

Ortmann, S. (2008) "Explaining non-transitions: the strategic behavior of political groups in Singapore and Hong Kong," Ph.D. Dissertation, University of Erlangen-Nuremberg.

Ott, D. (2000) *Small is Democratic: an examination of state and size in democratic development*, New York: Garland.

Parkin, F. (1983) *Marxism and Class Theory: a bourgeois critique*, New York: Columbia University Press.

Pei, M. (2007) "How will China democratize?" *Journal of Democracy*, 18(3): 53–7.

Preston, P. W. (1998) *Pacific Asia in the Global System: an introduction*, Oxford: Blackwell.

Przeworski, A. (1986) "Some problems in the study of the transition to democracy," in G. O'Donnell, P. Schmitter and L. Whitehead (eds) *Transitions from Authoritarian Rule: comparative perspectives*, Baltimore: Johns Hopkins University Press, pp. 47–63.

Przeworski, A. and Limongi, F. (1997) "Modernization: theories and facts," *World Politics*, 49 (2): 155–83.

Przeworski, A., Alvarez, M., Cheibub, J. A. and Limongi, F. (2000) *Democracy and Development: political institutions and well-being in the world 1950–1990*, Cambridge: Cambridge University Press.

Reid, A. (ed.) (1996) *Sojourners and Settlers: histories of Southeast Asia and the Chinese*, St. Leonards, NSW: Allen & Unwin.

Rich, R. (2007) *Pacific Asia in Quest of Democracy*, Boulder: Lynne Rienner.

Rigger, S. (1999) *Politics in Taiwan: voting for democracy*, London: Routledge.

Riggs, F. W. (1966) *Thailand: the modernization of a bureaucratic polity*, Honolulu: East West Center Press.

Rowen, H. S. (1998) "Is China becoming democratic?" *The American Enterprise Institute Online*, July/August. Online. Available HTTP: <http://www.taemag.com> (accessed 3 April 2008).

Rueschemeyer, D., Stephans, E. H. and Stephens, J. D. (1992) *Capitalist Development and Democracy*, Chicago: University of Chicago Press.

Saiedi, N. (1987) "A critique of Habermas' theory of practical rationality," *Studies in East European Thought*, 33(3): 251–65.

Schubert, G. (1994) *Taiwan—die chinesische Alternative*, Münster: Lit.

Schubert, G., Tetzlaff, R. and Vennewald, W. (eds) (1994) *Demokratisierung und politischer Wandel: Theorie und Anwendung des Konzeptes der strategischen und konfliktfähigen Gruppen (SKOG)*, Münster: Lit.

Sidel, J. (1996) "Siam and its twin? Democratization and bossism in contemporary Thailand and the Philippines," *IDS Bulletin*, 27(2): 56–63.

—— (2006) *Riots, Pogroms, Jihad: religious violence in Indonesia* (Ithaca: Cornell University Press).

—— (2008) "Social origins of dictatorship and democracy: colonial state and Chinese immigrant in the making of modern South East Asia," *Comparative Politics*, 40(2): 127–47.

Stubbs, R. (2005) *Rethinking Asia's Economic Miracle*, Basingstoke: Palgrave Macmillan.

Suehiro, A. (2008) *Catch-Up Industrialization: the trajectory and prospects of East Asian economies*, Honolulu: the University of Hawaii.

Thompson, M. R. (2001a) "To shoot or not to shoot: post-totalitarianism in China and Eastern Europe," *Comparative Politics*, 34(1): 63–83.

—— (2001b) "Whatever happened to 'Asian values'?" *Journal of Democracy*, 12: 154–65.

—— (2008) "Vanguard in a vacuum: students protests and developmentalist authoritarianism in Pacific Asia," paper prepared for the Workshop "Political Learning? Understanding Student Activism in Asia," Asian Political and International Studies Association (APISA), Kuala Lumpur, 20–21 December 2008.

Uhlin, A. (1997) *Indonesia and the "Third Wave" of Democratization*, New York: St. Martin's.

Vennewald, W. (1994) *Herrschaft der Technokraten und Professionals—Ohnmacht der Demokratie*, Opladen: Leske und Budrich.

Wade, R. (1990) *Governing the Market: economic theory and the role of government in East Asian industrialization*, Princeton: Princeton University Press.

—— (1998) "From "miracle" to "cronyism": explaining the great Asian slump," *Cambridge Journal of Economics*, 22(6): 693–706.

Weber, M. (1993 [1904/1905]) *The Sociology of Religion*, Boston: Beacon.

World Bank (1993) *The East Asian Miracle: economic growth and public policy*, New York: Oxford University Press.

—— (2008) "Gross national income per capita 2008, Atlas method and PPP." Online. Available HTTP: <http://siteresources.worldbank.org/DATASTATISTICS/Resources/GNIPC.pdf> (accessed 27 August 2009).

Zakaria, F. (1994) "A conversation with Lee Kuan Yew," *Foreign Affairs*, 73(2): 109–26.

6 Development and change in Korean democracy since the democratic transition in 1987

The Three Kims' politics and after

Hyug-Baeg Im

Introduction: development and underdevelopment of democracy in Korea

Korean democracy passed Samuel P. Huntington's "two turnover test" by smoothly handing over power to a new president in the election of 17 December 2007. Huntington notes that "a democracy may be viewed as consolidated if the party or group that takes power in the initial election at the time of transition loses a subsequent election and turns over power to those election winners, and if those election winners then peacefully turn over power to the winners of a later election" (Huntington 1991: 266–7). As Adam Przeworski argues, "democracy is a political system in which parties lose elections" (Przeworski 1991: 10). Thus, passing the "two turnovers" test is decisive evidence that an emerging democracy has succeeded in "institutionalizing uncertainty" or "subjecting all interests to competition" (Przeworski 1991: 14). South Korea (referred to simply as "Korea" hereafter) experienced its first turnover when it elected long-time opposition leader Kim Dae Jung to the presidency in 1997. Ten years later, Lee Myung Bak and the Grand National Party (GNP) retook power in the 2007 presidential election and the 2008 National Assembly election, completing the second turnover. In East Asia, only Korea and Taiwan have passed the two turnover test. Taiwan completed its two turnovers in a shorter period (12 years), but it still took only 20 years for Korea to complete the process. Japan, although acclaimed as the most advanced and stable democracy in Asia, has had only one turnover since the emergence of the "1955 regime," with the election of the non-Liberal Democratic Party politician Morihiro Hosokawa as prime minister in 1993.

Does passing the two turnover test mean that Korea has become a fully consolidated democracy? If democratic consolidation is defined as the institutionalization of electoral competition, then it can be said that Korean democracy is consolidated. Korea has proven itself a sustainable, durable, accountable, and free democracy over the 20 years since the democratic transition began in 1987. It has endured the severe economic crisis of 1997, a nuclear crisis involving North Korea, and a constitutional crisis that arose over the impeachment of President Roh Moo Hyun. Over time, Korea has become a freer and more accountable democracy, as demonstrated by its classification as a free country by Freedom House's *World Freedom Report*, which gave it a freedom score of one for political rights and two for civil liberties.

Nonetheless, there is still room for improvement in Korean democracy. Parties remain cliques of political aspirants. The party system has not yet been institutionalized, and electoral participation has decreased steadily since the democratic transition in 1987. Ideological orthodoxy remains firmly entrenched, thus impeding the politics of compromise. In this chapter, I analyze the development and change of Korean democracy since democratization in 1987, and explore ways to improve the quality of democracy in Korea in the twenty-first century.

Coexistence of tradition and modernity in Korean democracy since 1987

In the last half-century, Korea telescoped the stages of its industrialization, but did not achieve democratic transition until quite late in the third global wave of democratization. As a consequence of this compressed industrialization and late democratization, different historical times have coexisted, especially in terms of political governance. The traditional governance of the sedentary Confucian society has coexisted with the modern governance of the industrial society and even the post-modern governance of the "neonomadic" society (a term explained more fully later). Although Korean society has now entered the age of the post-industrial information society, Korean politics has not been able to completely jettison the legacies inherited from the politics of previous eras, such as high cost, low efficiency politics, unresponsive and unaccountable politics, low trust politics, closed network politics, and exclusionary politics.

After democracy was restored in 1987, modern political institutions such as political parties, parliament, and elections developed, but many traditional or pre-modern elements of political culture, behavior, consciousness, and institutions remained intact in the form of Confucian patrimonialism, clientelism, patriarchy, and closed-network politics. Within the pre-modern system, political leaders acted like patriarchs in large families, and strong regional ties dominated electoral politics. More recently, although Confucianism has not left Korea completely, modern political institutions and norms have been on the rise (Niemann and Burghart 2004).

However, political modernization is still incomplete. While Korea has achieved industrialization and democratization, it has yet to complete the major modernization project of nation-building. Korea is still a divided state, and indeed remains one of the few divided nations in the post-Cold War world. At the same time, many elements of post-modern politics have been introduced into Korea with globalization and the IT revolution. Korea is a country in which internet politics is vivid and active. Slimming down politics is the current watchword in Korea, and political parties have dissolved local party organizations and closed local party offices. The imperial party president no longer exists, and the power of party bosses has weakened as new politicians are elected over protégés of the party bosses through "people's primaries," or semi-open primaries. Since the dawn of the twenty-first century, the post-modern political agendas of gender equality, environmental protection, civil society, and peace have moved to the fore in electoral politics, and the breakdown of male-dominated politics is progressing rapidly as the number of female law-makers increases.

Korean democracy in the Three Kims era

Until the 2002 presidential election, the "Three Kims" (Kim Young Sam, Kim Dae Jung, and Kim Jong Pil) dominated Korean politics (Im 2004). Kim Young Sam and Kim Dae Jung led the democratization movement in the 1970s and 1980s, and Kim Jong Pil represented a moderate alternative to Park Chung Hee's dictatorship within the authoritarian ruling circle.

The Three Kims, as leaders of the first generation of Korean democracy, presided over a rapid and successful transition from authoritarian rule to liberal democracy by institutionalizing electoral competition and civilian control over the military and promoting political and civil liberties, including human rights. The political era of the Three Kims lasted 15 years, after which they handed over to the next generation a durable and sustainable democracy that is in no imminent danger of breakdown or protracted erosion. However, despite these achievements, the Three Kims also left the unfortunate legacy of a pre-modern political culture.

Development of liberal democracy

In the Three Kims era, Koreans developed a modern liberal democracy for the first time in their history. A democratic constitution was crafted through compromise among the key political forces and approved by an overwhelming majority of people. The new constitution guaranteed political rights and civil liberties, and limited the power of the president through the checks and balances of other institutions. Under Kim Young Sam's presidency, the military was forced to go back to barracks, where it was placed under firm civilian control. Fair and competitive elections were held regularly every four to five years, and government and elected officials were required to be more accountable to the people.

Civilianization

Korea has a long tradition of civilian control of the military. Confucianism is inherently anti-militaristic, which influenced the military policy of the Confucian Chosun dynasty and hence the absence of military coups during the whole period. Civilian control was also maintained during the Korean War and the government of Rhee Syng Man. This long tradition of civilian control was eventually broken by a military coup in 1961 led by General Park Chung Hee, which led to 30 years of military dictatorship. Reinstituting civilian control over the military was the first mission of the new democratic government, but it was never fully carried out. President Roh Tae Woo, a former general and a key player in the military coup in 1979 after the assassination of Park Chung Hee, was elected president in 1987 as a military-backed candidate. President Roh allowed a "reserved domain" for the military by securing the military's "organizational, financial and personal interests against civilian interference" (Croissant 2004: 370).

It was not until the Kim Young Sam presidency that the military was comprehensively purged from politics. Kim Young Sam, the first civilian president in 30 years, called his government a "civilian government" (*munminjungbu*) and launched a massive project to demilitarize and civilianize Korean politics. Kim Young Sam was expected to act cautiously in purging military officers and national security apparatus because of his indebtedness to the military forces in being elected to the presidency. However, he took decisive and quick action to disband the Hanahoe Club, the politicized military officer clique that was a pillar of authoritarianism and had occupied key strategic posts in the military and national security apparatus under the Chun Doo Hwan and Roh governments. Immediately after disbanding the Hanahoe Club, President Kim purged most of the Hanahoe members from the military and national security apparatus (Diamond and Shin 2000: 10). Kim Young Sam even prosecuted the two former presidents, Chun and Roh, on charges of corruption, military mutiny, treason for staging the December 1979 coup, and the massacre of civilians during the Kwangju uprising in 1980 (Roehrig 1998: 4–6). These military reforms were the greatest achievement of the first civilian president in what had been the most militarized country in the world.

With the quick and comprehensive purging of the politicized military officer group, President Kim ensured that Korea both avoided a democratic breakdown and reasserted civilian supremacy over the military by placing the "national security community" under the control of elected representatives. This effectively removed the "reserved domain" for the military in Korean politics, and deprived the military and the national security apparatus of their privileged status and prerogatives that had been outside the control of democratically elected civilian representatives.

Institutionalization of democratic competition

Joseph Schumpeter (1950) defined democracy as a form of government in which power is decided by a competitive struggle for people's votes. Korean democracy certainly satisfied this requirement during the Three Kims era.

Since the first democratic election in 1987, Koreans have elected a different president every five years and new members of the National Assembly every four years. In 1991, local assemblymen were elected for the first time since Park Chung Hee ended local elections. In 1995, the heads of local governments, governors, mayors, and county chiefs were added to the ballot in local elections, and since then three local elections have been held.

In addition to the increased frequency of elections and the expanded scope of elected positions, the fairness of electoral campaigns has been improved. Candidates now rely more on television or radio debates, and the public financing of campaigns has increased. Campaign spending has also become more transparent with successive political reforms. Przeworski (1991) argues that democracy becomes consolidated when it generates self-enforcing compliance with the outcome of an election, whereby the loser accepts his or her defeat and complies with the will of the people as expressed through the election. In Korea, elections have become "the only game in town" through which to obtain power.

Alternation of power

In the 1997 presidential election, Kim Dae Jung was elected to the presidency in his fourth bid for power, marking the first peaceful transfer of power to an opposition party candidate in 50 years. The election was a watershed in Korea's journey toward democratic consolidation, and his victory demonstrated the convertibility of power between rivals that is critical for an effectively functioning democracy. As the alternation of power between rival forces guarantees the uncertainty of the outcome of elections, it is one of the core conditions for democratic consolidation.

With the election of Kim Dae Jung, Korea became the first of the third-wave democracies in East Asia to experience the peaceful transfer of power to an opposition party. In that election, the Korean people rejected the candidate of the conservative establishment party that had ruled the country for decades. This was a historic event that broke the stigma of a Korean democracy ruled by "a dominant, corporatist party that tolerated a limited opposition but never ceded power" (Carothers 1997: 16).

The 1997 transfer of power had another historic meaning for democratic consolidation because it took place in the midst of a severe economic crisis. In late 1997, the Asian financial crisis that started in Thailand and Indonesia reached South Korea, resulting in the meltdown of the financial system and economic collapse. Korea avoided the worst-case scenario with help from the International Monetary Fund (IMF), which bailed out the financial system and the economy with massive loans totaling US$55 billion, but imposed strict fiscal and monetary conditions on the country. However, despite the extreme economic hardship that followed, the Korean people went to the polls and elected an opposition candidate, delegating to him the authority to overhaul the system of "crony capitalism" that had prevailed under authoritarian regimes and thereby extending the life of the new democracy. The election of 1997 showed the durability and improved accountability of Korean democracy, and demonstrated the Korean people's determination to live under democratic rule regardless of external events such as financial crises. The defeat of the ruling party candidate showed that the electoral mechanism of accountability was working, because the people held the ruling party accountable for the national economic crisis. Democracy helped Korea to carry out comprehensive reform without causing serious political instability by institutionalizing the electoral mechanism for legitimate power change (Haggard 2000; Kim 2001).

As mentioned, Korea passed Huntington's "two turnover test" with the election of the conservative candidate Lee Myung Bak to the presidency on 19 December 2007. Ten years after the first peaceful transfer of power, Korean liberals transferred power back to the conservatives. Widespread disenchantment with the Roh Moo Hyun government's poor performance on economic and social issues brought people out to the voting booth to punish the ruling party candidate and to transfer power to a pragmatic conservative candidate who promised to make economic growth and job creation a priority. In the 2007 presidential election, "retrospective voting" predominated over "prospective voting," which proved further that democratic accountability was working as the people once again punished the ruling party for its poor performance.

Legacies of Confucian patrimonialism

The question of why Koreans succeeded so spectacularly in installing democratic institutions in a short time but failed to internalize democratic norms, practice democracy within political parties, enforce the rule of law, or make the government transparent is an intriguing one. To use a computer analogy, why did Koreans in the Three Kims period operate the modern hardware of democratic institutions with the pre-modern software of patrimonialism, patriarchy, and paternalism?

The answer can be found in the resilience of Confucianism during the first generation of Korean democracy. According to Bung Ik Koh, although only about 2 percent of the Korean population would call themselves Confucian, "all men are Confucians" because the majority of Koreans actually observe basic Confucian rituals and subscribe to Confucian values (Koh 1996: 196–9). Confucianism has deep roots in the everyday life of Koreans, even though it has not been the state ideology for many years. Even today, "Confucianism saturates Korean people's lives and is the core of Korean culture" (Kim 1996: 225).

Despite industrialization and democratization, the legacy of Confucianism has survived in the minds of many Koreans, with its emphasis on education, secular life, the family, elite paternalism, and righteousness (Kwon and Cho 1994: 8). As one U.S. scholar observed, "Koreans operate with Western hardware and Confucian software" (Steinberg 1997: 151).

Confucian patrimonialism under the Chosun dynasty

Society during the Chosun dynasty was medieval agrarian in nature. It was a stationary society in which the total crop yield was fixed because the small amount of arable land could not be expanded. Thus, politics during the Chosun dynasty centered on how to distribute the fixed amount of crops—a zero-sum game. In this agrarian society, political coercion was the dominant force in deciding how crop yields would be distributed, and cutthroat power battles took place among the political elite to decide how wealth should be disbursed. In this situation, the peaceful transfer of power among political parties (*Boongdang*) was unthinkable. Parties were machines that perpetuated the inherited privileges of a handful of elite families (Kim 2002: 77), and every "*hwan guk*" (change of power) during the Chosun dynasty was accompanied by the death of hundreds of political opponents.

Politics in the Chosun era was also characterized by clientelistic ties among families, schools, and regions. This politics of closed networks was by nature exclusionary. Because political order was based on personal ties and bonds between family or sib members, it deterred the development of the impersonal ties and associations that are the basis of democratic civil society. Strong familism resulted in every individual dividing the society into "us" and "them." In this dichotomous society, family, birthplace, and school constituted an individual's identity, and it was thus difficult to form civil associations involving diverse interests and identities. A democratic community is a community primarily of strangers—rather than an exclusive community of in-group members—who ask that they be accorded fair treatment (Park 1997: 832).

In the Chosun era, the radius of trust in politics was very short because the strong trust within "inside" groups was based on distrust and exclusion of "outside" groups. The politics of exclusion and the zero-sum game generated a political environment that made compromise very hard. The agricultural stationary society of the Chosun era did not have the material base of an expanding economy to enable a positive-sum game of politics.

In the Chosun era, the centralized state coexisted with the regional strongholds of the Yangban literati. The relationship between the center and the provinces was both vertical and hierarchical, and as a result, the party system was formed on the basis of regional identification. The No-ron party that dominated most of the late Chosun period was based in the Kiho regions (Kyunggi and Honam provinces), whereas the opposition Nam-in party was based in the Youngnam region (Kyungsang provinces). Korean regionalism, as characterized by the life-or-death struggle for the center, was thus a central part of politics in the Chosun dynasty.

Finally, the agrarian Chosun society was characterized by strong patriarchy and paternalism. The state was regarded as an extended family with the king at its head. Family-based agricultural production generated a political structure of concentric circles in which the innermost circle was defined by family ties and the outer circles progressively included first regional ties, then school ties, and finally national ties. Under this political structure, patriarchy, cronyism, and the personalization of public authority were pervasive.

Confucianism as the state ideology justified the political order of the stationary agricultural society, and also provided the cultural base for factional strife among regional parties and for the rule of the individual, rather than the rule of law.

Confucian patrimonialism in post-transition democracy

Confucianism waned as an ideology and a moral code of conduct in Korean society with the advent of industrialization and democratization. No attempt was made to revive the Confucian codes of conduct that operated in the Chosun era, but the Confucian cultural legacy remained strong even after democratic transition (Koh 1996: 200).

In the Three Kims era, despite success in installing liberal democratic institutions, Koreans failed to develop democratic norms and practices, such as accountability, responsiveness, transparency, and the rule of law, precisely because of the Confucian cultural legacies that permeated the thinking of political leaders and the general populace. Confucian values became an obstacle to instituting democratic governance.

Nowhere was the residual strength of the Confucian legacy more apparent than in the resilience of regionalism in Korea. In the Three Kims era, every election was decided along regional lines (Im 2004: 185–7), and politics was reduced to a game between regional rivals. Regionalism was a major impediment to democratic development because voters did not support parties and candidates based on policy stances and ideologies, but on loyalty to a region or favorite son (Browne and Kim 2001: 20).

The Three Kims were partly responsible for the reemergence of regionalism as a dominant factor in deciding the outcome of elections, because all three chose "region" as the primary axis around which their parties were organized. After the democratic transition in 1987, democratization (democrats versus non-democrats) as a political issue lost its saliency for voters and the Three Kims had to find new issues to galvanize the electorate. Because class divisions had been suppressed and religious schisms were absent in Korean society, regional divisions became a means to mobilize voters (Im 2004: 188).

Regionalism created a virtually regional monopoly for the Three Kims' party. In the Cholla, Kyungsang, and Chungchong regions, where the Three Kims dominated electoral politics, party nomination virtually guaranteed election, and there was little inter-party competition. Even in the Seoul metropolitan area, home to more than 45 percent of the population, residents cast votes based on the party of their hometown.

Regionalism overshadowed the interests of class, religion, occupation, gender, and generation in elections. Regionalism also hindered political leaders from forming a broad, national support base, and thus hampered national integration (Im 2004: 189). Korean regionalism was based on Confucian familism (B. K. Kim 2000: 79), which entrapped Korean voters in regional competition. Korean voters expanded their concentric circles of identity from narrow blood (family) and school ties to broader regional sentiments when choosing candidates in election (B. K. Kim 2000: 79).

The second legacy of Confucian values for democracy was manifested in the system of delegative presidency. In Korea, successive democratically elected civilian presidents succumbed to the strong temptation to inflate their power. Each president ruled the country as if he had been delegated all the power from the sovereign people through election, acting as if free of constraints, putting himself above parties and organized interests, and thus transforming sovereign voters into passive observers. President Kim Young Sam in particular was infused with a strong delegative character, and along with his close associates made policies without consulting political parties, the legislature, or relevant interest groups.

The basic premise of delegative democracy is that once an individual is elected president, he or she is entitled to govern without regard for other democratic institutions. Under delegative democracy, although the vertical accountability of rulers to the ruled is secured through regular and contested elections, the "horizontal accountability" of office holders or state agencies to one another cannot be institutionalized. Delegative presidents do not acknowledge the power and authority of other elected bodies and do not recognize the rights of other representative bodies to enforce horizontal accountability through checks and balances. The Three Kims tried to put the National Assembly under their control by securing a solid majority in the legislature through party mergers and co-opting independent and opposition assemblymen into the governing party (Im 2000: 34).

Delegative politics also gave rise to "*daekwonjueui*" (the cult of ultimate power) in Korea. *Daekwon* (ultimate power) is undemocratic because, under democracy, power derives from the people and only they have the ultimate power. *Daekwonjueui* led to the mistaken view that to be elected president meant to be delegated all the power. As a result, Korean politics revolved inordinately around presidential elections, and the stakes in being elected president were so high as to make a presidential election virtually a life-or-death battle. Compromises and mutual trust were not possible, and the continuation of the zero-sum political game obstructed the workings of democracy (Croissant 2002: 14).

As mentioned, Confucianism was the major cultural source of delegative democracy. Indeed, Lucian Pye notes that Korean presidents acted like Confucian patriarchal fathers of the nation:

> Korean rulers, like Korean fathers, are expected to be embattled, needing to prove themselves in adversary contacts; but they are also expected to be masterful at all times, for like the Chinese figure, able to cope

single-handedly with all of his problems and demanding total adherence to his wishes. Yet, again like the Japanese leader-father, he is expected to be sympathetic, nurturing, and sensitive to the wishes of his followers-family, though at the same time vicious and aggressive in fighting external foes.

(Pye 1985: 67)

Pye's description of Korean presidents shares some characteristics with Guillermo O'Donnell's "delegative president," who regards himself as the embodiment of the nation, the custodian of national interests, and a paternalistic figure who stands above factional or partisan politics (O'Donnell 1999: 164–5). Confucian patriarchy or paternalism also views rulers as father figures upon whom people bestow all the power and who are expected to be the people's intermediary with God. Thus, delegative democracy fits well with Confucian values (Shin and Park 2001).

A third dimension of Confucian patrimonialism in the early days of Korean democracy was personal political parties. The Three Kims created and dissolved parties ten times: Kim Young Sam three times, Kim Dae Jung four times, and Kim Jong Pil three times. They repeated the same cycle of founding, dissolving, reestablishing, and renaming their parties at will (Shin 1999: 180), and ran their parties as if they were feudal lords. They reigned as imperial party presidents who monopolized the process of nominating candidates, appointed party officials and the chairmen of National Assembly committees, and allocated party finances. Moreover, they distributed political money to their followers in return for loyalty (Im 2000: 33).

The Three Kims' rule over their parties may have been somewhat justified under the authoritarian regime. To protect party members from intimidation, threats, and police surveillance and to maintain organizational integrity, the Three Kims may have needed to run and organize their parties in the way that an authoritarian dictator might. After democracy was installed, however, the Three Kims continued to lead their parties in an authoritarian manner. Because the parties were organized along regional lines, the Three Kims were able to maintain exclusive loyalty from their home provinces, and few party politicians could challenge their autocratic rule.

Yet no regional political party was able to win a stable majority in the National Assembly because of the electoral system of single member, simple majority. A regional party usually forged very loose alliances with other regional parties to win a presidential election, but such alliances usually broke down one or two years later (Kim and Im 2001: 31–2).

The volatile personal party politics of the Three Kims was a major impediment to the development of internal party democracy and an accountable party system. The regionalist political parties created by the Three Kims also prevented Korea from developing a policy-oriented party system. The party boss approach under the Three Kims was a symbol of the pre-modern political system: as party bosses, the Three Kims took care of their family (people), who in return were obligated to their father (leader) (Steinberg and Shin 2006: 524). The Three Kims' parties were thus strongly patrimonial, in that leadership and followership were both personalized.

Confucian orthodoxy and conformity remained strong in the post-democratic transition period, resulting in an emphasis on ideological purity and in turn a lower level of political tolerance in Korea than in other countries at a similar level of socioeconomic development (Han 1997: 83; Steinberg, 1997: 155). This cultural legacy also supported a strong vein of anti-communism among older generations. As a consequence, when the Cold War ended in other parts of the world, it remained a salient issue in Korea, and even today the anti-communist national security law remains intact. The Confucian legacy of ideological orthodoxy and conformity thus served as the main obstacle to the institution of a democracy characterized by diversity, pluralism, and tolerance (Han 1997: 83).

Anti-communism was an ideological barrier to entry into political society. The steadfast anti-communist stance narrowed the agendas discussed in democratic forums and obstructed efforts to find peaceful solutions to the problem of the Korean Peninsula. The residual anti-communist sentiment also pushed the McCarthyistic pro-communist "*Sakkalron*" (coloring one's ideology as pro-North and pro-communist) to the front of the electoral stage, thus distorting the political views of the candidates and limiting voters' ideological choices.

The ideological narrowness of Korean political society maintained the exclusionary character of Korean democracy, even though the country's democratic transition took place in the favorable international milieu of the cessation of the Cold War.

Change of democracy in the post-Three Kims era

The rise of the neo-nomadic society

Since the end of the Three Kims era, new political phenomena have risen to the fore in Korea. The election of Roh Moo Hyun signaled an end to the politics of the Three Kims generation, and a new generation of politicians is now putting its stamp on Korean political life (Larsen 2003). Post-modern and post-materialist political issues, such as generational shifts, gender equality, environmental protection, peace, civil society, and human rights have been placed at the top of the political agenda. These changes did not occur spontaneously after the exit of the Three Kims. Rather, the emergence of the new politics has been driven by profound social change. That social change is the result of the advent of what I call the "neo-nomadic society" in Korea (Im forthcoming). South Korea is one of the countries in which the IT revolution has advanced the fastest. The country ranks third in East Asia after the city-states of Singapore and Hong Kong in terms of the number of mobile phone and internet users and total amount of internet use. More than

30 million Koreans have become "netizens" who have everyday access to the internet, and the number of mobile phones exceeds the total population. Korea is the only country to boast a completed national information super-highway infrastructure, and its per capita VDSL use is the first in the world, surpassing even the United States. Korea is no longer a country that is catching up with advanced countries: it is at the forefront of the IT revolution.

Sparked by the digital revolution, globalization, and democratization, a neo-nomadic society has emerged in Korea. The French futurist Jacques Attali argues that with the digital revolution and globalization, human beings—equipped with notebook computers, mobile phones, the internet, and faxes—have ended 10,000 years of settled life and are once again becoming nomads who travel across occupations, environments, and national borders to pursue happiness. A nomad is defined by his or her identity, not by the place in which he or she lives (Attali 1998).

Koreans were a horse-riding nomadic people 5,000 years ago. Their nomadic temperament has been suppressed by long years of living in settlements, but it has reemerged with the advent of the digital revolution and globalization. The innovations coming out of "Teheran Valley" (Korea's version of Silicon Valley), the spectacular growth of mobile phone and internet use, and the phenomenal increase in digital access have all contributed to the transformation of Koreans into virtual nomads.

The inflow of foreign workers, flexible labor markets, free-trade agreements, and the opening of Korea's agricultural market through accession to the World Trade Organization (WTO) have compelled Korean workers to travel to find jobs, thus generating a working class of physical nomads, whereas the affluent have become hyper-nomads who travel all over the world in search of profits and wealth.

Moreover, with the advent of the digital revolution, the New Economy, the mass consumption of motor vehicles, the development of a complex national highway system and high-speed trains, a transportation revolution, and rapid urbanization, the nomadic Korean society has become highly mobile. People move and change residences, jobs, occupations, schools, and social class frequently. Social mobility is increasing rapidly as the New Economy creates new job categories and more flexible social classes. Advances in computing and the internet mean that many Korean people can work at home or work while traveling (K. D. Kim 2000: 22). Furthermore, the majority of Koreans now live in apartments, temporary residences fit for a highly mobile lifestyle. Few people buy apartments as lifetime residences (Yoon 2008). Thomas Friedman points out that Koreans form a "cybertribe" in the neo-nomadic world. With an internet-linked diasporic community (seven million Koreans) spread across the world, the Korean cybertribe combines speed, creativity, entrepreneurial talent, and global networking to generate enormous wealth (Friedman 2000).

The neo-nomadic society is transforming Korean political governance from a large, slow, isolated, closed, exclusionary bureaucracy into a small, fast, connected, open, and inclusive community. The core of the Korean neo-nomads comprises young people in their twenties and thirties. Young Koreans have variously become the N-generation (netizen generation), the P-generation (participation, passion, and potential power), and the M-generation (*m-tizen*: mobile citizen), participating actively in politics and communicating and debating in cyberspace through neo-nomadic devices such as the internet and mobile phones.

The Korea–Japan World Cup game in 2002 gave further momentum to the mobilization of young Koreans. During the World Cup, 24 million people spontaneously participated in street festivities, and although all generations were involved, the majority were "Red Devils" (the name of a Korean cheering group) and young Koreans in their teens, twenties, and thirties who were collectively termed the R (red devil) generation or the W (World Cup) generation. The mobilization of the R or W generation during the World Cup hinted at the future of governance in Korea—a festival in which everybody enjoys participating.

In part due to their mobilization during the World Cup, young Koreans who had been sarcastic, apathetic, and cynical about politics became politically active citizens. Following the World Cup, the W generation became members of the P generation, participating in the presidential election, candlelight demonstrations protesting against the U.S. Army's actions in the death of two Korean schoolgirls, and rallies against the Iraq War.

Netizens and m-tizens are the core of the Korean P generation. Netizens are intellectually open, inclusive, communicative, socially conscious, innovative, fast, mobile, and trustworthy youths. Netizens participate in politics through the organization of internet fan clubs such as NoSaMo (people who love Roh Moo Hyun) and demonstrations and discussions known as "*bungae moim*" (lightening meetings). Using the internet and mobile phones, netizens connect with and mobilize online communities to participate in offline activities, such as demonstrations, boycotts, and public debates.

"Confucius leaving Korea"

The political landscape in the new Korean neo-nomadic society is changing in several ways. First, the imperial presidency is disappearing from the political scene. Since his inauguration, President Roh has taken measures to end imperial president practices, refusing, for example, to take direct control of powerful state agencies such as the National Information Agency, the Public Prosecutor's Office, the National Police, and the Internal Revenue Office, thus enabling them to function in a politically neutral way. Under previous administrations, these state agencies were used by delegative presidents to strengthen their power and privilege, control their party, and intimidate opposition party politicians. Since President Roh took office, the ruling parties have not been under the strict control of the president and have enjoyed more autonomy in policy-making and legislative actions. The National

Assembly has acted as an effective counterbalance to the president. These changes have meant that today very few Koreans believe that Korea is still ruled by an imperial presidency.

Second, regionalism is waning as the dominating force in Korean politics. It was still a factor in the presidential election of 2002, with almost 95 percent of voters in Cholla province voting for Roh but more than 75 percent of voters in Kyungsang province voting for the opposition party candidate Lee Hoe Chang. In the National Assembly election of 15 April 2004, however, regionalism had begun to ebb as a political force everywhere except Kyungsang province. Instead, generational disagreement over the impeachment of Roh was the main factor deciding the outcome of the election that gave the ruling Woori Party the majority in the National Assembly for the first time since 1987 (Park 2004; Choi and Cho 2005; Lee 2007). In the recent election of 9 April 2008, regionalism was less of a factor in the electoral outcome than policy and ideological differences and the generational divide.

Third, the ideological orthodoxy sustained by Confucian culture has been retreating since the North–South Summit Meeting on 15 June 2000. Former president Kim Dae Jung's Sunshine Policy opened a new era of North–South reconciliation and cooperation, and since then many Koreans have become more tolerant of communist North Korea. At the same time, the number of older, more conservative Koreans wishing to maintain the ideological orthodoxy of anti-communism has declined. A full 40 percent of the National Assembly members elected in April 2004 identified themselves as progressives, and only 20 percent stated that they were conservatives. In the 2004 election, a left-wing party—the Democratic Labor Party (DLP)—gained a toehold in the National Assembly for the first time since the democratic transition in 1987, winning 10 seats and receiving 13 percent of the popular vote, making it the third largest party in Korea.

Advancing modernity: political reforms for modern liberal democracy

As pre-modern political culture and ideology have receded, various efforts to improve Korean democracy have been made since the end of the post-Three Kims era. Political parties have become smaller but more efficient, transparent, accountable, and responsive. The political society now accepts the reality of power sharing with the civil society, and Koreans in general have become more tolerant of diverse ideologies and cultural values and norms.

Party reform

Since the last days of the Kim Dae Jung presidency, the Korean political parties have overhauled their party governance (Im forthcoming). The party reform movement began with the ruling party. In the aftermath of a devastating defeat in the by-election of 25 October 2001, President Kim Dae Jung resigned as president of the ruling Millennium Democratic Party (MDP) under pressure from party reformists. In November 2001, the party formed a special reform committee and at the end of December produced a comprehensive reform program. The party governance reform abolished the post of party president, prohibited an incumbent president from concurrently holding the post of party chairman, prohibited the presidential candidate from being the chief party representative, and adopted a new nomination system in which presidential candidates are chosen by a "People's Nomination System."

This comprehensive reform program was intended to remove the elements of personal, feudal, and autocratic party leadership so characteristic of the Three Kims era and to expand the electoral base of the party. The most striking reform was the new People's Nominating System, which was actually a mixed system of open and closed primaries. The new system, which initiated a bottom-up process of nominating the party's presidential candidate, was a turning point in the conversion of the MDP from an elite party to a mass party.

The other major parties followed the MDP's reform program, similarly abolishing the post of the imperial party president and setting up mechanisms for intra-party democracy. They also adopted collegial systems of party leadership elected directly by rank-and-file party members. Under these systems, the candidate obtaining the most votes is the party chairman, but cannot wield the power formerly held by the party president. Instead, the floor leader, who is elected by National Assembly members, is empowered to set legislative strategies and party policies as the representative of the in-house party. This dual system of party leadership is intended to decentralize party decision-making and promote bottom-up processes of aggregating and representing constituency interests.

Another major party reform has been downsizing. The over-development of party organizations had been a major source of bureaucratization, "high cost, low efficiency politics," and political corruption. The major parties have slimmed down by scaling back the size of the central party secretariat and virtually abolishing local party branches. With these reforms, the Korean political parties have transformed themselves into neo-nomadic parties that aggregate, represent, and respond to constituency interests quickly, efficiently, and with less bureaucracy.

Political finance reform

In the 2002 presidential election, the major candidates relied less on outdoor campaigning in front of mobilized audiences and more on television and radio debates and advertisements through the mass media. The prominence of mass media and online campaigns has reduced the amount of campaign money needed, and has led the candidates to adopt a U.S.-style policy debate campaign.

However, illegal political contributions did not completely disappear in the 2002 election, and the disclosure of illegal campaign contributions to conservative party GNP candidates by major *chaebul* groups diminished public trust in the political system.

The campaign to end unlawful political financing dates back to mid-1993, when President Roh started the "*mani pulite*" (clean hands) campaign to end illegal contributions by ordering prosecutors to investigate the finances of both the ruling and opposition parties. The investigation by the prosecutor's office, combined with public pressure to establish a more transparent political financing system leading up to the National Assembly elections in April 2004, forced Korean politicians to reform the campaign financing system. The new political financing laws now require parties and candidates to report to the National Election Commission in a clear and verifiable manner all campaign contribution receipts, set limits on contribution, and encourage small donations. The government and the National Election Commission also encourage whistle-blowing on illegal campaign contributions and vote-buying by rewarding whistle-blowers with 50 times the amount of illegal money that they report and imposing a fine on both illegal donors and receivers that is 50 times the amount of money that they gave or received.

Thanks to these reforms, money played less of a role in the National Assembly elections of 15 April 2004 than in any other election. This National Assembly election was the cleanest election in Korean history, and marked a turning point for political transparency in Korea.

The advent of post-modernity: internet democracy

As mentioned, Korea is at the forefront of the IT revolution, and currently more than 30 million of the population of 47 million are netizens. Korean netizens make use of the internet to improve accountability and transparency in Korean politics. The internet delivers a broad swathe of information to citizens at fast speeds and a cheap cost, transmits the demands of the people to their representatives through two-way cyber communication, and enables politicians to respond to the people's demands regarding policy-making and legislation in a speedy manner. In addition, netizens use the internet as a collective place for monitoring, pressuring, and protesting that is available 24 hours a day, thereby enhancing political accountability.

Since the 1997 presidential election, Korean politicians have paid close attention to the internet revolution and have tried to appeal to netizen voters. In the presidential elections of 1997 and 2002, the National Assembly elections of 2004, and the local elections of 1998, politicians set up web pages to give information on themselves and their policies and to communicate with netizen voters.

In the aftermath of the 2002 election, the Korean political parties, recognizing the power of the internet in presidential elections, reorganized party governance using the internet. Parties and assemblymen opened cyber forums to communicate with constituents, to encourage the active participation of rank-and-file members in party policy-making, and to identify voter preferences. The parties also set up cyber polls enabling citizens to propose and vote on party policies.

The internet revolution has not only reformed representative democracy, but has also strengthened participatory democracy. Netizens have transformed themselves from passive consumers of political information into active producers and providers of information. In some cases, netizen groups such as NoSaMo and ParkSaMo (People who love Park Keun Hae) have replaced political parties or politicians as the organizers of electoral campaigns. Netizen voters lead electoral campaign by means of user-created content (UCC), user generated content (UGC), and user generated video (UGV). Web 2.0 has heralded a new age of political participation and information-sharing, and has expanded the political influence of minorities.

Concluding remarks

Korean democracy is at a crossroads. In the presidential election of 19 December 2007, the conservative GNP candidate Lee Myung Bak was elected to the presidency and GNP candidates gained a majority of seats to retake the National Assembly. This marked the end of the progressive period in Korea, ten years after the first transfer of power from conservatives to liberals.

The shift back to conservatism may be felt more in terms of economics than in politics. Lee Myung Bak and the GNP retook power from the progressives on a platform of neoliberal economic growth and populist redistribution policies. Lee Myung Bak and pragmatic conservatives were able to capture the votes of the rich Kangnam (South of the Han River) people and the poor Kangbuk people, capitalists and workers, the younger generation in their twenties and thirties, and the older generation in their fifties and sixties. This successful creation of a multi-class coalition enabled the GNP to retake power at its third attempt. This "new right" coalition can be described as neoliberal populist, but it is a very unstable combination. To sustain this multi-class coalition, the GNP government needs to produce both high economic growth and the redistribution of wealth. The success of Lee Myung Bak thus depends on the simultaneous achievement of these two contradictory objectives, one neoliberal (economic efficiency) and the other populist (wealth redistribution). Neoliberal policies by themselves would probably create wealth distribution problems and would worsen socio-economic polarization. However, if the distribution of wealth becomes more unequal, then populist supporters who voted for Lee, such as the poor, the young, and the unions, will probably withdraw their support.

With regard to political reform, even though the current conservative government could not completely reverse the trends of receding pre-modernity, advancing modernity, and accelerating post-modernity even if it wanted to, the passion and enthusiasm for political reform may cool. The extremely low voter turnout of 46 percent for the National Assembly elections of 9 April 2008—and the even more discouraging 19 percent voter turnout among those in their twenties—indicates political indifference, antipathy toward the political elite, and disenchantment with democracy among the younger generation. If the neoliberal economic policies of the Lee Myung Bak government, such as streamlining government, reducing taxes, deregulation, and the liberalization of the Korean economy, do not create jobs for young men and women and redistribute wealth, then protests on the internet may be on the horizon in Korea's near future. In this sense, the internet will play a vital role in preventing Korean democracy from reverting to authoritarianism.

Bibliography

Attali, J. (1998) *Dictionnaire du XXIe Siècle*, Paris: Libraire Artheme Fayard.

Browne, E. C. and Kim, S. W. (2001) "Regionalism in South Korean national assembly election: a vote components analysis of electoral change," paper presented at APSA Annual Meeting, San Francisco, 29 August–2 September 2001.

Carothers, T. (1997) "Democracy," *Foreign Policy*, 107: 11–18.

Choi, J. Y. and Cho, J. M. (2005) "Jiyukgyunyoului byunhwa ganeungsungeh gwanhan gochal (An empirical study on the possibility of change in regional cleavage)," *Korean Political Science Review*, 39(3): 375–94.

Croissant, A. (2002) "Strong presidents, weak democracy? Presidents, parliaments and political parties in South Korea," *Korea Observer*, 33(1): 1–46.

—— (2004) "Riding the tiger: civilian control and the military in democratizing Korea," *Armed Forces and Society*, 30(3): 357–81.

Diamond, L. and Shin, D. C. (2000) "Introduction: institutional reform and democratic consolidation in Korea," in L. Diamond and D. C. Shin (eds) *Institutional Reform and Democratic Consolidation in Korea*, Stanford, CA: Hoover Institution Press, pp.1–42.

Friedman, T. (2000) *The Lexus and Olive Tree: understanding globalization*, New York: Anchor Books.

Haggard, S. (2000) *The Political Economy of the Asian Economic Crisis*, Washington, DC: Institute for International Economics.

Han, S. J. (1997) "The public sphere and democracy in Korea: a debate on civil society," *Korea Journal*, 37(4): 78–97.

Huntington, S. P. (1991) *The Third Wave: democratization in the late twentieth century*, Norman: University of Oklahoma Press.

Im, H. B. (2000) "South Korean democratic consolidation in comparative perspective," in L. Diamond and B. K. Kim (eds) *Consolidating Democracy in South Korea*, Boulder, CO: Lynne Rienner, pp. 21–52.

—— (2004) "Faltering democratic consolidation in South Korea: Democracy at the end of three Kims' era," *Democratization*, 11(5): 179–98.

Im, H. B. (Forthcoming) "Democratic governance change in South Korea: from Confucian to neo-nomadic democracy," in *Confucian Culture and Democracy*, New York: Palgrave Macmillan.

Kim, B. K. (2000) "Party politics in South Korea's democracy: the crisis of success," in L. Diamond and B. K. Kim (eds) *Consolidating Democracy in South Korea*. Boulder, CO: Lynne Rienner, pp. 53–86.

—— (2001) "The public financial reform in Korea, Malaysia, Thailand: does democracy matter?" Paper presented at the Annual Meeting of the APSA, San Francisco, 28 August–2 September 2001.

Kim, B. K. and Im, H. B. (2001) " 'Crony capitalism' in South Korea, Thailand and Taiwan: myth and reality," *Journal of East Asian Studies*, 1(1): 5–52.

Kim, K. D. (2000) "Cyber sidaeeui doraewa salmeui jil (The advent of the cyber age and the quality of life)," in Asian Foundation (ed.) *Cyber Sidaeeui Salmeuijil* (Quality of life in the Cyber Age), Seoul: Asian Foundation, pp. 15–31.

Kim, K. O. (1996) "The reproduction of Confucian culture in contemporary Korea: an anthropological study," in W. M. Tu (ed.) *Confucian Traditions in East Asian Modernity: moral education and economic culture in Japan and the four mini-dragons*. Cambridge, MA: Harvard University Press, pp. 202–27.

Kim, S. J. (2002) "The genealogy of Confucian *moralpolitik* and its implications for modern civil society," in C. C. Armstrong (ed.) *Korean Society: civil society, democracy, and the state*, London: Routledge, pp. 57–91.

Koh, B. I. (1996) "Confucianism in contemporary Korea," in W. M. Tu (ed.) *Confucian Traditions in East Asian Modernity: moral education and economic culture in Japan and the four mini-dragons*, Cambridge, MA: Harvard University Press, pp. 191–201.

Kwon, T. H. and Cho, H. I. (1994) "Confucianism and Korean society: a historical basis of Korean democratization," paper presented at the International Conference on Democracy and Democratization in Asia, Université Catholique de Louvain, 30 May–1 June 1994.

Larsen, K. W. (2003) "The end and the beginning: prospects and problems for political reform in Roh Moo Hyun's Republic of Korea," paper presented at the conference on International Security and Domestic Reforms: Related Problems for South Korea, organized by the School of Advanced International Studies (SAIS) and the Korea Press Foundation, Washington DC, 1 May 2003.

Lee, J. J. (2007) "Hankook sunguwa sedaegaldeung (Korean elections and generational conflicts)," *Bigyominjujueui Youngu* (*Comparative Studies on Democracy*), 3(1): 51–92.

Niemann, U. and Burghart, S. (2004) "Is Confucius leaving Korea? Political changes and challenges after the general elections," *Asia Europe Journal*, 2: 337–9.

O'Donnell, G., (1999) "Delegative democracy," in G. O'Donnell (ed.) *Counterpoints: selected essays on authoritarianism and democratization*, Notre Dame: University of Notre Dame Press, pp. 159–74.

Park, H. C. (1997) "Community and the state: a Korean vision in a comparative perspective," unpublished paper.

Park, M. H. (2004) "17dae Chongsungwa jungdangjungchieui byunhwa: jiyukjueui jungdangchegyewa gwanryunhayu (17th National Assembly election and change in the party system: with reference to the regionalist party system)," *Jungchi, Jungbo Youngu* (*Studies on Politics and Information*), 7(1): 1–26.

Przeworski, A. (1991) *Democracy and the Market*, Cambridge: Cambridge University Press.

Pye, L. W. (1985) *Asian Power and Politics: the cultural dimensions of authority*, Cambridge, MA: Harvard University Press.

Roehrig, T. (1998) "Putting the Military on Trial: The Consolidation of Democracy in South Korea and Argentina," Online. Available HTTP: <http://www.ciaonet.org/conf/rot011> (accessed 10 April 2008).

Schumpeter, J. (1950) *Capitalism, Socialism and Democracy*, New York: Harper & Brothers.

Shin, D. C. (1999) *Mass Politics and Culture in Democratizing Korea*, Cambridge: Cambridge University Press.

Shin, K. Y. and Park, C. H. (2001) "Cultural tradition and democracy in South Korea," paper presented at the Korean Studies Association of Australia Conference 2001, Monash University, Australia, 24 September 2001.

Steinberg, D. I. (1997) "Civil society and human rights in Korea: on contemporary and classical orthodoxy and ideology," *Korea Journal*, 37(3): 145–65.

Steinberg, D. I. and Shin, M. (2006) "Tensions in South Korean political parties in transition: from entourage to ideology?" *Asian Survey*, 46(4): 517–37.

Yoon, Y. M. (2008) "Jungbohwa sahoe udiro gagoitna? (Where is the information society going toward?)" Online. Available HTTP: <http://www.ipv6.or.kr/archive/kripv6forum/html> (accessed 10 April 2008).

7 Thailand's conservative democratization

Kevin Hewison

Since its overthrow of the absolute monarchy in 1932, Thailand has had an astonishing democratic transition record: it has had more transitions to democracy than any other Asian country. It has also had more transitions *away* from democracy in the same period. While something of a joke, this highlights the fact that Thailand's widely anticipated democratic consolidation has repeatedly been confounded. But as the twentieth century ended, as a new constitution was implemented and the military weakened, there was increased confidence that the "consolidation process" had advanced so far that a "reversal of the democratic trend [seemed] increasingly unlikely" (Suchit 1999: 68).[1]

According to Linz and Stepan (1996: 3), a democratic transition is:

> complete when sufficient agreement has been reached about political procedures to produce an elected government, when a government comes to power that is a direct result of a free and popular vote, when this government *de facto* has the authority to generate new policies, and when the executive, legislative and judicial power generated by the new democracy does not have to share power with other bodies *de jure*.

They also note that democratization involves liberalization, asserting that the former is a wider process that includes the right to win control of government through free and fair elections that determine who governs.

In the decade since its 1997 constitution was promulgated, Thailand has failed on all of the counts specified by Linz and Stepan. Further, from 1997 to 2008, the country saw seven prime ministers (not counting interim prime ministers), a military coup in 2006, a new constitution developed under a military-dominated government in 2007, waves of street protests meant to overturn electoral outcomes and five-year political bans on 220 politicians and party executives.

There are several ways to interpret these events. This chapter begins by acknowledging that contestation over democratic practices amounts to a struggle for control of Thailand's political regime. A political regime is a particular organization of the state's power, embedded in the institutions of the state apparatus (see Hewison *et al.* 1993: 4–5). Although this approach shares common ground with that of Connors (2008a, 2008b), whereas he emphasizes the liberal aspects of this struggle in Thailand, this chapter concentrates on conservative and authoritarian power.

In a chapter of this length, it is impossible to discuss all aspects of the multiple discourses and struggles in Thailand's recent politics. Hence, the focus is on three elements of these struggles and debates, each of which is central to the future of Thailand's democratization: constitutions, judicialization, and the monarchy. Initially, a brief background of recent political events is provided (for further details, see Hewison 2007a, 2008; Connors 2008a).

Reshaping the regime: the rise of Thaksin

Thaksin Shinawatra, leader of the Thai Rak Thai (TRT) Party from 2001 to 2006, was elected prime minister in 2001 and again in 2005, before being overthrown by the military in 2006.[2] His electoral popularity and that of his party derives from an earlier period. The economic boom of the 1980s and early 1990s resulted in exceptionally rapid social change as business opportunities multiplied, employment grew and poverty declined. Political change was also rapid.

Following the 1991 coup, resistance to military political domination led to street protests in May 1992. When the military and police fired at demonstrators, the government was forced to resign (see Hewison 1997; Pasuk and Baker 2000). These events led to the development of a new constitution. Sometimes referred to as the "People's Constitution," the 1997 charter was the product of a political compromise. It was meant to provide a basis for further democratization, establishing checks and balances, encouraging participation, embedding the rule of law and establishing stable government (see McCargo 2002; Hewison 2007b).

Connors (2008a: 481) refers to the political compromise on the 1997 constitution as a "liberal–conservative" alliance that advanced a governance agenda that was meant to move electoral politics beyond a reliance on vote-buying and influential local figures. Although liberals cautiously introduced a division of powers and limited rights and liberties into the constitution, they agreed with conservatives that the military and monarchy should remain largely untouched, even if some liberals hoped they would modernize. The aim was to establish a political regime that was more recognizably democratic while maintaining ruling-class control over the state. To the surprise of the elite authors of this compromise, the electoral outcome of their efforts amounted to a serious challenge to the liberal–conservative pact and the political regime it had hoped to entrench. This challenge was mounted as the impacts of a serious economic downturn remade Thailand's capitalist landscape.

The economic crisis had political consequences. With bankruptcies, unemployment and poverty spiking, and the Democrat Party-led coalition government implementing unpopular IMF-mandated restructuring, opposition developed. There was considerable elite fear about the potential for social chaos. Domestic business leaders, intellectuals, workers, leaders of non-governmental organizations (NGOs), opposition politicians, and the king came together in a nationalist campaign against the government (Hewison 2000). The Democrats stood accused of destroying the economy, ceding sovereignty over economic policy-making to outsiders and selling off Thai assets to foreigners. Founded by Thaksin in 1998, TRT emerged as the political vehicle to save the domestic business class. The economic slump and fear of social conflict convinced the conservative, Bangkok-centered elite to support Thaksin.

One of the few business people not crippled by the crisis, Thaksin had the resources necessary to fund a new political party (Pasuk and Baker 2004; McCargo and Ukrist 2005). He recognized that to resurrect domestic capitalism, TRT needed to develop policies that appealed to poor and rural-based voters. In late 2000, TRT went to the electorate with a nationalist message and range of welfare policies. It developed a new social contract that enhanced social welfare for the poor while leading the elite to believe that its power would be reestablished (Hewison 2004). What many conservatives failed to realize was that a new political assertiveness would develop among the voting public, especially the poor (Pasuk and Baker 2008a: 18).

Once in power, Thaksin and TRT demonstrated the problems associated with this conservative myopia and the liberal–conservative compromise of the 1997 charter. Thaksin accrued tremendous power to himself as prime minister and to his cabinet, establishing the superiority of the executive over parliament and countervailing agencies. In fact, the drafters of the constitution had intended that there should be a strong party system and a powerful executive; however, TRT, with Thaksin in charge, was considered by some to be abusing the provisions and spirit of the constitution (Ginsburg 2008). Further, Thaksin and TRT leaders sought to neuter independent agencies, engaged in serious human rights abuses,[3] attempted to control sections of the media, and strengthened state security agencies. Critics emerged, but TRT's mass appeal and winner-take-all political strategy neutralized many of them.

Reshaping the regime: opposing Thaksin

The first sustained opposition to the TRT government was from state enterprise unions opposing the privatization policies that the government had begun to implement as the economy recovered. They drew attention to alleged corruption in the privatization process (Brown and Hewison 2005). But as TRT strengthened its electoral relationship with the poor in the run-up to the February 2005 election, its landslide victory seemed to make Thaksin and TRT invulnerable.

Surprisingly, just a few months later, an anti-government campaign emerged, led by disgruntled former Thaksin supporters. Significant among these opponents was former Thaksin acolyte and media entrepreneur Sondhi

Limthongkul. He accused the government of authoritarianism, conflicts of interest and corruption. Strikingly, Sondhi declared opposition to Thaksin as a crusade to protect the monarchy. Linking the king to political bickering was a risky strategy, with Sondhi gambling that patriotism could mediate a political alliance amid increasing elite consternation about Thaksin and his party. The earlier liberal–conservative compromise seemed doomed as conservatives began to oppose Thaksin. In December 2005, the king's call for the government to accept more criticism allowed Sondhi and his supporters to claim that their fight was for crown and nation.

The event that catapulted this opposition into a broader movement was the US$1.88 billion sale of the Shin Corporation, a Shinawatra business, to the Singaporean government's Temasek in January 2006. Many saw the tax-free sale as an outrageous example of Thaksin's nepotism and corruption (*Time* 10 April 2006). Outrage was strongest among the middle class, who saw Thaksin as escaping tax payment, while using their own taxes to boost TRT's electoral appeal by providing benefits to the poor. Some feared the creation of a "welfare state," imagining indolent villagers getting fat on state hand-outs. They also feared the rising political influence of the masses (Pasuk and Baker 2008a: 19, 21). An alliance was soon forged between the middle class and disgruntled conservatives.

The People's Alliance for Democracy (PAD) came to represent the interests of these two groups, and joined together Sondhi supporters and activist organizations. PAD demonstrations in 2006 brought thousands into the streets for well-organized rallies to accuse Thaksin of nepotism, corruption, censorship, and human rights violations. Repeatedly trumpeting Thaksin's alleged disrespect for the throne, the PAD called on the king to remove him and appoint a new prime minister (Connors 2008b). Sondhi's call to defend the monarchy was exceptionally powerful, playing to middle-class fears regarding the succession, and resulted in the resurgence of conservative political beliefs, which effectively ruptured the liberal–conservative alliance.

Thaksin responded to extra-parliamentary opposition by calling a snap election in April 2006, but at the PAD's urging, the major opposition parties, led by the Democrats, boycotted the polls. Essentially unopposed, TRT romped home, but alleging fraud, the PAD petitioned the Constitutional Court to suspend the results of the election (*Christian Science Monitor* 4 April 2006).

This brief account provides the background for the remainder of this chapter, which seeks to explain a conservative resurgence that sought to reinforce a conservative royalist regime. This renaissance is illustrated in three overlapping chronicles traversing the period from mid-2006 to late 2009, explaining the destruction of Thaksin, TRT and their political agenda. The chapter focuses on the struggle over the constitution, the politicization of the judiciary and the palace's enhanced political role.

The struggle over the constitution

The 1997 constitution, thrown out in the 2006 coup, is often identified as the most democratic of Thailand's many constitutions. Although correct, this is also a romanticization of the drafting process and political positioning of the basic law.

Scholars have long observed that constitutions are sites of political conflict. Writing of U.S. constitutionalism, DeBats (1983: 58–9) notes that the "Federalist revision of liberalism was in the service of a deliberate social conservatism," emphasizing property-holding as an element of freedom and sovereignty and the emergence of interest-based activism rather than a broader democratic involvement of citizens. Earlier, in 1938, Beard observed that the "prime consideration of any realistic constitutional history is economic: whose property, what property, and what forms of regulation and protection?" (cited in Belz 1972: 648). The development and operation of a constitution are contested processes, and the existence of a democratic constitution is no guarantee that political participation will be expanded and embedded. Indeed, constitutions can be used to *exclude* certain interests (see Hirschl 2004).

Constitution drafting in Thailand has traditionally been the preserve of the dominant political and military elites, and their interests have always prevailed. Even in the development of the 1997 document, elite control was maintained (Hewison 2007b). As already noted, Connors (2008a) considers the 1997 constitution to be the outcome of a liberal–conservative alliance. While liberals emphasized good governance, conservatives initially opposed expanded participation. The need to maintain order, stability, and unity along with the maintenance of the positions of the monarchy and military brought the conservatives into this alliance. More broadly, many reformers, NGOs, and intellectuals were also convinced that a "people's agenda" was being achieved, and middle-class angst about "money politics" and political rights was also addressed.

The electoral power of Thaksin and TRT challenged the liberal–conservative alliance. Thaksin's control of politics through election victories and the perception that he was bending rules or using them to his own and his party's advantage while empowering rural electorates caused a radical and conservative revision of the alliance. The liberals and conservatives, much of the urban middle class, and many activists came to oppose the government. They also agreed that the 1997 constitution needed to be reworked. Their enthusiastic support for the 2006 coup was one means to achieve this.

The coup set in motion a military-dominated process to develop a new constitution, with the junta establishing, tutoring, and controlling the bodies drafting the new constitution (*Nation* 20 December 2006[4]). Not surprisingly, the outcome was a regressive constitution. It weakened the executive branch, transferred considerable decision-making power to the bureaucracy and other unelected bodies, including the half-appointed senate and the judiciary, and enhanced the military's political role and budget (Hicken 2007; Thi 2007).

The junta also controlled the country's first-ever constitutional refer-endum. TRT-associated groups and coup opponents campaigned against the draft charter and were vigorously opposed and suppressed. When the consti-tution was approved, the Asian Human Rights Commission (AHRC 2007b) described a "heavy-handed undemocratic atmosphere," observing that the "junta . . . coerced, threatened, bought and cajoled part of the electorate." An editorial in the *Bangkok Post* (1 August 2007) said the process had a "facade of being a democratic choice," adding, "[t]his is not democracy, this is not the rule of law."

During the referendum campaign, fearing rejection of the charter, it was explained that the document was not permanent. Junta-allied National Legislative Assembly president Meechai Ruchupan said the charter could be amended later. An Army spokesman stated, "Whether the draft is good or bad is not the whole point. People can amend it later" (*Bangkok Post* 18 August 2007). Similar statements were heard in the run-up to the Decem-ber 2007 elections. Interestingly, the constitution permitted parliament to make amendments based on a simple majority vote. The People's Power Party (PPP), which inherited TRT's mantle following the latter's dissolution, campaigned in the election for changes to the charter. In particular, the PPP wanted amendments to provisions that gave the junta immunity from prosecution for its illegal coup. It also wanted a legal review of all junta announcements that had the force of law.

At the time, a PPP victory seemed improbable. But win they did, and the new government announced a committee to review the 2007 constitution (*Naewna* 8 February 2008). Immediately, though, the earlier conciliatory con-servative promises were forgotten. Various commentators agreed that changes were required, but they were wary of the PPP's motives, fearing that changes would benefit Thaksin and former TRT members. They opposed haste and, importantly, rejected the parliamentary route to amendment, favoring broader public involvement. Conservative groups began to insist that approval by referendum meant that the charter could not be changed (see *Bangkok Post* 5 May 2008).

With the appointment and election of new senate members, the PPP again proposed constitutional amendment (*Matichon* 7 March 2008). One of its executives went before the Supreme Court, charged with electoral fraud, so although the PPP raised questions regarding the dissolution of TRT in 2007, it faced the prospect of dissolution itself. It seemed that the PPP stand had considerable public support (*Bangkok Post* 27 March 2008). Opposition to amendment was initially led by a coalition of mostly appointed senators and the Democrats. However, the PAD soon returned to take on this issue.

The PAD had announced its "dissolution" two days after the 2006 coup, but was reactivated in March 2008, motivated by the government's push for constitutional change. Its first public gathering drew several thousand participants, and its leadership declared a campaign to stop constitutional amendment (*Bangkok Post* 29 March 2008). The PAD claimed that changes would benefit the PPP and its allies. Ominously, PAD leaders asserted that confrontation was unavoidable (*Bangkok Post* 20 and 24 April 2008).

As the amendment tug-of-war continued, in May, the PAD's Sondhi Limthongkul announced a "last war" against the "Thaksin regime," lodging an impeachment petition against those parliamentarians supporting constitutional revision. The PAD was supported by royalists including former prime minister Anand Punyarachun and former coup leader General Saprang Kalayanamitr (*Bangkok Post* 26 and 27 May 2008). The PAD's demonstration was protracted, lasting from 25 May until early December 2008. When the government proposed a joint panel with the Democrats to review charter changes and invited the PAD, the latter rejected the offer, stating that the constitution could *only* be amended *outside* parliament. Later, PAD leader Chamlong Srimuang announced that parliament offered no hope for the country and claimed that the government had acquired power "unconstitutionally" and had no right to amend the constitution (*Matichon* 7–18 June 2008).

Adding weight to the conservative opposition, Constitution Court judge Jarun Pukditanakul attacked the PPP's plans, asking whether a criminal should rewrite the Criminal Code and ill-intentioned people rewrite the charter. Military leaders, including Army commander General Anupong Paochinda, supported by Air Force Chief Chalit Phukpasuk, both junta alumni, also expressed doubts: "If the amendment is to happen, people must know whether that will serve the demands of any particular group . . . It is inappropriate to make changes for the sake of a small group of people" (*Bangkok Post* 17 July 2008). Within days, privy councilor and former premier Tanin Kraivixien and former Democrat prime minister Chuan Leekpai threw their support behind the opponents of amendment, arguing that the junta charter was well crafted, implying that no change was necessary (*Bangkok Post* 19 July 2008).

With such strong conservative support, the PAD leadership announced that its street protest would continue indefinitely. Proclaiming its opposition to any constitutional amendments, PAD leaders announced that there would be no negotiations with the government. The PAD's Suriyasai Katasila proclaimed, "our stance is to topple the nominee government and then to reform politics" (*Bangkok Post* 27 September 2008). For PAD, constitutional amendments could be made only after Thaksin—who had fled the country to the U.K.—had been "brought to justice" (*Bangkok Post* 1 October 2008).

The PAD's continuing street demonstration led to the government offering a limited compromise, suggesting that the constitution could be amended by an extra-parliamentary committee (*Matichon* 2 October 2008). The Democrats initially supported this approach but the PAD remained opposed, with PAD-associated civil society groups threatening violence if there was any move to amend the charter. PAD leaders announced a final push to oust the government (*Bangkok Post* 5 and 6 November 2008), beginning with 40,000 supporters massing to blockade parliament.[5] They said this was to block constitutional amendment, even though the prime minister denied such an agenda (*Bangkok Post* 23 November 2008).

The PAD's activism, highlighted by its occupation of Bangkok's airports, ended when the government fell following the dissolution of the PPP and two of its coalition partners by the Constitutional Court. Those who opposed the government, both liberals and conservatives, had succeeded, through a combination of legal and illegal tactics, in preventing any changes to a constitution that had grown out of a military coup and political repression, paving the way for a new government that came to power with the support of the military.

Judicialization or politicization?

Analysts including Ginsburg (2008), Dowdle (2009) and Leyland (2009) have identified a process of judicialization in Thailand that began with the 1997 constitution and has accelerated since April 2006.[6] As Pasuk and Baker (2008b) observe, a more assertive judiciary could be a positive development. However, a highly interventionist judiciary during periods of political conflict can lead to charges of political bias; they add that, "much of this judicial activity could be construed as politics by other means." This is certainly the case since 2006, as Thaksin and the "Thaksin regime" have been special targets of judicial sanctions. In this discussion, separating Shinawatra family cases from political cases is difficult, but then the protagonists did not separate them.

For all their efforts to destroy the Thaksin regime, from the 2006 coup to the December 2007 polls, the PPP's electoral success was a stinging rebuke to the forces that supported the coup. With a coalition of smaller parties, the PPP established a comfortable parliamentary majority, leaving the Democrats as the opposition.[7] Support for the PPP was strongest in the poorer northern and northeastern regions and in the working-class regions that encircle Bangkok (Pasuk and Baker 2008c). Assuredly, the margin was much closer than the 2005 landslide, but the 2007 vote represented a rejection of the coup, the military and the anti-TRT/PPP campaigns. The massive voter turnout could also be interpreted as popular support for electoral processes. However, for those who opposed Thaksin and TRT, this electoral outcome was unacceptable.

A series of judicial and extra-constitutional measures soon began, targeting the PPP. Just prior to the election, junta leader General Sonthi Boonyaratglin and the PAD leadership predicted a swathe of PPP disqualifications (*Nation* 1 January 2008). Indeed, three PPP candidates were the first to be yellow-carded.[8] Within days of the election, the Election Commission (EC) was investigating 83 cases, with 65 of them PPP winning candidates (*IHT* 3 January 2008). Meanwhile, the EC head predicted that electoral fraud charges against deputy PPP leader Yongyuth Tiyapairat would result in the party's dissolution (*Bangkok Post* 10 January 2008). Within a month, the EC found him guilty, with dissident EC commissioners claiming that the decision had been rushed, without hearing Yongyuth's witnesses (*Bangkok Post* 15, 17, and 27 February 2008). This verdict set in motion a legal process that eventually led to the dissolution of the PPP in December 2008.

When the PPP leadership suggested an "invisible hand" was at work and demanded that the EC be transparent, the military denied that a "coup by stealth" was underway and reasserted its strong support for the EC. The EC denied bias but replaced one of its investigation officers. For its part, the PAD warned that the PPP's electoral mandate meant little (Kate 2008; *Bangkok Post* and *Nation* 6–8 January 2008).

The National Commission to Counter Corruption (NCCC) soon launched legal proceedings against the new government, initially targeting the public health minister, who would become the first minister to be disqualified. The *Bangkok Post* (10 April 2008) explained that his mistake was an "unintentional blunder" in being a month late declaring his wife's assets. In late April, the NCCC also found that a deputy commerce minister had failed to properly declare a holding in a private company. That the company was apparently defunct carried no weight, and he was disqualified (*Bangkok Post* 25 April 2008).

At about the same time, the EC voted to dissolve two government coalition parties—Chart Thai and Matchimathipataya—passing the cases to the Constitutional Court. The Court was identified as a threat to the PPP as it was composed of judges considered Thaksin opponents and with links to military leaders (*Bangkok Post* 22 May 2008). In October, the Office of the Attorney General petitioned the Constitutional Court to dissolve the PPP (*Matichon* 11 October 2008). In May, the Constitutional Court found that Prime Minister Samak had breached the constitution in hosting a television cooking show and receiving small allowances (*Thai Post* 21 May 2008). This was a victory for the PAD, whose leaders called for even more legal action against the PPP, targeting anti-monarchy cases (see below).

The PAD now claimed that no prime minister from the coalition government was acceptable and that the government had to go (*Bangkok Post* 10–12 September 2008). To further this aim, it began publicly pressuring the judiciary and members of independent agencies. It insisted that investigations be sped up and called for increased political support. General Anupong complied, declaring his support for the Assets Scrutiny Committee (ASC), a critical junta-established agency. At the same time, just as the PAD harassed those it considered pro-Thaksin, its leaders were less concerned about legal decisions against their own number. When they faced charges, they were usually quickly bailed out or the courts rejected the serious charges against them, and they immediately returned to their rallies (*Times Online* 10 October 2008).

As soon as the PPP-led government took office, the ASC issued warnings of more charges against Thaksin, his family, and other TRT/PPP members. At the same time, former members of the junta announced that they would continue to "shield" it and prevent its closure by the government. When Thaksin proposed returning from exile, General Sonthi warned of further street demonstrations and the Attorney General's Department, headed by a junta ally, declared that Thaksin would be arrested on his return (*Matichon* 21 January 2008).

The ASC soon brought new charges against a swathe of PPP members and Thaksin (*Bangkok Post* 11 March and 1 April 2008). As its term neared its end, the ASC accelerated its work, with one panel recommending legal action without hearing 300 defense witnesses or considering 100 additional pieces of evidence. ASC secretary Kaewsan Atibodhi said the "evidence and witnesses are useless" (*Bangkok Post* 9 April 2008). When the ASC's tenure expired at the end of June, some 15 cases were pending against Thaksin (Crispin 2008a). When the ASC closed, PAD supporters cheered its members as heroes in the anti-Thaksin campaign (*Bangkok Post* 30 June 2008). At the same time, former junta members attended a farewell party for the ASC at the Army Club, promising to protect its legacy (*Bangkok Post* 1 July 2008). Meanwhile, the Constitutional Court ruled that the ASC's work, undertaken under junta rules, was legal.

Another legal tack taken against the government began in late May, after the government signed a joint communiqué with Cambodia and UNESCO for the World Heritage listing of the Preah Vihear temple complex. The PAD and Democrats protested and promoted a nationalist outcry. Various activists claimed, with no evidence produced, that the agreement was brokered to facilitate Thaksin's Cambodian business interests (*Bangkok Post* 15 July 2008). The Democrats brought a no-confidence debate in parliament (*Matichon* 24 and 25 June 2008).[9] Eventually, the foreign minister resigned after the Constitutional Court ruled against the government.

In July, Pojaman Shinawatra, Thaksin's wife, was convicted of tax evasion and sentenced to three years in jail. A day later, the Supreme Court's Criminal Division for Holders of Political Positions began hearing another case against Potjaman and Thaksin. The couple fled, with Thaksin claiming, "My cases have been pre-judged, to get rid of me and my family, who are regarded by a group of people as their political enemies, irrespective of the law and international principles of justice" (*Bangkok Post* 12 August 2008). Prosecutors then seized some US$2 billion in Shinawatra assets (*IHT* 25 August 2008). Arrest warrants were issued for Thaksin and his wife (*Matichon* 27 September 2008). In his absence, on 21 October, the Supreme Court found Thaksin guilty of violating conflict of interest rules and sentenced him to two years in prison (*Time* 21 October 2008).

With pro-PPP groups rallying against what they saw as a "judicial coup," the PAD occupied the airports on 25 November 2008. Just hours later, the Constitutional Court announced that party dissolution trials would proceed and demanded that evidence be submitted within hours (*Bangkok Post* 27 November 2008). The Court then set a 2 December deadline for closing statements, ruling that there was no need to hear witnesses or consider additional evidence. The Court's president announced that there would be no more hearings, meaning that some 200 witnesses would not be heard

(*Bangkok Post* 1 December 2008). The abrupt wrapping-up of the case made it clear that the parties would be dissolved. With pro-government groups threatening to protest at the Constitutional Court, newspapers warned of chaos if they were permitted to demonstrate, and the military announced the need to respect the Court's forthcoming judgment. The Air Force chief warned "If the power of the judiciary is not respected, there will be confusion. If the rules and court judgments are not followed, some decisive measures must be taken" (*Nation* 1 December 2001).

The Court announced its verdict on 2 December 2008. It dissolved the parties and revoked the political rights of 109 executives, banning them from politics for five years. This meant that some 146 TRT/PPP politicians had been banned by the Court in 2007 and 2008. Matchimathipataya party leader Anongwan Thepsuthin appeared stunned, asking:

> The verdict came out shortly after I read out my closing statement. Does this mean the court did not care about what the party had to say? What is going on with the judicial system? Chart Thai leader Banharn Silpa-archa claimed that the court's verdict had been made in advance.
>
> (*Bangkok Post* 3 December 2008)

Upon dissolution, as if following a script, PAD members left the airports, which resumed operations within 24 hours. The PAD announced: "The Constitution Court's verdict is clear proof that the previous administration's power was not obtained through democracy under the Constitution but was accomplished through electoral fraud and that the rally by the People's Alliance for Democracy was legitimate" (*Phujatkan* 2 December 2008).

General Anupong was reportedly relieved by the court's decision (*Bangkok Post* 3 December 2008), and he and senior military figures immediately entered into negotiations with banned politician Newin Chidchob and wealthy business people to encourage Newin's faction of the PPP to support the Democrats in forming a new government (*Bangkok Post* 4, 8, 10, and 13 December 2008). With broad business and military support, the Democrats formed a coalition government following Abhisit's election as prime minister by a parliamentary vote (*Bangkok Post* 16 December 2008).

Between 2006 and 2008, the judiciary brought down several ministers, convicted Thaksin and members of his family, banned four political parties that had all had electoral success, and ended the PPP-led government. It might be argued that these actions represent a flowering of a more activist judiciary enforcing the rule of law. However, as these cases progressed, there was a significant reluctance to take legal action against the PAD or other opponents of the PPP-led government.

When the PAD held rallies at government ministries and the Government House, seized a government television station, and then occupied airports, legal reactions were muted. General Anupong repeatedly refused to act on requests for assistance in managing demonstrations. Senior Democrats applauded the PAD's actions (*Bangkok Post* 9 September 2008). Anti-government legislators including Democrat leader Abhisit encouraged the PAD occupiers at Government House and criticized the government's use of police against demonstrators, ignoring the use of weapons by the PAD (*Bangkok Post* 30 August 2008).

Further, Democrats such as Korn Chatikavanij openly supported the PAD. He wrote:

> No point shying away from the obvious—after all . . . one of the PAD leaders . . . is a Democrat MP. Many other key speakers were our candidates in the recent general elections. Almost all of the tens of thousands . . . [of PAD demonstrators] are Democrat voters.

Referring to the PAD's illegal actions, Korn stated: "Did everything change as a result of the illicit acts? Not for me," adding, "I was saddened by the PAD decision to cross the legal line. Yet I understood it from the perspective of strategy." Acknowledging the PAD's significance for his party, Korn stated: "like it or not, the Democrats could not on our own have resisted the PPP." Korn admitted that the public did not support the PAD but retorted, "screw the opinion polls, the people attending the rally don't deserve to be vilified as criminals and I . . . visit[ed] them." While he criticized the PAD's airport occupation, Korn believed that the "disruption and economic damage" was limited because PAD members were "just sitting peacefully outside the airport," adding, "this damage can be repaired" (*Bangkok Post* 2 and 9 December 2008).

Sombat Thamronthanyawong, the president of the prestigious National Institute of Development Administration, also justified the PAD's illegal and violent actions, stating that "it is only natural that the PAD had to violate some laws." He added that while the "PAD did break the law and violate some people's rights" it was essentially a "political pressure group . . . acting as a check and balance for Thailand's future political reform . . . fighting against corrupt politicians" (*Bangkok Post* 30 August 2008).

These views make it clear that there had been a substantial politicization of the judiciary. As Ginsburg (2008: 31) observed, the shift in constitutional power means that "[u]nelected technocratic guardians are deciding who governs" and this inevitably means that these "institutions are themselves transformed by their new, high-profile mandates." The seeming technocratic structure of the legal decision-making "masks judicialized politics, and the guardians have inevitably been politicized as they are called on to determine who will govern."

Politics and the monarchy

The judiciary's remarkable and ongoing intervention in Thailand's political struggles was given a immense boost when the king first called for the courts to solve the problems created by the boycotted April 2006 election.

In its first round of anti-Thaksin demonstrations, the PAD had pinned its hopes on the king throwing Thaksin out and appointing his own prime minister and a new government (Connors 2008b). King Bhumibol claimed this would be undemocratic. Nevertheless, he declared the situation following the election a "political crisis," and added, "we have to find a way to solve the problem . . . This is not a democracy." He identified the judiciary as the body to set things right and called on them to clean up the political mess (*Nation* 25 April 2006). The judges heeded the king's advice, and on 8 May 2006 the Constitutional Court annulled the April elections and ordered new polls (forestalled by the 2006 coup). The judges then called on the Election Commissioners to resign (Vander Meer 2006). When they refused, the Criminal Court removed them from their posts and had them jailed. Apparently this was discussed in advance with palace representatives (AHRC 2007a; Asian Legal Resource Centre 2007), and even TRT critics referred to it as "judicial hijacking" (Vander Meer 2006).

From this moment, the leadership of the anti-Thaksin opposition shifted from the PAD to General Prem Tinsulanonda, a former prime minister and the president of the king's Privy Council.[10] Prem's relationship with the king and his Army links made him a powerful opponent. He made a series of speeches criticizing the government, and established control over the military. Supported by military leaders and privy councilors, Prem demanded that officers be loyal to the king (Prem 2006). The coup followed a few months later.

Even if it is officially denied, the palace's *political* role cannot be ignored.[11] The palace was critical in Thaksin's ousting through the military coup. Former National Security Council chief and royalist Prasong Soonsiri claimed that he and five senior military figures planned the coup from July 2006, with the PAD's Sondhi saying that this planning included the palace, General Prem and military figures (see *Nation* 2 October 2006; *Asia Times Online* 22 December 2006; and *Phujatkan Online* 25 August 2007). Coup troops advertised their support for the palace by displaying yellow ribbons; yellow being the king's color.[12] When the junta announced its reasons for the coup, the monarchy ranked high: "severe rifts and disunity among the Thai people . . . signs of rampant corruption, malfeasance, political interference in government agencies and independent organizations . . . [and] several actions verging on lèse-majesté."[13]

Following the coup, the palace's role was also important. The king approved the putsch within hours, deflating opposition. The military appointed General Surayudh Chulanond as prime minister, plucking him from the Privy Council. He then appointed a cabinet with numerous palace links. Led by General Prem, palace officials and royalists were mentors to the coup makers and their government, and royalists held numerous positions as the junta-backed government sought to neuter the "Thaksin regime." Most importantly, the writing of the 2007 constitution was placed in the hands of conservatives and royalists.

The PPP's 2007 election victory shocked royalists. During the initial jockeying to form a government, the king called for national unity and adherence to the junta's constitution (*Bangkok Post* 1 January 2008). Frantic attempts were made by anti-PPP groups to ensure a coalition agreement that would enable "control" of the PPP and ensure loyalty to the royalist agenda. At the top of the agenda was reverence for the monarchy, respect for General Prem, and no reprisals against the junta generals. The PPP rejected these demands while expressing loyalty to the king (*Xinhua* 28 December 2007).

Royalists then began attacking the PPP-led government. At the same time, lèse-majesté charges, which brought 3 to 15 years in prison, were made against PPP minister Jakrapob Penkair (*Bangkok Post* 21 and 22 February 2008). The Democrat Party highlighted these allegations (*Bangkok Post* 20 May 2008), and were supported by General Surayud, who had returned to the Privy Council, and military leaders (*Bangkok Post* 19 and 30 May 2008). After all military senior leaders had met and denounced him, Jakrapob resigned (*Nation* 2 June 2008). At the same time that they were attacking Jakrapob, the Democrats began to demand the censorship of websites deemed critical of the monarchy (*Thai Post* 20 May 2008).

The Democrats repeatedly made references to anti-monarchy websites, publications, and "movements," lending credibility to the PAD's claim that the monarchy was under threat. Senior Democrat Piraphand Salirathaviphak demanded amendments to the draconian lèse-majesté law, claiming that the monarchy was a national security matter (*Bangkok Post* 19 November 2008). Meanwhile, the Army warned community radio stations that they would be closed if they insulted the monarchy (*Bangkok Post* 5 November 2008).

As the PAD initiated further rallies, pro-PPP/Thaksin groups also mobilized, targeting Privy Council President Prem. Supreme Commander Boonsang Niempradita called these demonstrators "social garbage" and the media labeled them "hired thugs" and "extremists" (*Bangkok Post* 28 April 2008). The PAD seemed to comprise another category of demonstrator. Cloaked in the king's yellow and claiming to protect the monarchy, it continually warned against offending the crown (*Bangkok Post* 18 May 2008). Sondhi claimed that if the government was not dissolved, "the monarchy might collapse" (*Phujatkan* 26 August 2008).

After participants in a PAD rally were attacked by a pro-PPP crowd in Udornthani, it was reported that a PAD demonstrator was killed, although this claim was proved false. Even so, it stirred further support for the PAD, especially among intellectuals and the Bangkok elite (*Bangkok Post* 25 July 2008; *The Irrawaddy* 28 July 2008). General Prem, apparently an avid viewer of Sondhi's xenophobic ASTV, was moved to write a song about the political rift and death, while the *Bangkok Post* (6 September 2008) decried the violence.[14]

Throughout this period, Prem repeatedly met with military leaders, reminding them of their duty to protect the nation and monarchy (*Bangkok Post* 9 September 2006).

When Samak was forced to step down, the Democrats adopted a royalist strategy, calling for a national unity government, and were supported by General Anupong. The PAD briefly agreed, rejecting any dissolution of parliament.[15] Amid considerable maneuvering within the PPP, Somchai Wongsawat, Thaksin's brother-in-law, became prime minister (*Bangkok Post* 1 October 2008). Somchai offered the PAD a compromise, visiting General Prem as a sign of respect.

Immediately, however, the PAD sealed off parliament to prevent Somchai from presenting his constitutionally required policy statement, and there was a clash between police and armed demonstrators (*New York Times* 8 October 2008). Two protestors were killed, one of whom was a PAD security guard, who died when explosives in his car detonated.[16] To the surprise of many, Queen Sirikit immediately made donations to the injured PAD protestors, and she and a princess attended the funeral of one of those who died, along with hundreds of PAD supporters (*Nation* 13 October 2008). These royal acts allowed the PAD to proclaim that it was actively supported by the monarchy (*The Economist* 16 October 2008). Former prime minister and palace loyalist Anand Punyarachun attended the funeral of the PAD bomber (*Bangkok Post* 16 October 2008).

The government was blamed for the clash. Royalist Prawase Wasi called on Somchai to resign. General Anupong agreed and his call for the government's resignation was supported by the military chiefs (*Bangkok Post* 8–11 and 17 October 2008). As violence grew, Anupong asserted that the PAD had not perpetrated violence and remained steadfast: the military would not intervene except for "keeping peace and [in] order to protect the public and uphold important institutions like the monarchy" (*The Irrawaddy* 25 November 2008; *Bangkok Post* 26 November 2008).[17]

Recognizing that the Democrats might form a new government, PPP members of parliament petitioned for an early and special parliamentary session to select a new prime minister (*Bangkok Post* 2 December 2008), but their request went unanswered by the parliament's president and the palace (*Bangkok Post* 6 December 2008). The king did not make his usual birthday speech on 4 December, apparently because of illness (*Bangkok Post* 5 December 2008). At such a politically charged moment, not giving a speech was meaningful (*Asia Times Online* 6 December 2008). By not speaking, the king did not meet the dissolved PPP's interim prime minister.

This account makes it clear that the palace can no longer be considered "above politics," even if it would prefer to be in such a position. Political events in recent years have seen the monarchy move to the center of the political stage. Crispin argues that the speculation is that:

The military now marches mainly to the beat of the . . . Privy Council.

Both institutions would likely see their powers legally diminished in a post-Bhumibol era were a pro-Thaksin administration allowed to rule and amend laws without the resistance of a PAD-like protest movement.

(Crispin 2008b)

In other words, the palace's role has been to support the maintenance of a conservative political regime.

Conclusion

This broad-brush summary of the journey of democratization in Thailand cannot do justice to the full range of recent debates and struggles. By choosing to address the constitution, judiciary, and monarchy, the emphasis has been on the struggle to shape these for the establishment and maintenance of a conservative political regime.

In 1992, a civilian uprising saw a major diminution of the political dominance of the military. One of the principal outcomes of this uprising was the 1997 constitution, which was, as Connors (2008a) explains, the result of a liberal–conservative alliance. However, the logical outcome of this compromise, forged during an economic and political crisis, was a strong and electorally popular government led by Thaksin Shinawatra. Soon after Thaksin's 2005 landslide reelection, an alliance of opponents rejected both the 1997 constitution and the political compromise that had shaped it. This new alliance, while including liberals, came to be firmly dominated by conservatives and royalists.

The powerful interests—political and economic—of the conservatives close to the palace trumped the 1997 model of electoral democracy. Their aim was to reestablish a regime that included elections and political parties but where the interests of the conservatives were predominant, with the military required to maintain political order and the monarchy as the paramount symbol of loyalty. A kind of semi-democracy was reestablished, with the poor, the dispossessed, the working class, and rural people held to be unimportant for a conservative semi-democratic regime that emphasizes royalism, traditionalism, nationalism, and paternalism.

Notes

1 Suchit also pointed to specific weaknesses in Thailand's political structure: the fragile party system, unstable multi-party coalition governments, and "money politics."
2 There was another election in April 2006. TRT won after the opposition boycotted the polls. The courts declared the election invalid (see below).
3 Most reprehensible were extra-judicial killings in an anti-drug campaign, the government's ham-fisted efforts to control southern separatism and attacks on human rights activists (Human Rights Watch 2006; Connors 2009).
4 In referring to the local press, most of the citations are to stories that appeared in

several or most newspapers and in both Thai and English. Rather than burden the chapter with excessive citation, I have listed just one source. Readers will find similar stories in other sources for each date cited.

5 When postponing or moving the meeting was considered, Democrat Party leader Abhisit Vejjajiva opposed this, claiming that the president of parliament was "duty-bound" to hold the meeting. In January 2009, Abhisit changed his mind and his own government both postponed and moved a key meeting of parliament.

6 Here, "judiciary" includes the courts and other bodies established with watchdog mandates under the 1997 and 2007 constitutions.

7 Klein (2008) states: "only two parties, the PPP and the opposition Democrat Party, received double digit support. . . . Each received about 37 percent of the votes (the Democrats receiving about 200,000 less than the PPP out of a total 32 million votes cast)." This is misleading as it fails to report actual seats won. The initial official count gave the PPP 199 of 400 constituency seats and 34 of 80 party list seats, with the Democrats gaining 132 and 33 seats, respectively (see Pasuk and Baker 2008c: 21).

8 The EC issues yellow and red cards against candidates suspected of election fraud. Yellow cards are issued when there is indirect evidence of a candidate's involvement in fraud. The lack of direct evidence means a yellow-carded candidate may stand again. Red cards are issued when there is evidence of direct involvement. A new election is held and the red-carded candidate and his/her party are disqualified. The EC received 1,030 complaints regarding the 2007 election, with 352 considered to provide cause for investigation (*Bangkok Post* 30 December 2007). Cards continued to be issued throughout 2008, mainly to the PPP and its coalition parties.

9 The stewardship of Preah Vihear had been decided by the International Court of Justice in 1962, when Cambodia was considered the rightful custodian.

10 The Privy Council is made up of advisers selected by the king, mostly members of the royal family, former military leaders, and former bureaucrats (see Handley 2008).

11 The official line is: "the Thai monarchy has never been a player in politics. The king has gone to great lengths to demonstrate this point over the years. And it is this carefully cultivated political neutrality that gives his words such weight" (Tharit 2008).

12 In Thailand, each day is assigned a color. The king was born on Monday, 5 December 1927, in Cambridge, Massachusetts. Hence, the king's color is yellow.

13 "Statement by the Council for Democratic Reform." Online. Available HTTP: <http://www.cns.go.th/readnews_all.asp?page=2&cid=3&search=> (accessed 12 July 2007).

14 At this point, there had been one death. A pro-government demonstrator was allegedly beaten to death by PAD supporters.

15 Dissolution meant a new election, and the PAD wanted to avoid another PPP victory. It soon proposed a "people's government," in which elected politicians would make way for "qualified, non-partisan" outsiders (*Bangkok Post* 11–15 September 2008).

16 Police were attacked, shot, impaled, beaten and run over (*Bangkok Post* 10 October 2008). In addition to the two deaths, 8 to 10 persons suffered serious injuries, and 300 were treated for minor injuries and the effects of tear gas.

17 Independent observers noted that the "PAD has committed grave violations of domestic law and violated . . . human rights principles . . . They have been using weapons . . . with the aim to kill. This movement is turning into a criminal gang" (Human Rights Watch researcher Sunai Phasuk, cited in *The Irrawaddy* 27 November 2008). PAD demonstrators were also attacked several times including bomb and grenade attacks.

Bibliography

AHRC (Asian Human Rights Commission) (2007a) *Statement: THAILAND: recording reveals extent to which judiciary compromised; demands public response*, AS-141-2007, 26 June 2007.

—— (2007b) *Statement: THAILAND: A long road back to human rights and the rule of law*, AS-196-2007, 20 August 2007.

Asian Legal Resource Centre (2007) "Recording of conversation between Supreme Court Judge Pairote Navanuch, Supreme Court Secretary Virat Chinvinijkul and a senior government official on the eve of the 2006 Election Commission dismissal," *article2*, 6(3): 64–8.

Belz, H. (1972) "Changing conceptions of constitutionalism in the era of World War II and the Cold War," *The Journal of American History*, 59(3): 640–69.

Brown, A. and Hewison, K. (2005) " 'Economics is the deciding factor': labor politics in Thaksin's Thailand," *Pacific Affairs*, 78(3): 353–75.

Connors, M. K. (2008a) "Thailand—four elections and a coup," *Australian Journal of International Affairs*, 62(4): 478–96.

—— (2008b) "Article of faith: the failure of royal liberalism in Thailand," *Journal of Contemporary Asia*, 38(1): 143–65.

—— (2009) *Ambivalent about Rights: "accidental" killing machines, democracy and coup detat*. Hong Kong: City University of Hong Kong, Southeast Asia Research Center Working Paper No. 102, November.

Crispin, S. W. (2008a) " 'Crusading spirit' adrift on Thai political winds," *Asia Times Online*, 13 June 2008. Online. Available HTTP: <http://www.atimes.com/atimes/Southeast_Asia/JF13Ae03.html> (accessed 13 June 2008).

—— (2008b) "The politics of revenge in Thailand," *Asia Times Online*, 14 March 2008. Online. Available HTTP: <http://www.atimes.com/atimes/Southeast_Asia/JC14Ae01.html> (accessed 14 March 2008).

DeBats, D. (1983) "Liberal-democratic theory in America," in N. Winthrop (ed.), *Liberal Democratic Theory and its Critics*, London: Croom Helm, pp. 49–82.

Dowdle, M. W. (2009) "On the regulatory dynamics of judicialization: the problems and perils of exploring 'judicialization' in East and Southeast Asia," in T. Ginsburg and A. Chen (eds), *Administrative Law and Governance in Asia: comparative perspectives*, London: Routledge, pp. 23–37.

Ginsburg, T. (2008) *Constitutional Afterlife: the continuing impact of Thailand's post-political constitution*, Public Law and Legal Theory Working Paper No. 252, University of Chicago Law School.

Handley, P. (2008) "Princes, politicians, bureaucrats, generals: the evolution of the privy council under the constitutional monarchy," paper for the 10th International Conference on Thai Studies, Thammasat University, Bangkok, 9–11 January 2008.

Hewison, K. (2000) "Resisting globalization: a study of localism in Thailand," *The Pacific Review*, 13(2): 279–96.

—— (2004) "Crafting Thailand's new social contract," *The Pacific Review*, 17(4): 503–22.

—— (2007a) "Thailand after the 'good' coup," *Brown Journal of World Affairs*, 14(1): 237–47.

—— (2007b) "Constitutions, regimes and power in Thailand," *Democratization*, 14(5): 928–45.

—— (2008) "A book, the king and the 2006 coup," *Journal of Contemporary Asia*, 38(1): 190–211.

Hewison, K. (ed.) (1997) *Political Change in Thailand*, London: Routledge.

Hewison, K., Rodan, G. and Robison, R. (1993) "Introduction: changing forms of state power in Southeast Asia," in K. Hewison, R. Robison and G. Rodan (eds), *Southeast Asia in the 1990s: authoritarianism, democracy and capitalism*, Sydney: Allen & Unwin, pp. 2–8.

Hicken, A. (2007) "The 2007 Thai constitution: a return to the past," unpublished paper, Department of Political Science, University of Michigan.

Hirschl, R. (2004) "The political origins of the new constitutionalism," *Indiana Journal of Global Legal Studies*, 11(1): 73–84.

Human Rights Watch (2006) "Authorities must ensure independent and effective murder investigation," 13 January 2006. Online. Available HTTP: <http://hrw.org/english/docs/2006/01/13/thaila12433.htm> (accessed 14 April 2007).

Kate, D. T. (2008) "Worries about Thailand's invisible hand," *Asia Sentinel*, 4 January 2008. Online. Available HTTP: <http://www.asiasentinel.com/index.php?option=com_content&task=view&id = 969&Itemid=185> (accessed 6 January 2008).

Klein, J. (2008) "In Thailand: a reality check," Asia Foundation Thailand website, 3 December 2008. Online. Available HTTP: <http://asiafoundation.org/in-asia/2008/12/03/in-thailand-a-reality-check/> (accessed 13 December 2008).

Leyland, P. (2009) "The emergence of administrative justice under the 1997 Thai constitution," in T. Ginsburg and A. Chen (eds), *Administrative Law and Governance in Asia: comparative perspectives*, London: Routledge, pp. 230–56.

Linz, J. and Stepan, A. (1996) *Problems of Democratic Transition and Consolidation*, Washington, DC: Johns Hopkins University Press.

McCargo, D. (ed.) (2002) *Reforming Thai Politics*, Copenhagen: NIAS.

McCargo, D. and Ukrist, P. (2005) *The Thaksinization of Thailand*, Copenhagen: NIAS.

Pasuk Phongpaichit and Baker, C. (2000) *Thailand's Crisis*, Chiangmai: Silkworm.

—— (2004) *Thaksin*, Chiangmai: Silkworm.

—— (2008a) "Thailand: fighting over democracy," *Economic & Political Weekly*, 13 December 2008, pp. 18–21.

—— (2008b) "Thailand on trial," *The Wall Street Journal*, 11–13 July 2008.

—— (2008c) "The mask-play election: generals, politicians, and voters at Thailand's 2007 poll," paper presented at the Contemporary Thailand Workshop, University of North Carolina at Chapel Hill, 12 November 2008.

Prem Tinsulanonda (2006) "A special lecture to CRMA cadets at Chulachomklao Royal Military Academy," 14 July 2006. Online. Available HTTP: <http://www.crma.ac.th/speech/speech.html> (accessed 28 August 2007).

Suchit Boonbongkarn (1999) "Thailand's successful reforms," *Journal of Democracy*, 10(4): 54–68.

Tharit Charungvat (2008) "The Thai monarchy," *International Herald Tribune*, 18 December 2008.

Thi, Awzar (pseud.) (2007) "The draft 2007 constitution of Thailand: a Generals' Charter in Judges' clothing," *article2*, 6(3): 42–52.

Vander Meer, J. (2006) "Thaksin in the dock," *Asia Sentinel*, 9 August 2006. Online. Available HTTP: <http://www.asiasentinel.com/index.php?option=com_content&task=view&id=82&Itemid=31> (accessed 15 April 2008).

Part II

Democracy in East Asia?

Achievements and enduring challenges

8 Democracy and disorder

Will democratization bring greater regional instability to East Asia?[1]

Amitav Acharya

If . . . the consent of the citizens is required to decide whether or not war is to be declared, it is very natural that they will have great hesitation in embarking on so dangerous an enterprise.

Immanuel Kant (1986)

To be safe, democracy must kill its enemy when it can and where it can.
U.S. Secretary of War and Noble Peace Prize Winner,
Elihu Root (Cited in Russett 1993)

What difference does it make to the dead, the orphans and the homeless, whether the mad destruction is wrought under the name of totalitarianism or the holy name of liberty or democracy?

Mahatma Gandhi (1942)

The nexus between democracy and stability has received far less attention than other drivers of East Asia's regional order, such as the balance of power, economic interdependence, and regional institutions.[2] In the academic world, scholars studying democratization in East Asia have been more concerned with exploring the domestic context of and the factors behind democratization (such as the impact of economic growth, the role of the middle class, and the functions of a largely national civil society) than with its external underpinnings and consequences (Acharya 1999; Lynch 2006: 5).[3]

International relations scholars, especially those debating the "Democratic Peace" thesis, have neglected the East Asian regional context in developing their arguments about whether democracy is a force for peace or a recipe for disorder. Preoccupied as they are with large-N statistical studies, the debates about Democratic Peace have produced little insight into any *regional* dynamics, and few attempts have been made to examine democracy and regional peace and security in East Asia (an important exception is Goldsmith 2007; see also Friedman 2000 on China; and Acharya 2003 and Emmerson 2009 on Southeast Asia).[4]

In the world of policy-making, the nexus between democracy and economic performance sparked debate in the 1990s when Singapore's Lee Kuan Yew was challenged by the Philippines' Fidel Ramos over the former's claim that democracy breeds indiscipline and poor economic performance (Acharya 1999).[5] The 1997 financial crisis forced Lee to acknowledge the existence of "bad Asian values" in authoritarian Asian societies, such as corruption, nepotism, and a lack of transparency; values that were widely blamed for the crisis. This "democracy-versus-growth" debate has been replaced by concerns (if not a debate as yet) over the relationship between democracy and democratization on the one hand and regional stability and security on the other. The downfall of the Suharto regime in Indonesia in 1998 as a direct consequence of the financial crisis set in motion the democratization of Southeast Asia's most populous nation. In the aftermath of Suharto's ousting, tensions between Jakarta and its neighbors Singapore and Malaysia fueled perceptions that democratization in the region might be a recipe not just for domestic disorder, but also for inter-state conflict. Neighbors such as Singapore feared that Jakarta might abandon its support for Association of Southeast Asian Nations (ASEAN) or, at worst, revert to a Sukarno-style belligerent nationalist posture toward its neighbors. At the same time, concerns emerged about the implications of Taiwan's democratic transition, which some viewed as having heightened the prospects for conflict with China by creating an alternative political model of growth and prosperity that made Beijing nervous and insecure. Moreover, the issue of democratic change in Burma, and more generally the issue of human rights and democratization in Southeast Asia, polarized ASEAN and strained its relations with an otherwise sympathetic West.

Assessing the relationship between democracy and regional conflict has several implications for academics and policy-makers concerned with East Asia. First, until now, economic interdependence and regional institutions have driven the search for stable peace in the region, but the question remains as to whether there can be a true East Asian community in the absence of shared democratic values and politics. Second, international support for democracy in the region has been lukewarm at best (even after the Cold War years when support for authoritarian rule in the West outweighed support for democracy). This is partly based on a fear of the allegedly destabilizing effects of democratization, whether justified or not. A third implication concerns the role of Asian regional institutions in promoting democracy. Democratic transitions can enhance or undermine regional cooperation and institution-building. If democracy causes disorder, then Asian regional institutions may justifiably shy away from the promotion of democracy and hold fast to the principle of non-intervention in the internal affairs of their member states. Indeed, this is precisely what they have done thus far. But if democracy induces peace, then it may be time for these institutions to embrace democratic ideals and devise plans for their defense in regional affairs.

In this chapter, I argue that the available evidence does not support the pessimism about the effects of democratization on regional order in East

Asia. The pessimists fail to consider several mitigating factors that check the allegedly destabilizing consequences of democratization and accentuate its peace-causing effects. These are not necessarily liberal forces, such as economic interdependence (Wan 2002; Lind 2005; Goldsmith 2007) or regional institutions (Acharya 2002; Ba 2009), although these forces do matter. Rather, they are factors created by the effects of democratization itself that may mitigate the potential for conflict that is supposedly inherent in the democratization process. These mitigating factors do not necessarily correspond to the normative and institutionalist logic underpinning the Democratic Peace theory, and have been largely overlooked by critics of the theory.

Some initial caveats and clarifications are necessary. First, in this chapter I am concerned mainly with inter-state conflict. With the exception of Appendix 1, which offers a preliminary estimate of the number of deaths caused by authoritarian and democratic regimes in East Asia (and note that authoritarianism wins the contest), I do not address how democratization affects domestic conflict. I acknowledge that domestic change and internal conflicts linked to democratic transition can be a major determinant of inter-state conflict, as domestically insecure regimes tend to export their conflicts and expose their countries to foreign intervention. But lack of space precludes a consideration of the fuller implications of democratization for domestic order. Second, my focus here is on East Asia, which does not include the South Asian states. (It has been argued that India and Pakistan and India and Sri Lanka have been embroiled in military conflicts despite the presence of democratic regimes, the most notable being the Kargil conflict between India and Pakistan under Prime Minister Nawaz Sharif, see Friedman 2000.) Third, I am concerned primarily with dyadic inter-state conflict (which is the main focus of both the supporters and critics of Democratic Peace theory), although this cannot be entirely separated from domestic violence. I am less concerned with the general issue of regional instability, such as strategic relations with outside major powers that may be affected by democratization and may undermine regional security. Hence, I do not examine arguments about the rise in anti-Americanism caused by democratization in South Korea and the Philippines, which may affect the alliances of these countries with the United States, an outcome that some would view as detrimental to regional stability. This is an important subject, but perhaps worthy of a separate examination.

Finally, I offer a qualitative analysis that focuses on and generalizes from individual cases of democratic transition in Asia and its impact on peace and stability. My approach in this respect is different from the quantitative studies that are commonplace in the literature on Democratic Peace. The factors linking democratization and order that I highlight are sensitive to the East Asian regional context and broader than those identified in the standard Democratic Peace literature that has dominated the debate on democracy and peace at the global level. As such, this chapter not only challenges the Democratic Peace theory and its critics, but also encourages a move beyond the narrowly focused and quantitative research of Democratic Peace scholars and their critics to focus on regional cases and dynamics.

Conceptual linkages

As might be expected, the meanings of democratic transition and democratization vary and remain contested in the academic literature. I use the definition of Linz and Stepan (1996: 3; Lynch 2006: 3) that "a democratic transition is complete when sufficient agreement has been reached about political procedures to produce an elected government, when a government comes to power that is the direct result of a free and popular vote, and when this government *de facto* has the authority to generate new policies, and when the executive, legislative, and judicial power generated by the new democracy does not have to share power with other bodies *de jure*." Democratization is different from liberalization. Liberalization is characterized by a tolerance of opposition and the activities of organized labor groups, legal safeguards for individuals, the release of political prisoners, and the return of exiles. Although it includes these elements, democratization goes further, entailing "free competitive elections, the results of which determine who governs" (Linz and Stepan 1996: 3).

Much of the recent debate in Western academic and policy-making circles on democracy, democratization, and international order has revolved around the claims of Democratic Peace theory (see, for example, Ray 1995; Brown *et al.* 1996; Weart 1998). Although the exact formulation of the theory is itself contested, simply put it argues that democracies tend not to fight other democracies (as opposed to the broader claim that democracies tend to be more pacific than autocracies, a proposition that is much more controversial and harder to defend). Academic writing on Democratic Peace offers two reasons for the pacific tendency of democracies; one normative and the other institutional (Maoz and Russett 1993). The normative argument holds that democracies tend to externalize domestic values and practices, such as tolerance of diversity, competition, the peaceful settlement of disputes, and respect for liberty. This explains why democracies seek and maintain peaceful relations with other democratic states who possess similar values. The institutional argument focuses on the constraints placed on the leaders of democratic states in going to war, such as parliamentary scrutiny, media criticism, and the pressure of public opinion, which might view war as a waste of public resources. If states in a dyadic relationship are both democracies, then the normative and institutional constraints on war are magnified, especially as the governments of these states will be tied to common values and practices that engender trust and a sense of community. This explains the rarity of war between democracies.

The Democratic Peace thesis has its fair share of critics. Much of the criticism focuses on key terminology, such as how democracy is defined and what constitutes a war. Believers in Democratic Peace have often been accused of tautology in defining these terms in ways that support and safeguard the Democratic Peace proposition. This is not the place to revisit the debate on Democratic Peace: suffice it to state that although it is a useful starting point, the theory does not serve as an adequate framework for analyzing the international consequences of democratization in East Asia for several reasons.

For a long time, the relative paucity of durable liberal democracies in East Asia meant that there was a very small sample with which to test the causal arguments of the Democratic Peace theory. Friedman notes that as democracies in East Asia are physically isolated from each other by extensive stretches of water, and as wars usually take place between neighbors, the Democratic Peace logic in Asia is "circular or not significant" (Friedman 2000: 228).[6] Moreover, many East Asian democracies, despite allowing regular elections, are "illiberal" in terms of multi-party competition and civil liberties (for example, Singapore, and Malaysia up to a point), which begs the question of whether the logic of Democratic Peace can really be applied here. After all, in some versions of the Democratic Peace argument the pacific impulse of democracies toward each other is the product of liberalism, in that political systems that guarantee political and civil liberties, especially open criticism of governments, ensure that "citizens have leverage over war decisions" rather than simply holding regular controlled elections.[7]

Other reasons can be found to support the argument that the normative and institutionalist logic underpinning the Democratic Peace theory does not easily fit the East Asian regional context. As far as the normative argument goes, the internalization of norms—any norms—takes time, and the relative newness of democratic regimes in East Asia makes it difficult to speak of the externalization of democratic norms in the foreign policy behavior of many democracies, such as Thailand, the Philippines, South Korea, Taiwan, and Indonesia. Democratic norms may have a more significant impact on the foreign policy of older democracies such as Japan and India, but India's behavior toward its immediate South Asian neighbors belies such expectations. To date, no study has assessed the impact of the domestic norms of the democratic states of Asia on their foreign policy behavior.

The institutional argument is negated by the fact that the parliamentary scrutiny of foreign policy is less institutionalized and binding in Asia than in Western democracies, especially the United States. In most Asian states, the legislature plays an insignificant role in foreign policy-making (although this may be changing, as is evident in the role of the Indonesian national legislature and recent efforts by legislators in semi-authoritarian states such as Singapore and Malaysia on the issue of Burma). Moreover, and this is a general criticism of Democratic Peace theory, the very institutions that are supposed to rein in the warmongering of democratic regimes—whether parliament, the media, or public opinion—can be manipulated to encourage conflict.

Against this backdrop, an aspect of the academic debate on democracy and regional stability that seems to have more resonance in East Asia is not the theory of Democratic Peace itself, but the criticism that it receives from those who believe that democratization, if not mature democracy, is a prescription for disorder. The best known of the academic perspectives is that held by Mansfield and Snyder. In their view, democratization increases the danger of war (Mansfield and Snyder 1995, 2002), with Snyder separately blaming heightened nationalism for instability and war during democratic transitions (Snyder 2000). Mansfield and Snyder claim that:

> Countries do not become mature democracies overnight. More typically, they go through a rocky transitional period, where democratic control over foreign policy is partial, where mass politics mixes in a volatile way with authoritarian elite politics, and where democratization suffers reversals. In this transitional phase of democratization, countries become more aggressive and war-prone, not less, and they do fight wars with democratic states.
>
> (Mansfield and Snyder 1995: 5)

In their 2002 article, Mansfield and Snyder reiterate this argument with the statement that "transitions from dictatorship to more pluralistic political systems coincided with the rise of national independence movements, spurring separatist warfare that often spilled over across international borders" (Mansfield and Snyder 2002: 297).

Yet this linking of democratization and violence does not take into account the possible mitigating factors of democratization. In an earlier essay that went well beyond the literature on Democratic Peace theory and its critics, I identified some of the possible consequences, both negative and positive, of democratization for regionalism and regional order in Southeast Asia (Acharya 2003). Expanding on this framework, I here present a list of possible consequences of democratization for regional conflict and stability.

The consequences that cause conflict include both revived or freshly created inter-state tensions, and the effects of democratic transitions on regional cooperation and the mechanisms that ensure the peaceful settlement of disputes. Newly democratic states have a tendency to export their "revolutions," either actively or passively (by showing sympathy for pro-democracy struggles in their region), which makes their authoritarian neighbors fearful and hostile. Heightened nationalism, which, as Mansfield and Snyder (1995) point out, is often a feature of newly democratic states, can also fuel inter-state tensions. Further, the advent of a new and legitimate regime may revive tensions over issues "settled" by an unpopular ousted regime. As far as regional cooperation and cooperative institutions are concerned, preoccupation with democratization may divert the attention and resources of leaders away from regional cooperation. Further, regional institutions led or promoted by an authoritarian regime may be opposed by a newly democratic regime and its civil society allies and newly empowered civil society groups.

Regional cooperation that is founded on close interpersonal ties and informal contacts among leaders and elites will also face disruption if the key regime anchoring them is removed from office. In a related vein, regional institutions established and maintained by authoritarian states may lose legitimacy and support from the populations of member states that enjoy greater domestic political openness.

Democratization may also call into question the sanctity of existing regional norms and the relevance of existing institutional mechanisms. Leaders of separatist movements who become the democratically chosen leaders of new states created by the collapse of an authoritarian polity are likely to be hostile toward a regional grouping that had previously not supported their cause or even acquiesced with their suppression out of deference to regional norms. Uneven democratization within a regional grouping may polarize members over key political issues, including the promotion of human rights and democracy through regional means. Another factor is the trans-boundary spillover effect of domestic strife that often accompanies the democratization process, with the cross-border outflow of political or ethnic refugees in particular being a source of bilateral tension.

Although these dangers may be present in any democratization process, they may also be offset by a number of mitigating forces generated by the very same process. The rulers of a newly democratizing state are likely to focus on internal consolidation and economic reconstruction (especially if it has been under a long and ruinous authoritarian rule) to fulfill promises made during the struggle for democracy. In such situations, war would be regarded as wasteful. Democratization also creates more domestic transparency in ways that are beneficial to regional understanding and trust. The transition to democratic rule brings in its wake a greater availability of information about a state's national security and financial policies and assets, which may serve to reduce suspicions among its neighbors and expand regional security and economic cooperation. The rule of law in the domestic context often leads to demands for rule-based interactions in the regional arena, which can be more conducive to regional collective problem-solving. Democratization also creates a deeper basis for regional socialization by according space to civil society and accommodating its concerns. The ruling elite in democratizing states is likely to co-opt civil society and accept its transnational links, thereby increasing the chance of more effective responses to transnational issues. The ruling elite is also likely to accord a higher priority to maintaining and enhancing its international legitimacy than to regaining territory from neighbors or to seeking unilateral gains. During the struggle for democratic change, opposition leaders may accept and use international liberal norms, such as the pacific settlement of disputes, and interdependence, which may further offset the impact of nationalism produced by democratization.

Moreover, the nationalism that accompanies democratization may be a *positive nationalism* (pride in having achieved an open polity, being able to say we are a "democratic nation," winning respect from the international community, and avoiding the derogatory labels of authoritarian regime or "dictator"), rather than a negative nationalism. Democratizing states are more likely to subject themselves to international mediation and arbitration in their internal and inter-state conflicts, and democratizing states are as much—if not more—likely to adopt cooperative security and regional integration strategies toward their neighbors. This last factor, known as the "cooperative security" effect of democratization, has been a significant trend in three recent cases of democratic transitions in East Asia: those of Thailand, South Korea, and Indonesia.

East Asian cases

A comparison and correlation of democratic transition and the incidence of inter-state war (as judged by the yardstick of Mansfield and Snyder (1995) of at least 1,000 battle deaths) involving South Korea and Taiwan in Northeast Asia and the Philippines, Thailand, Cambodia, and Indonesia in Southeast

Table 8.1 Democratization in East Asia: key dates

Country	Key date	Event
Philippines	February 1986	Corazon Aquino replaces Fidel Marcos
South Korea	June 1987	Direct presidential elections under Roh Tae Woo (29 June 1987)
Taiwan	July 1987	On 30 October 1986, Chiang Ching-Kuo announced that the Kuomintang (KMT) state would lift the martial law in July 1987. The first elections in which parties other than the KMT were allowed to contest were held in 1989.
Thailand	July 1988	Chatichai Choonhavan becomes the first elected prime minister, replacing Prem Tinsulanonda. He led the country and the coalition government until the military coup in 1991.
	May 1992	Anand Panyarachun replaces Sunthorn/Suchinda.
	September 1992	Chuan Leekpai is elected to office.
Cambodia	July 1993	The Ranariddh-Hun Sen coalition government replaces the United Nations Transitional Authority in Cambodia (UNTAC) following elections.
Indonesia	July 1999	The first parliamentary elections after the collapse of the Suharto regime in May 1998, organized by Habibie (7 June 1999).
	October 1999	The first (indirect) presidential elections (on 20 October 1999). Habibie had resigned after losing a vote of confidence on 19 October 1999.

Asia, throws one factor into particular relief: there is not a single instance in East Asia of a newly democratic regime initiating outright war with a neighbor. Neither is there much evidence (with the possible exception of Taiwan) of significantly increased tensions with neighbors caused by growing nationalism in the democratizing country that Mansfield and Snyder (1995) predict. Drawing upon the foregoing conceptual discussion, I present a matrix of indicators to assess the war and peace behavior of selected East Asian nations that have gone through democratic transitions.

Northeast Asia

I first turn to Northeast Asia and compare the cases of South Korea and Taiwan. At first glance, it would appear that democratization has had opposite effects on the prospects for inter-state conflict for these two nations. Arguably, Taiwanese democratization has led to greater Taiwanese nationalism and stronger assertions of Taiwanese identity, thereby aggravating tensions with mainland China. In contrast, South Korean democratization brought into power a government (that of Kim Dae Jung) that sued for peace with its North Korean adversary (Chung 2002, 2003).

In the case of Taiwan, Yuan-Kang Wang blames democratization for the missile crisis of 1995–1996. As he puts it, "democratization in Taiwan led it to increasingly demand more international recognition of state sovereignty . . . [and] made for a rocky period in cross-strait relations, culminating in the testfiring of missiles by China in the waters near Taiwan during 1995–1996" (Wang 2004). Moreover, democratic politics resulted in the molding of political parties along ethnic lines, thereby causing domestic polarization and further provoking mainland China (Tsang and Tien 1999). Other analysts attribute greater cross-strait antagonism to changing conceptions of national identity in Taiwan brought about by democratization (Horowitz *et al.* 2007).

However, these trends should be contrasted with the important pacific effects of Taiwanese democratization. As Hughes (1999: 134) notes, one of the early results of democratization (evident by 1994) was that the ruling Kuomintang (KMT; then under Lee Teng-hui) came to be "constrained by public opinion against taking undue risks and limiting cross-strait transactions," while the opposition Democratic Progressive Party (DPP) "appeared to be constrained in its advocacy of Taiwan independence by its rejection at the polls." This was of course before the DPP won the presidency and embarked on the campaign to build Taiwanese identity, but even after the DPP obtained power, the constraining effect of public opinion on its mainland policy persisted, despite the discernable growth of a "Taiwanese identity." It may have been this effect, rather than fear of Chinese retaliation alone, that pulled Chen Shui-bian's government from the brink of conflict with mainland China that would have resulted from Taiwan's unilateral declaration of independence. A related point here is the "constructed" nature

Table 8.2 Destabilizing and conflict-causing consequences of democratization

Did the newly democratic country	South Korea	Taiwan	The Philippines	Thailand	Indonesia
Fight a war with its neighbor(s) within the first 10 years of transition?	No	No[a]	No	No[b]	No
Attempt to destabilize the region by exporting its "revolution"?	No	No	No	Maybe[c]	No
Revive territorial claims thought to have been "settled" by the authoritarian predecessor?	No	No	No	No	No
Find itself distracted from, or expressed lack of interest in, regional cooperation?	No	N/A	No	No	No[d]
Reduce its adherence to existing regional norms and institutional mechanisms for regional cooperation?	N/A	N/A	No	No	Yes[e]
Experience opposition from its civil society toward existing regional institutions?	No	N/A	Yes, to ASEAN and APEC over East Timor and Burma	Yes, to ASEAN over Burma	Yes, to ASEAN over Burma

Notes:
a A military crisis with China occurred in 1996 over Lee Teng-Hui's revision of the One China policy, and subsequently due to tensions over DPP's plans for independence.
b Limited border conflicts with Laos in 1987–1988, and with Burma in 2001, neither of which can be attributed to democratization.
c Thailand did seek to promote democracy in the region, which caused tensions with Burma.
d This appeared to be the case initially under the government of Abdurrahman Wahid.
e Especially the non-interference norm and the ASEAN Way, but this may have spurred ASEAN to engage in greater institutionalization.

Table 8.3 Stabilizing and cooperative security effects of democratization

Did the newly democratic country	South Korea	Taiwan	The Philippines	Thailand	Indonesia
Sign a peace or reconciliation treaty (bilateral or multilateral) with a hostile neighbor or a domestic insurgent group within its first 10 years?			Yes, with the Moro National Liberation Front (MNLF)	Yes, Paris Peace Agreement on Cambodia, 1991	Yes, Bali Concord II, 2003
Adopt cooperative security strategies toward a hostile state?	Yes		Yes	Yes	Yes
Allow greater domestic transparency and oversight of foreign and defense policy?	Yes			Yes	Yes
Push for more rule-based interactions in regional institutions?	N/A		Yes	Yes	Yes
Subject itself to international mediation and peacemaking efforts?	Yes		MNLF	Yes	Yes, Aceh
Accord space to the civil society and accept at least some of its transnational links and demands?	Yes	Yes		Yes	Yes

of Taiwanese identity. To the extent that Taiwanese identity has been identified as a conflict-causing variable induced by democratization, and to the
extent that it was deliberately promoted by the DPP to improve its electoral
prospects, electoral defeat would mean a retreat from the DPP's strategy. If
the growth of a Taiwanese identity has been partly due to top-down regime
manipulation (through textbooks and officially backed campaigns, for
example) rather than an entirely spontaneous occurrence among the masses,
then it would be reversible under different political conditions and national
leadership, and indeed may already have happened as an outcome of
Taiwan's latest elections.

Like Taiwan, the case of South Korea involves the issue of reunification,
but the Korean reunification dynamic is different from the cross-strait situation. The driving force in the Korean case is the more prosperous and democratic South Korea, whereas in the cross-strait context the party driving
reunification is the less prosperous (at least until now) and authoritarian
China. Moreover, South Korea's desire for national reunification is not
embedded in ethnic politics or a competing national identity, as is the case in
Taiwan.

South Korea offers clearer evidence that democratization does not necessarily trigger nationalist sentiments that then pressure governments to take an
aggressive stance toward an adversary. On the contrary, democratization has
been accompanied by a desire for peace and the accommodation of the
North among the South Korean population, and has produced successive
governments (although not all) in Seoul that are dovish, rather than hawkish,
toward the North (Horowitz *et al.* 2007). The South Korean case shows that
national identity-building under conditions of democratization need not be
exclusionary, as might have been the case initially in Taiwan, but can be
inclusionary. In other words, democratization can engender *positive nationalism*, (as opposed the negative nationalism stressed by Mansfield and Snyder
(1995), and can encourage the forging of a common identity in divided
societies with ideologically different regimes.

The main reason for the positive nationalism in South Korea is the opening
up of its national security establishment and security discourses, which is a
direct outcome of democratization. This of course did not happen overnight.
Although Roh Tae Woo and Kim Young Sam allowed free elections, the
security discourse and policy-making in the country remained more or less
the same as under authoritarian rule, and was monopolized by a narrow and
military-dominated elite. Things really changed under the presidency of Kim
Dae Jung. Democratization opened up a space for alternative views and
approaches to national security and the problem of the Korean peninsula.
Kim Dae Jung's "sunshine policy" toward North Korea might not have been
a direct product of democratization, but was influenced by these alternative
discourses and ideas. Although tensions between the North and the South
remain, North Korea's covert actions against the South and its assassinations
of South Koreans have declined since South Korea became democratic. It is

thus defensible to link democratization with improved relations between the two Koreas.

South Korea's case is important also because it shows the *cooperative security effect of democratization*. Cooperative security involves taking an inclusive approach to security: it is *security with*, as opposed to *security against*, one's adversary. Under the logic of cooperative security, newly democratic regimes, rather than directing any newly generated nationalist feelings in their societies against their neighbors, may actually use them for peace and cooperation. This effect may be generated by several factors. One is the "transnational moral debt" of the leaders presiding over the transition to democracy. This applies not just to leaders (like Kim Dae Jung) who were severely persecuted by their authoritarian predecessors and sheltered by the West, but also more generally to leaders who received significant goodwill and support from the international community, including civil society groups, both before and after the collapse of authoritarian rule. These leaders may seek to distance themselves from the hard-line policy of their predecessors, and may also cultivate a new foreign policy image of moderation and accommodation that is more consistent with their democratic credentials. Moreover, they carry a moral obligation not to disappoint the international community by engaging in domestic or external violence. Kim Dae Jung's "sunshine policy," pursued despite stiff resistance from the United States, can be viewed as an example of the cooperative security effect of democratization.

Southeast Asia

Both of the Northeast Asian cases involve the issue of "national reunification," rather than conventional inter-state relations. Hence, care must be taken in using them to make generalizations about the link between democratization and inter-state conflict in other parts of Asia. The Southeast Asian cases of democratic transition differ because no reunification is involved, yet here too there is little evidence that democratization has fuelled conflict with neighbors. I discuss the cases of Thailand, Cambodia, and Indonesia. The Philippines is left out because there has been no dyadic conflict between the Philippines and its ASEAN neighbors since the Sabah dispute with Malaysia in the late 1960s and early 1970s (Sino-Philippine tensions over the Spratlys had little to do with democratization in the Philippines). The case of the Philippines is more relevant to discussions of the implications of democratization for foreign military alliances and bases, although it should be pointed out that although democratic transition in the Philippines initially led to greater opposition to the presence of foreign military bases, 9/11 engendered positive public sentiment toward U.S.–Philippines security cooperation against terrorism and separatism in the south of the country.

Thailand is a good starting point for examining the effects of democratization in Southeast Asia. Democratization in Thailand was neither linear nor terminal, but it was the government of Chatichai Choonhavan (the first elected premier after the military regime of Prem Tinsulanonda allowed elections in 1988) that pursued the "battlefields to marketplaces" approach toward Vietnam. This broke the diplomatic deadlock in the Cambodia conflict and provided an opening for ASEAN's eventual reconciliation with Vietnam in perhaps the most peace-inducing development in the recent history of Southeast Asia. It may be difficult to separate the effects of democratization from economic and even geopolitical motives linked to national security or regime security. Indeed, critics of Chatichai's policy argue that he was merely reviving the historic strategy of Thai economic and strategic dominance of mainland Southeast Asia embodied in the *Suwannaphum* (literally, golden land) concept. In the end, however, any such designs that Thailand might have harbored failed to bear fruit. Alternatively, the battlefields-to-marketplaces policy can be seen as an example, albeit a weak one, of the "cooperative security" effect of democratization. At the very least, it counters the view that democratization is a natural or automatic catalyst of nationalism that spills over into conflict with neighbors.

The Chuan Leekpai government that came into office after the outbreak of the Asian economic crisis just over a decade later in 1997 is a clear example of a newly elected regime pursuing a foreign policy agenda that self-consciously reflects and promotes its democratic credentials, including the soft promotion of democracy in neighboring authoritarian states. Asada Jayanama, then a top Thai diplomat, stated at the time: "We want to encourage Indonesia to move towards democratization because then we'll have three important democratic countries in Southeast Asia: Indonesia, Thailand, and the Philippines. That will change the picture" (cited in Acharya 2001: 5). The "picture" to which he was referring was the balance of authoritarian or semi-authoritarian regimes and democratic governments in ASEAN. The majority enjoyed by the former had sustained ASEAN's principle of non-interference, which had shielded the dictatorship in Burma from international pressure and isolation. In a similar vein, Chuan's Foreign Minister, Surin Pitsuwan, hoped that Thailand's democratic system would "be an inspiration to freedom and democracy-loving peoples in other countries, without interfering in their internal affairs." Despite ostensibly affirming the non-interference principle, Surin was actually pushing for a "flexible engagement" approach for ASEAN that challenged the non-interference principle and which, by his own admission, was a reflection of Thailand's "commitment to freedom and democracy" (Pitsuwan 1998: 5). The "flexible engagement" concept to reform the workings of ASEAN was also partly directed at Burma, in an apparent repudiation of ASEAN's existing policy of "constructive engagement" toward the Burmese junta.

Although the flexible engagement approach caused some apprehension in Burma and discomfort among other ASEAN members, particularly Singapore, it did not lead to conflict with Burma or the unraveling of ASEAN. The Chuan government did pursue a less friendly attitude toward Burma, and even went so far as to engage in a brief military conflict with the country in 2001 during the last days of his government. But it was a limited border skirmish in which less than ten people died and had little to do with the democracy-promoting agenda of the government, which had in any case become considerably muted by this time. Thailand was largely restrained from pursuing the "flexible engagement" policy and was sensitive to the prior salience of ASEAN regionalism. Overall, the recent history of Thailand shows that democratization need not lead to increased conflict with neighbors, and may even produce a cooperative security effect.

In turning to the international effects of democratization in Cambodia, one must start by noting the special circumstances under which the country was brought under democratic rule. Democratization was a necessary part of the overall restoration of the country, the normalization of its politics, and the restoration of its sovereign status following the decade-long (1979–1989) Vietnamese invasion and occupation. Moreover, democratization was brought about under the direct auspices of an international institution, the United Nations Transitional Authority in Cambodia (UNTAC). ASEAN also played a significant role in the peace process that led to the creation of UNTAC, thereby becoming a stakeholder in the democratic future of Cambodia. After UNTAC supervised the first elections in 1993, the democratic system was fragile for a time until Cambodia settled into the familiar Southeast Asian pattern of strongman rule under Hun Sen. However, throughout the process of democratization, there was little sign of Cambodia pursuing nationalist policies designed to cause tension and conflict with neighbors, including its historic rivals Vietnam and Thailand. This was true even of the very unstable system that followed UNTAC under the co-prime ministers Hun Sen and Prince Ranariddh and under Hun Sen's subsequent solo rule. Since the advent of democracy, Cambodia's relations with Vietnam have proven to be remarkably stable and free of violence. This is in no small measure due to Cambodia's membership of ASEAN, which accepted Vietnam as a member (in 1994) not long after the democratic transition in Cambodia took place. Cambodia itself became an ASEAN member in 1999, after an earlier date of admission in 1997 had to be postponed due to the breakdown of the coalition government in Phnom Penh. This may well suggest that guidance from—and obligation to—international and regional institutions during the process of democratization may offset the tendency of a newly democratic regime to channel its nationalism into conflict with its neighbors and instead induce restraint and peaceful conduct. There is little doubt that international pressure, including the recognition that violence against neighbors would have alienated the international community that was providing so much assistance to the country and the regime, would have been a particular consideration for the Cambodian government during the early years of transition to democracy. Added to this is the imperative that a new regime must focus on economic reconstruction to secure its domestic legitimacy.

Electoral politics has led to heightened nationalism in Cambodia and Thailand that the two countries have recently directed against each other. In June 2008, the armed forces of the two countries clashed over the contested

Preah Vihear temple complex on their border (Osborne 2008). A 1962 International Court of Justice ruling awarded the temple to Cambodia. The Thai government under Samak Sundarvej, who succeeded the ousted prime minister Thaksin Shinawatra (and who remained loyal to him), had initially supported Cambodia's application to UNESCO for the recognition of the temple complex as a UNESCO world heritage site, but later bowed to public pressure (generated by the military-backed anti-Thaksin opposition seeking to undermine it) and reversed its stance, sending troops to the border in an attempt to assert Thai sovereignty over the temple. Cambodia's own military response reflected Hun Sen's desire to garner domestic public support in the run-up to the national elections in 2008. ASEAN membership seems to have been a factor in restraining the two sides from escalating the issue further into outright war. However, the nationalist domestic pressure in Thailand behind the conflict had little to do with democratization per se, as neither the royalists nor the pro-Thaksin elements were acting out of any democratic impulse.

The most significant evidence in Southeast Asia of why democratization does not lead to conflict and why it may even produce a cooperative security effect comes from its largest nation, Indonesia. Post-Suharto Indonesia has firmly confounded all expectations, not the least those of Singapore, which bemoaned the loss of its long-time friend and the "father of ASEAN" Suharto and predicted a relapse into Sukarno-era nationalism. Indonesia's relations with Singapore did indeed deteriorate sharply after the ousting of Suharto in 1998, with his successor Jusuf Habibie (who was but an unelected president) deriding the island republic as a "little red dot." The first (indirectly) elected post-Suharto President, Abdurrahman Wahid, also took a dim view of Singapore, accusing it of selfishness. Yet these attitudes reflected a feeling of contemptuousness, rather than of belligerence, toward Singapore. They were not induced by a democracy-promoting agenda or by democratization-induced nationalist pride, although both of these traits are present in post-Suharto Indonesia. Rather, the issues at stake were bilateral, such as the extradition of wealthy Chinese Indonesians who kept their money in Singapore out of the reach of Indonesian authorities, and sand imports by Singapore from Indonesia that caused environmental damage to Indonesian islands.

The "little red dot" episode notwithstanding, since democratization Indonesia's foreign policy has been non-provocative and peaceful, thanks to the "transnational moral debt" imperative mentioned earlier, which includes international pressure and the political legitimacy concerns of the democratic government (Kai 2008). Indonesia has not reneged on any of Suharto's commitments to regional cooperation. On the contrary, Jakarta has played a major role in strengthening ASEAN through a cooperative security approach, which is embodied in its proposal for an ASEAN Security Community. Interestingly, this concept, despite its dilution due to opposition from authoritarian member states, still makes a pitch for enshrining democracy and human rights as part of ASEAN's normative framework. In other words, rather than defecting, Indonesia has become a reinvigorated promoter of regionalism, albeit with a more liberal purpose for what has traditionally been a distinctively illiberal regional grouping. Indonesian nationalists might have been heartened by ASEAN's refusal to condemn the bloody actions of the Indonesian-backed militias in East Timor during the referendum for independence there in 1999. They may also have liked ASEAN's formal declaration of support for Indonesia's territorial integrity in 2000 and its refusal to support the independence of Aceh. Yet Indonesia also provides evidence that democratization may increase a country's tolerance for the international community's criticism of—and involvement in—its domestic affairs, as is evident in the country's allowance of outside mediation and monitoring in the long-standing internal conflict in Aceh. The embracing of regional restraint by the post-Suharto Indonesian governments has much to do with elite and societal pride in having overthrown authoritarian rule and gained the international respectability that goes with democratization.

Stabilizing factors

I have argued that the process of democratization engenders forces that mitigate or constrain pressures on newly democratic regimes to engage in conflict with other states. Although the cases discussed vary widely and there are important differences between Northeast Asia and Southeast Asia in this regard, the "transnational moral burden" of newly democratic regimes, positive nationalism, and the "cooperative security effect" of democratization are evident across both sub-regions. Beyond these are other factors worthy of consideration, including economic prosperity, economic interdependence, and regional institutions. These are not offered as alternative explanations of why war has not accompanied democratic transitions in East Asia, but as stabilizing forces that have cushioned the destabilizing effects of democratization.

The relative economic prosperity of states undergoing democratic transition is a factor that has inhibited conflict in South Korea and Taiwan, although this does not explain the lack of bellicosity in the case of relatively poorer democratizing countries such as the Philippines and Indonesia. The role of economic interdependence may be more important. Lind (2005) suggests that "economic interdependence stabilizes democratic transitions." Goldsmith (2007) finds considerable evidence for the pacific effects of economic interdependence in East Asia in reinforcing the "liberal peace." I believe that economic interdependence works better as a stabilizing force for democratic transition in Northeast Asia, and specifically in the relationships of South Korea and Taiwan with more powerful neighbors like Japan and China. It is less important in Southeast Asia. The absence of war among ASEAN members since 1967 has occurred without significant intra-ASEAN economic interdependence.

In Southeast Asia, the key stabilizing force is the impact of regionalism and regional institutions. Whereas Northeast Asia lacks a sub-regional mechanism for cooperative security, in Southeast Asia ASEAN membership has served as a check on the nationalist impulses of newly democratic regimes. The role of ASEAN also suggests that the regional context of democratization matters. The democratization of its key member states— Thailand, the Philippines, and Indonesia—has had a paradoxical impact on ASEAN. On the one hand, it has produced growing criticism of the "ASEAN Way" of non-interference and informal socialization, which has been credited with conflict prevention and dispute settlement in the region. On the other hand, democratization has led to fresh ideas for reforming ASEAN, such as Surin Pitsuwan's call for "flexible engagement." The debate over non-interference in ASEAN has highlighted the interesting trend that the strongest supporters of a more relaxed sovereignty are those countries that have undergone a major democratic transition. Thus, Thailand and the Philippines and now Indonesia are among the main supporters of a more open and flexible ASEAN approach to sovereignty and non-interference. Although the debate over non-interference has divided ASEAN, over the long term it could prove to be a blessing in disguise. The criticism of the "ASEAN Way" has resulted in calls for greater transparency within the association and the development of a new culture of peer criticism and review. Thanks to this debate, ASEAN is now developing mechanisms to secure greater transparency and achieve more effective crisis prevention and conflict management. The ASEAN experience also suggests that democratization need not cause too much ideological polarization and conflict within other East Asian and Asia-Pacific regional institutions and frameworks such as the ASEAN Regional Forum and the East Asian Community.

Conclusion

My goal in this chapter has not been to establish whether democratization leads to peace, but to suggest that the danger of conflict that accompanies the transition to democracy may be mitigated by other factors generated by the democratization process. Contrary to the claims of those who believe that democratization causes greater inter-state conflict and regional disorder, I contend that it may actually have pacific effects. I do not offer any firm conclusions or predictions about the impact of democratization on regional stability—that would require much more extensive research into long-term trends than is undertaken here. But I hope with this chapter to stimulate discussion and debate by identifying a range of possible factors that might shape the nexus between democratization and regional order, including especially *those factors that may contribute toward a positive co-relationship*, which have not thus far been adequately highlighted in the academic literature or policy debates on East Asian security.

In terms of theoretical framework, I have argued that the propositions of Democratic Peace theory are not especially helpful in investigating the consequences of democratization for regional order in East Asia, although they cannot be entirely disregarded. Rather, one must look outside the standard Democratic Peace literature to understand why democratic transitions have not been as violent as the likes of Lee Kuan Yew might have led us to expect.

In South Korea, Indonesia, and to a lesser extent Thailand, there are clear signs that democratization has been accompanied by a more cooperative strategy toward problem neighbors. The reasons for this vary, but generally include a desire to discredit and establish a distance from the foreign policies of authoritarian predecessors; the pressure to build domestic legitimacy through economic performance, which would be undermined by war; and the moral debt of the new regime to the international community, including donors and civil society groups that backed the opposition to authoritarian rule. To be sure, foreign adventures sometime help to divert attention from domestic problems and help the legitimacy of new regimes, but this occurs only if the new regime fails to achieve legitimacy through peaceful means. Peace with neighbors may be a better way to create the necessary regional climate for improved domestic economic performance.

A key test of my argument will be China. Will a democratizing China pose a threat to regional order? The answer depends very much on the pathway of this transition, which cannot be predicted. However, historical record offers no reason to assume that democratization in China will generate a virulent negative nationalism directed against China's neighbors.[8] Nationalism in China is already rising, even before democratic transition has taken place. This nationalism is partly the product of regime manipulation, but is also generated by economic development and the growth of Chinese national power. There is a possibility that the nationalism that would be generated by democratic transition might create pressure to take Taiwan by force, but there is also reason to hope that a democratic China would exude a positive nationalism and adopt the cooperative security approach, thus making it a more attractive home for the Taiwanese to rejoin.

Finally, the international community should overcome its fear of democracy and democratization in East Asia. Western nations and international institutions have played an insignificant role in promoting democratization in East Asia. During the Cold War, U.S. policy toward democratization among its former allies, such as South Korea, Taiwan, Thailand, and the Philippines, was ambiguous or hostile. Asian regional institutions have similarly discouraged democratization in their neighborhood, and the role of Asian democracies such as Japan and India in promoting democracy in the region has been indifferent or negative (witness their tolerance of or support for the Burmese dictatorship). Among the reasons for the lukewarm support for democratization from the international community and regional organizations are geopolitical rivalries (such as between India, Japan, and China over Burma) and the salience of the non-interference norm (as with ASEAN), but also the belief that democratization could cause regional disorder. Yet this view is misplaced, as this chapter argues and demonstrates. Mine is not an argument, however, in support of the overt promotion of democracy for geopolitical reasons. The temptation of this approach is evident in recent efforts by Japan and Australia to develop an "alliance for democracy" involving the United States and extending to India (Masaki 2007). This strategic concept risks turning the Democratic Peace approach into a Democratic War approach, and could potentially endanger regional stability by severely provoking China without actually promoting democracy in the region. Reforming regional multilateral institutions to engage in a greater acceptance and diffusion of democratic values and norms within a cooperative security framework is a better approach.

Appendix 1

Democracy and death: East Asia 1945–2008 (estimates)

Although this chapter has not dealt with the impact of democratization on domestic conflicts and deaths, the result of preliminary and ongoing research undertaken by the author shows political violence to have claimed far more lives under authoritarian regimes than under democratic governments. Note that there is no consolidated comparative data on these killings and data is extremely hard to gather. The numbers in the following table are indicative but not exact, but I stand by the overall trend.

Table 8.4 Democracy and death in East Asia: 1945–2008[a] (estimates)

Country	Authoritarian Rule (Includes occupation)	Democracy
South Korea	1,000[b]	Negligible
Taiwan	1947: 21,000[c] 1954–55: 5,000	Negligible
The Philippines	(1950–52) 9,000; (Marcos Regime 1966–87): 35,000 + 40,000 = 75,000	1989 onward: 38,600[d]
Thailand	1973–80 Junta rule: 1,577[e]	2003–2008: 936[f]
Indonesia	Sukarno (1945–67) 5,000 + 5000 + 1000 + 30,000 = 41,000[g] Suharto (1965–66) 500,000[i] Suharto (1967–98) 150,000[j]	Starting from Habibie 1999– 2006: 2,017[h]
Cambodia	1970–75: 156,000[k] 1975–78 Pol Pot Famine and Massacre: 1,000,000[l] 1978–89: 65,000[m]	1989–1998: >20,425[n]

Notes:
a Data Source (unless otherwise stated): Sivard, R. L. (1996) *World Military and Social Expenditures, 1996*, Washington, DC: World Priorities, Inc., p. 19.

b Including the death toll of Gwangju massacre of May 18, 1980.
c Including the "2.28 incident" of 1947 when Taiwan was under KMT martial law, which committed approximately 20,000 deaths.
d *The Philippines Government vs. Moro Islamic Liberation Front (MILF)*, ending 2007. Data source: Stockholm International Peace Research Institute.
e 1973 Democracy Movement, 14 October Incident. Data source: Wyatt (2004).
f UCDP data estimate given above is not counting deliberate targeting of civilians, or one-sided violence, which has occurred throughout the conflict. At the same time, due to the difficulty of identifying the specific organization responsible for the attacks, it is possible that some violence by non-insurgent related actors may be included in the estimate above.
g Including the "9.30" Movement in 1965, which committed at least half a million deaths.
h UCDP (Uppsala Conflict Data Program—http://www.pcr.uu.se/research/UCDP/) has only collected detailed information on battle-deaths for the time period after fighting resumed in 1999. That is the basis for the total battle-death estimate given. Also, in the province of Aceh, it was estimated that over 4,300 people had been killed in 1998–2002. Most of these victims were civilians and not victims of battle-related incidents but rather one-sided violence or rioting.
i These killings followed the abortive coup in the night of 30 September/1 October 1965. "In the course of little more than five months from late 1965 to early 1966, anti-communist Indonesians killed about half a million of their fellow citizens" [source: Cribb, R. and Ford, M. (2010) "The killings of 1965–66," *Inside Indonesia*, 99 (January–March 2010), HTTP available at http://insideindonesia.org/content/view/1267/47/ (accessed 10 February 2010)]. Most of the victims were Indonesia's left, especially members and sympathisers of the Communist Party (PKI). Most of the killings were done or coordinated by anti-communist sections of the Indonesian army. Although Sukarno was not stripped of all his powers till March 1967, Suharto was firmly in control of the army from early October 1965. Hence, the approximately half a million deaths related to the coup should be counted under Suharto although technically Sukarno was still in office.
j This number includes the deaths of Annex Timor; famine and massacre through 1975 invasion to 1982.
k North Vietnam & U.S. intervention during the civil war period.
l Some estimates put the figures of death under Pol Pot rule, including deaths from disease and starvation, at over 2 million. See for example, http://www.historyplace.com/worldhistory/genocide/pol-pot.htm (accessed 10 February 2010)
m Vietnam vs. Cambodia war period.
n UCDP data.

Notes

1 Revised version of a paper delivered at the conference on "The Experiment with Democracy in East and Southeast Asia: Two Decades After," Centre for Asian Studies, University of Hong Kong, 2–3 May, 2008.
2 Collectively, economic interdependence, multilateral institutions, and democracy constitute the drivers of liberal peace in the Kantian sense, and even a superficial glance at the literature on East Asian security reveals a far greater focus on interdependence and institutions, especially the latter, than on democracy or more generally the relationship between domestic political change and international relations in the region.
3 For an important study of Southeast Asian democratization that focuses on domestic forces, see Hewison *et al.* (1993). For a study of the "international dimensions" of democratization, see Whitehead (1996).
4 Benjamin Goldsmith's (2007) quantitative analysis concludes that although the liberal peace argument is not irrelevant to Asia, there is only limited evidence that democracy (or international institutions) has pacific effects, especially compared with trade (interdependence or commercial liberalism). He suggests that the Democratic Peace argument is more pertinent to analyzing the relationship between Asian

countries and the outside world than to relationships among the Asian countries. My own qualitative analysis suggests that there is a strong correlation between democratization and regional order, which implies a stronger influence of democracy and democratization on peaceful inter-state relations.

5 Lee Kuan Yew stated that "I do not believe that democracy necessarily leads to development. I believe that what a country needs to develop is discipline more than democracy" (cited in Time 1993; see Far Eastern Economic Review 1992; van Putten and Noomen 1994; Inoguchi and Newman 1997).

6 Friedman's general argument is that there can be no correlation between democracy and peace in general, and certainly not in East Asia, because Democratic Peace theory as formulated by Western scholars may not apply to Asia. In his view, Western Democratic Peace theory is based on a misreading of Kant. In identifying why republics may not pursue a belligerent policy, Kant stressed caution and mutual interaction between states rather than democracy per se. From this perspective, the cost of war would be a more important factor than democracy in restraining governments from fighting. Applying this logic to East Asia, Friedman holds up ASEAN as a model of this dynamic. If we accept this view, then multilateralism may be a more important factor in East Asian stability than democracy, and the cost of war more important than democracy. Yet at the same time—and going somewhat against his own critique of Democratic Peace—Friedman believes that a democratic China and democratic Japan could build "a structure of peace" (Friedman 2000: 224–55).

7 John Owen (1994) makes the point that illiberal democracies (e.g. the ancient Greek city states, which valued heroism and warrior ethic, or the contemporary Balkan countries, which define themselves "not as abstract individuals, but according to religious categories") are unlikely to enjoy Democratic Peace by this logic. Democratic Peace is also less likely to hold for societies imbued with a predominantly communitarian ethic.

8 Although I agree with Lynch (2006) that there is no "East Asian path to democratization," democratization usually has a snowball effect, and regionally similar patterns are common in southern Europe, Latin America, and post-communist Europe. If it takes place at all, Chinese democratization will be stable due to the country's greater prosperity, and will be realized through the South Korean and Taiwan pathway rather than the "people's power" phenomenon that took hold in the Philippines or Indonesia, although even in cases in which people power was the driver there is scant evidence of warlike behavior on the part of the democratic regimes that resulted.

Bibliography

Acharya, A. (1999) "Southeast Asia's democratic moment? The impact of the Asian economic crisis on human rights and democratization," *Asian Survey*, 39(3): 418–32.

—— (2001) "Democratization and regional stability in Southeast Asia," paper presented to the Forum on Regional Strategic and Political Developments, Institute of Southeast Asian Studies, Singapore, 25 July 2001.

—— (2002) "Regional institutions and Asian security order: norms, power and prospects for peaceful change," in M. Alagappa (ed.) *Asian Security Order: Instrumental and Normative Features*. Stanford, CA: Stanford University Press, pp. 210–40.

—— (2003) "Democratization and the prospects for participatory regionalism in Southeast Asia," *Third World Quarterly*, 24(2): 375–90.

Ba, A. (2009) *(Re)negotiating East and Southeast Asia: region, regionalism, and the Association of Southeast Asian Nations*, Stanford, CA: Stanford University Press.

Brown, M. E., Lynn-Jones, S. M. and Miller, S. E. (eds) (1996) *Debating the Democratic Peace*, Cambridge, MA: MIT Press.

Chung, C. P. (2002) "Democratization in South Korea and Taiwan: the effect of social division on inter-Korean and cross-strait relations," IDSS Working Paper (No. 24), Institute of Defense and Strategic Studies, Nanyang Technological University, May 2002.

—— (2003) "Democratization in South Korea and inter-Korean Relations," *Pacific Affairs*, 76(2): 9–35.

Emmerson, D. K. (2009) *Hard Choices: Security, Democracy and Regionalism in Southeast Asia*, Stanford, CA: Walter H. Shorenstein Asia-Pacific Research Centre.

Far Eastern Economic Review (1992) "Discipline versus democracy," *Far Eastern Economic Review*, (December).

Friedman, E. (2000) "Immanuel Kant's relevance to an enduring Asia-Pacific peace," in E. Friedman and B. L. McCormick (eds) *What if China Does Not Democratize? Implications for war and peace*, Armonk, NY: M. E. Sharpe, pp. 224–55.

Gandhi, M. K. (1942) *Non-violence in Peace and War*, Ahmedabad: Navajivan Publishing House.

Goldsmith, B. E. (2007) "A liberal peace in Asia?" *Journal of Peace Research*, 44(1): 5–27.

Hewison, K., Robison, R. and Rodan, G. (eds) (1993) *Southeast Asia in the 1990s: authoritarianism, democracy and capitalism*, St. Leonard, NSW: Allen and Unwin.

Horowitz, S., Heo, U. and Tan, A. C. (eds) (2007) *Identity and Change in East Asian Conflicts: the cases of China, Taiwan, and the Koreas*, New York: Palgrave Macmillan.

Hughes, C. R. (1999) "Democratization and Beijing's Taiwan policy," in S. Tsang and H. M. Tien (eds) *Democratization in Taiwan: implications for China*, Basingstoke: Macmillan.

Inoguchi, T. and Newman, E. (1997) "Introduction: 'Asian values' and democracy in Asia," in Proceedings of a Conference organized as part of the First Shizuoka Asia-Pacific Forum: The Future of the Asia-Pacific Region by the Shizuoka Prefectural Government and the Organizing Committee of the Asia-Pacific Forum, Hamamatsu, Shizuoka, Japan, 28 March 1997.

Kai, H. (2008) "Indonesia's foreign policy after Soeharto: international pressure, democratization, and policy change," *International Relations of the Asia-Pacific*, 8(1): 47–72.

Kant, I. (1986) "Perpetual peace: a philosophical sketch," in John M. Vasquez, (ed.) *Classics of International Relations*, 3rd edn, Upper Saddle River, NJ: Prentice Hall.

Lind, J. (2005) "Logrolling for peace: how economic interdependence overcomes the dangers of democratization,"paper presented at the annual meeting of the International Studies Association, Hilton Hawaiian Village, Honolulu, Hawaii, 5 March 2005.

Linz, J. and Stepan, A. (1996) *Problems of Democratic Transition and Consolidation: southern Europe, South America and post-communist Europe*, Baltimore, MD: Johns Hopkins University Press.

Lynch, D. (2006) *Rising China and Asian Democratization*, Stanford, CA: Stanford University Press.

Mansfield, E. D. and Snyder, J. (1995) "Democratization and the danger of war," *International Security*, 20(1): 5–38.

—— (2002) "Democratic transitions, institutional strength, and war," *International Organization*, 56(2): 297–337.

Maoz, Z. and Russett, B. (1993) "Normative and structural causes of democratic peace, 1946–86," *American Political Science Review*, 87: 624–38.

Masaki, H. (2007) "The emerging axis of democracy," *Asia Times Online* (15 May 2007). Online. Available HTTP: <http://www.atimes.com/atimes/Japan/IC15D h01.html> (accessed 19 June 2009).

Osborne, M. (2008) "Preah Vihear: the Thai-Cambodia temple dispute," Online. Available HTTP: <http://www.opendemocracy.net/article/preah-vihear-the-thai-cambodia-temple-dispute> (accessed 19 June 2009).

Owen, J. M. (1994) "How liberalism produces democratic peace," *International Security*, 19(2): 87–125.

Pitsuwan, S. (1998) "The role of human rights in Thailand's foreign policy," statement presented at the Seminar on the Promotion and Protection of Human Rights by Human Rights Commissions, Bangkok, 2 October 1998. Online. Available HTTP: <http://www.hk-consulate.go/th/speech.htm> (accessed 28 August 2000).

van Putten, C. and Noomen, W. (1994) "Introduction: East Asian governments: governing the market, governing the media?" *International Communication Gazette*, 53(1–2): 1–5.

Ray, J. L. (1995) *Democracy and International Conflict*, Columbia: University of South Carolina Press.

Russett, B. (1993) *Grasping the Democratic Peace: principles for a post-cold war world*, Princeton, NJ: Princeton University Press.

Snyder, J. (2000) *From Voting to Violence*, New York: W.W. Norton.

Time (1993) "Asia's different drum," *Time*, (14 June), p. 18.

Tsang, S. and Tien, H. M. (eds) (1999) *Democratization in Taiwan: implications for China*, Basingstoke: Macmillan.

Wan, M. (2002) "Economic interdependence and economic cooperation," in M. Alagappa (ed.) *Asian Security Order: instrumental and normative features*, Stanford: Stanford University, pp. 210–40.

Wang, Y. K. (2004) "Taiwan's democratization and cross-strait security," *Orbis*, 48(2): 293–304.

Weart, S. (1998) *Never at War: why democracies will not fight one another*, New Haven, CT: Yale University Press.

Whitehead, L. (1996) *The International Dimensions of Democratization*, Oxford: Oxford University Press.

Wyatt, D. K. (2004) *Thailand: a short history*, New Haven, CT: Yale University Press.

9 Democracy's double edge

Financing social policy in industrial East Asia

Joseph Wong

This chapter examines the relationship between democratic politics and social policy reform in industrial East Asia, specifically, Taiwan and South Korea. Theoretical and empirical debates about the relationship between political democracy and the welfare state are not new. The conventional welfare state literature presupposes that class struggle and power resource mobilization are necessarily mediated through democratic political institutions. Democracy, in this respect, is an assumed pre-requisite to the formation of the modern welfare state (Cutright 1965; Stephens 1979; Korpi 1983; Jackman 1986; Esping-Andersen 1990). More recent scholarship on social policy reform among recently democratizing countries, however, offers a less sanguine viewpoint. In many of these countries, the transition to procedural democracy has failed to produce more substantive democracies, and political equality has not translated into greater socioeconomic equity in nations in Latin America, the former Soviet states, Africa, and parts of Southeast Asia (Weyland 1996; Chalmers *et al.* 1997; Cook 2007). Among late-developing countries, democracy has had little to no effect on welfare state formation, giving rise to serious tensions concerning the institutional bases of democracy and the resulting quality of democracy as understood by citizens. What does democratization deliver?

These contending perspectives—democracy as a prerequisite versus democracy as a null variable—represent two poles that anchor the ongoing debate about the relationship between democracy and social policy reform. This chapter takes a more nuanced and disaggregated approach to evaluate this debate, using the cases of Taiwan and South Korea. On the one hand, democratic reform provides an important window of opportunity for significant social policy innovation. In Taiwan and Korea, the transition to democracy during the late 1980s and into the early 1990s was catalytic in steering reform agendas towards social policy. On the other hand, democratic politics limits the range of policy options available to policy-makers charged with resolving the inevitable challenges that emerge in sustaining social protection systems. In Taiwan and Korea, policy-makers have been constrained in their capacity to initiate much-needed reforms in social policy areas such as health and pension provision. That much of the recent policy conflict in both places has centered on financing issues has only served to further limit the extent to which policy-makers can resolve pressing policy problems.

This chapter contends that democracy both facilitates and constrains social policy reform. Democratic reform in Taiwan has compelled its government to institute a universal National Health Insurance (NHI) program, while democracy in Korea has resulted in the creation of the National Pension Program (NPP). Yet, democratic politics has also tied the hands of reformers, hampering their efforts to adjust and adapt existing social policies to address current fiscal crises. Taiwan's healthcare system and Korea's pension program are on the brink of financial disaster, and government policy-makers have been unable to adequately resolve these fiscal challenges because of political concerns. In instances of social policy innovation and constraint, the democratic imperatives of electoral competition, the politics of social mobilization and the logic of policy path dependency have shaped (and continue to shape) what policymakers can and cannot do. In other words, there is a *consistent political logic* at play here, and it is precisely this political logic that gives democracy a double edge with regard to social policy reform.

The first section of this chapter outlines the origins of universal healthcare in Taiwan and pension coverage in Korea. Section two highlights the sources and severity of the current financial crises affecting these social programs. The third section analyzes the possible policy solutions and constraints that have, for the most part, limited the scope of reform for social policymakers in Taiwan and Korea. The concluding section develops the argument that democracy is double-edged when it comes to social policy reform and welfare state development. This section also draws broader conclusions regarding the countervailing implications of democratic politics, especially for social policy reform.

Origins of universalism

Healthcare reform in Taiwan was initiated during the authoritarian period when the Kuomintang (KMT) party ruled with little political contestation. Social insurance, which included medical care coverage, was initially extended to government employees and military servicemen as early as the late 1950s and 1960s to ensure loyalty among key constituencies and clients of the KMT party-state. Insurance provision was not extended to workers until Taiwan's economic boom years, although coverage remained far from universal, even into the 1980s. Self-employed workers, including farmers, and dependents, including children and spouses, were excluded from any form of social medical insurance. By 1985, only 25 percent of Taiwan's population enjoyed health insurance benefits; the vast majority was forced to purchase healthcare provision on the "open"—and thus inflated—market (Lin 1997; Wong 2004a).

This pattern of gradual and limited reform also characterized the South

Korean experience in pension reform during the pre-democratic period. Pension benefits were first extended to government employees in 1960. Coverage was later extended under separate administrative programs, first to military personnel in 1963 followed by private school teachers in 1973. Just after the imposition of the repressive Yushin constitution in 1972, President Park Chung-Hee proposed to implement a limited pension system for industrial workers (Lee 1997). Kwon (1998) argues that the authoritarian developmental state essentially offered old-age income security to industrial workers in exchange for their political support for the military regime, or more accurately, to guarantee their acquiescence to it. Park's plan was soon scrapped, however, because of rapid inflation resulting from Korea's monetary strategy, which aimed at combating the recession at home and OPEC price spikes abroad. Pension coverage thus remained limited in Korea throughout the 1970s and 1980s. As in Taiwan, the vast majority of firm employees and self-employed workers remained excluded. It was not until the mid-1980s, when Korea's fiscal situation had improved, that the government again considered implementing a social insurance-based model for old-age income security. The National Pension Act was promulgated in 1986, near the end of the authoritarian Chun Doo-Hwan regime. The program was not implemented, however, until 1988, just after Roh Tae-Woo became president in Korea's first direct and open presidential election in December 1987.

The universalization of health insurance in Taiwan and the rapid expansion and eventual universalization of pension coverage in South Korea coincided with the introduction of democratic reform during the late 1980s. Policy-makers and political actors in both places confronted a new set of political incentives, which in turn compelled them to steer social policy reform towards universalism. The logic of democratic politics facilitated welfare reform.

National health insurance in Taiwan

The first step towards universalizing health insurance coverage in Taiwan was initiated by a mass farmers' movement in 1985. Rural dwellers and farmers demanded political reform, and more importantly, greater state involvement in the provision of social protection and social welfare coverage (Hsiao 1994). Taiwan's focus on industrial development during the 1970s and 1980s meant that the socioeconomic gap between cities and the countryside had grown quite significantly, which undermined the KMT's growth-with-equity pact that had, in part, legitimated its authoritarian rule throughout the postwar period. As the ruling KMT historically had depended on rural political support, the authoritarian state had little choice but to respond to the movement. Health insurance was thus extended to farmers, first on a pilot project basis and soon after with the formal extension of medical insurance benefits to the countryside. Taiwan's health insurance coverage rate consequently increased from 25 percent in 1985 to 38 percent three years later in 1988 (Lin 1997).

Around the same time, the opposition grassroots *tangwai* movement formed a political party in 1986, the Democratic Progressive Party (DPP), and the KMT party-state lifted martial law a year later, which signaled the start of meaningful democratic reform in Taiwan. Supplementary elections were extended in 1989, followed by full Legislative Yuan elections in 1992 and a direct contest for the presidency in 1996 (Chao and Myers 1998). Thus, in a relatively short period of time, the ruling KMT party faced the prospect of real electoral competition from a relatively well-mobilized opposition. The KMT could no longer rely on a strategy of minimizing dissent or forcing consent, but instead needed for the first time to actively win electoral support.

The KMT began planning the National Health Insurance (NHI) program in 1986, with a target date for implementation set for 2000. This was a conspicuous policy turnaround for the ruling party; after all, this was the same leadership that earlier had eschewed any efforts to universalize medical insurance coverage, citing fiscal reasons. This was an attempt by the KMT government to solidify its political support in the countryside and win support across the island more generally. The KMT announced in 1988 that it had moved forward the implementation date of the NHI program by five years, from 2000 to 1995, which coincided with Taiwan's first presidential election, scheduled for March 1996. President Lee Teng-hui implored the Legislative Yuan to pass the NHI bill on the eve of its deliberations in 1994 (Wong 2004a).

The KMT's move to universalize the NHI scheme was intended to high-light the ruling party's record in promoting economic growth with equity in Taiwan, to reaffirm the notion that the KMT was the party best suited to continue overseeing the development of Taiwan's economy, and to promote social stability. Universalizing health insurance provision was also a preemptive strategy to co-opt part of the DPP's electoral platform. The KMT ably worked health insurance reform into its own reform agenda, thus blunting the DPP's nominally social democratic credentials. Moreover, the NHI program was expected to be extremely popular; the program's consistently high public approval ratings indicate that this was indeed the case. It made good political sense, under what were increasingly democratic and competitive circumstances, for the ruling party to initiate universal healthcare reform when it did (Wong 2004a).

The NHI program began operating in the spring of 1995. Briefly, it provides universal coverage (97 percent of the population), and includes non-working dependents. It is financed through insurance contributions, which are shared among employers and employees, and government subsidies for self-employed workers. The premium rate was set at 4.25 percent of one's reported monthly income, a *de facto* payroll tax drawn directly from an individual's monthly income. The NHI program is funded through a single-pipe financing stream, meaning that all premium contributions are pooled in a single fund and managed by the public National Health Insurance Corporation (NHIC). This organizational structure is intended to maximize risk and financial pooling. Finally, patients are not restricted in their choice of healthcare provider, although they are subjected to a nominal user or co-pay fee. Under Taiwan's NHI program, direct out-of-pocket payments at the point of healthcare delivery are comparatively low.

National pension program in Korea

The political process by which pension benefits were extended in Korea is not dissimilar to that of Taiwan's efforts in creating the NHI program. As mentioned, the National Pension Act was passed by the Korean National Assembly in 1986, although the implementation of the National Pension Program (NPP) was initially delayed. In fact, the NPP was not revisited until Korea began to undergo democratic reform in 1987, and was then initiated by President Roh Tae-Woo.

The spring and summer of 1987 saw widespread grassroots mobilization in Korea. The opposition *minjung* movement, comprising students, workers, and middle-class activists, took to the streets demanding political and socio-economic reform. Activists contended that the authoritarian state and its big business allies had increasingly betrayed the interests of the common Korean citizen. In this respect, democracy was inextricably tied to socioeconomic reform and the call to redefine citizenship. President Roh capitulated in June of 1987, announcing plans for direct presidential elections later that year, followed by National Assembly elections in the spring of 1988. Roh's announcement marked Korea's democratic opening.

The presidential election of 1987 was very close, with the incumbent Roh winning by only a plurality of votes, while his opponents in the election, Kim Young-Sam and Kim Dae-Jung, effectively split the opposition's electoral support. The 1987 elections ushered in new policy debates that centered on social welfare policy reform, debates that had previously been silenced by the authoritarian ruling party. The NPP reform initiative was part of a larger social policy reform package promised by Roh, which included, among other initiatives, the expansion of medical insurance coverage. Social mobilization ensured that his promises were not empty ones. The NPP was implemented in January of 1988, a few months before Korea's first National Assembly elections, and around the same time, medical insurance coverage was also extended to include rural self-employed workers (farmers). The NPP of 1988 was initially quite limited in scope, covering workers employed in small firms (with 10 or more employees) in addition to those working in larger firms and the Korean *chaebol* sector. Coverage expanded quite rapidly thereafter, first to workers in very small firms (with five or more employees) in 1992, followed by farmers in 1995. Although far from universal, the expansion of the NPP was nonetheless received favorably by industrial workers and farmers, and thus won the ruling party considerable political support throughout the early 1990s. Like the KMT in Taiwan, the ruling party in Korea essentially initiated a social policy about-face to solidify and win over key electoral constituencies.

The second major expansion in Korea's pension program occurred during the late 1990s, around the time of Kim Dae-Jung's election to the presidency. Similar to that in Taiwan, the labor market in Korea is characterized by a sizable informal sector and large number of self-employed workers and employees of "micro" firms (fewer than five employees). Thus, the initial extension of pension benefits to firm-based workers during the late 1980s in effect excluded self-employed and micro-firm workers, who accounted for roughly 50 percent of Korea's labor force (Kwon 1998). In 1997, Kim Dae-Jung ran on an electoral platform that featured social policy reform in health, pension, and unemployment security. Upon winning the presidency, Kim immediately brokered a deal among business, labor, and middle-class activist groups in which corporate lay-offs were allowed in exchange for healthcare reform and the expansion of the NPP. Subsequently, medical insurance funds were integrated to increase risk- and financial-pooling (Wong 2004a), and the NPP was further extended in 1999 to self-employed and micro-firm workers. With Kim's initiative, Korea's pension system became universal in reach.

The universal NPP is managed by the National Pension Service (formerly the National Pension Corporation). The program is organized as an insurance scheme based on Korea's earlier social insurance pension programs for government employees and military personnel. The NPP was designed to "provide high benefits against low contributions" (NPS 2005: 3). The pension system is thus financed through premium contributions, shared among employers and employees. The contribution rate was initially set at 3 percent of monthly income in 1988, necessarily low in order to bring employers (i.e. industry) on board. The premium rate has gradually increased over time and is presently set at 9 percent of one's reported monthly income. Self-employed workers must bear the entire premium contribution. The retirement or pensionable age is currently 60 years. For a pensioner with 40 years of contributions, the pension income replacement rate is 60 percent of the average of her/his income over the course of the entire insured period (as of 1999). Finally, one's pension benefit amount is calculated from the combination of (1) one's average income and (2) a redistributive component derived from the average income of all insured persons. In this way, the Korean NPP is redistributed across income groups and is not simply a forced savings mechanism (NPS 2005).

The political logic

The pattern of universal social policy reform in Taiwan and Korea has been shaped by a common political logic inherent in the practice of democratic politics. First, *electoral competition* in both places compelled the incumbent ruling parties, the KMT in Taiwan and Democratic Justice Party (DJP) in Korea, to universalize social policy. Both parties formulated electoral platforms that featured social policy reform both in response to grassroots political mobilization and to strategically co-opt the reform initiatives of their opposition.

Second, the link between the expansion of social welfare policy protection and the institutionalization of new electoral incentives was further strengthened by the presence of *non-programmatic parties* in Taiwan and Korea. Although both the KMT and DJP had initiated welfare expansion during the late 1980s, these two parties blocked any attempts at welfare universalism during their authoritarian rule. That they effectively ran on social policy reform platforms in the era of democracy reflected the absence of socioeconomic cleavages in Taiwan's and Korea's political party systems. Unlike in Europe, where social class categories tend to shape party ideologies, the KMT and DJP enjoyed a sort of ideological flexibility and political space that enabled them to turn to social policy appeals with few political costs or accusations of ideological inconsistency. This peculiar political logic of social policy reform is relatively unique to these East Asian cases (Wong 2004b).

Third, social policy reform in Taiwan and Korea was driven in part by *bottom-up societal mobilization*. The farmers' movement in Taiwan, followed by the democracy movement more generally, solidified public support for welfare expansion. Public opinion in Taiwan tended to favor welfare expansion over economic growth around the time of Taiwan's democratic transition (Chu 1992). In Korea, the *minjung* movement integrated socioeconomic policy reform into its overall democratic vision. Labor mobilization, along with that of farmers, during the late 1980s was crucial in this regard. Civic groups such as the Citizens' Coalition for Economic Justice were also critical actors in appealing to Kim Dae-Jung to promote social welfare reform in the period leading up to his 1997 bid for the presidency. Simply put, electoral incentives in Taiwan and Korea were linked to societal demands for welfare state deepening, and it therefore made good electoral sense for political actors to expand the state's social policy commitments.

Fourth, the choice of social insurance schemes for the universalization of medical care coverage in Taiwan and expansion of pension coverage in Korea was a function of *policy path dependency*. Earlier policy decisions to create social insurance for government workers and military personnel dating back to the 1950s provided the institutional bases and structures for subsequent social policy innovations. In addition, the gradual and piecemeal nature of coverage expansion throughout the postwar period reinforced this particular policy trajectory. By adding coverage rather than structurally reworking the extant system, the range of policy options was effectively narrowed. Additive reform represented for government policy-makers the reform path of least resistance. They were able to transform the provision of social policy through existing institutions, which lowered the transaction costs associated with wholesale institutional change (Peng and Wong 2008).

Crisis

The successful implementation of the NHI scheme in Taiwan and the NPP in Korea marked a watershed in social welfare policy in each case. Given the conventional wisdom that the welfare state was in decline, the reforms in Taiwan and Korea offered important countervailing evidence. With respect to healthcare in Taiwan, the NHI facilitated redistribution across disparate income groups, especially as utilization rates for healthcare resources grew substantially and disproportionately among lower-income households (Chiang and Cheng 1997). The NHI was also very popular, maintaining a 70 percent public approval rating throughout the late 1990s and into the early 2000s. Pension reform in Korea was similarly beneficial in promoting greater equity across demographic and income groups. The NPP was also a success in terms of public popularity. Both programs, however, soon faced severe financial crises. Declining revenues and rising outlays threatened the long-term sustainability of both social protection programs.

Healthcare in Taiwan

In its first three years of operation, the NHI enjoyed a budget surplus, although the size of this surplus shrank considerably over that period. Between 1998 and 2003, there was only one year, 2000, in which the revenue generated from insurance contributions was higher than insurance expenditures, and even then the surplus for that year was minuscule. Perpetual deficits throughout the late 1990s depleted the government's NHI reserve fund such that by 1999, the NHI reserve posted negative funds (Wong 2004a: 114).

The financial crisis of the NHI was caused by three key factors. First, supply-side pressures increased financial outlays. Because healthcare providers were compensated through a fee-for-service scheme, providers were perversely incentivized to "over-doctor" patients to increase their own incomes. Between 1995 and 1998, for example, the average cost per outpatient visit increased from NT$530 to NT$588, and the average cost for each inpatient case increased from NT$29,418 to NT$34,851, despite greater economies of scale in delivery (BNHI 1999: 188–9). In addition, physicians tended to prescribe treatments that were not listed on the NHI benefits schedule, which enabled them to charge patients directly and at unregulated (and thus inflated) prices. These sorts of loopholes were exploited by various healthcare providers. Hospitals, for instance, were allowed to negotiate drug prices directly with pharmaceutical companies and in turn to sell these drugs at a much higher price than their actual purchasing price. Nearly 50 percent of hospital physicians prescribed four to five drugs for upper respiratory infections per visit, and 10 percent prescribed more than eight drug products per visit. According to a study conducted by the Department of Health in 2002, in only 14 of 103,024 outpatient visits monitored were no drugs prescribed. In other words, 99.99 percent of outpatient visits resulted in at least one drug prescription (Cheng 2003: 68).

Supply-side pressures to over-doctor were reinforced by demand-side waste, even though the initial NHI proposal included several demand-side containment strategies. The NHI legislation, passed in 2004, called for a referral

system by which patients were restricted from visiting more expensive medical centers and hospitals without first obtaining a primary care physician's
referral. In addition, the original NHI program required that patients pay
a larger out-of-pocket co-pay levy based on percentage costs rather than a
flat rate. These demand-side measures were intended to curb excessive and
potentially wasteful utilization of medical care resources. Both measures
were scaled back, however, soon after the NHI was implemented in the
spring of 1995, because of opposition from social movement groups, especially labor organizations (Wong 2004a). Healthcare provision in the NHI
program was therefore made very accessible, with low barriers to utilization.
On the one hand, greater accessibility was crucial for facilitating greater
socioeconomic equity among disparate income groups. On the other hand,
the absence of effective demand-side constraints resulted in excessive resource
utilization rates. People living in Taiwan visited the doctor for outpatient
services on average 14 times per year (as of 2001); the Organisation for Economic Co-operation and Development (OECD) average, meanwhile, was
around six annual visits. This naturally translated into rising costs. Cheng
(2003: 65) shows that whereas Taiwan's population grew by 5 percent between
1994 and 2000, hospital utilization rates—the most expensive level of care—
increased disproportionately by 17 percent for outpatient visits, 56 percent for
outpatient surgery and over 42 percent for emergency room services.

   Both supply-side and demand-side pressures contributed equally to the
challenges of managing spiraling costs and expenditures in Taiwan's medical
insurance system. The NHI also faced tremendous challenges on the revenue
side of the equation, specifically with respect to the effective collection of
premium contributions (Ku 1998). As a social insurance scheme, the NHI's
primary revenue stream was the monthly premium contributions of workers.
Assessing and collecting the premiums of those employed by a company or
the government was fairly straightforward. However, assessing premium
contributions for self-employed workers—who account for roughly half of
Taiwan's entire labor market—was very problematic. There was (and is) no
rigid reporting mechanism to ensure that self-employed workers honestly
disclosed their earned income (Chu 2000). Hence, self-employed workers
tended to underreport their income, and Taiwan's taxation system was unable
to correct for this. As a result, actual premium contributions fell well short of
anticipated revenues.

Pensions in Korea

Financial pressures in pay-as-you-go pension systems are generally felt over a
longer period of time. In contrast to healthcare, where medical care interventions are reimbursed immediately, payouts for old-age pension benefits
are spread over a longer temporal horizon. Nonetheless, Korea's National
Pension Program (NPP) confronted financial shortfalls soon after its implementation. The NPP needed more revenue. Consequently, the pension

contribution rate for employees of private enterprises, which had initially been set at 3 percent of one's monthly income in 1988, was raised to 6 percent in 1993 and increased again to 9 percent in 1998. The contribution rate for individually insured (i.e. self-employed) workers was initially set at 3 percent of monthly income in 1995, but this too was increased annually thereafter, reaching 9 percent in 2005 (NPS 2005).

The Korean government had severely underestimated the revenue needed for the NPP to maintain its benefits commitment over the longer term. Three reasons stand out. First, it made political-strategic sense for the Roh Tae-Woo administration of the late 1980s to initially keep premium contributions low while committing to relatively high levels of benefits. Given the long-term nature of pension programs, this sort of short-sighted financial arrangement could be done. The imperative to raise premium rates would be the next administration's political problem.

The NPP's financial crisis was not solely due to political shortsightedness, however. Demographic shifts also mattered. Policy-makers had greatly underestimated the increase in the population of older persons. In 1980, only 3.8 percent of Korea's total population was over the age of 65, but by 2000, this number had nearly doubled. In addition, the fertility rate in Korea also more than halved, decreasing from 2.83 to just 1.24, during the same time period (KNSO 2005). Koreans are living longer and having fewer children. Demographic projections now suggest that nearly one quarter of Korea's total population will be over the age of 65 by the year 2030. Its population is poised to become one of the oldest in the world, and this demographic shift represents one of the most rapid transformations among all advanced industrial countries. Although the NPP was able to maintain its benefits commitment in the short term, it is clear that the current financial situation makes the program unsustainable over the long run.

Third, income underreporting among self-employed workers has posed a major challenge for the NPP and its financial stability over the longer term. As in Taiwan, self-employed workers account for a significant portion of Korea's labor market. Table 9.1 shows that over 55 percent of those enrolled in the NPP system in 2004 were classified as "individually insured persons," an adequate proxy for Korea's self-employed sector.

Table 9.1 Number of insured persons, year ending 2004

Insured category	No. of insured	% of total
Workplace-based insured persons	7,580,649	44.40
Individually insured persons (self-employed)	9,412,566	55.10
Voluntarily insured persons	77,002	0.45
Total	17,070,217	100.00

Source: National Pension Service. (2005) *National Pension Scheme in Korea*, Seoul: NPS, p. 12.

Korea's weak fiscal institutions have prevented the government from ensuring effective income-reporting and tax collection among self-employed and micro-firm workers. Moreover, the unwillingness of the state to remedy its weak fiscal administrative capacity has exacerbated the financial crises of the NPP. This problem, incidentally, also extends to medical insurance premiums and income tax collection more generally. As in Taiwan, self-employed workers in Korea tend to underreport their income, which creates a perpetual fiscal gap between expected and actual revenues collected through social insurance contributions. Resolving this structural-administrative problem has not been easy, nor has there been sufficient political will to properly address this issue. Institutionalizing a system to accurately monitor and assess the income of self-employed workers continues to be a key policy challenge for policy-makers working on social insurance reform in Korea and Taiwan.

Now comes the hard part: reform constraints

Democracy in Taiwan and Korea has narrowed the range of policy options available to reformers, constraining their efforts to resolve important challenges in healthcare and pension provision. Democratic politics—the imperatives of electoral competition, the legalization of associational life, the reinvigoration of civil society, and the stickiness of prior policy decisions—has made it near impossible for social policy reformers to effectively rectify the issue of financial instability in what are expensive social programs such as health and pension plans. Indeed, democratic constraints have been particularly pronounced when it comes to issues of financing. No one prefers to pay more and receive less.

Adapting the NHI in Taiwan

To restore the financial stability of the NHI, three policy solutions were available to health policy-makers. First, the state could shift the financial burden of the healthcare system to the (quasi) private sector and thus reduce the program's strain on government coffers. Second, health policy-makers could rein in expenditures by implementing cost containment measures. Third, the Bureau of National Health Insurance (BNHI) could raise revenues. Each of these three solutions was implemented with limited success, and always at great political cost to the governing administration.

In Taiwan, the most comprehensive reform option, marketization and privatization, was briefly considered during the late 1990s, specifically between 1997 and 1999. The KMT government drafted new legislation that proposed to create a multiple-carrier system in which the publicly managed BNHI would be one of several competing insurers. Marketization of the insurance system entailed structural incentives for carriers to maximize cost effectiveness. The reform initiative would recast the BNHI as a private, non-profit foundation, thus alleviating the government of its *de facto* role as the healthcare financier of last resort. The marketization and privatization reform effort came at what appeared then to be a fortuitous time. The NHI's continued financial crisis, combined with a more general discourse of welfare state retrenchment (i.e. economic liberalization), offered what seemed to be an auspicious window of opportunity for this specific initiative to be passed in the democratically elected legislature.

It turned out, however, that this was not the case. Civil society organizations—most notably the NHI Coalition, an alliance of over 200 social movement groups—opposed the government's reform proposal. Legislators quickly followed suit. Politicians from all political camps, even those among the governing KMT, moved to oppose or radically amend the government's multiple-carrier reform. Bureaucrats within the Department of Health (DOH) also maintained a conservative "go-slow" position in the debate, signaling their reticence toward the government's reform plan (Wong 2004a). Although the government's proposal was not technically defeated in the legislature, by 1999, the multiple-carrier legislation was mired in competing proposals and faced a groundswell of social opposition, and the reform initiative soon became a dead issue. No subsequent administration has dared to revisit the marketization and privatization reform scheme (Wong 2004a).

Cost containment subsequently became the focus of reform. For instance, DOH officials introduced in 1999 new provider payment systems in an effort to move the NHI away from the fee-for-service scheme originally implemented in 1995. Many believed that the fee-for-service program motivated providers to over-doctor patients, and therefore the gradual use of global budgeting would provide an effective supply-side constraint. Under the global budget scheme, healthcare providers and the BNHI would negotiate on an annual basis the total budget allocation for services rendered in each category of care. In other words, providers were incentivized to keep their insurance claims (and thus, their services) within specified budget allocations. Global budgeting was gradually phased in, despite some opposition from physician groups and hospitals. More recently, the BNHI reduced its allocated compensation for hospital services because of fiscal reasons, which has resulted in tremendous opposition from the politically powerful hospital sector. Hospitals have adjusted, however, by cream skimming—taking on healthier patients rather than those most in need of medical care—and by threatening to lower their overall quality of care provision. Indeed, decreased quality of care is one of the main hazards of any global budgeting system.

DOH officials also adjusted demand-side cost containment measures. Most notably, the government looked to gradually raise co-pay rates as a means to curb excessive utilization. Proponents of this tactic contended that people would be less likely to overuse healthcare resources if they were required to make an out-of-pocket payment over and above the coverage afforded by medical insurance. The expectation then was that co-pay rate adjustments would also increase revenue streams. Reformers anticipated little political opposition to co-pay reform as the adjustments were to be made administratively within the BNHI and the DOH, and thus did not require legislative approval. Moreover, the incremental nature of the adjustments—just a few extra dollars per visit—was thought to be tolerable, especially given the comparatively high levels of access patients already enjoyed. Simply put, this was reform by stealth. However, revenues did not increase substantially and utilization rates did not decrease, in part because the rise in co-pay rates was relatively marginal. Politically speaking, efforts to raise co-pays have met with continual opposition from both politicians, regardless of affiliation, and social activist groups, especially those representing workers and middle-class organizations. Demand-side measures, therefore, have had little effect in ameliorating the NHI's financial shortfall, and come with tremendous political costs.

Generating increased revenues through insurance premiums was another key policy priority. Given the inability of the state to effectively assess and collect premiums from self-employed workers, reformers reasoned that an across-the-board premium rate increase was the only way to substantially increase revenues. Although there was consensus on this particular policy measure, there was little political will to carry out the adjustment. Raising premium rates was a hard political sell. For instance, the initial premium rate of 4.25 percent (of one's monthly income) set in 1995 was based on a five-year actuarial calculation. In other words, the premium rate would have to be adjusted in 2000. According to the NHI Act, the BNHI and DOH reserved the authority to unilaterally adjust the premium from 4.25 percent up to 6 percent without legislative consent. Premium rate adjustments were intended to be a matter of public administration, not political negotiation. However, the original premium rate of 4.25 percent was not adjusted in 2000, as that was an important presidential election year and no candidate dared to propose a premium rate adjustment. Politics mattered more than actuarial forecasts. Chen Shui-Bian of the Democratic Progressive Party (DPP), who won the 2000 presidential election, remained hesitant for political reasons to raise the premium rate even after the election, although the NHI's financial situation continued to worsen.

For two years, political imperatives won out over financial necessity. Only in 2002, after the NHI had posted a deficit for two consecutive years, did the DPP government endeavor to raise the NHI premium levy, increasing it from 4.25 percent of one's monthly income to 4.55 percent. This administrative reform met with tremendous opposition from social movement groups. In addition, the opposition KMT party—ironically, the same party that proposed to privatize the NHI during the late 1990s—attempted to pass a resolution in the Legislative Yuan to reduce the NHI premium rate to the original 4.25 percent. The KMT also demanded that all administrative adjustments be subjected thereafter to legislative oversight. This was a political strategy with little regard for the financial realities of the ailing NHI system. It also effectively portrayed the KMT as the defender of the welfare state, putting the DPP on the defensive. The DPP's modest efforts to adjust the NHI premium rate proved to be politically costly for the government, especially in terms of support from its grassroots base. Hence, the political will to continue premium rate adjustments into the future all but disappeared, even though actuarial forecasts required another adjustment in five years' time. Put another way, whereas social policy expansion made good political sense in Taiwan's democracy, raising the cost burden to maintain social policy commitments was a poor political strategy.

Legislative deadlock in Korean pension reform

The reform logic at play in Korea's pension program was not dissimilar to that of healthcare reform in Taiwan during the late 1990s and into the early 2000s. As with the NHI in Taiwan, the NPP needed to raise revenues and curb expected outlays. As part of its 1998 financial stabilization reform plan, the Korean government scaled back the size of its commitment to old-age benefits, decreasing the income replacement rate from the original 70 percent to 60 percent. This decrease was to be gradually spread out over 10 years between 1998 and 2008. In addition, the National Pension Corporation (now the National Pension Service) decided to gradually raise the pensionable age from 60 to 65 years. This reform effort was not popular in Korea. Still, these NPP adjustments coincided with the further expansion of pension eligibility to self-employed workers in 1999, a measure that was initiated by the Kim Dae-Jung administration. In this respect, the government was able to justify the scaling back of benefits (income replacement rate) and toughening up of eligibility requirements (pensionable age) with the argument that universal expansion in NPP coverage required a new financial formula. Although the reform was not popular, the explanation was minimally acceptable to Koreans. The expansion of coverage to include the sizable self-employed sector ensured that a significant portion of the population would benefit from the reform and thus it was less likely to raise political objections. Kim had strategically tied together financial reform in the NPP with the program's universal expansion, thus minimizing opposition.

Five years later, the Roh Moo-Hyun administration, which was elected in 2002, proposed a new reform initiative for the still financially strapped NPP scheme. In 2003, the National Pension Service posited that the pension income replacement rate needed to be decreased again, from 60 percent to just 50 percent, and that this scaled-back pension arrangement had to be implemented by 2008. In other words, the income replacement rate for Korea's NPP would have decreased from 70 percent to 50 percent in just 10 years. In addition, the Roh administration recommended an increase in the insurance premium contribution rate, from 9 percent of one's monthly income to 15.9 percent by 2030. In other words, the premium rates for firm employees would increase from just 3 percent in 1988 to nearly 16 percent. For self-employed workers, a similarly sized increase would be borne, but in an even shorter time period, from 1995 to 2030 (NPS 2005). Although the financial realities of the Korean NPP system warranted, and continue to warrant, drastic increases in a short period of time, the political fallout from these adjustments has been overwhelmingly negative. This is especially the case given the Roh government's proposal to decrease the NPP's income replacement rate by yet another 10 percent (from 60 percent to 50 percent). The trust of the general populace in the ability of the Korean government to effectively manage pensions has waned considerably.

The Roh government's reform proposal, not surprisingly, met with tremendous resistance. Civil society groups mobilized quickly, and industrial labor movements were energized. The conservative opposition party, the Grand National Party (GNP), mobilized its rank and file within the National Assembly to oppose the proposed adjustments. Interestingly, the nominally conservative GNP came up with a counterproposal, a new NPP scheme that would be financed through general tax revenues. This was a highly unlikely prospect given the state's terribly weak fiscal institutions, but appealing nonetheless. In response, government policy-makers considered splitting the NPP into two funds, one for firm employees and another for self-employed workers. The intention was to force self-employed workers to take greater financial responsibility for their future pensions, rather than free-riding upon the contributions of firm employees. However, because the self-employed sector accounts for approximately 50 percent of Korea's labor market, this reform idea was not politically feasible. For political reasons endemic to the practice of democracy, the hands of government policy-makers were tied. The Roh government's reform proposal was not passed by the National Assembly, and is not expected to gain legislative approval anytime in the future.

Conclusion: democracy's double edge

This chapter has examined the relationship between democracy and social policy. The empirical evidence drawn from the cases of Taiwan and South Korea clearly suggests that there are strong *relationships* between democratic politics and welfare state development. I emphasize the plural for what should now be obvious reasons. Democracy clearly matters in shaping a welfare state, but *how* it matters is not unidirectional, nor is it consistent in its causal effects. Democracy is double-edged in that it can both facilitate social welfare policy innovation and constrain social policy options. What makes this double-edged notion even more compelling in the context of social policy reform in Taiwan and Korea is that the same intrinsic qualities of democracy— the imperatives of electoral competition, the intervention of civil society actors, and the logic of path dependency—account for its facilitative and constraining roles.

First, political competition, specifically electoral competition, restructured the political game in Taiwan and South Korea. The introduction of elections during the late 1980s in both places forced the incumbent ruling parties to adjust their legitimating strategies from those that suppressed dissent to those that could effectively win support. Parties were increasingly accountable for their promises and actions. Vying parties also needed to be more responsive to important electoral constituencies. Appealing policies thus mattered to win electoral support. That the political parties in Taiwan and Korea are non-programmatic in terms of left–right cleavage also means that political entrepreneurs were not ideologically bound to any *a priori* position when it came to social policy issues. Parties could therefore co-opt their opponents' social policy platforms without being ideologically inconsistent or with little political cost, as long as this strategy made good political, and ultimately electoral, sense. For example, this sort of electoral imperative compelled the then ruling parties, the KMT in Taiwan and DJP in Korea, to initiate social policy reform during the late 1980s, and a similar logic led Kim Dae-Jung to universalize pensions in Korea after 1997. Yet, it was also the same impera-tives of electoral competition that tied the hands of policy reformers in Taiwan and Korea during the late 1990s and into the early 2000s, when their health and pensions programs experienced tremendous financial instability.

Second, democratization in Taiwan and Korea has ensured the develop-ment of vital civil societies there, which in turn have played a significant role in shaping social policy reform trajectories in both places. Social mobilization among farmers, workers, intellectuals, and middle-class activists preceded governmental efforts to expand the scope of the welfare state during the late 1980s. Similarly, Kim Dae-Jung's alliance with progressive civic groups, including labor, in the wake of the 1997 financial crisis bound him to signifi-cant social policy promises. However, social activism during the late 1990s forced the KMT government and subsequently the DPP administration in Taiwan to backpedal on their efforts to implement comprehensive cost containment measures in the NHI program. The DPP's initiative in 2002 to raise the NHI premium rate also met with tremendous societal opposition and came with great political costs, so much so that administrations now think twice before adjusting the premium rate, actuarial calculations not-withstanding. Social movement mobilization in Korea, in tandem with the opposition party in the National Assembly, has blocked the government's efforts to adjust premiums and benefits in the NPP scheme, despite the clear fiscal necessity for some adjustment.

Third, social policy reform trajectories in Taiwan and South Korea have been shaped by the interaction of democratic political imperatives and the constraining effects of path dependency. Here I want to distinguish bet-ween two types of path-dependent logic: institutional and distributional path dependency.

The logic of *institutional path dependency* means that earlier policy decisions implemented by the authoritarian states in Taiwan and Korea reduced the number of available institutional options for social welfare design during subsequent efforts in social policy reform. The social insurance model, for instance, was adopted early on in both places, and not surprisingly has persisted into the present period as the model of choice. The social insurance schemes in Taiwan and Korea reflect the legacy of weak fiscal institutions. In addition, the piecemeal nature of expansion from the 1960s through the 1980s institutionalized the extant social insurance structure, as earlier efforts at expansion were achieved through the addition of new groups rather than the total restructuring of the social program. The logic of institutional path dependency was particularly powerful during the period of democratic reform and welfare expansion in Taiwan and Korea. As political elites needed to respond to societal demands quickly, policy-makers tended to favor models that were readily available for emulation. In other words, institutional path dependency was reinforced by the imperative of political expediency. The transaction costs of institutional change were simply too high.

Distributional path dependency in Taiwan and Korea refers to the political mobilization of group interests (and representative interlocutors) for the purpose of maintaining certain distributional outcomes. Drawing on Paul Pierson's (1996) work on path dependency and the politics of welfare state adjustment, I argue that the cases of the democratization of Taiwan and Korea demonstrate how early social policy decisions regarding financing and spending shape people's distributional expectations when it comes to the costs and benefits of social protection. People are extremely sensitive to proposed adjustments in how much they pay versus the amount of benefits they receive. Social policy reformers in Taiwan and Korea have faced various sources of opposition whenever they have looked to adjust their respective health and pension programs. That these distributional coalitions have translated into electoral coalitions, at least from the perspective of the vote-seeking political elites, means that the implementation of certain policy measures, although necessary for the maintenance of expensive social policy programs such as health and pension plans, has ultimately come at great political (or electoral) cost. In brief, under democratic conditions in which people (i.e. voters, groups) have been able to effectively mobilize, the constraining effects of path dependency—both institutional and distributional—have been amplified.

Bibliography

BNHI (Bureau of National Health Insurance) (1999) *National Health Insurance Annual Statistical Report*, Taipei: Bureau of National Health Insurance.

Chalmers, D., Vilas, C. M., Hite, K., Martin, S. B., Piester, K. and Segarra, M. (eds) (1997) *The New Politics of Inequality in Latin America*, Oxford: Oxford University Press.

Chao, L. and Myers, R. (1998) *The First Chinese Democracy: political life in the Republic of China on Taiwan*, Baltimore: Johns Hopkins University Press.

Cheng, T. M. (2003) "Taiwan's new national health insurance program: genesis and experience so far," *Health Affairs*, 22(3): 61–76.

Chiang, T. L. and Cheng, S. H. (1997) "The effect of universal health insurance on healthcare utilization in Taiwan," *Journal of the American Medical Association*, 278(2): 89–93.

Chu, T. M. (2000) "Analysis of financing social insurance in Taiwan," paper presented at the International Symposium on Reform and Perspectives of Social Insurance, Taipei, 29 September 2000.

Chu, Y. H. (1992) *Crafting Democracy in Taiwan*, Taipei: Institute for National Policy Research.

Cook, L. (2007) *Postcommunist Welfare States: reform politics in Russia and Eastern Europe*, Ithaca: Cornell University Press.

Cutright, P. (1965) "Political structure, economic development and national social security programs," *American Journal of Sociology*, 70(5): 537–50.

Esping-Andersen, E. (1990) *The Three Worlds of Welfare Capitalism*, Princeton: Princeton University Press.

Hsiao, H. H. (1994) "Political liberalization and the farmers' movement in Taiwan," in E. Friedman (ed.) *The Politics of Democratization: generalizing East Asian experiences*, Boulder, CO: Westview Press, pp. 202–20.

Jackman, R. (1986) "Elections and the democratic class struggle," *World Politics*, 39(1): 123–46.

KNSO (Korean National Statistics Office) (2005) *Future Household Projection*, Seoul: Korean National Statistics Office.

Korpi, W. (1983) *The Democratic Class Struggle*, London: Routledge.

Ku, Y. W. (1998) "Can we afford it? The development of national health insurance in Taiwan," in R. Goodman, G. White, and H. J. Kwon (eds) *The East Asian Welfare Model: welfare orientalism and the state*, London: Routledge, pp. 119–38.

Kwon, H. J. (1998) "Democracy and the politics of social welfare: a comparative analysis of welfare systems in East Asia," in R. Goodman, G. White, and H. J. Kwon. (eds) *The East Asian Welfare Model: welfare orientalism and the state*, London: Routledge, pp. 27–74.

Lee, S. K. (1997) "A comparative study of welfare programs for old-age income security in Korea and Taiwan," Ph.D. dissertation, Department of Sociology, University of Wisconsin-Madison.

Lin, K. M. (1997) "From authoritarianism to statism: the politics of national health insurance in Taiwan," Ph.D. dissertation, Department of Sociology, Yale University.

NPS (National Pension Service) (2005) *National Pension Scheme in Korea*, Seoul: NPS.

Peng, I. and Wong, J. (2008) "Institutions and institutional purpose: continuities and change in East Asian social policy," *Politics and Society*, 36(1): 61–88.

Pierson, P. (1996) "The new politics of the welfare state," *World Politics*, 48(2): 143–79.

Stephens, J. D. (1979) *The Transition from Capitalism to Socialism*, London: Macmillan.

Weyland, K. (1996) *Democracy without Equity: failures of reform in Brazil*, Pittsburgh: University of Pittsburgh Press.

Wong, J. (2004a) *Healthy Democracies: welfare politics in Taiwan and South Korea*, Ithaca, NY: Cornell University Press.

—— (2004b) "Democratization and the left: comparing East Asia and Latin America," *Comparative Political Studies*, 37(10): 1213–37.

10 Devolution and democracy

A fragile connection

Ledivina V. Cariño

The Local Government Code of 1991 was one of the best legacies of the People Power Revolution of 1986 in the Philippines. As the country chose democracy as the path to development, the Code changed its largely decentralized structure and chose devolution as the road towards democratic local governance. But does devolution necessarily lead to democracy? In analyzing whether this connection indeed exists, I have viewed devolution as an increase in the power of elected local government units (LGUs) and democratization as enhancing popular power, advancing justice and equity, upholding the rule of law, and being accountable to the governed. In an earlier study, I found that the record is mixed (Cariño 2007).

On the one hand, devolution has indeed enabled stronger and more government and citizen action for the public interest. Armed with devolution, many LGUs have devised programs that respond to and address the needs of their constituents while listening to their advice and allowing them space to dissent and criticize as free citizens. Civil society has initiated and supported some of these programs, not only by giving a voice to the citizenry for current tasks, but also by building up social capital for future collective action.

On the other hand, power has been misapplied as local bosses, now operating with less central oversight, have manipulated resources for their particularistic interests. Furthermore, accountability programs and local revenue generation have not been as prominent as new spending, leading to active local governments more dependent on the national level.

In this chapter, I continue that exploration, this time narrowing my study to LGU performance in community-based coastal resources management (CBCRM). In CBCRM, the residents of a coastal community participate in the planning and implementation of programs for the use, distribution, and conservation of their fisheries, coral reefs, and other marine resources. CBCRMs build upon traditional knowledge and community norms as well as scientific findings provided by outsiders such as an environmental non-governmental organizations (NGOs), academic institutions, governmental offices at national and local levels, and, often, a funding agency. Throughout the archipelago, these programs have proven that coastal communities can protect the environment guided by democratic principles. It would seem that

CBCRM areas manifest the Lincolnian ideal of government by, of, and for the people.

So what is the problem? In CBCRM areas, two ingredients for democratic governance are already present: laws enabling people's participation in governance, and actually empowered communities.[1] However, community-based programs are small islands of democracy that need wider societal support for initiation, enforcement, and sustainability. Much of that continuing support must come from local governments. However, and this is the fragile link I alluded to in the title, devolution has not always produced local governments attuned to democratic governance. While democratic procedures are enshrined, elite interests, often represented by local officials themselves, make existing law a tool to suppress the people's initiatives for justice and participation (cf. Peerenboom 2010). This rule of law seems not to allow for horizontal accountability, by which governments are held responsible for violations of its letter and spirit (Chu 2008: 8). Also, the LGUs may regard the people's efforts to democratically govern themselves as a means of diminishing their power as officials. Ferrer and Nozawa (1995: 11) explain this as a power struggle, and ask how "government who basically holds the power (can) facilitate effectively a process that will in effect result in government sharing or relinquishing its powers directly to local communities." However, democracy is power-sharing, in contrast to authoritarian systems where the government concentrates all power unto itself. The actions of a local government as regards CBCRM are thus a proper testing arena for linking devolution to democratization. Where local governments support people power, devolution will indeed strengthen the democratic initiatives embodied in the CBCRM.

This chapter seeks to study if and how local government units have used their devolved powers to advance democracy in CBCRM areas. Local democratic governance is demonstrated by LGUs that wield power to support the rights of their less privileged constituents, promote justice and fairness, especially in resolving conflicts, practice responsiveness and accountability, and foster a long-term vision of environmental protection and human development.

For this purpose, I have conducted a reanalysis of research on the progress and problems of CBCRM. These cover more than 20 individual case studies and eight summative works encompassing more than 300 coastal areas. The CBCRM communities mentioned here have not been randomly picked. Their common characteristics are their access to external funding and support from researchers able to write up their experiences. While my sample makes no claim to be representative, the geographic distribution of the cases is very similar to the national distribution of known marine sanctuary, fish sanctuary, and marine reserve sites in the country as of 2000 (see Table 10.1).

The papers I analyze have been written from the viewpoint of support groups such as NGOs, community development analysts, environmentalists, and natural scientists, i.e. people initially uninterested in devolution. Because

Table 10.1 Philippine marine reserve sites

Area	Total[a] 2000		Sample[b] Various dates	
	Number	%	Number	%
Luzon	113	26	8	28
Visayas	240	56	16	55
Mindanao	78	18	5	17
Total	431	100	29	100

a Crawford *et al.* 2000
b Various: see References

of this, the role of local governments was not their main focus of analysis. Nevertheless, they often discovered that the attitude and performance of LGUs were critical to the success or failure of the program. Thus, the role of local governments frequently became more than a side issue. White *et al.*'s (2007) conclusion is instructive:

> Regardless of how MPAs (marine-protected areas) are established, local support systems need to be in place and functional. Thus, a common thread is the importance of being part of a larger ICM (integrated coastal management) system beyond the immediate community-based MPA. This larger ICM system is the local government planning and implementation framework.
>
> (White *et al.* 2007: 94)

White *et al.* (2007) introduce the benchmark system that embodies the national ICM strategy adopted by the Department of Environment and Natural Resources (DENR) and the League of Municipalities of the Philippines (LMP). The system standardizes the approach that each local government must adopt to support the coastal management effort.

It would seem at first glance that they view the problem as merely technical, necessitating that LGUs simply learn and undertake a set of steps for effective CRM interventions. However, in a later article on best practices for coral reef MPAs, Christie and White (2007: 1054) recognize that approach as merely "instrumental co-management," and point out that "governments have generally not perceived co-management as a means to introduce more democratic principles into fisheries management," adding that "co-management processes that are not attendant to power dynamics and establishment of conflict resolution mechanisms run the risk of breaking down."

I follow this latter lead here, since, as I shall show below, most of the problems CBCRM areas face in dealing with local governments stem less from the latter's lack of technical ability than from their lack of commitment to democracy.

Background: CBCRM areas and the state of the Philippines

The Philippines stands out in the Third World for standing firm on the idea that democracy is its route to development. But between proclamation and performance is a chasm that shows a political system mired in corruption, elite privileges, regulatory capture, and promotion of self-interest. The shortcomings show up glaringly in how the country treats the poor and the environment. Poverty among Filipino families has been decreasing but remains high, falling from 44 percent in 1985 to 34 percent in 2000. The number of poor families has increased by 356,000 between 1997 and 2000. This is because the country still grows at a fast clip of 2.5 percent per year. Even worse, poverty lives amid increasing inequality. The ratio of the average per capita income of the richest decile to the poorest has increased from 18 in 1985 to 24 in 2000 (Reyes 2007).

Nowhere is the state of poverty starker than in the rural areas, where three-quarters of the poor live. Slightly more than 40 percent of all rural families live below the poverty line. Poverty incidence is highest (56 percent in 2000) among families whose heads are engaged in agriculture, fisheries, forestry, and related work (Reyes 2007).

The Philippines is an archipelago of over 7,000 islands and occupies close to 2 percent of the world's total land area. About 60 percent of the population resides in coastal areas. The Food and Agriculture Organization (FAO) maintains that the Philippines is at the epicenter of the world's marine biodiversity, with a higher concentration of species per unit area than its much larger neighbor, Indonesia (One Ocean, no date).

However, as White *et al.* (2002: 1) put it, the Philippines' "18,000-kilometer coastline is under siege." Of 27,000 square kilometers of coral reefs, as much as 70 percent are considered to be in poor or fair condition, with only 5 percent in excellent condition as of 1991. Based on FAO estimates, by 2010, Philippine fish supply will drop from 1.95 million tons to 0.94 million and per capita annual consumption of fish will plunge to 10.45 kg (Indab and Suarez-Aspilla 2004). Illegal fishing methods, over-fishing, siltation, pollution, and mangrove forest and coral reef destruction are major attacks on the environment. Fisheries-related food production has been static despite the increase in the number of commercial vessels, municipal fishers, and fishpond coverage. Municipal fish catch has also been on the decline (White *et al.* 2007). Coupled with a high population growth rate, this explains the growing poverty among artisanal fisherfolk.

Into this breach has emerged the CBCRM movement, in which, again, the Philippines is a leading exponent. Its beginnings can be traced to the marine sanctuary established in 1974 in Sumilon, Cebu, as a research facility of Silliman University. Sumilon is acclaimed internationally for showing that fish sanctuaries improve the condition of coral reefs, increase the available fish, and improve the fish catch in adjacent areas (since the sanctuary is a no-take area) (White *et al.* 2002). The results of these and other experiments increased awareness of both coastal degradation and of programs that can tackle it. Government, academe, international organizations, and environmental groups have since joined in.

By the 1980s, the concern was centered not only on improvements in the environment, but also on the welfare of the people engaged in it. Thus, the management of the marine-protected areas incorporated community development techniques. Generally, a non-governmental organization (NGO) enters a coastal community and delivers an ecological awareness seminar and other types of public education to the people. There then follows a long process of dialogue and community consultation until a core of residents form a "people's organization" (PO) to manage the coastal resource. The PO sets its own rules for fishing practice and coastal preservation, and drafts an ordinance for the municipal council (the local legislative body) to make them binding on the whole community. Its members become "fish wardens" authorized to report and even charge violators. Implementation can be difficult, as most rules include a marine sanctuary with no fishing permitted, the return of captured fish fry, and bans on destructive fishing methods, overfishing, and other practices that the community has used for a long time. Marine sanctuaries pay off in terms of improved coral reefs and reinvigoration of the fishing stocks in the area and the surrounding bay. However, the fish do not return immediately, leading to a period of deprivation, requiring increased commitment to a future orientation. Community commitment and participation are crucial to the success of the movement. Thus, with the technical issues resolved, the movement grows into more democracy.

The Philippines leads the world in creating marine-protected areas (MPAs), although their actual number is not known. Crawford *et al.* (2000) list 431 sites as of 2000. However, in 2006, the MPA Database (CCEF 2006), which purports to be the definitive list, included only 332 sites, of which 306 were municipal-government declared and the rest national. Christie and White (2007) report 312 municipal-government declared MPAs, an increase of six in one year. They also report that among the MPAs the Coastal Conservation and Education Foundation (CCEF) surveyed between 2001 and 2006:

- 131 or 56 percent are at level one (MPA declared) or level two (MPA legally established with management beginning);
- 84 (36 percent) are at level three (MPA enforced for two years or more)
- 20 (9 percent) are at level four (MPA consistently enforced with community and government participation);
- Zero are at level five (MPA sustainability for five years or more).

The low level attained by most of the MPAs indicates the fragility of their existence and of the support provided by LGUs. Considering that MPAs have been in the country since the 1970s, the fact that only 20 have consistent community and government support and none is judged not to have been sustained beyond five years is ominous.

The government responsibility for CRM

Coastal resources management is now a local function. The Local Government Code of 1991 gave to municipal governments the exclusive authority to grant fishery privileges in municipal waters (up to 15 km from the coastline) and to impose rentals, charges, and fees. This allows marine reserves to be established through a municipal ordinance without the need for central approval. Aside from regulatory measures, LGUs can also provide funds for fisheries and environmental management from their 20 percent Development Fund. They can give seats to POs for CRM in the local development councils, one-fourth of whose members must come from NGOs and POs.

The Fisheries Code of 1998 created local Fisheries and Aquatic Resources Management Councils (FARMCs), another multi-sectoral council for local level planning, development, and administration of municipal waters. This body is composed of fisherfolk organizations, NGOs, LGUs, and central government agencies, with the local chief executive as the chair. FARMCs provide assistance in the preparation of municipal fishery development plans, recommend the enactment of municipal fishery ordinances, provide assistance in the enforcement of fishery laws, rules, and regulations, and advise the LGUs on fishery issues. They can also recommend the creation of MPAs in municipal waters. The Fisheries Code provides that a municipality may declare at least 15 percent of bays or any fishing ground and habitat area as a sanctuary where no fishing is allowed.

These Codes have prompted Christie *et al.* (2007) to call the Philippine scheme "the most decentralized marine governance in the world." The statement is not necessarily made in praise, because with bays usually transcending a single LGU's boundaries, the concern of one LGU for its fishers and waters may actually work against the wider interests of coastal management itself. Both Codes allow for this eventuality by recommending inter-governmental cooperation. Yet few local governments have been willing to, in effect, give up some of their powers to make a cooperative undertaking with their neighbors' work.

The performance of local governments in CBCRM

Local governments are expected to play several roles in making community-based coastal resource management work in their territories. These cover passing the required ordinances, enforcing rules and implementing coastal resource management programs, and dealing with conflict and dissent related to these programs. I shall survey the performance of LGUs described in the literature and then appraise the devolution–democracy connection their behavior illustrates.

Enacting CBCRM-pertinent ordinances

All of the sample communities have the municipal ordinance without which the efforts of the people to organize for CRM cannot be enforced. In two areas, ordinances supporting CBCRM can be traced to the strength of the community organizations that were able to get their members elected as mayors and municipal councilors. Led by these officials, the municipal government of Guiuan, Eastern Samar wrote a marine reserve and fishery ordinance which became a model for seven other towns surrounding it (Bersales 1996). Meanwhile, the municipality of Governor Generoso, Davao, banned commercial fishing and imposed maximum penalties for illegal fishing within all 90,000 hectares of its municipal waters. It then implemented community-based fishery resource management with the promotion of indigenous devices which serve both as markers around the 15-kilometer boundary of the municipal waters and as artificial reefs that attract fishes. It also reallocated the municipal budget to support CBCRM, providing for livelihood support and a food security program for fishers and other poor inhabitants (de la Cerna 2004).

Seven others show the leadership exerted by mayors and municipal councils already attuned to community participation and environmental conservation. (1) In Culasi, Antique, the municipal government supported the creation of the Fishermen's Association of Malalison Island, which persuaded the NGO and research institution to choose the area as their project site for the Community Fisheries Resource Management Project. Its municipal ordinance designated a one-kilometer area between Culasi and Malalison as a TURF (Territorial Use Rights in Fisheries) area (Agbayani and Homicillada 1995). (2) In Caliling, Negros Occidental, the LGU passed Municipal Ordinance 96–25 declaring its marine protected area (MPA).This was not a passive activity, because it followed a campaign of public hearings where the officials themselves presented priority issues for discussion and approval by the citizens in attendance (Luchavez 1995). (3) The Sagay Protected Seascape of Negros was initiated by municipal officials. Ironically, they had a hard time convincing the people of its importance, but it is now adjudged as one of the most successful MPAs by a panel of experts convened by the Coastal Resources Management Project-Philippines (Crawford *et al.* 2000). (4) In Donsol, Sorsogon, CBCRM was started in 11 barangays and gained momentum upon the election of a new mayor. (5) Palapag Bay in Northern Samar was the first municipality to have a Coastal Resource Management Council (CRMC). It was established in 1993 after a municipality-wide consultation and was the origin of ordinances instituting marine sanctuaries, formally creating CRMCs at village and municipal levels, and prohibiting the catching of certain local fry. The case analysts attributed the success of Palapag Bay to, among others, "supportive local officials, particularly the mayor, municipal council members and barangay (village) officials," as well as several barangay chapters of FISHERS (Fishermen's Endeavor for the

Rehabilitation of the Sea in Northern Samar), and the national fishers' organization, *Pambansang Kilusan ng mga Samahang Magsasaka* (National Organization of Farmers' Federations, PAKISAMA). PAKISAMA brought lessons from Palapag into the national Fisheries Code which duly mandated the formation of CRMCs (Baritua and Cusi 1995: 59). (6) Ulugan Bay, Puerto Princesa, Palawan incorporated a master plan for community-based eco-tourism in its municipal ordinance. It was championed by the City Agriculturist, the only special mention of a civil servant in the cases. Apart from him, Puerto Princesa authorities also closely monitored the development of the plan (UNESCO-CSI 2002). (7) The ordinance passed under the Sustainable Coastal Area Development (SCAD) program in Prieto Diaz, Sorsogon was a comprehensive resource management plan. Local politicians were active in negotiations, although the analyst thought this support fortuitous and still urged caution in dealing with power-holders (Rivera 1998). These cases all show leadership by local officials who have been committed to environmental issues, even prior to election.

Three cases show the participation of the barangay council along with the municipal government and academic institutions and/or NGOs. These include: the Selinog Island Marine Reserve, featuring the collaborative effort of the governments of Barangay Selinog and Dapitan City (Indab and Suarez-Aspilla 2004); the three-year marine sanctuary management plan of Gilutongan Island (the island's barangays and the municipality of Cordova, Cebu) (White *et al.* 2007); and a marine sanctuary where fishing was not allowed and a marine reserve where non-destructive fishing technologies could be used, which started as a resolution of Barangay San Salvador and moved up as a municipal ordinance of Masinloc, Zambales (Katon *et al.* 1997).

In other cases, local governments did not immediately accept the idea of CBCRM and the voluntary sector and research institutions had to engage in extensive political education and research before they would give their support. Apo Island, being one of the earliest projects, had to show its mettle first, but:

is now a classic example of a highly successful community based coral reef fishery and marine biodiversity conservation project ... due to the collaborative partnership among an organized fisher community, a local government and an NGO academic institution, serving primarily as technical and social facilitator-adviser
(White *et al.* 2007: 99; see also Indab and Suarez-Aspilla 2004)

In Bolinao, Pangasinan, marine science and community development units of the University of the Philippines (UP) considered the municipal government their priority group in training on the concepts and tools of CRM. However, Ferrer *et al.* (1996) cite the difficulty of vesting main responsibility in government, which they claimed had to be reminded of its responsibility and prodded to do the right thing. Nevertheless, Bolinao became a model for another municipality. Puerto Galera, Mindoro became convinced of the benefits of CBCRM and formulated its ordinance only after the municipal council, barangay captains, and other citizens attended a workshop at UP's Bolinao Lab (UNESCO-CSI 2002).

The municipal council of Calatagan, Batangas also balked at first at the demands of community organizations and NGOs to declare Pagapas Bay a marine reserve. However, faced with the results of the rapid rural systems appraisal done by the NGO/PO combined, they even extended the scope of the reserve to cover all of the town's municipal waters (Melgar and Rodriguez 1996). Similarly, Cimagala (1995) reports having to undergo several meetings with LGUs just to generate support for municipal ordinances in Bohol Province, despite the leadership already exerted by its governor.

In the case of Baliangao, two CRM ordinances were already in place before the community-based project began. However, this was solely at the instance of the mayor; the people assented because of "feudal relations within the community" where what the mayor says, goes (Heinen and Laranjo 1996: 18). This suggests that not all ordinances may be the result of a democratic process.

Enforcing and implementing CBCRM

With an ordinance in place, the focus shifts to enforcement and implementation. This requires staff, funds, equipment, and a working enforcement mechanism for coastal resources management. (1) For Bais Bay, the government of Bais City continued the programs of environmental education and mangrove regeneration despite the withdrawal of funding by the Canadian International Development Agency (CIDA). It raised the environmental consciousness of its civil servants, paid community organizers for the CBCRM program, built boardwalks, and donated seeds. It also added two marine sanctuaries, fully embracing the CBCRM program as its own. It now serves as a learning site of the USAID Coastal Resources Management Project (Calumpong 1995). (2) The Gilutongan Marine Sanctuary, now one of the prime dive sites in the Philippines, is judiciously managed by the municipal government of Cordova, Cebu. It has provided funds and personnel for managing the marine sanctuary, for reef monitoring activities, for information, education, and communication for divers and other guests, and for supplies and the maintenance of a guardhouse, anchor buoys and coastal law enforcement patrols. It has also shared diving fees with the barangay council of Gilutongan Island, which, for its part, also funds medicine, alternative livelihood, information, education, communication (IEC), and law enforcement (White *et al.* 2007). (3) Apo and Selinog Islands are successful reserves and models of management, protecting their MPAs from fishers who violate the law. This is traced to strong support from the political leadership, active community involvement in managing the protected area, a clear legal basis, an intensified information and education campaign, and networking between

LGUs, national government agencies, and NGOs/academe (Indab and Suarez-Aspilla 2004). (4) The municipal government of Masinloc "extended visible support through the legislation on marine sanctuary and reserve, mediation in fisher-related conflicts, provision of facilities and equipment for patrolling coastal waters, and extension of financial support to the marine guards" (Katon *et al.* 1997: 23). Even though Masinloc Bay is a protected seascape under central jurisdiction and the Protected Area Management Board is headed by a central official, the Masinloc mayor remained an active member. He sustained project initiatives after the phase-out of the NGO and received a national award for his management of the San Salvador marine sanctuary (Katon *et al.* 1997). All had not been rosy, however, as another account said the LGU was simply a reactive mechanism to citizen demands. Further, the police force allegedly connived with the violators instead of enforcing fisheries rules (Dizon and Miranda 1996).

A program with popular participation as one of its hallmarks requires mechanisms for institutionalizing popular involvement and CBCRM development-planning. Such a council was established in four areas. (1) A Bolinao Marine Sanctuary Committee was created by the mayor and provided with a budget in 1996. It was instrumental in endorsing CBCRM activities in the municipality and in undertaking participatory coastal development-planning (McManus *et al.* 1998). (2) Coastal Zone Management Councils were created in the seven towns of Eastern Samar. Each council was tasked with formulating, reviewing, and lobbying for fishery ordinances in their respective municipalities and making concrete plans for CRM (Bersales 1996). (3) Barili Bay created a stakeholders' forum with government, NGO and PO participation. The forum has addressed resource use conflicts (Gutierrez *et al.* 1996). (4) Malalison also formed strategic alliances between the LGU, academe, the community, and the funder (Agbayani and Homicillada 1995).

Against these positive developments are complaints about the LGUs' lack of political will to enforce rules. This was the experience in Barili Bay (Gutierrez *et al.* 1996), Malalison (Agbayani and Homicillada 1995), San Salvador (Dizon and Miranda 1996), Cogtong Bay (Katon *et al.* 1998), and Sagay (Crawford *et al.* 2000). In most of these cases, fines were either not imposed or were too small to deter violators, a problem even in the success story of the provincial and municipal governments of Negros Oriental (Ablong and Waltemath 1995). Also, the Bohol Sea is not completely protected (despite successes in Apo and Selinog Islands) due to a lack of government support, boundary disputes, and incomplete implementation of the law on the delineation of municipal waters.

The lack of will has been unmasked as due to a conflict of interests among local officials. Ormoc Bay could hardly be protected in Albuera, Leyte, when its mayor and council members were trawl operators (Yap 1995). In Barili Bay, the barangay captain was a commercial fishing operator, and was forced by his constituents to sign a memorandum of agreement instituting a ban on his boat fishing within 3 km of the shoreline (Gutierrez *et al.* 1996). In

Carigara Bay, local politicians hindered the operation of the fishery program of the Leyte-Samar Rural Development Workers Association as a threat to their political standing (Yap 1995). Even in the success story of Palapag, enforcement could not proceed against a violation committed by a relative of a high-level local official and the intervention of the vice governor. This led to the transfer of civil servants from the area (Baritua and Cusi 1995).

Politics rears its ugly head in the poor management of other sites. The Baliangao mayor suspended the implementation of CBCRM ordinances on various occasions in a move to court support from his constituents. However, he became more supportive after dialogues with NGO/PO members (Heinen and Laranjo 1996). Meanwhile, the Barili mayor's membership of a different faction from the provincial governor confused POs seeking support for CBCRM from both leaders (Gutierrez *et al.* 1996). For their part, poor central–local relations affected Mabini and Candijay, Bohol, the municipalities around Cogtong Bay. Since Cogtong Bay is part of the Rainfed Resources Development Project of DENR, the coastal resource management program proceeded with little involvement of the municipal governments. However, they made themselves visible by intensifying tax collection efforts and impos- ing small fines on illegal fishing, using local ordinances which tended to undermine CBCRM efforts and demoralized fishers' association members (Janiola 1996).

Change in political leadership also affected CBCRM operations. The shift from strong leadership to lack of support occurred in Sagay (Crawford *et al.* 2000), Cogtong Bay (Katon *et al.* 1998), Sumilon (White *et al.* 2007), and Calatagan (Melgar and Rodriguez 1996). The new Calatagan mayor did not activate the Resource Management Board and instead asked the group to seek accreditation for membership of the Municipal Development Council. This shows that he perceived the multi-sectoral organization (despite the mayor being presiding officer) as being outside the framework of government rather than one of its major components. The opposite happened in Donsol, Sorsogon when the new mayor provided strong support for the program (World Wildlife Fund, no date).

The municipal civil service may also become a stumbling block for CBCRM implementation. Luchavez (1995) decried "an obstructive, unmotivated gov- ernment bureaucracy" in Caliling, with no policeman assigned to enforcement nor any members of the fishers' association deputized as fish wardens. The government approved a water project, but did not fund it, dooming mangrove reforestation. Instead of administering the program, a barangay official pil- fered pipes. In Pangil Bay, the civil service misinformed the people about cooperatives and almost derailed the establishment of the mechanism for citizen participation (Gauran 1996).

No municipality has followed the example of the provincial government of Negros Oriental, which created a Resource Management Division (RMD) to continue the work of the Central Visayas Regional Project (CVRP) after its termination. RMD is a regular part of the local bureaucracy, with funds, personnel, and equipment provided by the province. RMD, backed up by the governor, continued to support the CBCRM NGO and promoted the program to all the municipalities of the province. Because of its work, Negros Oriental increased the number of its marine reserves from 10 at the end of CVRP in 1992 to 19 by 1996 (Vogt and Willoughby 1998).

Dealing with conflict and dissent

With CBCRM standing for environmental sustainability, the welfare of fishers and popular empowerment, one may be tempted to clothe it in pure virtue. However, as in all programs, conflicts in interpretation and implementation require study, deliberation, and consultation to reach the best approximation of the public interest. Conflicts may arise relative to jurisdiction (at the central, provincial, or municipal level, and inter-municipal boundary disputes), resident versus migrant interests, fisheries versus other economic pursuits, and so on. Effective local governance would be indexed by the ability of local officials to handle conflicts with a view to listening to all sides and determining with the participants where the public interest lies.

Bolinao shows that the community organizations, with their supporters from academe, an NGO, and a funding agency won over the local officials for a point of conflict when a corporation sought to establish a cement plant near the coast. The organizations persuaded the local government to undertake a consultative process in which they in effect trained the officials on how to conduct one. Eventually, the LGU rejected the cement plant. More than that, the municipal council liked the consultative process so much that it adopted the participatory process for other legislation (McManus *et al.* 1998).

The alliance between academe, the community, the funder, and the local government also developed in Malalison after another conflict, this time when the provincial government objected to the original draft ordinance on the grounds that it could be detrimental to other barangays. The draft was accepted and the ordinance passed after dialogue with the barangays and the provincial council (Agbayani and Homicillada 1995). This case shows that an ordinance can also be the subject of objections for public-interest reasons.

Another problem involved the use of *kunay*, a type of beach seine that can be harmful to small fish. The people's organization in San Salvador opposed its use, but kunay owners circulated a draft resolution in its favor. The mayor called a general assembly to resolve the issue and *kunay* owners lost community support (Katon *et al.* 1997).

A major source of conflict—but a great resource if cooperation can be mustered—is the fact that many bays touch several municipalities. As Stuart Green, a Philippine coastal fisheries manager, put it:

> The geopolitical boundaries and way the country's political units are laid out are all wrong for the ecosystem approach! . . . The way municipal governments are all given their own jurisdiction . . . is good for

short-term municipal government-led management, but long-term and larger management will be almost impossible because of the way they are laid out and the sea is divided up into tiny little pockets with very powerful leaders who want to do it their way.

(Christie *et al.* 2007: 244)

Protecting marine areas covering more than one municipality requires not only the basic commitment of LGUs to the environment, anti-poverty, and a vision for the future, but also the ability to give up exclusive power and cooperate with adjacent jurisdictions competing for the same scarce resources. Following Green's prediction, only one inter-municipal agreement seems to be successful. This is the agreement reached in Panguil Bay, which covers 76 coastal barangays in two chartered cities and 10 municipalities in three provinces—Zamboanga del Sur, Lanao del Norte, and Misamis Occidental. The Fishery Sector Program run by an NGO immediately and continuously coordinated all its decisions with LGUs and national agencies from the start of implementation. Decisions involved all levels, from the communities, the municipal/city/provincial governments and national agencies to the NGOs working in the area. The people's organizations all acquired a juridical personality for greater strength in negotiating with governments and for sustainability. In Misamis Occidental, strict enforcement has occurred "upon the insistent demand by the barangay residents, the local government units and the Department of Agriculture." It is not without its problems: for instance, TURFs cannot be implemented due to the lack of local zoning. Still, the municipal/city councils are informed of and involved in all decisions, and this large bay system seems to be working (Gauran 1996: 33).

Other inter-municipal agreements have run into problems. (1) Although its total population is around just 3,000 people, Daram Island in Samar covers three municipalities and 72 sectoral people's organizations, 23 barangay-level federations, three municipal people's organization federations, three municipal-level coastal resource management councils, one inter-municipal council, and a provincial PO federation. The analyst reports continuous negative propaganda and indifference from the LGUs. Moreover, the mayors wanted a share of the NGO's funding; Magpayo also alludes to corruption from the barangay to the provincial level. The problems Daram's Fishery Integrated Resource Management for Economic Development program faced vis-à-vis LGUs were alleviated only when the citizen groups held successful general assemblies at the village level, apprehended violators, broadcast their activities and demands via local radio, and engaged in constant dialogue with local officials (Magpayo 1995).

(2) Batan Bay in Aklan covers five municipalities. Its Intermunicipal Coastal Resource Management Council (ICRMC) is composed of local government officials, national government agencies, NGOs, and POs, mainly fisher organizations. However, the ICRMC has not been active because of factionalism among local government leaders (Lopez-Rodriguez 1996).

(3) After difficult negotiations, the three municipalities surrounding Pagapas Bay in Batangas Province agreed to pass the same municipal ordinance. They further agreed to form the NALICA (Nasugbu, Lian, and Calatagan) Coastal Resource Management Council which the mayors take turns chairing. The Congressman gave the municipalities an equal share of his pork barrel funds for the NALICA CRMC. The NALICA Executive Committee then added the same amount to their budgets from local funds and put up a secretariat composed of the information officers of their respective municipalities. Nevertheless, the CRMC met an early demise. At the presentation of the first year's accomplishments, the people's organization complained that the CRMC had not paid attention to the municipalities' lack of a program and reluctance to apprehend commercial fishing boat owners who intruded into their area. It limped on to its second year, when failures were raised again. The POs looked at problems of implementation "as an issue to be raised against government for its failure to protect the resource and undertake programs to rehabilitate it" while the NGO thought the responsibility should be shared by all stakeholders, and not only by the LGUs as the main protectors of the environment. It was ironic that it was the differing perceptions of the NGO and the POs on the role of LGUs in the program that finally killed the alliance, with the NGO withdrawing from the area (Melgar and Rodriguez 1996: 125).

(4) Bais Bay Basin has a coordinating body composed of two municipalities and Bais City, and has representatives from fishers' associations, women's groups, NGOs, and the three LGUs involved. However, the coordinating body met only once and failed to function as intended due to boundary disputes over Manjuyod and Bais City (Calumpong 1995).

An appraisal of the local governments' role in CBCRM and democracy

If we go by the indicators of democracy posited above, there is evidence of some LGUs using their devolved powers to advance democracy. Some examples show their commitment to the public interest values carried by CBCRM programs, their openness to citizen demands and complaints, their use of transparent and fair means of conflict resolution, and their creation of participatory mechanisms to make CRM work. In a few cases, political leaders showed prior knowledge and commitment to community participation and environmental conservation, or a willingness to learn participatory coastal resource management and to uphold it in their administration. They also shared power with the active citizenry by accepting their draft ordinances, inviting them to consultative councils, and listening to their demands to strengthen their local fisheries and marine programs. In addition, they have put resources into the program, signifying not just nominal acceptance, but an active commitment to make it work. Thus, they have increased the number of marine reserves beyond those started by initiators external to the municipality, drawn up livelihood programs to complement CRM, conducted information and education campaigns to further advance the program, and enforced the difficult rules CRM entails.

However, many more LGUs fall short of using their power to advance the public good, especially after taking the relatively easy first step of enacting an ordinance. The economic and political interests of some have taken precedence over their responsibility to enforce the law. Many officials cannot separate themselves from their family or class connections. After all, to be leaders in a coastal village is practically to have fishing interests. Elite families usually own the big commercial boats prohibited within municipal waters by the new Codes and the demands of the aroused fisherfolk. In other cases, they have lacked the political will to do the right thing, perhaps because the ones to be favored are only small fishers who do not count for very much during elections.

Even when they have shown concrete support for the program, municipal leaders have not paid enough attention to sustainability. They still see CRM as an *ad hoc* program with consultative mechanisms that have temporary lives. Meanwhile, the budget and personnel devoted to it are provided on a year-by-year basis rather than being made an integral part of the municipal bureaucracy. This may sound more like a technical than a political problem. However, the tendency not to use the civil service as a mechanism to advance newly recognized public causes suggests an inability to regard it as also an instrument of power for the public good. Local governments generally fail to wield the civil service as a democratic weapon complementing popular empowerment.

Conflicts are bound to arise in the administration of any program. The instruments used for dealing with conflict and dissent also show a government's commitment to democracy. Where conflicts are resolved well, the LGUs concerned have used a consultative process that gave voice to all sides. A particular kind of conflict that has festered in most cases is the one where power must be shared across jurisdictions. The coordinating efforts made in all cases except Panguil Bay seem to have failed due to disputes over jurisdictions, political factionalism, an inability to form a vision of the public good beyond one's territory, and sometimes, just a surrender to the sheer difficulty of sharing power even with one's peers. This may seem impossible to transcend unless one realizes that the people's organizations that have federated to make the system work are more numerous and have probably given up more to prop up their federations.

On the whole then, there are many positive signs of LGUs using their devolved powers to advance democracy. However, the connection is still fragile, and a lot remains to be done, as the issues I have raised above have shown.

Moving from fragility to strength

I started with the idea that local democracy has been fostered by progressive laws and the active citizenship of the people themselves, helped by the voluntary sector and academe with physical and social technology to protect and properly use their coastal resources. In many cases, the local governments have lagged behind the people in furthering democratic governance in this crucial policy area. The key to this is not only to find supportive local officials in the government of the day, but to change the local governments themselves so that any incumbent government finds it hard to ignore the democratic thrust CBCRM imposes on it. The cases reviewed here suggest a lack of widespread political education, functioning participatory representative councils, strong local bureaucracies, and central support for the devolution regime. All these are needed to move LGUs from fragility to strength.

Political education for democracy

Personal commitment to CBCRM goals has played a primary role in enacting and enforcing CBCRM ordinances. However, the gains of one administration have been reversed when officials not as personally committed to the same values take the helm. What is needed, therefore, is institutional commitment that transcends the terms of office of local officials. This requires political education, not just of incumbent officials, but also of the leadership of the entire municipality from which future officials may be drawn. More comprehensively, inclusion in the educational curricula of the environment and human rights values would produce boys and girls who grow up to be men and women enlightened by dedication to these values. Such political education must also include learning the substance and processes of democracy so that officials are elected not to perpetuate feudal relations but for their policy commitments and public-interested criteria.[2]

Deliberation through multi-sectoral councils

Just as in other important policy issues, the public interest embodied in coastal resource management does not preclude conflicts in the production and allocation of benefits. The interests of fisheries and eco-tourism are not necessarily compatible, as they require different priorities in provision of infrastructure, enabling acts of government, etc. Councils whose members represent different viewpoints can allow for a discussion and hearing of the different views. However, the Philippine record for such multi-sectoral councils has not been very good. Despite the requirement of the Local Government Code, many have not been formed, or when formed, may not meet regularly as required. When actually meeting, they become copies of Congress and the local government councils in that rather than producing comprehensive plans and programs emerging out of a balancing of different interests, they come up with the simple formula of dividing by n, or quid pro quo measures. NGO representatives may even join in this travesty (Cariño *et al.* 2004). Thus, these councils need to be strengthened as actual deliberative bodies with clout. They have to be provided with a regular budget and personnel, training in participatory conflict resolution such as that shown in Bolinao, and the active participation of NGOs and POs to keep officials to their commitments.

Strengthening the local bureaucracy

Many local governments have been confined to the passing of municipal ordinances and occasional enforcement. In rare cases, they assign one or two personnel to CRM, provide them with some funds and buying equipment or supplies according to the demands of the NGO/POs around them. This suggests a perception of CRM as a supplemental program that is not necessary to the regular functioning of coastal LGUs. This contrasts with the example of Negros Oriental, whose sustained efforts in protecting the marine environment has made it a model for other provinces. As Ablong and Waltemath (1995: 46) aver, "Sustainable CRM requires the active support of a permanent office which can be responsible for providing qualified long-term support to the community." Because of this crucial support, the municipal governments of Negros Oriental have been encouraged to set up MPAs. In a smaller way, barangays have also been encouraged by the support of the City Agriculturist of Puerto Princesa City in Palawan.

These instances should not remain isolated. The Local Government Code enjoins that:

> every local government unit shall exercise the powers expressly granted, those necessarily implied therefrom, as well as powers necessary, appropriate or incidental to its efficient and effective governance, and those which are essential to the promotion of the general welfare.

The institutionalization of CBCRM in the local civil service is important for sustaining the commitment and gains already accruing from marine reserves, enforcement of fishing ordinances, and other aspects of coastal resources management.

Standard setting and monitoring by central-level agencies

Devolution is a national policy that is supposed to change not only LGUs but national agencies as well. We have found programs along this line in the area of CBCRM. The Department of Environment and Natural Resources, along with the League of Provinces of the Philippines, has set up an award mechanism to recognize provinces that have shown initiative in pushing for the conservation and enrichment of their marine environment. DENR has also drawn up a benchmarking system with the League of Municipalities of the Philippines. This could be harmonized with the CCEF standard for evaluating MPAs. The suggestion is not for the central government to take over such voluntary sector initiatives, but for it to support them, and in so supporting them, to disseminate knowledge about CBCRM and, if possible, to provide crucial resources so that the NGOs, people's organizations, and funders can further garner LGU support.

In CBCRM, the people have led the way towards concretizing democracy for marginalized fishers and their poor communities. Under the Local Government Code and the Fisheries Code, local government units have received devolved powers that allow them to also deliver democracy to the people. This four-pronged approach will go a long way towards strengthening the link between devolution and democracy.

Notes

1 This is not to say that the people's organizations have no problems. There have been factionalism, members—and leaders—violating their own rules, and instances showing the tragedy of the commons, where many fisher-folks refuse to operate under the organization's norms, but reap their benefits nonetheless.
2 Such political education must include the democratic dispositions: (a) an inquiring and open-minded outlook; (b) being prepared to look at things from other people's viewpoint and to consider their interests; (c) being disposed to respond to differences and disagreements with others on the basis of reason; (d) being inclined to be actively involved in matters of community concern; and (e) being willing to take responsibility for one's decisions and actions (Cam 2008).

Bibliography

Ablong. W. E. and Waltemath, M. (1995) "Establishment of marine reserves in Negros Oriental," in C. M. Foltz, R. S. Pomeroy and C. V. Barber (eds) *Proceedings of the Visayas-Wide Conference on Community-Based Coastal Resources Management and Fisheries Co-Management*, pp. 42–7. Online. Available HTTP: <http://www.co-management.org/rr8cont.htm> (accessed 12 March 2008).

Agbayani, R. F. and Homicillada, W. (1995) "Community organizing and fishery resource management on Malalison Island," in C. M. Foltz, R. S. Pomeroy and C. V. Barber (eds) *Proceedings of the Visayas-Wide Conference on Community-Based Coastal Resources Management and Fisheries Co-Management*, pp. 11–20. Online. Available HTTP: <http://www.co-management.org/rr8cont.htm> (accessed 12 March 2008).

Baritua, J. and Cusi, A. (1995) "Resource management council formation in Samar," in C. M. Foltz, R. S. Pomeroy and C. V. Barber (eds) *Proceedings of the Visayas-Wide Conference on Community-Based Coastal Resources Management and Fisheries Co-Management*, pp. 57–62. Online. Available HTTP: <http://www.co-management.org/rr8cont.htm> (accessed 12 March 2008).

Bersales, J. E. R. (1996) "Coastal resource management: the experience from Northern Samar," in E. M. Ferrer, L. P. de la Cruz and M. A. Domingo (eds) *Seeds of Hope: a collection of case studies on community-based coastal resources management in the Philippines*, Quezon City: College of Social Work and Community Development, University of the Philippines and NGO Technical Working Group for Fisheries Reform and Advocacy, pp. 99–110.

Calumpong, H. P. (1995) "Landscape approach to coastal management in Bais Bay, Negros Oriental," in C. M. Foltz, R. S. Pomeroy and C. V. Barber (eds) *Proceedings of the Visayas-Wide Conference on Community-Based Coastal Resources Manage-ment and Fisheries Co-Management*, pp. 49–56. Online. Available HTTP: <http://www.co-management.org/rr8cont.htm> (accessed 12 March 2008).

Cam, P. (2008) "Educating for democracy," paper presented at the Sixth National Social Science Congress, Philippine Social Science Council, Quezon City, Philippines, May 2008.

Cariño, L. V. (2007) "Devolution toward democracy: lessons for theory and practice from the Philippines," in G. S. Cheema and D. A. Rondinelli (eds) *Decentralizing Governance: emerging concepts and practices*, Washington, DC: Brookings Institu-tion Press and Ash Institute for Democratic Governance and Innovation, John F. Kennedy School of Government, Harvard University, pp. 92–115.

Cariño, B. V., Corpuz, A. G. and Manasan, R. G. (2004) "Preparatory work for the proposed technical assistance on strengthening provincial planning and expend-iture management," report submitted to the Asian Development Bank.

CCEF (Coastal Conservation and Education Foundation) (2006) "Marine protected coast, reef and management database." Online. Available HTTP: <http://www.coast.ph/MPA> (accessed 20 April 2006).

Christie, P. and White, A. T. (2007) "Best practices for improved governance of coral reef marine protected areas," *Coral Reefs*, 26(4):1047–56.

Christie, P., Fluharty, D. L., White, A. T., Eisma-Osorio, L. and Jatulan, W. (2007) "Assessing the feasibility of ecosystem-based fisheries management in tropical contexts," *Marine Policy*, 31: 239–50.

Chu Y. H. (2008) "East-Asia's struggling democracies: a view from the citizens," paper presented at the Conference on the Experiments with Democracy in East and Southeast Asia: Two Decades After, organized by the Centre of Asian Studies, University of Hong Kong, 2–3 May 2008.

Cimagala, C. T. (1995) "Wildlife protection and conservation: the Tahong-Tahong experience," in C. M. Foltz, R. S. Pomeroy and C. V. Barber (eds) *Proceedings of the Visayas-Wide Conference on Community-Based Coastal Resources Management and Fisheries Co-Management*, pp. 29–33. Online. Available HTTP: <http://www.co-management.org/rr8cont.htm> (accessed 12 March 2008).

Crawford, B., Balgos, M. and Pagdilao, C. R. (2000) "Community-based marine sanc-tuaries in the Philippines: a report of focus group discussions," Coastal Resources Center, University of Rhode Island and Philippine Council for Marine and Aquatic Research and Development.

de la Cerna, J. (2004) "Philippines, municipality of Governor Generoso, Province of Davao Oriental, community-based ecological enterprise through participatory governance of municipal waters," Online. Available HTTP: <http://www.toolkitparticipation.nl/cases/81> (accessed 12 March 2008).

Dizon, J. C. A. M. and Miranda, G. C. (1996) "The coastal resource management experience in San Salvador Island," in E. M. Ferrer, L. P. de la Cruz and M. A. Domingo (eds) *Seeds of Hope*, Quezon City: College of Social Work and Com-munity Development, University of the Philippines and NGO Technical Working Group for Fisheries Reform and Advocacy, pp. 129–58.

Ferrer, E. M. and Nozawa, C. M. C. (1995) "Community in the Philippines: key concepts, methods and lessons learned." Online. Available HTTP: <http://idrinfo.idrc.ca/archive/corpdocs/121922/Key-concepts.htm> (accessed 12 March 2008).

Ferrer, E. M., McManus, L. T., de la Cruz, L. P and Cadavos, A. G. (1996) "The Bolinao community-based coastal resource management project (initial phase):

towards an interdisciplinary approach," in E. M. Ferrer, L. P. de la Cruz and M. A. Domingo (eds) *Seeds of Hope*, Quezon City: College of Social Work and Community Development, University of the Philippines and NGO Technical Working Group for Fisheries Reform and Advocacy, pp. 159–86.

Gauran, D. T. (1996) "Fishery sector program—community-based coastal resource management in Panguil Bay, Mindanao," in E. M. Ferrer, L. P. de la Cruz and M. A. Domingo (eds) *Seeds of Hope*, Quezon City: College of Social Work and Community Development, University of the Philippines and NGO Technical Working Group for Fisheries Reform and Advocacy, pp. 23–8.

Gutierrez, J. S., Rivera, R. A. and de la Cruz, Q. L. (1996) "The sustainable coastal area development program in Barili, Cebu," in E. M. Ferrer, L. P. de la Cruz and M. A. Domingo (eds) *Seeds of Hope*, Quezon City: College of Social Work and Community Development, University of the Philippines and NGO Technical Working Group for Fisheries Reform and Advocacy, pp. 83–98.

Heinen, A. and Laranjo, A. (1996) "Marine sanctuary establishment: the case of Baliangao Wetland Park in Danao Bay," in E. M. Ferrer, L. P. de la Cruz and M. A. Domingo (eds) *Seeds of Hope*, Quezon City: College of Social Work and Community Development, University of the Philippines and NGO Technical Working Group for Fisheries Reform and Advocacy, pp. 3–20.

Indab, J. D. and Suarez-Aspilla, P. B. (2004) "Community-based marine protected areas in the Bohol (Mindanao) Sea, Philippines," *NAGA, WorldFish Center Quarterly*, 27(1): 4–8.

Janiola, E., Jr. (1996) "Mangrove rehabilitation and coastal resource management in Cogtong Bay: addressing mangrove management issues through community participation," in E. M. Ferrer, L. P. de la Cruz and M. A. Domingo (eds) *Seeds of Hope*, Quezon City: College of Social Work and Community Development, University of the Philippines and NGO Technical Working Group for Fisheries Reform and Advocacy, pp. 49–66.

Katon, B. M., Pomeroy, R. S. and Salamanca, A. (1997) *The Marine Conservation Project for San Salvador: a case study of fisheries co-management in the Philippines*, Manila: International Center for Aquatic Living Resources (ICLARM) and Haribon Foundation.

Katon, B. M., Pomeroy, R. S., Ring, M. W. and Garces, L. (1998) *Mangrove Rehabilitation and Coastal Resource Management Project of Mabini-Sandijay: a case study of fisheries co-management arrangements in Cogtong Bay, Philippines*, International Center for Living Aquatic Resources Management. Online. Available HTTP: <http://www.co-management.org/download/working/wp33/content.pdf> (accessed 26 March 2008).

Lopez-Rodriguez, L. (1996) "The fishers of Talangban: women's roles and gender issues in community-based coastal resources management," in E. M. Ferrer, L. P. de la Cruz and M. A. Domingo (eds) *Seeds of Hope*, Quezon City: College of Social Work and Community Development, University of the Philippines and NGO Technical Working Group for Fisheries Reform and Advocacy, pp. 67–82.

Luchavez, T. F. (1995) "Ecosystems rehabilitation and resource management in Caliling, Negros Occidental," in C. M. Foltz, R. S. Pomeroy and C. V. Barber (eds) *Proceedings of the Visayas-Wide Conference on Community-Based Coastal Resources Management and Fisheries Co-Management*, pp. 22–8. Online. Available HTTP: <http://www.co-management.org/rr8cont.htm> (accessed 12 March 2008).

McManus, L. T., Yambao, A. C., Salmo III, S. and Aliño, P. (1998) "Participatory coastal development planning in Bolinao, Northern Philippines: a potent tool for conflict resolution," International Workshop on Community-Based Natural Resource Management. Washington DC, United States, May 1998. Online. Available HTTP: <http://srdis.ciesin.columbia.edu/cases/Philippines-Paper.html> (accessed 12 March 2008).

Magpayo, N. P. (1995) "Fishery integrated resource management for economic development (FIRMED)," in C. M. Foltz, R. S. Pomeroy and C. V. Barber (eds) *Proceedings of the Visayas-Wide Conference on Community-Based Coastal Resources Management and Fisheries Co-Management*, pp. 63–8. Online. Available HTTP: <http://www.co-management.org/rr8cont.htm> (accessed 12 March 2008).

Melgar, M. and Rodriguez, M. (1996) "The formation of Coastal Resource Management Council for the CBCRM of Pagapas Bay," in E. M. Ferrer, L. P. de la Cruz and M. A. Domingo (eds) *Seeds of Hope*, Quezon City: College of Social Work and Community Development, University of the Philippines and NGO Technical Working Group for Fisheries Reform and Advocacy, pp. 115–28.

One Ocean (no date) "The Philippine marine biodiversity." Online. Available HTTP: <http://www.oneocean.org/flash/philippine_biodiversity.html> (accessed 29 March 2008).

Peerenboom, R. (2010) "Rule of law and democracy: lessons for China from Asian experiences," this volume.

Reyes, C. M. (2007). *An Initial Verdict on our Fight against Poverty*, Makati City: Philippine Institute for Development Studies, Research Paper Series No. 2007–02.

Rivera, R. (1998) "Re-inventing power and politics in coastal communities: a case study on the Sustainable Coastal Area Development (SCAD) Program in Prieto Diaz, Bicol, Philippines," *The World Bank/WBI's CBNRM Initiative*. Online. Available HTTP: <http://srdis.ciesin.columbia.edu/cases/phiippines-005.html> (accessed 12 March 2008).

UNESCO-CSI (2002) "Environment and development in coastal regions and in small islands." Online. Available HTTP: <http://www.unesco.org/csi/act/other/philippi.htm> (accessed 12 March 2008).

Vogt, H. P. and Willoughby, N. (1998) "Involving fishing communities in marine protected area development: the establishment of marine reserves in Negros Oriental, Philippines." Online. Available HTTP: <http://srdis.ciesin.columbia.edu/cases/philippines-001.html> (accessed 12 March 2008).

White, A. T., Salamanca, A. and Courtney, C. A. (2002) "Experience with coastal and marine protected area planning and management in the Philippines." Online. Available HTTP: <http://pdf.usaid.gov/pdf_docs/PNACM048.pdf> (accessed 12 March 2008).

White, A. T., Gomez, E., Alcala, A. C. and Russ, G. (2007) "Evolution and lessons from fisheries and coastal management in the Philippines," in T. McClanahan and J. C. Castilla (eds) *Fisheries Management: progress toward sustainability*, Oxford: Blackwell, pp. 88–111.

World Wildlife Fund (no date) "Community-based tourism program, Donsol, Sorsogon."

Yap, N. (1995) "Community organizing in Leyte: The Labrador experience," in C. M. Foltz, R. S. Pomeroy and C. V. Barber (eds) *Proceedings of the Visayas-Wide Conference on Community-Based Coastal Resources Management and Fisheries Co-Management*. Online. Available HTTP: <http://www.co-management.org/rr8cont.htm> (accessed 12 March 2008), pp. 69–72.

11 Rule of law and democracy

Lessons for China from Asian experiences [1]

Randall Peerenboom

Foreign leaders, academics and pundits often suggest that the successful democracies in Asia, such as Taiwan, may provide inspiration for China. On the contrary, Chinese leaders and citizens are not likely to be inspired by what they see elsewhere in Asia or other regions. Rather, they are more likely to conclude that the best approach is to continue to follow the "East Asian Model" and postpone democratization until the country is richer and more stable.[2]

This chapter suggests that the quality of democracy—as measured by economic growth, political stability, institutional development, human rights protection and other indicators of human well-being—is relatively low in low- and middle-income Asian democracies. Although it is generally higher in high-income countries, even in the rich countries there are significant problem areas. Most notably, there are serious shortcomings in rule of law, institutionalized "grand corruption," and a tendency toward an excessively powerful executive branch insufficiently constrained by institutional checks and balances.

Moreover, describing East Asian democracies as "liberal democracies" is conceptually confusing and obscures important differences. East Asian states, particularly those with a Confucian influence, are generally less liberal than the average in their income class at all levels of income (Peerenboom 2007: 42–3, 67–9). Even the established democracies in Taiwan, South Korea, and Japan are less liberal than democracies in Euro-America (Peerenboom *et al.* 2006). All three are rights-based as opposed to majoritarian democracies in that they take rights seriously, but rights are often interpreted in more collective or communitarian ways than in the preferred way of Euro-American liberals, which emphasizes individual autonomy and freedom. Whether described as collectivist, communitarian, or in some other way, Asian democracies deserve their own distinctive label(s).

Legal reforms, economic growth, and democratization

Rule of law and democracy tend to be mutually reinforcing.[3] However, rule of law need not necessarily march in lockstep with democracy, and in Asia and the Middle East, several of the legal systems that score highest in terms of rule of law are not democracies, or are illiberal democracies. Singapore and even more clearly Hong Kong show that liberal democracy, or even a nonliberal version of democracy, is not a precondition for a legal system that generally complies with the requirements of a thin rule of law. Despite the limitations on democracy, the use of the legal system to suppress opposition, a nonliberal interpretation on many rights issues, and a two rating on the zero to ten Polity IV scale, Singapore's legal system is regularly ranked as one of the best in the world. It was ranked in the top ninety-ninth percentile on the World Bank rule of law index in 1996, and in the ninety-third percentile in 2002. By way of broad comparison, the U.S. and the average OECD rankings were in the ninety-first to ninety-second percentiles for 1996 and 2002.

Like Singapore, Hong Kong has a well-developed legal system that is largely the product of British colonialism. Until the handover to the PRC in 1997, the system was widely considered to be an exemplar of rule of law, notwithstanding the lack of democracy and a restricted scope of individual rights under British rule. After the handover, the legal system continues to score highly on the World Bank rule of law index, with only a slight drop from 90.4 in 1996 to 86.6 in 2002.

Among Arab countries, Oman, Qatar, Bahrain, Kuwait, and the United Arab Emirates are in the top quartile on the World Bank rule of law index, but have a zero ranking on the Polity IV index.

Conversely, just as non-democracies may have strong rule of law legal systems, democracies may have legal systems that fall far short of rule of law. Guatemala, Kenya, and Papua New Guinea, for example, all score highly on democracy (8–10 on the Polity IV index) and yet poorly on rule of law (below the twenty-fifth percentile on the World Bank rule of law index). Eight other countries receive an 8–10 score on the Polity IV index and yet score below the fiftieth percentile of countries on rule of law, including the Philippines.

Moreover, both democracy and rule of law are clearly related to wealth. Empirical studies have yet to sort out the complicated causal ways in which democracy, rule of law, and wealth interact to support each other.[4] However, one of the striking features of the successful transitions in Taiwan, South Korea, and, until recently, Thailand is that the transition to democratization has come only after economic growth reached relatively high levels.

In contrast, those countries that have attempted to democratize at lower levels have generally failed in the past, often reverting to authoritarianism. Indonesia tried democracy between 1950 and 1957, just after independence from the Dutch. The experiment ended when Sukarno declared martial law. Thailand went through numerous cycles of democratic elections followed by military-led coups—there have been nearly twenty coups attempts since 1932, including one in 2005 that pushed out the populist billionaire Thaksin and was followed by civil demonstrations that brought down two governments led by Thaksin associates, resulting in the fifth head of state in two years.

South Korea held elections in the 1960s and early 1970s before returning to authoritarian rule. The less-than-successful experiments with democracy in the Philippines from 1935 led to Marcos declaring martial law in 1972. Further south, General Zia reclaimed power in Bangladesh in 1975 when the democratically elected government was unable to make good on its promise of rapid development. Adopting neoliberal economic principles and promising rapid economic growth, Zia himself won the 1978 elections in a landslide. However, he was replaced by General Ershad in 1982.

Nowadays, those states that have attempted elections at low levels of wealth and with weak institutions continue to limp along with low levels of economic development, pressing social order problems and massive discontent over the political system, as in the Philippines, Indonesia, India, Cambodia, Bangladesh, Nepal, and now Timor-Leste.

The experience of Asian countries is consistent with the experience of many countries elsewhere. As Pinkney points out:

> What is remarkable is that almost all third world countries have had at least nominally pluralist political systems at some time in their history, yet the majority did not (or could not) build on these to establish durable forms of democracy.
>
> (Pinkney 2003: 65)

Empirical studies demonstrate that democracies are unstable at relatively low levels of wealth (Barro 1996; Przeworski *et al.* 2000). Poor democracies are particularly vulnerable to economic downturns. The longer the economic decline, the more likely the regime is to fail. Economic difficulties also adversely affect authoritarian regimes, but to a lesser degree. Democracies are also more sensitive to overall income inequality. And whereas both democracies and authoritarian regimes are threatened when the rich get richer, in general, only democracies are threatened when the poor get poorer (see also Boix and Stokes 2003).

That wealth matters does not mean that there is a particular point at which countries necessarily become democratic. There have been and still are rich authoritarian or semi-democratic states in Asia and elsewhere. Obviously, many countries have become democratic at very low levels of wealth. And while per capita income is the best predictor of the survivability of democracies, a few countries have managed to sustain democracy against the odds, including India, Costa Rica, Mauritius, Botswana, Jamaica, Trinidad and Tobago, and Papua New Guinea. Other than India, these are all small countries with populations of less than five million, several having less than one million citizens. With some exceptions, they tend to be relatively wealthy by developing country standards, to have distributed wealth reasonably equitably, and to have invested in human capital and effective institutions.

Of course, not all authoritarian systems have succeeded in achieving economic growth, implementing rule of law, or making progress on human rights and other indicators of human well-being. Whether cause or result, most very poor countries are authoritarian.[5] As neither poor authoritarian regimes nor poor democratic ones are particularly good at ensuring growth, perhaps there is no need for a tradeoff between democracy and development.[6] If faced with a choice between a bad democratic government and a bad authoritarian one, most people would no doubt opt for a bad democratic one. Authoritarianism is certainly more risky. You are more likely to get miracles or disasters. Of the regimes that grew at an average rate of 7 percent per year for at least ten years between 1950 and 1990, all were authoritarian except for the Bahamas (where tourism, money-laundering, and tax-haven revenues provided high per capita growth, albeit for a small population). On the other hand, 8 of the 10 countries with the lowest growth rates over a 10-year period were also authoritarian (Przeworksi *et al.* 2000: 176–7).

Chinese and other Asians need not be reminded that authoritarian regimes can go badly astray. Laos, Myanmar, and North Korea are unfortunate reminders of this possibility. At minimum, successful reforms require governments that are willing to invest in institutions and people, sound economic policies, and some luck. But we do not need to base our assessment of China on general empirical studies or a blind choice between an authoritarian regime likely to produce miraculous growth and one likely to fail miserably. There is a 25 year track record for China, and an even longer track record for Japan and the other Asian tigers. Fortunately for Chinese citizens, China is following the path of Japan, South Korea, Taiwan, Hong Kong, and Singapore—not Laos, Myanmar, and North Korea, or for that matter the Philippines, Indonesia, Cambodia, Bangladesh, and India.

Democracy in Asia: inspiration or warning?

"Messy" elections

The affirmative view of democracy places a great deal of faith in elections as a means of holding government officials accountable, resolving social conflicts, and addressing social justice through the empowerment of the least well-off. Anyone who believes most Chinese citizens are likely to see elections as the answer to their problems based on the experiences of Asian countries should think again. Elections, while providing scandal for the media, hardly inspire confidence or match the inflated rhetoric about the ability of democracy to hold government officials accountable or allow citizens to pursue their own personal version of human flourishing. Recent presidential elections in Asia have been particularly disheartening.

In the 2004 elections in Taiwan, Chen Shui-bian seemed willing to risk confrontation with China just to stay in office, continually challenging Beijing and Washington with calls for a national referendum and constitutional changes, despite stern warnings from Beijing and Washington to avoid further provocation. Even close observers of Taiwanese politics—used to, as they are, fisticuffs and chair-throwing by members of the legislature—were shocked by the dirty politics in which the KMT compared Chen to Hitler, and then the bizarre shooting of the president and vice president by a slow-moving bullet on the day before elections (Lawrance 2004). Capitalizing on the sympathy vote from the shooting, Chen claimed victory by less than 30,000 votes out of a total of 13.3 million. After weeks of protests and demonstrations, both peaceful and otherwise, by supporters of the LDP, Chen was finally sworn into office, where he presided over a deeply divided public. With his poll numbers plummeting as the economy faltered and his party embroiled in corruption scandals, Chen continued to test the waters and the patience of Washington and Beijing by taking a series of small steps toward independence. His party was then overwhelmingly defeated in the next election where both party heads had been formally charged with corruption and misuse of government funds. The winner, Ma Ying-jeou, was ultimately acquitted, as the practice for which he was charged was a long-standing and widely accepted one. Former president Chen and other LPP members, however, have been less fortunate. The large number of LPP prosecutions has led to claims of politicization of the legal system and unflattering comparisons of the current LDP administration to its more dictatorial predecessors.

In the Philippines, where former actor Joseph Estrada was impeached and forced out of office after being linked to illegal payoffs from gambling lords, President Arroyo squared off against another leading film actor, Fernando Poe, a high school drop-out who had never held public office, although he did once play a town mayor in the movies. Poe studiously avoided the issues in a campaign long on symbolism and short on substance on the part of both candidates. Just over one year later, President Arroyo herself faced impeachment over alleged election fraud and corruption. Former president and estranged ally Corazon Aquino led the demonstrations in the streets. Although Arroyo's control of the House of Representatives allowed her to survive the impeachment vote, polls showed 8 out of 10 Filipinos no longer trusted her and 7 out of 10 wanted her impeached. A few months later, Arroyo declared a state of emergency after she survived the third coup attempt of her five years in office.

Meanwhile, in South Korea, President Roh was impeached on charges of illegal campaigning, corruption among his aides, and mismanagement of the economy, before being acquitted and reinstated. However, his subsequent attempt to replace several cabinet members without following constitutional procedures gave rise to complaints of amateurism and unflattering comparisons to the heavy-handed ways of former dictators. He remained in office until 2008 when he was succeeded by Lee Myung-bak. Within months, Lee's pro-U.S., pro-free-market policies led to the largest demonstrations in two decades, plummeting poll ratings, and offers of resignation from his entire cabinet.

The 2004 presidential elections in Indonesia featured two former military men. One of them, General Wiranto, the head of Suharto's former Golkar

Party, stood accused of being a war criminal for his role in East Timor. Far from being disqualifying, the accusations seem to have caused some Indonesians to support him in a show of nationalist resistance to foreign pressure. In the final runoff, former General Susilo Bambang Yodhoyono won in a landslide over the incumbent Megawati, who failed during her tenure to resolve domestic security issues, reduce corruption, or meet heightened expectations for social justice.

In India, the voters threw out the BJP despite a growth rate of 8 percent, opting instead for the Congress Party led by the Italian-born Sonia Gandhi, widow of the assassinated former Prime Minister Rajiv Gandhi—who then promptly decided not to take office. The ensuing turmoil caused the single biggest one-day drop in the stock markets ever, although the markets recovered when Gandhi named an economist known for his market-orientation to head her party. The elections—marred by the deaths of over twenty women and children in a stampede to secure sarees, a bomb that killed 11 people attending a political rally in Kashmir followed by boycotts of the polls by separatist militants, the murder of 26 policemen by Maoist guerillas in Jharkhand, the shooting deaths of three political party members in Bihar, and the usual charges of rampant vote-buying—were described as relatively clean and successful by Indian standards (*Economist* 2004).

In Nepal, the problems go beyond mere messy elections. A Maoist insurgency, one of the lowest levels of economic development in Asia, and an unstable monarchy have all hindered democratic consolidation. Real-life events, as reported by the CIA, read like the desperate attempts of Hollywood screenwriters to come up with novel plot lines in this jaded age of weary worldliness:

> In 2001, the crown prince massacred ten members of the royal family, including the king and queen, and then took his own life. In October 2002, the new king dismissed the prime minister and his cabinet for "incompetence" after they dissolved the parliament and were subsequently unable to hold elections because of the ongoing insurgency. While stopping short of reestablishing parliament, the king in June 2004 reinstated the most recently elected prime minister who formed a four-party coalition government, which the king subsequently tasked with paving the way for elections to be held in spring of 2005. Citing dissatisfaction with the government's lack of progress in addressing the Maoist insurgency, the king in February 2005 dissolved the government and assumed power in the Kingdom.
>
> (CIA 2005)

Following massive demonstrations, parliament was reconvened in 2007. After two postponements due in part to uprisings, elections in 2008 swept the Maoist rebels, considered by many to be terrorists, into power. The Maoists' decision to end the monarchy, supported by many, led to bombings by royalists.

Democracy proponents often argue in the face of poor economic performance, massive demonstrations, calls for regime change, and elections marred by violence and vote-buying, that democracy is "messy" (Lawrance 2004; Gilley 2004). However, the same apologists for democracy are quick to criticize every shortcoming under an authoritarian regime, and to call for immediate elections as a solution. One can only imagine the scorn that would be heaped on anyone so bold as to offer in response to political violence, widespread corruption, and other social maladies in authoritarian states, the limp excuse that "authoritarianism is messy." At minimum, the performance of both democratic and non-democratic regimes should be scrutinized and evaluated objectively and without bias.

Disappointing results, especially in countries that democratized at low levels of wealth

In turning from elections to the actual performance of Asian democracies, Chinese leaders and citizens are likely to draw three conclusions. First, based on the dismal performance of countries that have attempted to democratize at low levels of wealth both in the past and more recently, for China to democratize now would be folly given the current level of wealth and the lack of other conditions generally associated with successful consolidation.

Far from being an inspiration, India is generally seen as a warning of what happens when countries democratize prematurely. Compared to China, India is poorer, less politically stable, and generally perceived as more corrupt, chaotic, and poorly governed. Fairly or not, many Chinese attribute the differences largely to democracy. The *Economist* summarized the ills besetting Indian democracy as follows:

> not just . . . constituencies handed down like family heirlooms; but also . . . venal, sometimes thuggish and often outright criminal candidates; . . . parties appealing not on the basis of policies but of narrow regional or caste interests; . . . coalitions formed not out of like-minded ideologies but out of naked power-seeking.
>
> (*Economist* 2004)

Scholars often wonder how India has managed to sustain democracy. Part of the explanation seems to be that the state is too weak to overcome the various centers of power and no single group is sufficiently powerful to dominate the others. However, as Lele and Quadir note:

> The literature on democracy and development . . . rarely mentions the most obvious and perhaps the only necessary condition for the survival of formal democracy. It can survive and thrive anywhere as long as it protects the interests of the entrenched and dominant classes and as long

as they can hold economic, political and ideological sway over the subaltern classes.

(Lele and Quadir 2004: 3)

Whatever the explanation, democracy has not addressed pressing issues of extreme poverty for many citizens, led to a just and efficient legal system, or put an end to ethnic conflicts, religious tensions, or caste-based discrimination.

Nor are the Chinese likely to be inspired by the Philippines. The government is notoriously weak, corrupt, and inept. The country is politically unstable. Democracy remains elitist. Effective participation by citizens is limited (Angeles 2004; Rocamora 2004). Political parties are weak and lack a coherent ideology, with members jumping ship as their fortunes change. Parties "revolve around political stars rather than around ideologies. They nurture networks of followers or supporters who are dependent on them for money, jobs, favors or political access, not party members loyal to party principles . . ." (David 1994: 24–5).

In Indonesia, the nature of democracy is contested, with the debates fragmented and confused (Lindsey 2004: 312). There is no consensus on what the purpose or purposes of the state should be. Significant differences separate Islamists (with a wide range of views within the Muslim community), labor, liberal democratic supporters of the IMF vision, and nationalists who see legal reforms and good governance as forms of neo-imperialism (Linnan 2007).

In comparison to China, Indonesia remains very poor and very poorly governed (Lindsey 2007). Since democratization, there has been a general deterioration in social order, a rise in crime, an upsurge in vigilante groups, and widespread unrest among Muslims in several provinces. Democracy has not resolved the critical problems of deeply entrenched corruption and clientelism, which are undermining the independence of the judiciary and efforts to implement rule of law. Transitional justice issues remain unresolved. The government has refused to extradite those accused of war crimes to the special tribunal in Dili. Indonesian courts have acquitted or imposed light sentences on senior officers in charge of East Timor. The U.S. State Department described the trials as seriously flawed and lacking credibility. The legal system as a whole is extremely weak. Judges are incompetent, corruption widespread, and the litigation process slow and inefficient, with cases often taking as long as seven years to complete. Senior judges stubbornly resist reforms that would decrease their power and opportunities for rent-seeking. The public prosecutor is seen as highly corrupt, incompetent, and militaristic. The police force suffers from lack of competence and corruption. The Ombudsmen Commission has received considerable foreign donor support, even though it has been relatively ineffective, because donors think it serves the purpose of transparency and provides the kinds of checks on government that are important in a liberal democracy. The bar association is deeply divided and has not been a source for reforms. The state is simply too weak to carry out significant institutional reforms.

Linnan observes that the international donor community has assumed a similar conception of the state and civil society as in developed Western states—an independent and liberal civil society in opposition to a largely secular and limited neutral state. He suggests that donors may be unwilling to accept non-Western conceptions of the state and civil society, as in socialist China or in Indonesia where Islam, communitarianism, and a post-colonial concern with nationalism play a more important role. The combination of communitarianism and nationalism leads to a more corporatist relationship between social organizations and the state that challenges the typical, if somewhat overstated, emphasis on civil society as independent from and in opposition to the state. It also leads to a greater emphasis on collective goals. As he notes:

> communitarianism is not the pallid conceptual variety of Anglo-American jurisprudence. Instead, it reflects two factors: first, how society works differently under circumstances when average per capita GDP is less than US$1,000; and second, the fact that the vast majority of Indonesia's population is not further removed than one generation from a rural village setting in which cooperation-intensive rice agriculture shaped society.
>
> (Linnan 2007: 271)

Indonesia might eventually prove successful in consolidating liberal democracy. However, other possible scenarios include: the emergence of a hard-line Islamic regime; the rise of a military regime that might use the specter of Islamic fundamentalism, the failure of the government to achieve economic growth, or the breakdown of law and order to grab power; a turn toward more authoritarian methods by the democratically elected president to deal with the growing insurgency and the breakdown in law and order; or the emergence of a nonliberal, more communitarian or collectivist regime of the type found in Singapore, Taiwan, South Korea, and Japan.

In Cambodia, economic growth lags far behind that of China. The economy is heavily dependent on tourism, textiles, and foreign aid. Growth slowed dramatically in 1997 and 1998 due to the regional economic crisis, civil violence, and political infighting. Although growth picked up in 1999, the first full year of peace in 30 years, longer-term prospects for the economy are less promising. The failure to invest in human capital and institutions has left Cambodians ill-prepared for the ruthless competition of the marketplace (CIA 2005).

Bangladesh remains poor, overpopulated, and poorly governed. Political infighting and corruption at all levels of government have hampered economic and political reforms. Incompetent governance has led to violent protests and a marked decrease in political stability, as indicated by its drop from the twenty-seventh percentile in 1998 to the twelfth percentile in 2004 on the World Bank indicator on political stability and absence of violence.

The government's reaction has been harsh, as reflected in the worsening civil and political rights record, with Bangladesh dropping from the forty-fifth percentile in 1998 to the 29 percent percentile in 2004 on the World Bank voice and accountability index. Other indicators have also moved significantly lower over the same period. Bangladesh plummeted from the forty-third percentile to the eleventh percentile on control of corruption, from the forty-first percentile to the thirteenth percentile on regulatory quality, and from the thirty-ninth percentile to the twenty-sixth percentile on government effectiveness, while its legal system remained stuck in the bottom quartile on the rule of law index.[7] In 2007, a bloodless coup sought to put an end to fighting that threatened to reduce the country to anarchy, resulting in a military-backed caretaker regime that suspended parliamentary elections until a more convenient time when the political situation would be more stable.

Democracy and human rights

One of the main arguments in favor of democracy is that democracies generally better protect human rights. It is true that many empirical studies show that democracy is one of the factors generally associated with better rights protection. However, at lower of levels of wealth, democracy frequently does not produce the desired results. The transition to democracy often leads to chaos and repression.

A number of quantitative studies demonstrate that the third wave has not led to a decrease in political repression, with some studies showing that political terror and violations of personal integrity rights actually increased in the 1980s (McCann and Gibney 1996: 23–5; Reilly 2003). Other studies have found that there are non-linear effects to democratization: transitional or illiberal democracies increase repressive action. Fein (1995) described this phenomenon as "more murder in the middle"—as political space opens, the ruling regime is subject to greater threats to its power and so resorts to violence.

More recent studies have also concluded that the level of democracy matters: below a certain level, democratic regimes oppress as much as non-democratic regimes.[8] Bueno de Mesquita *et al.* found:

> that improvements in a state's level of democracy short of full democracy do not promote greater respect for integrity rights. Only those states with the highest levels of democracy, not simply those conventionally defined as democratic, are correlated with better human rights practices.
>
> (de Mesquita *et al.* 2005: 439)

Describing their conclusions as "somewhat melancholy ones from the standpoint of state building and human rights," they dispel the notion that rushing to hold elections will lead to a marked improvement in human rights.

The experiences of Asian countries are largely consistent with the findings of these multi-country studies. Unlike China, India appears to deserve its level-four PTS rating (Peerenboom 2007). In Indonesia, there have been numerous human rights violations since the fall of Suharto, most notably with respect to ethnic violence and the tragedy in East Timor. Although Cambodia held elections in 1993 and 1998, the period was marked by battles between government armed forces and the Khmer Rouge, resulting in continued human rights violations. The government offered amnesty to key leaders and supporters of the Khmer Rouge, much to the dismay of many rights advocates. Nevertheless, stability remained an issue with a preemptive coup led by Hun Sen in 1997 in which more than fifty people were killed, many of them shot in the back of the head after arrest.

In the Philippines, there have been numerous rights violations, including disappearances, extrajudicial killings, arbitrary arrests, and prolonged detention, as the government struggles to defeat insurgents. Consistent with popular views in other countries threatened by political instability, most Filipino citizens apparently do not consider the government's tough treatment of insurgents and terrorists to be human rights violations.

Amnesty International has reported massive human rights violations in Nepal by both the military and Maoist guerrillas, including the killing and kidnapping of civilians, torture of prisoners, and destruction of property. In defense of the government's suspension of constitutional freedoms and harsh actions, Nepal's Prime Minister declared: "You can't make an omelet without breaking eggs. We don't want human rights abuses but we are fighting terrorists and we have to be tough" (Lak 2002).

Of course, not all of the news is bad. Asian democracies generally have fewer political prisoners than in authoritarian regimes; citizens enjoy greater freedom of speech, association, and assembly; and the media is subject to fewer restrictions, although it is generally still considerably less free than in Euro-America. While courts in authoritarian states often enjoy a high degree of independence over commercial matters and other run-of-the-mill cases, they are generally restricted to one degree or another in politically sensitive cases (Ginsburg and Moustafa 2008). Thus, in South Korea and Taiwan, only after democratization did the courts emerge as independent and authoritative forces capable of handling even politically sensitive issues involving controversial constitutional amendments and the criminal liability of past presidents impartially (Wang 2002; Ginsburg 2003; Hahm 2004).

On the other hand, in other countries, democratization at lower levels of wealth has exacerbated or at least failed to resolve shortcomings in the legal system, including problems with the authority and independence of the judiciary. In Indonesia, corporatist ties between judges and the political, military, and business elite have undermined the authority and independence of the judiciary (Dick 2007). In the Philippines, the courts continue to be so heavily influenced by the politics of populist, people-power movements that basic rule of law principles are threatened (Pangalangan 2004). Democratization alone is clearly not sufficient to ensure an independent and authoritative judiciary.

To be sure, not all of the problems in Asian countries are due to democracy, any more than all of the problems in authoritarian states are due to authoritarianism. There is also a danger of comparing the performance of Asian democracies against some Western ideal, or failing to account for the general negative impact of low levels of wealth on political stability, good governance, and the protection of rights.

At higher levels of wealth, democracy has certain economic advantages. While the average growth rate of authoritarian regimes is slightly higher than that for democracies above US$3,000 per capita GDP, growth is labor-extensive and labor-exploitive. The labor force grows faster, but the marginal worker is less productive and the average worker much less productive than in democracies (Przeworski *et al.* 2000: 270). In contrast, democracies take better advantage of technology and get more out of their workers. China of course has plenty of labor. Nevertheless, the various advantages of democracies once a higher level of wealth is obtained suggest that at some point China will be better off democratizing.[9]

A second lesson, however, is that China is likely to develop its own variety of democracy, which will most likely be closer to the nonliberal elitist democracy found in other Asian countries than to the liberal democracy found in Euro-America (Gu 1997). As former Singaporean Ambassador Chan Heng Chee has observed:

> developing countries may benefit from a "postponement" of democracy and when it eventually does arrive, Asian democracy must be expected to look different from the Western type: it will be less permissive, more authoritarian, stressing the common good rather than individual rights, often with a single dominant party and nearly always with a centralized bureaucracy and "strong state."
>
> (Chan 1993)

What kind of democracy? From imperial to imperiled to impeached

There are significant differences in East Asian democracies. Nevertheless, some of the more common features may be relevant for the future of democracy in China. One such feature is that East Asian democracy emphasizes a strong state rather than the more limited liberal state. Weakened by colonialism, war, and internal strife, Asian states have turned to democracy as a way of strengthening the state. National security, state sovereignty, and the dignity of the people remain key concerns throughout Asia, and especially in China.

State legitimacy is largely performance-based. The priority is on economic growth. The government is obligated to provide for the material well-being of citizens. At the same time, in contrast to the liberal state, the state is more involved in setting a moral agenda and creating the conditions for a harmonious society. There is less emphasis on individual rights and more on collective interests, including social stability.

The majority of citizens want strong leaders who can deliver the goods, and are willing to give them great leeway in pursuing their goals. There is less concern with formal checks and balances. Citizens elect imperial presidents with wide discretionary powers whom they can trust to exercise sound judgment because of their moral character—the modern-day equivalent of the sage and virtuous Confucian *junzi*. Four of five Koreans, for instance, agree that the "moral and human qualities of a political leader are more important than his ideas," with nearly two-thirds agreeing that "if we have political leaders who are morally upright, we can let them decide everything" (Helgesen 2002: 82). Not surprisingly, few Koreans opposed at the time President Kim Young Sam's extralegal measures to attack corruption (Bell 2000: 153). Showing a similar disregard for rule of law principles, President Kim Dae-jung used a general tax audit of all the major news media companies as a cover for persecution of his political opponents and encouraged, in the name of popular sovereignty, civic groups to violate laws preventing unregistered political groups from engaging in political campaigns (Hahm 2004). Similarly, Ling and Shih (1998) have argued that democracy in Taiwan is a way of installing a virtuous and benevolent ruling elite.

Meanwhile, in Thailand, the commitment to rule of law and separation of powers remains weak. A majority would accept government control over the judiciary or even parliament to promote the well-being of the nation (Albritton and Bureekul 2003). Indeed, support for Thaksin and his allies remains strong in Thailand, despite the opposition from the urban elite. More generally, Chu *et al.* (2001) found that only a minority of people living in East Asian third-wave democracies believe national government officials always or most of the time abide by the law, or that they are not corrupt, the notable exception being much-maligned Singapore. Few people believe the judiciary is capable of holding government officials accountable.

In contrast to broad-based forms of participatory or deliberative democracy, democracy in East Asia relies more heavily on good governance by a technocratic elite (Peng 1998; Bell 2000). Many Asian citizens have not internalized the democratic values required for deliberative democracy, including toleration of diverse viewpoints. Two-thirds of Koreans believe that too many competing groups will destroy social harmony, while almost half believe that "if people have too many different ways of thinking, society will be chaotic" (Helgesen 2002: 82). Some 40 percent believe that "the government should decide whether certain ideas should be allowed to be discussed in society" (Park and Shin 2004). Three out of four Thais view a diversity of political and social views as threatening, while almost half are unwilling to tolerate minority viewpoints (Albritton and Bureekul 2003).[10]

The willingness to defer to government leaders leads to the tyranny of the elite and grand political corruption. Yet the public is quick to turn on leaders who abuse the people's trust or whose morally upright image is tarnished by corruption scandals. The high-handed ways of strong executives also lead to conflicts between the president and members of his own party and conflicts with other elites. The president then goes from imperial to imperiled to impeached in short order, and is subject to a vote of no confidence, or limps along as a lame duck with little public support.

In short, democracy in East Asia is often a story of grand political corruption, of clientelism and the dominance of the elite and business interests, and of imperial presidents with little regard for rule of law. Thus, a third lesson likely to be drawn from the experiences of East Asian democracies is that democracy is no panacea, even in those countries typically cited as success stories, and won't be in China either.

Conclusion: a critical appraisal of democracy

Advocates of the affirmative view of modernity continue to tout democracy as appropriate for all countries. Yet despite the vast amount of resources spent on promoting democracy around the world and the initial excitement surrounding the most recent wave of democratization, most third-wave democracies have turned out to be stunningly disappointing. The empirical reality —studiously ignored by those who confuse the slogan "democracy and freedom for all" with a sound foreign policy and development strategy—has simply not lived up to the hype. It is true that many countries have democratized in the sense of holding some form of national elections from time to time. But the number of cases of successful consolidation of liberal democracy is small, and is dwarfed by the number of failures (Carothers 2004; Diamond 2008).

As in the previous waves of democratization, several third-wave democracies have reverted back to various forms of authoritarianism or have become mired in highly dysfunctional states of formal democracy. Many, if not most, democracies today are illiberal democracies. It is often difficult to tell them apart from authoritarian regimes except for the holding of periodic elections where the outcome is tightly controlled. The vast majority of democratic governments remain corrupt and inefficient. Few have managed to achieve sustained economic growth.

One of the cardinal principles of democratic transition theory is that successful transitions to democracy must not attempt to radically alter the property rights of the bourgeoisie or go too far in limiting the power of the military (O'Donnell and Schmitter 1986: 69). As a result, most transitions to democracy do not result in significant reallocation of political and economic resources. In many countries, elites from the previous regime continue to control political power and key state resources.

Even when a new elite takes over, the avenues for public participation generally remain restricted and ineffectual. In many Latin American countries, strong clientelist and paternalistic states dominate civil society. In Africa and parts of Asia, the state is frequently weak, but so is civil society, often divided as it is along ethnic lines. Social groups generally lack the resources and skills to participate effectively in the policy-making processes. Internal disagreements and a general distrust of the state also undermine effective coordination. After democratization, civil society, once united in opposition to the authoritarian state, becomes fragmented. Entrenched conservative interests quickly organize and challenge more progressive groups in the public sphere. A variety of single-interest social groups compete for financing and to be heard on issues ranging from women's rights to public schooling to environmental degradation. When former opposition leaders become government leaders, they typically lose patience with human rights activists and other critical voices constantly reminding the government how far short it falls of inspirational ideals for a progressive society.[11] Political parties are frequently fractured, and dominated by personalities rather than substantive policy platforms. Elections do nothing to address the abject poverty, obscene inequality, and horrific human suffering so often found in developing democracies. The bottom line is a hollowing out of democracy, which all too often benefits a few, who become increasingly rich, at the expense of the many.

The political dominance of the business elite and the rise of money politics in newly established democracies undermine the democratic potential of elections, making a mockery of the equality and fair competition inherent in the slogan of "one person, one vote," just as they do in long-standing democracies where the reality is often closer to "one dollar, one vote." Democracy then serves a legitimating function for an entrenched hierarchical order in which government officials and business leaders have a closer and more mutually rewarding relationship to foreign business interests than to their own constituents and fellow citizens.[12] Many poor people internalize arguments that they as individuals are responsible for their dire straits, undermining efforts to create a movement to address larger structural reforms needed to address poverty, including the need to pay greater heed to global injustice. In those few newly established democracies fortunate enough to enjoy sustained growth, the middle class facilitates political stability, but often at the expense of more radical popular movements.

Critics decry the large gap between *formal or electoral* democracy, where elections are controlled by and serve the interests of elites, and *substantive or progressive* democracy, which gives equal voice to the marginalized and addresses the disparities in resources, power, and opportunities. Yet the commonly offered solution to the twin problems of democracy and inequality—more democracy, and in particular, more "empowerment" of the disenfranchised—is inadequate. Allowing greater voice to the poor, while desirable, is no magic cure.

Given the harsh reality in most developing democracies, it is hardly surprising that the majority of citizens have little faith in their governments and are fed up with politics. In Asia, between 75 percent and 92 percent of citizens are dissatisfied with the government in democratic Japan, South Korea, India, Indonesia, and the Philippines (Pew Global Attitudes Project 2002). It is tempting to attribute the problems of developing democracies to growing pains: surely over time these troubles will be overcome. There are, however, two serious problems with this pollyannish view. First, describing these dysfunctional, often failed states, as being in "transition to democracy" is simply no longer credible, and fails to capture the depth of their problems or the depressing reality that many countries are caught in a stable but bleak cycle of poverty, government malfeasance, and despair (Diamond 1996; Carothers 2003).

In light of the poor empirical record of democracies, the dominant view through the 1960s, 1970s, and early 1980s that there are preconditions to successful democratization is now making a comeback—although no one is sure what the necessary preconditions are or how to satisfy them. At minimum, no one is saying that economic wealth is the only relevant factor, or that it is a necessary or sufficient condition. An institutionalized market economy; a reasonably high level of wealth; a robust and democratically oriented civil society; cultural values that promote tolerance, civility, and compromise; ethnic and religious harmony; elites willing to compromise and to distribute resources and opportunities more equally; political stability; and functional institutions, including a legal system that meets the requirement of rule of law and government institutions that practice good governance—all may be desirable, and may facilitate democratic consolidation (see also Thompson's chapter in this volume arguing that democratic consolidation in Asia is explained largely by the path dependency of the different roads taken to democracy). But what happens when those conditions are not present?[13]

The second problem with the view that fledgling democracies will work out the kinks over time and then all will be well is that the crisis with democracy is not limited to developing countries. Developed countries have their own share of problems. According to the Eurobarometer, the majority of EU citizens do not have much trust in the parliament, the national government, the judiciary, or the press (although expectations may be higher in developed democracies). A mere 17 percent trust political parties. The overwhelming majority of citizens in the newer EU countries are dissatisfied with the way democracy works in their countries, while a full 40 percent of all EU citizens are not satisfied (Eurobarometer 2005).

Many people around the world, in rich and poor countries, are deeply dissatisfied with democracy, but they see few viable alternatives. Democracy seems to be "the only game in town," even if a losing one for most.

For the Chinese and Vietnamese, and increasingly for others trapped in dead-end democracies in Asia and elsewhere, the markets before democracy approach of China and other East Asian countries understandably holds some attraction. This does not mean that Chinese and Vietnamese citizens would not some day prefer democracy to the current political system. It simply means that democracy is not the main issue at present for most people.

However, China may democratize at some point in the future, just as other East Asian states have.[14]

Notes

1 This chapter draws on parts of Chapter 2 and Chapter 7 of Peerenboom (2007).
2 The East Asian model involves the sequencing of economic growth, legal reforms, democratization, and constitutionalism, with different rights being taken seriously at different times in the process. For a more detailed discussion, see Peeren-boom (2007).
3 Rigobon and Rodrik (2005) found that greater rule of law produces more dem-ocracy and vice versa, but the effects are not strong. Barro (1997) notes that there is little empirical evidence that rule of law promotes political freedom.
4 Rigobon and Rodrik (2005) found that while democracy and rule of law are both related to higher GDP levels, the impact of rule of law is much stronger. For a discussion of other studies, see Peerenboom (2005) and the citations therein. See also Polterovich and Popov (2007), noting that free and partly free former Soviet countries experienced deeper recessions and higher inequality than those that were not free, and that, in general, democratization stimulates economic growth in countries with strong law and order, whereas democratization under-mines growth in countries with poor law and order.
5 Przeworski *et al.* (2000: 158) note that 96 percent of countries with per capita GDP of under US$1,000 are dictatorships.
6 Burkhart and Lewis-Beck (1994) conclude that economic development causes democracy, but democracy does not cause economic development. Barro (1997) found that at extremely low levels of development, introducing greater political freedoms, contributes to growth. That is, in the worst dictatorships, the lack of limitations on government power deters investment and growth. However, once a moderate amount of political freedom has been attained, democracy inhibits growth. At higher levels of development, the demand for democracy rises. Personn and Tabellini (2006) found that democratization and economic liberalization in isolation each lead to higher growth. However, sequencing also matters: countries that first liberalize the economy before extending political rights do better than those that democratize and then carry out economic reforms. They thus conclude that reformers of closed authoritarian regimes ought to give priority to economic liberalization.
7 On the positive side, the UNDP (2005: 46) points out that Bangladesh was able to make notable improvements in human development, admittedly from a very low base, despite low growth.
8 Davenport and Armstrong (2002) found that "authorities do not perceive any change in the costs and benefits of repression until the highest levels of democracy have been achieved" (see also Zanger 2000; Keith and Poe 2002).
9 Although Rodrik (2007) did not find evidence that democracy promotes growth, he did find that democracies have more predictable growth rates and economic performance, handle adverse shocks better, pay higher wages, and deliver better distributional outcomes. However, as the success of East Asian states on these issues shows, much depends on the nature of the authoritarian regime.
10 However, only 25 percent agree that free speech is not worth it if that means having to put up with a threat of social disorder, while over 90 percent believe that political leaders should tolerate the views of challengers, suggesting that Thais are aware of the misuse of restrictions on free speech in the name of public order and the use of defamation laws to curtail political opposition.
11 Bell and Keenan (2004: 346–7) point out that once in power, even the rights-

friendly Nelson Mandela criticized NGOs, claiming that "many of our non-governmental organizations are not in fact NGOs, both because they have no popular base and [due to] the actuality that they rely on the domestic and foreign governments, rather than the people, for their material sustenance."

12 As Rapley (2004) and Dezalay and Garth (2002) note, many elite in developing countries—often trained in prestigious American universities—support neoliberal policies.

13 I have discussed these and other factors elsewhere, concluding that China is not likely to become democratic in the near future, although democratization in the long run is likely (Peerenboom 2002: 513–46).

14 For a discussion of the implications of China democratizing or not, see Peerenboom (2007). Clearly, democracy will not be a panacea for all of the legal, governance, environmental, economic, and political problems that China is now confronting. While in some cases, democratization may play a positive role, in others, it could exacerbate these problems.

Bibliography

Albritton, R. B. and Bureekul, T. (2003) "The meaning of democracy in a developing nation." Online. Available HTTP: <http://www.kpi.ac.th/en/meaning_of_democracy1.htm> (accessed 10 January 2004).

Angeles, L. C. (2004) "Grassroots democracy and community empowerment: the quest for sustainable poverty reduction in Asia," in J. Lele and F. Quadir (eds) *Democracy and Civil Society in Asia (Vols I & II)*, New York: Palgrave Macmillan, pp. 182–211.

Barro, R. (1996) "Democracy: a recipe for growth?" in M. G. Quibria and J. M. Dowling (eds) *Current Issues in Economic Development: an Asian perspective*, New York: Oxford University Press, pp. 67–106.

—— (1997) *Determinants of Economic Growth*, Cambridge, MA: MIT Press.

Bell, C. and Keenan, J. (2004) "Human rights nongovernmental organizations and the problems of transition," *Human Rights Quarterly*, 26(2): 330–74.

Bell, D. (2000) *East Meets West: human rights and democracy in East Asia*, Princeton: Princeton University Press.

Boix, C. and Stokes, S. (2003) "Endogenous democratization," *World Politics*, 55(3): 517–49.

Burkhart, R. E. and Lewis-Beck, M. S. (1994) "Comparative democracy: the economic development thesis," *American Political Science Review*, 88(4): 903–10.

Carothers, T. (2003) *Promoting the Rule of Law Abroad—the problem of knowledge*, Washington, DC: Carnegie Endowment for International Peace.

—— (2004) *Critical Mission: essays on democracy promotion*, Washington, DC: Carnegie Endowment for International Peace.

Chan, H. C. (1993) *Democracy and Capitalism: Asian and American perspectives*, Singapore: Institute of Southeast Asian Studies.

Chu, Y. H., Diamond, L. and Shin, D. C. (2001) "Halting progress in Korea and Taiwan," *Journal of Democracy*, 12(1): 122–36.

CIA (2005) *The World Factbook*. Online. Available HTTP: <http://www.cia.gov/cia/publications/factbook/docs/faqs.html> (accessed 5 October 2005).

Davenport, C. and Armstrong, D. (2002) "Democracy and the violation of human rights: a statistical analysis of the third wave." Online. Available HTTP: <http://apsaproceedings.cup.org/Site/abstracts/011/011002ArmstrongD.htms> (accessed 1 December 2002).

David, R. (1994) "Redemocratization in the wake of the 1986 people power revolution: errors and dilemmas," *Karasnlan*, 11: 20.

De Mesquita, B. B., Downs, G. W., Smith, A. and Cherif, F. M. (2005) "Thinking inside the box: a closer look at democracy and human rights." *International Studies Quarterly*, 49(3): 439–58.

Dezalay, Y. and Garth, B. G. (2002) *The Internationalization of Palace Wars: lawyers, economists, and the contest to transform Latin American states*, Chicago: University of Chicago.

Diamond, L. (1996) "Is the third wave over?" *Journal of Democracy*, 7(3): 20–37.

—— (2008) *The Spirit of Democracy*, New York: Henry Hold and Company.

Dick, H. (2007) "Why law reforms fail: Indonesia's anti-corruption reforms?" in T. Lindsey (ed.) *Law Reform in Developing and Transitional States*, London: Routledge, pp. 42–64.

Economist (2004) "Asia: the greatest show on earth; India's election," *Economist* (17 April 2004).

Eurobarometer (2005) "Eurobarometer," Issue 62. Online. Available HTTP: <http://europa.eu.int/comm/public_opinion/archives/eb/eb62/eb_62_en.pdf> (accessed 1 October 2005).

Fein, H. (1995) "More murder in the middle: life-integrity violations and democracy in the world, 1987," *Human Rights Quarterly*, 17 (1): 170–91.

Gilley, B. (2004) *China's Democratic Future*, New York: Columbia University Press.

Ginsburg, T. (2003) *Judicial Review in New Democracies: constitutional courts in Asian cases*, New York: Cambridge University Press.

Ginsburg, T. and Moustafa, T. (eds) (2008) *Politics of Courts in Authoritarian Regimes*, Cambridge: Cambridge University Press.

Gu, E. (1997) "Elitist democracy and China's democratization," *Democratization*, 4(2): 84–112.

Hahm, C. (2004) "Rule of law in South Korea: rhetoric and implementation," in R. Peerenboom (ed.) *Asian Discourses of Rule of Law: theories and implementation of rule of law in twelve Asian countries, France and the U.S.*, London: Routledge-Curzon, pp. 385–416.

Helgesen, G. (2002) "Imported democracy: the South Korean experience," in C. Kinnvall and K. Jonsson (eds) *Globalization and Democratization in Asia: the construction of identity*, London and New York: Routledge, pp. 73–91.

Keith, L. C. and Poe, S. C. (2002) "Personal integrity abuse during domestic crises." Online. Available HTTP: <http://apsaproceedings.cup.org/Site/papers/046/046004PoeSteven0.pdf> (accessed 2 November 2002).

Lak, D. (2002) "Kingdom on the brink of catastrophe," *South China Morning Post*, (12 May 2002).

Lawrance, A. (2004) "Nobody said democracy is a tea party," *South China Morning Post*, (27 March 2004).

Lele, J. and Quadir, F. (eds) (2004). *Democracy and Civil Society in Asia (Vols I & II)*, New York: Palgrave Macmillan.

Lindsey, T. (2004) "Indonesia: devaluing Asian values, rewriting rule of law," in R. Peerenboom (ed.) *Asian Discourses of Rule of Law: theories and implementation of rule of law in twelve Asian countries, France and the U.S.*, London: Routledge-Curzon, pp. 286–324.

—— (2007) "Legal infrastructure and governance reform in post-crisis Asia: the case of Indonesia," in T. Lindsey (ed.) *Law Reforms in Developing and Transitional States*, London: Routledge, pp. 3–41.

Ling, L. H. M. and Shih, C. Y. (1998) "Confucianism with a liberal face: the meaning of democratic policies in postcolonial Taiwan," *Review of Politics*, 60(1): 55–83.

Linnan, D. K. (2007) "Like a fish needs a bicycle: public law theory, civil society and governance reform in Indonesia," in T. Lindsey (ed.) *Law Reforms in Developing and Transitional States*, London: Routledge, pp. 268–90.

McCann, J. A. and Gibney, M. (1996) "An overview of political terror in the developing world, 1980–91," in D. L. Cingranelli (ed.) *Policy Studies and Developing Countries*, Greenwich, CT: Jai Press, pp. 23–5.

O'Donnell, G. A. and Schmitter, P. (ed.) (1986) *Transitions from Authoritarian Rule: tentative conclusions about uncertain democracies*, Baltimore: Johns Hopkins University Press.

Pangalangan, R. C. (2004) "The Philippine 'people power' constitution, rule of law, and the limits of liberal constitutionalism," in R. Peerenboom (ed.) *Asian Discourses of Rule of Law: theories and implementation of rule of law in twelve Asian countries, France and the U.S.*, London: RoutledgeCurzon, pp. 371–84.

Park, C. M. and Shin, D. S. (2004) "Do Asian values deter popular support for democracy? The case of South Korea," paper presented at the AAS Annual Meeting, San Diego, CA, 4–7 March 2004. Online. Available HTTP: <http://www.aasianst.org/absts/2004abst/Interarea/intertoc.htm> (accessed 8 March 2004).

Peerenboom, R. (2002) *China's Long March toward Rule of Law*, Cambridge: Cambridge University Press.

—— (2005) "Human rights and rule of law: what's the relationship?" *Georgetown Journal of International Law*, 36(3): 809–946.

—— (2007) *China Modernizes: threat to the West or model for the rest?* Oxford: Oxford University Press.

Peerenboom, R., Petersen, C. and Chen, A. Y. (eds) (2006) *Human Rights in Asia*, New York: Routledge.

Peng, Y. L. (1998) "Democracy and Chinese political discourses," *Modern China*, 24(4): 408–44.

Personn, T. and Tabellini, G. (2006) "Democracy and development: the devil is in the detail," NBER Working Paper, no. 11993.

Pew Global Attitudes Project (2002) "What do Asians think about their own lives?" in *What the World Thinks in 2002*. Online. Available HTTP: <http://international.ucla.edu/asia/news/02pewpolla.asp> (accessed 10 November 2002).

Pinkney, R. (2003) *Democracy in the Third World* (2nd edn), Boulder: Lynne Rienner.

Polterovich, V. and Popov, V. (2007) "Democratization, quality of institutions and economic growth." Online. Available HTTP: <http://ssrn.com/abstract=1036841> (accessed 1 November 2008).

Przeworski, A., Alvarez, M. E., Cheibub, J. A. and Limongi, F. (2000) *Democracy and Development: political institutions and well-being in the world, 1950–1990*, Cambridge: Cambridge University Press.

Rapley, J. (2004) *Globalization and Inequality: neoliberalism's downward spiral*, Boulder, CO: Lynne Rienner.

Reilly, D. (2003) "Diffusing human rights: the nexus of domestic and international influences," paper presented at the Annual Meeting of the American Political Science Association, Philadelphia, PA, 27 August 2003. Online. Available HTTP:

<http://www.allacademic.com/meta/p62741_index.html> (accessed 30 August 2003).

Rigobon, R. and Rodrik, D. (2005) "Rule of law, democracy, openness, and income: estimating the interrelationships," *Economics of Transition*, 13(3): 533–64.

Rocamora, J. (2004) "Formal democracy and its alternatives in the Philippines: parties, elections and social movements," in J. Lele and F. Quadir (eds) *Democracy and Civil Society in Asia (Vols I & II)*, New York: Palgrave Macmillan, pp. 196–222.

Rodrik, D. (2007) *One Economics, Many Recipes*, Princeton: Princeton University Press.

UNDP (United Nations Development Program) (2005) *Human Development Report 2005*, New York: UNDP.

Wang, T. S. (2002) "The legal development of Taiwan in the 20th century: Toward a Liberal and Democratic Country," *Pacific Rim Law and Policy Journal*, 11(3): 531–60.

Zanger, S. C. (2000) "A global analysis of the effect of regime changes on life integrity violations, 1977–93," *Journal of Peace Research*, 37(2): 213–33.

12 Group rights and democracy in Southeast Asia

Chua Beng Huat

Looking even briefly around Asia, two phenomena are readily observable. First, unlike the situation in many African countries, losers do not protest and refuse to accept general election results. The electoral process has progressively stabilized throughout most of Asia. Touted recently as the "most democratic" of elections in Bangladesh's history was the January 2009 election, in which the Awami League won an overwhelming majority of seats in the National Assembly. The trend towards electoral stability began in Asia in the late 1990s, with South Korea and Taiwan transiting from military-backed authoritarian rule to democracy and the peaceful change of the ruling party in government. In 1997, South Korea instituted a one-term presidency system, and over the past decade, the ruling party in Taiwan has alternated between the Democratic Progressive Party and Kuomingtang (KMT). Equally dramatic was the severe curtailing of the power of the long-ruling coalition party, the *Barisan Nasional*, in Malaysia in the March 2008 general election, when it lost its two-thirds majority in the federal parliament for the first time since the late 1960s. This loss was traumatic for the party, so much so that Prime Minister Abdullah Badawi was forced to hand over power to his deputy, Najib Razak, prematurely. In Indonesia, the military has returned to the barracks after the successful completion of two rounds of presidential elections following the ousting of the late President Suharto in 1998. Finally, the only long-ruling government that has not suffered any loss of electoral political power is the People's Action Party (PAP) government in Singapore.

The case of Thailand is unique. First, in 2007, the popularly elected government of Prime Minister Thaksin Shinawatra of the Thai Rak Thai (TRT) Party was overthrown in a bloodless coup. After a year of lackluster military administration, a general election was held in 2008. Winning by a landslide was the People's Power Party, constituted by Thaksin loyalists and given the same overwhelming support by the rural poor and urban working class that the now-outlawed TRT had once received. A coalition comprising the military, royalists loyal to the aging incumbent Thai king, and the urban business and middle classes in Bangkok under the banner of the People's Alliance for Democracy (PAD) immediately held public demonstrations against the duly elected government. The long siege of Parliament House culminated in the occupation of the Bangkok International Airport in December with impunity, as security forces, including the military and police, refused to abide by the government's emergency order to forcefully remove the demonstrators. The anti-democratic character of the PAD became immediately apparent, however, when they demanded constitutional changes that would require only one-third of Parliament to be popularly elected and the remaining two-thirds to be appointed. This proposal was immediately criticized in the press and by the Thai people, who were not about to give up their democratic right to vote so readily, having paid heavily, with the succession of repressive military regimes, for the right to democratic government. Nevertheless, the PAD coalition successfully removed the popularly elected government based on a legal technicality. The constitutional court, finding that members of the ruling party had violated electoral laws by vote-buying, ruled that these office bearers of the ruling party resign from Parliament and be barred from electoral contests for the next five years. This created the opportunity for a coalition of smaller parties, with the support of members of the ruling party coalition who had switched sides, to cobble together a slim majority in Parliament to form a new government in December 2008. The situation is, however, far from stable, with pro-Thaksin supporters threatening to continue political action, including mass demonstrations, until a new election is held.

The second observable phenomenon is the persistence of violent conflicts between ethnic and religious minorities and the state in many Asian countries. Violence continues in the southern Philippines, where there is a high concentration of Muslims in a predominantly Catholic nation, and has intensified in southern Thailand, where a Muslim minority is fighting the predominantly Thai-Buddhist state. Other examples include the continuation of conflict in Sri Lanka after the collapse of a very short period of negotiated truce and, most recently, the violent riots in Tibet, where Tibetans confronted the Han-dominated state, the People's Republic of China (PRC). State violence against ethnic and religious minorities has gone on for so long that it has fallen off the global media screen, for the most part. The struggles of different minority groups in Myanmar against the military state were displaced from public attention by the uprising of Buddhist monks in early 2008.

Considering the two phenomena together, it is obvious that the stabilization of electoral politics, an index of successful democratization, does not resolve ethnic issues within a democratizing state. Indeed, violent conflict might even intensify. Ethnic minorities wanting autonomy often express a desire for independent statehood. This aspiration unavoidably comes into conflict with the need perceived by the democratizing state to centralize power and authority over the national territory and every individual under a supposedly common citizenship. There is thus a logical impasse between minority group formation and citizenship formation. Whereas the former emphasizes collective membership, citizenship is individualized in the modern state, and whereas minority, or ethnic group, solidarity emphasizes constraint in individual cultural practices and choice, modern citizenship emphasizes individual rights and freedoms with minimal state intervention. Thus, although political liberalism has very shallow roots, particularly in East and Southeast Asian states, these "modern" states implicitly operate with a liberal conception of citizenship, which conflicts with the minority groups' claims to cultural difference and its political implications.

With the exception of Thailand (Hong 2008), all countries in Southeast Asia are postcolonial nations, with boundaries that were arbitrarily established by the colonial regimes without regard to the territorial claims of the existing ethnic groups. Consequently, the new nations are constituted by different ethnic groups, and by default, are multiethnic. Conflict between group rights and citizenship rights is endemic, which accounts for the sustained violent conflicts between the state and ethnic and/or religious minorities. This chapter examines three cases in which ethnic conflicts with different historical backgrounds have been dealt with by states in various ways, resulting in different future trajectories. However, it is necessary to first examine some of the contradictory demands of individual and group rights.

Multiculturalism and citizenship

To radically cut a very long history short, the evolution of the modern state in the West since the issuing of the Magna Carta, from the formation of the first parliament in Britain and the Declaration of Independence of the United States of America, which became the first republican nation, to the French Revolution, has progressively shaped and defined the relationship of the citizen to the state in terms of progressively safeguarding the rights of individual citizens from encroachment by the state, that is, creating a liberal democracy with minimal state intervention. Indeed, liberalism is conventionally associated with democracy, as evidenced in the term "liberal democracy." That all democracies must be liberal has become so widely taken for granted that it has become close to impossible for political thinkers in the West to imagine how a "non-liberal" democracy might look. The hegemony of liberalism is demonstrated in Fukuyma's (1992) grandiose claim that the liberal-democratic-capitalist society has brought about "the end of history." Although the end of history is hardly at hand, the modern nation state unavoidably contains within it elements of liberal individualism, at least minimally, with the electoral process of one person, one vote, the equality of individuals in the eyes of the law, and the rights of belief and expression, even though these rights are constantly subject to modification, if not violation, by the incumbent government.

Liberal individualism is, of course, not without its critics in Europe and Anglo-America. The asocial individual, unconstrained by the society and culture within which he/she exists but endowed with "natural" rights and freedom to define, at will, what is "good" for him/herself is, Gray (1995: 5) argues, ontologically, someone "without history or ethnicity, denuded of the special attachments that in the real human world give us the particular identities we have"; that is, ontologically such an individual does not exist, is but a conceptual fiction upon which is built an entire discourse of individual rights. Gray's critique may be read as a mode of social realism: individuals are embedded and bound by the cultural practices of the community in which they reside and which constitute them as who they are, that is, with identity, realized in and through the reproduction of their everyday life. Therefore, any conceptualization of social and political life should begin with the community-embedded individual—living in and part of a community.[1] However, liberal individualism is so entrenched in the United States that an American philosopher confesses, "I have grown weary of that game. I simply cannot muster energy for yet one more attempt to show the incoherence of liberal political philosophy or practice" (Hauerwas 2002).

One area in which the critique of liberal individualism has had some traction in the West is in the debate over multiculturalism. As Kymlicka (2005) observes, in the past, Western nations have feared the presence of ethnic group loyalties, particularly when their members are concentrated in specific geographical locations. Such loyalties and territoriality are necessary conditions for the rise of the sub-nationalism or ethno-nationalism of the ethnic group in question, which might in turn give rise to secessionist aspirations that threaten the nation. Consequently:

> efforts [have been] made to erode this sense of distinct nationhood, including restricting minority language rights, abolishing traditional forms of regional self-government, and encouraging members of the dominant group to settle in the minority group's homeland so that the minority becomes outnumbered even in its traditional territory.
>
> (Kymlika 2005: 23)

However, today, the same Western countries "have accepted the principle that these substate national identities will endure into the indefinite future, and that their sense of nationhood and nationalist aspirations must be accommodated in some way or other" (Kymlika 2005: 23).

Kymlicka also points out that the willingness of Western nations to accommodate sub-national identities is based on a liberal democratic ideology, which recognizes first, the equal rights of individuals, whether they are members of a minority or majority group; second, that in the past, minorities have been dominated and thus unfairly treated by the majority; and, third, that the democratic state enables minority groups to have different points of access to power. However, he contends that an overriding ideological element is the radical reduction of national security concerns in the West:

> It is difficult to think of a single Western democracy where the state fears that a national minority would collaborate with a neighboring enemy and potential aggressor . . . As a result, the question of whether national minorities and indigenous peoples would be loyal in the event of invasion

by a neighboring state has been removed from the table ... In the absence of any grounds for treating minority nationalism as a security threat, the politics of sub-state nationalism in the West is just that—normal day-to-day politics.

(Kymlika 2005: 34)

The Asian context

Compared to nation states in Europe that evolved over a long period of time, those in Asia are of recent origin. Prior to the Second World War, Asian nations were either imperial states, such as dynastic China and Japan, or colonized territories, where governance was inevitably authoritarian. Japan's defeat in the Pacific War led to contemporary democratic Japan, which remains a constitutional monarchy. In China, although the decaying Qing Dynasty was finally overthrown in the Republican Revolution of 1911, the new Republic of China struggled simultaneously to bring warlords under control, fight the rising Communist Party, and resist territorial invasion by foreign powers, eventually losing the civil war to the communists, who established the present-day PRC in 1949 and drove the republicans to the island of Taiwan. The civil war in Korea from 1950–1953, a proxy war between communism and Western capitalism, euphemistically called the "free world," resulted in a divided nation, where a peace treaty is yet to be signed. Those on either side of these divisions are unlikely to readily give up their current political position. Divided Korea and the tension across the Taiwan Strait continue to remind us of the unresolved ideological differences between communism and democracy in Asia.

The postcolonial nations, all of which were born in the aftermath of the Second World War, often emerged after long and violent anti-colonial struggles. Military leaders who were at the forefront of these struggles often assumed that, having shed blood in support of the revolution, it was their right to lead the new nations, usurping the power to govern if necessary. Many of these new states in Southeast Asia had experimented with electoral democracy immediately after political independence but this resulted in violence and grief and subsequently, the establishment of military-backed authoritarian regimes, such as in the Philippines and Indonesia. Others, including Singapore and Malaysia, significantly modified the rules of the democratic game, with extensive gerrymandering at every election, for example, to shore up a hegemonic single-party state, either co-opting or marginalizing the opposition.

Liberalism therefore has very shallow roots in the newly minted Asian nations, which have a tendency to tightly embrace their citizens, constantly inscribing on the latter a "national" identity, incorporating them into a bounded "national" territory, and attempting to build the "nation" as a community in which members supposedly share the same destiny. Such prevailing nationalist ideological conditions are not conducive to liberalism, which preaches maximum individual freedom in a minimalist state. Liberalism threatens the geographical, demographic, and ideological boundaries that these new nations are fighting to establish and maintain. It is seen as a threat, and thus is an ideology to be avoided, if not rejected outright, even though election as the only legitimate route to political office has to be adopted. The preferred ideological framework is, not surprisingly, some version of reinvented local traditional values: *panca sila* and *gotong royong* in Indonesia, "Asian values" in Singapore and Malaysia, and "socialism with a Chinese character" in the PRC.

In international relations, half a century after the end of the Second World War, nation states in Asia remain "projects-in-progress," with many national boundaries still in dispute. Examples include the border between India and the PRC, the cross-strait tension between Taiwan and the PRC, and divided Korea. Minor disputes include those between Philippines and Malaysia on the status of Labuan and between Singapore and Malaysia over an outcrop that contains no more than a lighthouse (Jayakumar and Koh 2009). Current international relations between neighboring countries remain entangled with the history of past conflicts. For instance, different interpretations of the history of Japanese aggression in Asia, especially in the PRC and Korea, continue to affect international relations between East Asian states. The formation of the Association of Southeast Asian Nations (ASEAN) has helped maintain regional peace, although individual member states face domestic conflicts. Nevertheless, military expenditure continues to increase in each of the 10 member states, contributing to the uncertainty among them of each other's territorial ambitions.

To summarize, today, with very few exceptions, Asian nations profess democracy. They have adopted the electoral process but not liberalism as a national ideology. However, as stated, they operate implicitly with the idea of the governing of individual citizens, in spite of the absence of a belief in liberal individualism, as it is the individual as a citizen who is endowed with rights and obligations vis-à-vis the state. Most states do not protect the rights of minority ethnic and religious groups to preserve their different cultural beliefs and practices. Also, sub-national loyalties continue to be seen as a threat to the unity of the hard-won unitary nation state that has emerged only after bloody struggles, resulting in continuing violent ethnic conflicts, as noted in the introduction to this chapter. It would be unreasonable to expect contemporary Asia to be a place wherein sub-nationalities are respected by the majority and guaranteed by the state, and multiculturalism flourishes, if contemporary Western liberal democracies were taken as the reference. However, one should not treat Western history, experience, and trajectories as universal; rather, it would be best to "provincialize" them and examine concrete instances in Asia where some mode of recognition and tolerance of difference within a unitary or federal state is in practice with some success. I will now examine three heuristic instances from Southeast Asia: Singapore, where multiculturalism has been the official policy since political independence; Malaysia, where three race-based parties have shared political power as a coalition under the presumed "supremacy" of the indigenous Malay majority; and Aceh, where years of violent ethnic and religious conflict have resulted in local autonomy within a unitary Indonesian state.

Singapore: a constitutional multiracial nation

In 1965, when Singapore achieved political independence, its resident population was approximately 75 percent *Huaren* (ethnic Chinese), 17 percent Malay, and 7 percent Indian, with a small percentage of other ethnic groups. The demographic reality was reconstituted into distinct "racial"[2] groups (Chinese, Malay, Indian, Other; CMIO) of a constitutional "multiracial" state, with Malays constitutionally recognized as the indigenous population of the new nation.[3] As most nations today have multiracial populations but few have adopted multiracialism as an official policy, it should be apparent that such an official policy is not necessitated simply by the presence of a multiracial population. Multiracialism is a conscious ideological construction, necessitated perhaps by the prevailing regional geopolitical conditions at the time of Singapore's independence.

The political system of the island-nation is based entirely on the template of a modern nation state—an elected parliamentary democracy with a constitutional guarantee of all conventional equalities and freedoms of individuals, that is, all of the liberal rights, "regardless of race, language or religion."[4] In social and cultural policy and administration, however, the equality of individuals is often superseded or suppressed by the logic of multiracialism, which stresses the formal equality of racial groups. For example, since the 1970s, when English was instituted as the primary medium of instruction for all educational institutions, every primary and secondary school student must also learn his/her so-called mother tongue: Mandarin for *Huaren*, Malay for Malays, and, recognizing the much greater linguistic differences among Indians, a number of languages including Tamil, Bengali, and Hindi. This highly ideological policy is couched in the questionable belief that teaching the mother tongue is a means to instill in students "traditional" Asian values, which will supposedly provide them with cultural ballast to combat the insidious "Westernization" of Singaporeans.[5]

With multiracialism and multiculturalism as part of the national ideology, "race" has been maintained at a very high level of visibility in Singapore to signify "deep divisions" within the nation.[6] Given the racial divisions, the potential for racial conflicts can be imagined as a permanent possibility, which creates political-discursive and interventionist space for the state to closely monitor and police racial boundaries. The government has set itself up as an autonomous, neutral umpire that allocates resources and adjudicates disputes among the races. To appreciate the political effects of this structural autonomy, one needs to understand the ideological use of the idea of "racial harmony"; peaceful coexistence stands as a sign of tolerance of difference among Singaporeans.

To avoid racial conflict, each racial group must pay, voluntarily or not, the cost of producing racial harmony as a public good. These costs are uneven and dissimilar. For *Huaren*, race-group equality administratively reduces the overwhelming demographic majority to being just one of three racial groups. The displacement of Mandarin by English as the national lingua franca severely disadvantaged the sizeable population among the *Huaren* who are either/both Mandarin-educated and/or speakers of other Chinese dialects.[7] In this sense, there is a "minoritization" of the non-English-speaking within the *Huaren* demographic majority. For Malays, their special status as indigenous people is double-edged. It brings greater political attention to the Malay-Muslim community, which, following administrative reorganization, is now under direct government control through the Minister for Muslim Affairs. Under the Minister's purview is the Islamic Religious Council of Singapore, which oversees religious rulings pertaining to Islamic law, which is administered by the Shariah Court. Below these state organizations are community welfare organizations, which cater to the needy in the community. A relatively "unified community" is constantly projected publicly at considerable cost to differences within it.[8] Thus, outside the Malay-Muslim population, the organizations appear to operate in unison in promoting community cohesion and interests. Finally, as the smallest visible racial group, Indians feel discriminated against in many ways. For example, Lee Kuan Yew stated, when he was ready to retire from being prime minister in the early 1990s, that Singapore was not ready for an Indian-Singaporean prime minister. The question is whether it will ever be ready. Indians, however, are absolutely essential in providing the rationale for multiracialism as state policy. Without the Indian group, the racial politics of Singapore would have been reduced to a simple majority–minority dynamic of Chinese versus Malays, with all the untoward implications of domination and marginalization. The presence of the Indian community thus provides the substantive and conceptual space for a discourse of racial equality and racial harmony.

The uneven and dissimilar costs of the multiracialism policy to the three racial groups are underwritten, that is, made bearable, by the idea of racial harmony as a politically and ethically undeniable public good. The risk of disrupting harmony has rendered the entire domain of race politically sensitive. Public voicing of grievances by individuals or groups within a discourse of race have been quickly suppressed and the individuals publicly chastised, and even criminalized as "racial chauvinists" who threaten racial harmony.[9] Racial harmony thus operates as a repressive device for preempting public debate and negotiation and therefore the resolution of issues that commonly plague a multiracial society, such as racial discrimination in employment, the historical legacy of structural inequality, and the "real" sentiments among the racial groups toward each other. Suppressing rather than encouraging public discussion, the concept of racial harmony is thus maintained by the passive tolerance of visible and recognizable differences, without the encouragement of cultural exchange, deep understanding, or the crossing of cultural boundaries as befits a liberal conceptualization of "multicultural-ism."[10] Within the logic of the government of groups, racial equality and harmony have been fashioned into a political and social administrative device rather than serving as principles of group equality.

However, for state-promoted multiracialism to be effective, it must be socially productive. Most importantly, it should engender "cultural" security for the racial groups and their members. Among those who are concerned that their race-culture might be threatened by modern/Western values and eroded by ever-expanding hedonistic consumerism, official multiracialism assures them of their race-cultural security and continuity. The official guarantee of such continuity is thus constantly on display through government policies in different arenas, including elite bilingual schools where Mandarin and English are taught as first languages and government administrative assistance in the building of Islamic mosques.

With the equality of both individuals as citizens and racial groups in place, the PAP government is able to exploit the potential contradictions that arise from the conflicting logic of the two equalities to arrive at preferred decisions, depending on the context. For example, the need to maintain the equality of racial groups may be used as a rationale for the displacement of individual rights; individuals, as members of a racial group, are presumed to be represented by it, and should express grievances through the group. This enables the PAP government to move away from liberal political notions toward its version of communitarianism (Chua 1995, 2004). However, the equality of individuals is invoked explicitly in the ideology of meritocracy, which individualizes education and economic success/failure, denying any social systemic structural disadvantages and/or discrimination of any racial group.[11] This has enabled the government to maintain a highly neo-liberal (individualistic and free market) orientation in the economic sphere.

Conceptually, an ideological formation is the result of the "naturalization of the historical." This transformation essentializes the existing social order as a "natural" state, freezing existing structural formation from further historical development. Thus, there has been little, if any, autonomous development in race relations in Singapore since the official ideology of multiracialism was established. All changes in race relations have been, therefore, by fiat, through government policies.

Malaysia: multiracial coalition in crisis

As a consequence of British colonization, Malaysia has, like Singapore, a similar population composition, with Malays, *Huaren*, and Indians, although the proportion of Malays, rather than Chinese, is larger. Since 1957, initially as the Federation of Malaya and subsequently as Malaysia in 1963, the country has been governed by an alliance of three race-based political parties: the

United Malay National Organization (UMNO), the Malaysia Chinese Association (MCA), and the Malaysia Indian Congress (MIC). The Alliance was the result of a political bargain brokered at the point of political independence from British colonial rule. As the indigenous people of Malaya, Malays were to be politically dominant; *Huaren* would continue to drive the economy, as reflected in the appointment of a *Huaren* as the first finance minister; and Indians would be assured of a parliamentary presence, including representation in the cabinet. Racial divisions were thus built into the political structure from the formation of the independent nation. However, unlike Singapore, this structure was not based on the principle of race-group equality. Rather, it reflected the unequal strengths of the three racial groups in different spheres at the time of independence. It was an arrangement that recognized and attempted to make permanent the inequalities among the racial groups, with Malay political supremacy, *Huaren* predominance in the economic sphere, and Indians as junior partners. Such a pragmatic "bargain" has turned out to be highly unstable as the nation has developed.

Buoyant economic growth throughout the 1960s contributed to the continuing political dominance of the Alliance. However, the same economic development also disrupted the political bargain. Malays began to demand a greater share of the economy, while *Huaren* became dissatisfied with their political marginalization. Things came to a head in the 1969 general election, when the Alliance lost its all-important two-thirds majority in the federal parliament, which had enabled it to implement policies and introduce changes to the constitution at will. The election result precipitated one of the worst racial riots in Malaysian history because, it is generally believed, the Malays feared their displacement from political dominance in their own homeland.

A state of emergency was immediately imposed and the political and economic spheres were radically restructured. In the interest of consolidating racial peace, several smaller political parties joined the Alliance to form a supra-coalition, the Barisan Nasional (BN; National Front). Since then, the BN has continued to govern Malaysia at the federal national level. Over the years, the UMNO has established itself as the dominant party and primary driving force in the BN, while elected members of other parties and races have been rewarded with junior political offices. While a handful of Chinese and Indians continue to hold cabinet positions, no Chinese has ever been appointed finance minister again. A New Economic Policy (NEP) was instituted in 1970, which was a 20-year plan (1970–1990) to redistribute wealth in favor of Malays until they owned 30 percent of the national wealth and, in the process, cultivate a Malay business and professional class. The NEP opened up opportunities for the UMNO to enrich itself through proxy companies and also created a political economy characterized by corruption and cronyism in which successive BN governments readily offered handouts to the favored. Selected Malays received undervalued shares of privatized

state-owned companies, were given privileged access to government contracts, and provided with easy loan terms to start businesses. In addition,
generous scholarships, at home and abroad, were given to Malay youth
(Shiraishi 2008). The NEP was thus a financially very costly exercise and had
to be financed by heavy borrowing from domestic and foreign funds.

Initially there was a significant amount of goodwill among *Huaren* regarding the notion that the expansion of wealth among Malays was necessary to
attain long-term racial peace, even though the enacted policy was detrimental
to their own interests. However, the NEP has proved to be a corrupt instrument for wealth creation for only an elite class of favored Malay individuals,
making them very wealthy. After three decades of such corruption and the
intensification of income inequalities brought about by the globalization of
capitalism, the NEP has become intolerable for the majority of the population, including many Malays. In a survey reported in January 2009, almost
60 percent of Malays surveyed disagreed that their power is threatened by
non-Malays, while approximately 66 percent of the respondents said the
threat comes from corrupt Malay leaders (*Straits Times* 14 January 2009).

The weakness of the national economy was exposed by the 1997 Asian
financial crisis, as were serious disagreements among the UMNO leadership
that had hitherto been hidden by a united front. The most significant disagreement was between then Prime Minister Mahathir Mohamad and his
deputy, Anwar Ibrahim, around the issue of economic restructuring. The
prime minister bailed out several high-profile Malay entrepreneurs and their
businesses with public funds and worked hard to forestall IMF intervention
by imposing capital control. The disagreement led to Anwar's removal from
politics, and he was subsequently arrested on charges of corruption and
sodomy.

Throughout the period of Anwar's dismissal, arrest, trial, and subsequent
conviction, massive street demonstrations were held in Kuala Lumpur, the
capital city, with calls for "*Reformasi*." The jailing of Anwar provided the
spur for the mobilization of civil activists, particularly around issues of
human rights and political and media freedom. It ultimately brought together
the political opposition and civil activists, who established a new multiracial
party, the *Parti Keadilan Nasional* (National Justice Party), led by Anwar's
wife, Dr. Wan Azizah Wan Ismail, and drawing in Malays who had become
disenchanted with the UMNO. The new party managed to engineer
an informal coalition of opposition parties, including the *Parti Islam
SeMalaysia* (PAS), the Democratic Action Party, nominally multiracial but in
truth an ethnic-Chinese party, and *Parti Rakyat Malaysia* (Malaysia People's
Party). It contested the 1999 general election with the explicit aim of
reducing the two-third BN majority in the federal parliament. It did not
succeed in doing so, but did manage to reduce the total number of UMNO
members of parliament significantly by defeating nine cabinet and deputy
ministers. This was to be a prelude of things to come.

Since the 1970s, the religious environment has changed in Malaysia, with

Muslims becoming more assertive. Reflecting this are the widely reported incidents of the progressive encroachment of Islam into the lives of non-Malays. One issue is conversion and its consequences. For example, recently, Indians and Chinese have had to go to court seeking the return of the bodies of their husbands or fathers who had supposedly converted to Islam, without the knowledge of family members. They have invariably lost their case to the Muslim religious authorities. The same holds true for non-Muslim women, who have fought for custody of their children in cases of divorce from converted husbands. Another religious issue is the destruction of Indian Hindu temples, allegedly erected on public land, without regard for local sentiment. Such destruction led to a massive "illegal" demonstration, resulting in the jailing of five organizers under the Internal Security Act, which entitles the government to detain people without trial. All of these events took place in quick succession just before the general election in March 2008.

In the 2008 general election, cleared of sodomy charges and out of jail, Anwar provided political leadership for *Parti Keadilan*, although he remained banned from contesting the election. He successfully convinced the various non-BN political parties to form a coalition, the *Pakatan Rakyak* (Citizen/People Coalition). This time, capitalizing on the grievances of the various classes and religious and racial groups, *Pakatan Rakyak* successfully prevented the BN from maintaining its two-thirds majority in the federal parliament. It also defeated the BN in five state legislature elections and formed the respective state governments. The election upset for the BN and UMNO was the result of the aggregate effects of the political, economic, and religious issues that had been rationalized in terms of the racial composition of the population. The election results threw the UMNO into disarray.

The case of Malaysia's multiracialism has many lessons to teach regarding race relations. In contrast to Singapore, where the claim of Malays to indigenous status is largely symbolic, in Malaysia, the claim of Malays to such status has effectively rendered the citizenship of *Huaren* and Indians as "lesser" than that of Malays. This is reflected in the unequal position of the three races in the initial Alliance and subsequently in all BN governments. However, results of the 2008 general election suggest that the unequal race-based coalition of the BN, and in general, racially divided politics in Malaysia, may have run its course. Nevertheless, *Pakatan Rakyat* remains a race- and religious-based party, and it is too early to see its electoral success as heralding a new "multiracial" politics. There is intense internal debate in the PAS, the Malay/Islamic party, with a segment of the party leadership viewing membership in the multiracial coalition, *Pakatan Rakyak*, as the future, and others remaining committed to an Islamic Malaysia with tolerance of others.

Ironically, at this point, the most optimistic note is provided by former Prime Minister Abdullah Badawi, whose own tenure in office was cut short by the 2008 election results. He rightly argued that the hegemonic more than two-thirds parliamentary dominance of the BN could not last forever, as the population was maturing politically with better education and economic conditions, and that the election was a reflection of a maturing democracy. Furthermore, the BN remains in power, albeit with a reduced parliamentary majority, but unlike the case in 1969 there is racial and political stability. From the present vantage point, Malaysian politics appears to be stabilizing towards a two-party state, with each party a multiracial coalition, although with a Malay leader at the helm. If the *Pakatan Rakyak* were to form the government after the next general election, disrupting the continuing domination of the BN, then the democratization of Malaysia would be complete.

Aceh, Indonesia: self-governing within a unitary state

Anthony Reid, an international scholar on Acehnese history, notes that Aceh has been "subjected to military occupation for most of the previous 130 years" (2006: 1), from Dutch colonialism to the New Order under the late President Suharto, and after that, the years of President Megawati. However, after Aceh suffered the worst earthquake and tsunami in its history in December 2004, a peace agreement was signed on 15 August 2005 between the Gerakan Aceh Mederka (GAM, Free Aceh Movement) and Indonesia's central government, mediated by former Finnish president Martti Ahtisaari and ratified as a new law three months later. It is neither possible nor necessary for the purpose of this chapter to recall in detail the long history of the violent conflict between the Acehnese people and the Indonesian state. A brief outline suffices to give some idea of the depth of the conflict, the better to appreciate the significance of the settlement.

Aceh's population of about four million is composed almost entirely of Acehnese. Javanese constitute a small minority, and mostly serve as government officials. Acehnese are distinguished by their "language, history and *adat* (customs)" (Reid 2006: 8–13). The closest Austronesian (Malayo-Polynesian) linguistic relative to Acehnese is Cham, which is found in today's Central Vietnam, rather than in Sumatra. This suggests that Acehnese were originally Islamized-Cham migrants from mainland Southeast Asia to northern Sumatran ports, following the marine trade route that linked the Middle East to southern China between the eighth and fourteenth centuries. The Kingdom of Aceh was purportedly founded by one of the sons of the King of Champa after the fall of the kingdom to the Vietnamese in 1471. However, the lingua franca of the archipelago has always been Malay, and this "may have preserved Acehnese as the intimate language of the village and family, and of poetic recitation" (Reid 2006: 8).

Regarding religion and *adat*, Acehnese are deeply committed to preserving the two as separate spheres. According to Reid, even during the colonial period, there were two elites upholding the two normative systems: the *ulama*, religious leaders, were in charge of administering Islamic law, while the village heads and district chiefs governed the customary system of landholding and inheritance. The division of the realms did not exempt their leaders from competition for power and dominance, which provided the Dutch colonial regime with the opportunity to "divide and conquer," working with the chiefs while using military force against the religious leaders, who put up stiff resistance against colonial rule as a "holy war against the foreign infidels" (McGibbon 2006: 318). In 1945, when Indonesia was under Japanese occupation, the *ulama* mobilized traditional religious elements against the chiefs and eliminated them, became unrivalled and gained control of local government when independence was achieved after the Second World War.

Conflict with the central government of the newly independent Indonesia followed quickly: while the *ulama* sought to create a just society based upon Islamic precepts, Jakarta's nationalist elite tended to be dominated by Western-educated leaders who harbored deep reservations about what they saw as the "fanatical" brand of Islam in Aceh (McGibbon 2006: 319). This precipitated a rebellion in Aceh, the *Darul Islam* (House of Islam) rebellion, led by the religious leader Daud Beureu'eh. The rebellion was subsequently quelled by the central government, which promised special status for Aceh; a promise it never fulfilled. During the 1965 coup and massacre of the members of the Parti Kommunist Indonesia (PKI), the *ulama* forged an unholy alliance with the military. This raised the *ulama*'s hope that the new military-backed New Order regime would accommodate the aspirations of Acehnese for special status on account of their ethnic and religious distinctiveness. Their hope was dashed once again.

After almost a decade of relative calm, a new political movement, the GAM, became active, and included many of the members of the earlier rebellion.[12] Aceh was declared a Military Operation Zone, and the repression and abuse of Acehnese intensified throughout the New Order period. The industrialization of Aceh, the extraction of oil revenues from it by the central government, and the continuing impoverishment of the local population contributed to the support for the rebellion. Ideologically, the idea that the Indonesian state was "an agent of alien Javanese oppression and an heir to Dutch colonialism" was concretized in military action, which in turn consolidated the identity of Aceh and Acehnese as a "national" community (Aspinall 2006: 161). After the collapse of the Suharto regime in 1998, the demand for independence intensified, organized largely by students and NGOs, and the insurgent GAM gained popular support and recruits. The combination of these forces posed a serious challenge to the Indonesian state. The two subsequent presidents, Habibe and Wahid, tried to rein in the military operations in Aceh but the next elected president, Megawati, reopened the door for the military to continue security activities while negotiations with the GAM for a ceasefire and special status for Aceh continued through international mediation. Throughout these negotiations, the GAM was not willing to give up its demand for independence or to completely disarm its members. Continuing violence finally led to the imposition of martial law in 2003, leaving the military with "a free hand to resolve the conflict in its own way" (Jemadu 2006: 284).

The cycle of violence finally came to an end with the tsunami of

26 December 2004, which killed hundreds of thousands of Acehnese. Newly elected President Susilo Bambang Yudhoyono refused to adopt the "security" approach. Goodwill prevailed during a series of negotiations mediated by Martti Ahtisaari, former president of Finland, and a Memorandum of Understanding (MOU) was signed. The MOU gives Aceh full local autonomy. Economically, Aceh has the right to raise funds with external loans, set and raise taxes to fund official internal activities, conduct trade and business internationally, and seek foreign direct investment. Aceh is to enjoy direct and unhindered access to foreign countries by sea and air, and is entitled to 70 percent of the revenues generated from oil and gas deposits and other natural resources. Politically, Aceh is entitled to use its own symbols, including a flag, crest, and anthem. All central government decisions that concern Aceh are to be executed in consultation with and with the consent of the Aceh provincial legislature and, importantly, Acehnese have the right to form local political parties to contest provincial elections. The MOU states that the GAM is to demobilize and disarm its forces completely and amnesty is to be granted to all of its members, and those imprisoned as a consequence of the armed conflict are to be released. In addition, various measures to rehabilitate individuals affected by the conflict will be undertaken. Correspondingly, the military presence is to be reduced radically to the necessary minimum, and any future movement of military forces of more than a platoon will require prior notification to the Head of the independent Monitoring Mission to be set up by the European Union and members of ASEAN.

The MOU was further reinforced by the provincial election in January 2008, in which the leaders of the demobilized GAM won all the seats contested and are now members of the governing legislature of *Nanggroe Aceh Darussalam* (State of Aceh, Abode of Peace).

In contrast to Singapore and Malaysia, where the central concern has been the management of a multiracial citizenry, the case of Aceh is one in which a unitary state, Indonesia, has had to deal with a territorially concentrated ethnic group with secessionist aspirations. Similar to other regions in Asia, the area is characterized by a long history of violent conflicts. Unfortunately, in most Asian nations—including Thailand, the Philippines, Sri Lanka, and the PRC—the central government continues to seek military and security solutions rather than political ones, and is unwilling to recognize the deep cultural differences of the territorially embedded ethnic/religious groups and their desire for the preservation of their cultural practices and identity through local autonomy. Indeed, it is often the failure of the central government to respect this local desire that pushes the ethnic/religious group into demanding an independent state. The case of Aceh demonstrates the possibility of a political solution for local autonomy without threatening the unitary state of Indonesia. In this case, the popularly elected local autonomous government is free to espouse Islam as the official religion, in contrast to the secular central government, which implicitly espouses the equality of individuals regardless of race and religion.[13]

Conclusion

To contest Kymlicka's Eurocentric argument that Western liberalism and democracy are essential ingredients in explaining the successful management of ethnic and religious differences, I have offered three instances from Southeast Asia in which the management of such differences has been successful, in different ways, within polities that maintain the electoral process for the selection of leaders but do not have liberalism as the national ideology. In each of these cases, the management mechanism is unique, emerging from the historical and political context.

Singapore is what might be called a "settler" nation, in which the current population includes the descendents of migrants. However, in contrast to settler nations in the West, such as Australia, Canada, or the United States, the majority of the present population is not descended from white colonizers. Singapore is located in a region in which Malays are the indigenous people and make up the regional majority. This geopolitical situation dictated that the new island-nation, in which *Huaren* comprise the overwhelming majority, had to adopt multiracialism as a constitutional principle. The state thus strives to maintain equality among the various ethnic groups through a number of policies, including an equal number of national holidays for all the visible groups, ethnic quotas in public housing estates that reflect the proportions of each group in the total population, and ethnic self-help groups in which the members of each group contribute financially to the group's organizations and programs and cater to the needy among the group. The division of the population into three distinct racial groups—Chinese, Malay, and Indian—has enabled the single-party government of Singapore to develop this division into a basis of governance that is greatly to the advantage of the incumbent political party and enhances its ability to stay in power.

Malaysia's population has the same Chinese, Malay, and Indian composition. However, the majority, Malays, are also the indigenous population. In the new postcolonial state, *Huaren* and the Indian populations were made unequal, junior partners of a ruling alliance of three racially exclusive political parties. The three race-based parties were crucial in maintaining stability in the early years of nationhood. However, the pragmatic assigning of power in the political and economic spheres to Malays and *Huaren*, respectively, ultimately proved untenable, as members of neither racial group were willing to be confined to secondary status in either sphere. The three-party alliance fell apart after little more than a decade. The subsequent reorganization of the political sphere spawned supra-coalitions of multiple political parties of different class and ethnic composition, of which there remain two: the long ruling Barisan Nasional (BN) and newly established Pakatan Rayak. After the 2008 general election, the BN lost its hegemonic position in the federal parliament, although it remains in power. This is arguably the result of the maturing of the democratic process in Malaysia—the loss of the all-important two-thirds parliamentary majority of the BN is no longer seen as a threat to Malay supremacy in the political sphere but has been accepted by the people, without violent incidents occurring. Going forward, an optimistic projection is a polity of two political parties, each a supra-coalition of constituent multiracial and multi-religious political parties, perhaps always with a Malay leader in symbolic recognition of the indigenous claim of the Malays in their homeland.

Finally, following the dashing of the hopes of Acehnese for the recognition of their distinctiveness from the rest of Indonesia and the abuse they suffered at the hands of authoritarian and military repression by the central government, Acehnese "Indonesian nationalist" sentiment during the decolonization struggle against the Dutch was radically transformed into the demand for Aceh independence, by violent means if necessary. However, the local and national effort required for reconstruction after the devastating tsunami in 2004 provided an additional impetus to the ongoing discussion for a political solution that was supported by the then newly elected President Yudhoyono, who suspended military action against the GAM. With the political will of both parties, the armed struggle finally came to an end, with Aceh gaining local autonomy within a unitary Indonesian state. The political legitimacy of the leaders of the armed struggle was consolidated through subsequent provincial elections.

The three cases discussed above are concrete illustrations showing that the successful management of ethnic differences in any nation state is the result of local developments in the social, economic, and political spheres over a significant span of time. In each case, the electoral process for the selection and replacement of political office holders has seen steady improvement. However, in none of the cases is liberalism the foundational ideology of the state or even the contesting political parties. These three Southeast Asian examples are clearly at variance with Kymlicka's "essential" conditions for successful multiculturalism in Europe and Anglo-America; rather, they suggest that there can be no in-principle general solution to the management of difference, and that liberalism need not be the ideology underpinning a society. For the many Asian nations in which sub-national violent conflicts continue, the case of Aceh is perhaps the most encouraging, as it points to the possibility of a peaceful political solution ending years of violence.

Notes

1 The literature on the liberalism/communitarianism debate is relatively large but there is no need to review it here. See Mudhall and Swift (1992).
2 Although the less discriminatory and politically correct term is "ethnic" groups, the term "racial" is the one used by the Singapore government and has become common parlance among Singaporeans. It is therefore adopted here.
3 Certain privileges are granted to Malays as the indigenous population, including free education at all levels. However, middle-class Malay university students have not had free tuition since the early 1990s. This change would suggest that these privileges are not permanent.

4 There was one exception. The Islamic population was to be governed by separate legislation, the Administration of Muslim Law Act, in religious and family matters. See Suzaina Kadir (2004).
5 Another education experiment to contain "westoxification" was the introduction to the school curriculum of religious studies as moral education. This initiative was quickly dropped when it was found that students were becoming more religious as a result of the lessons, thus possibly creating a climate of greater religious intolerance. See Tong (1992).
6 Indeed, the perpetuation of such divisions is commonly cited, by detractors of multiculturalism everywhere, as an argument against multiculturalism as public policy.
7 As the late doyen of Singapore bilingual theater Kuo Pao Kun asked: "Has any other majority population ever committed such an extraordinary act of voluntary uprooting, preferring to its own language (a major world language) one which its former colonizer forced upon it?" (cited in Lim 2007).
8 The persistent differences and grievances of the different sectors among the Malay-Muslim population are seldom aired in public, lest the apparent disunity be exploited by the other racial communities to weaken the Malay-Muslim community's bargaining position. See Suzaina Kadir (2004: 364–9).
9 In the 1997 general election, one of the candidates from the Workers' Party was publicly labeled a "Chinese chauvinist" by the ruling party, on account of his having expressed his opinion about the social and economic disadvantages suffered by those who are monolingual Mandarin speakers in the face of the ascendancy of English as the lingua franca. He is now a fugitive from the law for his failure to pay indemnity, resulting from a series of libel suits brought against him by several members of the ruling party, including cabinet ministers. In another instance, four Malay primary school students were denied entry on the first day of school in 2003 when they turned up wearing the *tudung*, the Islamic headdress for girls and women. See *Straits Times*, 1 February 2003.
10 Supporters of multiculturalism in the West tend to have such a liberal conception in mind. See Will Kymlicka (2005).
11 For a critical analysis of the structural economic disadvantage of Malays in Singapore, see Rahim (1998).
12 William Nessen (2006) suggests that there is long continuity of leadership and membership in the Acehnese independence struggle since the 1950s.
13 To the best of my knowledge, the case in the West most comparable to that of Aceh is Quebec, in Canada, where the struggle for local autonomy based on the ethnic difference between the minority Francophone and majority Anglophone populations remains a central political issue in this federated state.

Bibliography

Aspinall, E. (2006) "Violence and identity formation in Aceh under Indonesian rule," in A. Reid (ed.) *Verandah of Violence: the background of the Aceh problem*, Singapore: National University of Singapore Press, pp. 149–76.
Chua, B. H. (1995) *Communitarian Ideology and Democracy in Singapore*, London: Routledge.
—— (2004) "Communitarianism without competitive politics in Singapore," in B. H. Chua (ed.) *Communitarian Politics in Asia*, London: Routledge, pp. 78–101.
Fukuyama, F. (1992) *The End of History and the Last Man*, London: Penguin.
Gray, J. (1995) *Enlightenment's Wake: politics and culture at the close of the modern age*, London: Routledge.

Hauerwas, S. (2002) "On being a Christian and an American," in R. Madsen, W. M. Sullivan, A. Swidler, and S. M. Tipton (eds) *Meaning and Modernity: religion, polity and self*, Berkeley: University of California Press, pp. 224–35.

Hong, L. (2008) "Invisible semicolony: the postcolonial condition and royal national history in Thailand," *Postcolonial Studies*, 11(3): 315–28.

Jayakumar, S. and Koh, T. (2009) *Pedra Blanca: the road to the world court*, Singapore: National University of Singapore Press.

Jemadu, A. (2006) "Democratization, the Indonesian armed forces and the resolving of the Aceh conflict," in A. Reid (ed.) *Verandah of Violence: the background of the Aceh problem*, Singapore: National University of Singapore Press, pp. 272–91.

Kadir, S. (2004) "Islam, state and society in Singapore," *Inter-Asia Cultural Studies*, 5(3): 357–71.

Kymlicka, W. (2005) "Liberal multiculturalism: western models, global trends and Asian debates," in W. Kymlicka and B. He (eds) *Multiculturalism in Asia*, Oxford: Oxford University Press, pp. 22–55.

Lim, S. H. (2007) "Queering Chineseness: searching for roots and the politics of shame in (post)colonial Singapore," in E. Jurriëns and J. de Kloet (eds) *Cosmopatriots: on distant belongings and close encounters*, Amsterdam; New York: Rodopi.

McGibbon, R. (2006) "Local leadership and the Aceh conflict," in A. Reid (ed.) *Verandah of Violence: the background of the Aceh problem*, Singapore: National University of Singapore Press, pp. 315–59.

Mudhall, S. and Swift, A. (1992) *Liberals and Communitarians*, Oxford: Oxford University Press.

Nessen, W. (2006) "Sentiments made visible: the rise and reason of Aceh's national liberation movement," in A. Reid (ed.) *Verandah of Violence: the background of the Aceh problem*, Singapore: National University of Singapore Press, pp. 177–98.

Rahim, L. Z. (1998) *The Singapore Dilemma: the political and educational marginality of Malay community*, Singapore: Oxford University Press.

Reid, A. (2006) "Introduction," in A. Reid (ed.) *Verandah of Violence: the background of the Aceh problem*, Singapore: National University of Singapore Press, pp. 1–21.

Shiraishi T. (2008) "The rise of the middle classes in Southeast Asia," in S. Takashi and P. Pasuk (eds) *The Rise of Middle Classes in Southeast Asia*, Kyoto: Kyoto University Press, pp. 1–23.

Tong, C. K. (1992) "The rationalization of religion in Singapore," in K. C. Ban, A. Pakir, and C. K. Tong (eds) *Imagining Singapore*, Singapore: Times Academic Press, pp. 276–98.

13 Diagnosing the micro foundation of democracy in Asia

Evidence from the AsiaBarometer survey,[1] 2003–2008

Satoru Mikami and Takashi Inoguchi

Introduction

The end of the Cold War had a tremendous impact on countries around the world. Regime types and political units (national boundaries) fluctuated wildly. It was certainly a modern emancipation period that opened the window of opportunity for democratization in many hitherto authoritarian states. Indeed, the number of countries that introduced multi-party systems with or without the pressures of a popular uprising rapidly increased at the time. After two decades of trials, however, progress varies from region to region. While new institutions such as free and fair elections and a free and independent mass media took root rather quickly in Latin America and Eastern Europe, electoral fraud and outright repression have resurfaced in Africa and the Middle East.

The most "representative" region that reflects the variety of results of democratic experiments around the world is Asia, where we find (1) stable democracies whose transitions preceded the third wave (e.g. Japan, India, and Sri Lanka); (2) newer democracies that have persisted since the third wave (e.g. the Philippines, South Korea, Taiwan, Indonesia, Bangladesh, and Mongolia); (3) unstable pendulums that repeat regime changes since the third wave (e.g. Thailand, Pakistan, and Nepal); (4) stable authoritarians that have survived the pressure of democratization (e.g. Singapore, Malaysia, China, Laos, Myanmar, North Korea, Bhutan, Vietnam, and the Maldives); (5) war-torn countries that eventually began to construct governance systems with the help of international society (e.g. Afghanistan and Cambodia); (6) new states that emerged as a result of the breakup of larger political units at the time of the third wave (e.g. Tajikistan, Kazakhstan, Turkmenistan, Kyrgyzstan, and Uzbekistan); and finally (7) the special cases of Hong Kong and Macau. In short, Asia contains a measure of diversity in terms of political regimes, inhibiting an easy conclusion about the viability of democracy in the region, unlike in regions where democracy is either taken for granted (such as Europe) or is out of the question (such as the Middle East).

The aim of this chapter is thus to examine the achievements of these democratic experiments in Asia from the viewpoint of the ordinary citizen. There are at least two reasons such an approach might be useful. First of all, although tracking macro-political events such as the occurrence or non-occurrence of democratization of the state and the success or failure to maintain a democratic regime can provide us with some insights into the viability of democracy in the period subsequent to these observations, these events themselves are nothing but the subject we should explain. They are external symptoms that manifested themselves in state-level political institutions and practices, or macro-political consequences of underlying tendencies that cannot necessarily be explained by simply regressing them on local history. To make inferences on whether there is some potential for democratization in present authoritarian states or whether the foundations of democratic institutions are being eroded in existing democracies, we might need to shift the analysis from the national level to the individual level. Researchers of democratic consolidation have also paid considerable attention to mass public attitudes (Linz and Stepan 1996).

The second legitimization of inquiry into individual attitudes stems from the classical system theory. According to Easton (1965), individual citizens function both as targets of governance and as principals (albeit nominal) who input "support" and "demand" into the government as their agent and receive output from it. Any system, whether democratic or not, needs a certain level of support for its stable maintenance. A lack thereof can paralyze output functions, even though it does not necessarily lead to a revolution. If this framework is valid, support for a democratic system, as a kind of "support" with a context-dependent effect, can be a barometer of the health of existing democratic institutions and an indicator of the potential for future democratization in present authoritarian states. Furthermore, in real political life, we often encounter situations in which people's attitudes play a pivotal role in deciding the course of a country's political development, especially when incumbents try to transform a democratic political system into a non-democratic one, or when existing authoritarian leaders try to maintain their rule using plebiscites. In these circumstances, if a majority of people exhibit "support" for democracy, the democratic regime tends to survive, while a transition to democracy is more likely to occur in an authoritarian state.

Based on these theoretical and practical considerations, this chapter examines the micro foundation of democracy using survey data. The structure of this chapter is as follows. The first section reviews existing studies related to the political function of mass public attitudes, distinguishes both levels of analysis and the components of attitudes, then derives competing culturalist, structuralist, and behaviorist hypotheses on the determinants of democratic attitudes. We then introduce the data used in this study (*AsiaBarometer 2003–2008*) and explain how we operationalize the dependent variable:

citizens' attitudes toward democracy. The third section first describes the levels of popular support for democracy measured in each of the 42 available surveys, then shows the results of a series of multiple regressions that explore the origins of democratic attitudes for each sample. The results show that complex patterns exist in Asia, which inhibit the simple application of existing theories on political attitudes. We therefore suggest that there is a need to recast the framework for analyzing political attitudes in Asia. The final section summarizes our findings and considers their implications for the prospects for democracy in Asia.

Theoretical overview

Scholarly attention to the relationship between political regime and political attitudes or culture is not new. Needless to say, theories of political culture and system theory have been at least partly motivated by the search for factors that are conducive to the stability, longevity, and efficient functioning of democracy. Even scholars of democratic transition and consolidation and of the breakdown of democratic regimes, who are normally characterized by their emphasis on the role of strategic behavior in crafting and maintaining democracy, have already paid considerable attention to the importance of related concepts such as commitment. Their work can be classified into studies on (1) elite loyalty; and (2) mass public attitudes toward democracy. The most well-known studies from the elite-centered perspective include that carried out by Juan Linz, who examined how disloyal behavior among political elites in the face of seemingly intractable problems was critical in the breakdown of democratic regimes in interwar-period Europe, post-WWII Latin America, and Southern Europe (Linz 1978). In the context of transition from authoritarian rule, Adam Przeworski (1986) modeled the dynamics of commitment shift among political elites using a variant of the threshold model.

On the other hand, scholars have been slow to focus on mass-level attitudes in the study of transition. Nonetheless, since a mass of micro-level data have become available owing to the various barometer projects conducted around the world (e.g. the World Values Survey, Eurobarometer, Latinobarometro, Afrobarometer, etc.), empirical and systematic works have mushroomed lately (Diamond 1999; Tessler and Gao 2005; Welzel and Inglehart 2006; Mattes and Bratton 2007; Tsunekawa and Washida 2007). Welzel (2007), for example, demonstrated that "emancipative" mass attitudes have a significantly positive effect on subsequent democracy both before and after transition, using World Values Survey data. One of the authors of this chapter also found evidence that an increase in the proportion of people who prioritize, as the task of government, respect for plurality and freedom rather than the maintenance of order and substantive (economic) achievement enhances the likelihood of democratic regime survival, even controlling for the powerful effect of the level of economic development (Mikami 2008). This study joins this academic trend and diagnoses the micro-foundation of democracy using the AsiaBarometer Survey, which was organized by Takashi Inoguchi in 2003 and has covered 29 Asian countries and regions (including Hong Kong and Taiwan) and three Pacific rim states (the United States, Russia and Australia) to date.[2]

In addition to the distinction between elite political culture and mass political culture, however, we also need to be aware of (1) the unit of analysis and (2) the components of political attitudes, because theories and concepts concerning input from the general public are sometimes mutually overlapping and somewhat confusing. They can refer both to individual attitudes and to national character as the aggregate or average of individual ones, and can be defined to encompass a wide variety of aspects, ranging from estimation of the political situation to the sense of political obligation and efficacy. In this study, "political culture" refers to the aggregated or averaged individual "political attitudes" at the national level, while attitudes toward democracy, such as support for or commitment to a democratic regime, are defined as elements of the wider concept of individual "political attitudes," which can be aggregated or averaged at the national level to constitute one component of "political culture." Figure 13.1 graphically illustrates the relationships between units of analysis as well as the location of various concepts involved in the study of political culture or attitudes. Examples of concepts that have emerged from studies in which the unit of analysis is national include the thesis that a balanced mixture of participant and subject culture (civic culture) is best for democratic rule (Almond and Verba 1963), and the proposition that value changes (e.g. from materialism to post-materialism) or an increase or decrease in human networks and interpersonal trust (i.e. social capital) affect the likelihood of collective action, which in turn, if united as a civil society, can be a key to the healthy functioning of democratic institutions. Also, studies on legitimacy and the argument that "national unity," "horizontal legitimacy," or "stateness" is an indispensable precondition for democratization (Rustow, 1970; Holsti 1996; Linz and Stepan 1996) can be classified as national-level analyses.

The unit of analysis in this chapter, on the other hand, is basically individuals within each country although we also try to compare aggregate levels of support for democracy across countries. In what follows, we chiefly investigate the determinants of individual sympathy for a democratic system while taking the positive effects of higher levels of support for democracy for granted. One possible explanation for this causality is, as shown in Figure 13.1, the assertion that certain religions (e.g. Islam and Catholicism) or traditions (e.g. Confucianism) are inherently incompatible with democratic rule (Huntington 1991: 300–11). Due to its emphasis on the group over the individual, authority over liberty, and responsibilities over rights, Confucianism is regarded as undemocratic or anti-democratic. The problem with Islam, which is said to contain elements that may be rather congenial to democracy, revolves around its rejection of the division between religious and political life and the superiority of religious authority over secular government. These

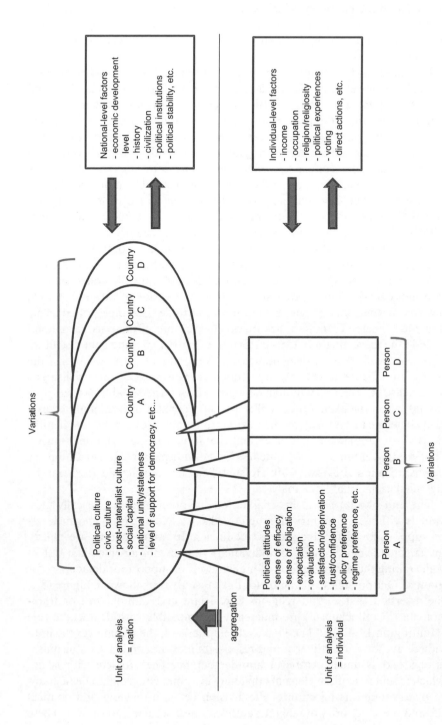

Figure 13.1 Units of analysis and components of political attitudes.

are the two most often cited undemocratic cultures, but others might also contradict democratic principles.

An alternative explanation is based on respondents' socioeconomic status as measured by income, occupation, and education, which as a structure might determine what people think and how they behave. For instance, researchers of the "comparative-historical school" assert that the middle class or working class was traditionally an inherent supporter of democracy due to their class interests: politically excluded segments of a society usually try to promote and defend a more open system (Moore 1966; Rueschemeyer *et al.* 1992). However, since exploited classes do not necessarily choose a democratic method for their redemption, as exemplified by the Mugabe regime in Zimbabwe, we prefer to keep an open mind as to the effect of citizens' socioeconomic status on their attitudes toward democracy.

Still another possible explanation comes from endogenous relationships within political attitudes themselves. That is, the perceived functioning of the political system and a sense of political efficacy can have some degree of influence on regime preference. However, these effects should vary depending on the type of regime in which respondents live. In democracies, a lack of political efficacy should engender a feeling of despair and disillusionment with the democratic scheme, leading to a susceptibility to non-democratic initiatives. By contrast, under a non-democratic system, people who sense political inefficacy can develop a desire for democracy in the expectation that democratic institutions will provide more effective avenues for influencing politics. In addition, perceptions of the functioning of the political system can have, by definition, different effects depending on the type of current political regime. In democracies, perceived untrustworthiness of politicians and officials who have been elected or chosen according to the democratic rules of the game may well generate discontent with the products of democracy and promote undemocratic attitudes, while greater trust in incumbents reinforces the idea that democracy works. By contrast, citizens living in non-democratic systems are expected to become democratic sympathizers if they lose confidence in the benevolence of those who occupy political office under authoritarianism. Based on the foregoing theoretical considerations, we explore the following three sets of questions in the remainder of this chapter.

1 Religious factors: to what extent can observance of one or more religions practiced in Asia, or religiosity itself, be hostile to supportive attitudes toward democracy?
2 Structural factors: which segments of society in terms of occupation are more democratic than others? What influence, if any, can being wealthy or highly educated have on attitudes toward democracy?
3 Political factors: do newly acquired political attitudes, especially a sense of efficacy and trust in an incumbent's benevolence, formed through the experiments of democratic politics during the past several decades have any influence on regime preferences?

252 Satoru Mikami and Takashi Inoguchi

Before we examine these questions empirically, however, we must first consider how to measure our dependent variable: attitudes toward a democratic system.

Methodological considerations

In general, supportive attitudes can differ both qualitatively and quantitatively. This applies also to the case under consideration. Mere support for a democratic regime and commitment to it are not the same attitudes. They differ in that the former can be volatile while the latter is, by definition, exclusive and unconditional. Commitment is exclusive, in that positive reaction is reserved only for a democratic system. While simple support can be indifferent and ambivalent among various alternatives, commitment must reject, by definition, all non-democratic alternatives. Commitment is also unconditional in that no matter what kind of problem the country faces or no matter how strongly people feel a lack of individual power in a larger community, commitment to a democratic system must be robust and the alternatives must be vehemently denied, even as a tentative solution. Meanwhile, mere support can switch sides depending on the conditions surrounding the system.

Thus described, commitment should logically enhance the stability of the political system with which its principles coincide and undermine the stability of the systems its principles contradict. With respect to a democratic political system, an individual's commitment to democracy should boost the support for the existing democratic system, whereas it should limit the possible support base for an authoritarian regime, thereby undermining the stability of the authoritarian state. If this argument holds, it seems to be obvious that what is important in considering the viability of democracy or the possibility of democratization is commitment to, rather than support for, democracy, because mere support for democracy ultimately guarantees nothing. Indeed, it is commitment that is stressed in the study of democratic transition and consolidation.

However, to move from an abstract theory to a verifiable hypothesis, we have to translate the notion into an empirically measurable and testable indicator. Here, focusing on a qualified concept such as commitment introduces a thorny problem, especially in a cross-national comparison. Let us show the difficulty with the actual question that we used to tap people's attitudes toward democracy:

Q. I'm going to describe various types of political systems. Please indicate for each system whether you think it would be very good, fairly good, or bad for this country.

1 Governance by a powerful leader without the restriction of parliament or elections.

2   A system whereby decisions affecting the country are made by experts (such as bureaucrats with expertise in a particular field) according to what they think is best for the country.
3   Military government.
4   A democratic political system.

This is the standard question on regime preference used in various barometer projects.[3] The first three systems—an unfettered leadership system, technocracy, and military government—are non-democratic alternatives, while the last one is the benchmark question to which most people, we assume, would positively respond (i.e. "very good" or "good"). If we are to take the aforementioned exclusivity and the unconditional nature of commitment, the first way that comes to our mind is to use the combination of responses that say "yes" only to a democratic system and "no" to all non-democratic alternatives. However, this approach entails one serious problem: that is, the non-exhaustiveness of the non-democratic alternatives included in this question. Non-democracies can take a wide variety of forms, including one-party dictatorship, absolute monarchy, and theocracy. Since resistance to various kinds of non-democracies can vary from person to person, it is perfectly conceivable that the same person rejects one type of non-democratic regime while accepting other variants of authoritarianism. Therefore, it is possible that the seemingly exclusive support for "democracy" is just a coincidence resulting from the fact that the respondent's favorite type of authoritarianism was not included in the list. Moreover, the difference in resistance to non-democratic alternatives may correlate with nationality due to the idiosyncratic political history shared by the population. In other words, vulnerability to authoritarianism's seduction is culturally and historically contingent, enabling a certain type of non-democratic regime to be accepted in the country where others are totally rejected. Therefore, the particular combination of responses cannot retain universality as a measure of commitment to democracy. Also, a latent variable approach through confirmatory factor analysis cannot solve the problem because it is apparent that the structures of factor loadings differ from country to country, inhibiting meaningful comparison of structured means of "commitment" measured as a latent variable.

   Therefore, we have no choice but to abandon the concept of commitment as a testable variable. Instead, we use support for democracy as a more practical dependent variable. Although more fickle, support is easier to capture because the response to the regime preference question is to a certain degree the indicator in its own right. However, this does not mean that we can take the answer at face value. Clearly, it is not sufficient to count on a positive answer to the question on the desirability of a democratic system because, first of all, the definition of the term "democracy" is hotly contested and consequently has quite a vague meaning for most ordinary people. Given the universal acceptance of the word "democracy" around the world, most people are expected to approve of it if they are straightforwardly asked about its desirability. Also, it seems highly doubtful that ordinary people can explicitly differentiate between support for the government, the regime, or the political community, and define democracy as one type of political regime without associating "something good" against the expectation of political scientists.

Thus, we have to be tactical in measuring support for a democratic system. But how then should we do it? Our answer is to use separately each of the questions on the desirability of non-democratic systems. In tapping popular attitudes toward democracy, we consider this approach more efficient than directly asking about a democratic system because by suggesting specific features of non-democratic alternatives while avoiding the word "democracy," we should be able to observe how people react to the violation of democratic principles without preoccupations.

Whether or not citizens can explicitly reject non-democratic alternatives also has practical implications. As mentioned in the earlier part of this chapter, when potential dictators or existing ones resort to plebiscite to transform a democratic political system into a non-democratic one, or to maintain existing authoritarian systems, they typically disguise their authoritarian intentions by describing their initiatives as a progress toward "the true democracy." Thus, it is crucially important for the persistence of a democratic regime or transition from authoritarian rule that ordinary people can discern the non-democratic aspects of pseudo-democratic systems and reject them explicitly. Or, even though the impact of rejection is not that significant, dictators should certainly have difficulty in implementing their projects in the face of public opposition.

This approach also has an advantage in terms of comparability across nations. Independence of irrelevant alternatives, to use the terminology of statistics, is not required because no particular combination of authoritarianism is used in this method. The consequences which might be brought about depending on the response to each of the three non-democratic systems proposed should be the same across different countries even though their implications for actual lives may be different from country to country. If the probability of rejection of a certain type of authoritarianism is low, this means that the country is likely to succumb to that particular type of authoritarianism. For these reasons, we use the rejection of each of the three non-democratic alternatives as a set of binary dependent variables (coded 1 if the answer is "bad" and 0 if otherwise) which indicate respondents' support for democracy.[4]

On the other hand, the three sets of possible determinants enumerated in the previous section are operationalized as follows. First, we constructed a series of dummy variables to tap 10 major religions (Catholic, Greek Orthodox, other Christian, Sunni Muslim, Shia Muslim, Hindu, Mahayana Buddhist, Theravada Buddhist, Taoism, and non-membership). We did not flag Confucianism because the respondents who selected this category were a tiny minority. We then chose appropriate dummies to insert into the equation, depending on the distribution of the religious structure within each sample.[5] Second, with regard to socioeconomic factors, we first categorized respondents' occupation according to an 18-category variable, from which we constructed a pair of dummy variables for "self-employed" and "unemployed." The reference category is "employed." We also inserted ordinal variables for income and education, respectively, whose scales inevitably differ from country to country.[6] Third, to measure respondents' sense of political inefficacy and the untrustworthiness of democratically installed politicians and officials, we used 5-point ordinal variables which indicate the degree of agreement to six statements: (1) Generally speaking, people like me don't have the power to influence government policy or actions; (2) Politics and government are so complicated that sometimes I don't understand what's happening; (3) Since so many people vote in elections, it really doesn't matter whether I vote or not; (4) There is widespread corruption among those who govern the country; (5) Generally speaking, the people who are elected to the [national parliament] stop thinking about the public once they're elected; and (6) Government officials pay little attention to what citizens like me think.[7] Finally, as control variables, we included dummy variables for gender (male = 1) and age, ranging from 20 to 69.[8] The surveys were conducted through face-to-face interviews (other than for Japan 2003) during the period from 2003 to 2008, using, basically, a stratified multi-stage random sampling method. Although in some countries—Brunei, Vietnam, Myanmar, and Laos—the questions were skipped for political reasons, we were able to collect data from 24 societies in East, Southeast, South, and Central Asia, as well as from the Pacific-rim countries of the USA, Russia, and Australia. All cases that included at least one missing value are listwise deleted from the following analyses. The resulting sample sizes and major religions are listed in Table 13.1.

Results

Attitudes toward democracy

We start with a description of the distributions of dependent variables. It is helpful to examine first the responses to the straightforward question on the desirability of democracy for the sake of comparison with the more indirect method of assessing attitudes toward democracy. Figure 13.2 depicts the proportion of respondents who approved of a democratic system. The results are ordered from left to right according to roughly equal records of political history. On the far left are fairly long-standing democracies such as Japan, India, and Sri Lanka, with the U.S.A. and Australia also being included in this group. The next group is the "third-wave" democracies, such as South Korea and Taiwan, as well as Indonesia and Mongolia, which have at least so far retained their newly acquired democratic rule. Then come the "unstable pendulums," such as Pakistan, Nepal, and Thailand, which are followed by post-conflict societies such as Afghanistan and Cambodia. Adjacent to them are

Table 13.1 Complete sample sizes and structures of religious distribution

	Country	Year	n	Major religions
Long-standing democracies	Australia	2008	753	Catholic (24%), other Christian (30%), none (36%)
	India	2003	782	Hindu (88%)
	India	2005	1,164	Hindu (91%)
	India	2008	1,039	Hindu (90%)
	Japan	2003	747	Mahayana Buddhist (13%), none (74%)
	Japan	2004	579	Mahayana Buddhist (25%), none (72%)
	Japan	2006	680	Mahayana Buddhist (36%), none (59%)
	Japan	2008	747	Mahayana Buddhist (32%), none (63%)
	SriLanka	2003	681	Theravada Buddhist (62%), Sunni Muslim (11%), Catholic (9%)
	U.S.A.	2008	823	Catholic (29%), other Christian (49%), none (13%)
"Third wave" democracies	Bangladesh	2005	938	Sunni Muslim (84%), Hindu (15%)
	Indonesia	2004	746	Sunni Muslim (91%)
	Indonesia	2007	935	Sunni Muslim (91%)
	Mongolia	2005	673	Mahayana Buddhist (74%), none (18%)
	Philippines	2004	671	Catholic (88%), other Christian (11%)
	Philippines	2007	817	Catholic (86%), other Christian (11%)
	South Korea	2003	727	Catholic (9%), other Christian (23%), Mahayana Buddhist (26%), none (41%)
	South Korea	2004	743	Catholic (9%), other Christian (24%), Mahayana Buddhist (20%), none (46%)
	South Korea	2006	950	Catholic (8%), other Christian (25%), Mahayana Buddhist (22%), none (43%)
	Taiwan	2006	957	Mahayana Buddhist (31%), Taoism (41%), none (24%)
Unstable "pendulums"	Nepal	2005	660	Hindu (80%), Mahayana Buddhist (11%)
	Pakistan	2005	903	Sunni Muslim (95%)
	Thailand	2004	764	Mahayana Buddhist (40%), Theravada Buddhist (58%)
	Thailand	2007	986	Mahayana Buddhist (54%), Theravada Buddhist (43%)

Post "failed-states"	Afghanistan	2005	697	Sunni Muslim (88%), Shiite Muslim (12%)
	Cambodia	2004	786	Mahayana Buddhist (1%), Theravada Buddhist (97%)
	Cambodia	2007	992	Mahayana Buddhist (13%), Theravada Buddhist (84%)
Newly independent authoritarians	Kazakhstan	2005	646	Sunni Muslim (38%), other Christian (33%), none (22%)
	Kyrgyzstan	2005	644	Sunni Muslim (77%), other Christian (13%)
	Russia	2008	891	Greek Orthodox (79%), none (14%)
	Uzbekistan	2003	590	Sunni Muslim (65%), other Christian (20%), none (12%)
	Uzbekistan	2005	589	Sunni Muslim (71%), other Christian (16%), none (9%)
Exceptional case	Hong Kong	2006	916	other Christian (10%), Mahayana Buddhist (13%), none (73%)
Stable authoritarians	Bhutan	2005	523	Mahayana Buddhist (93%)
	China	2003	767	Mahayana Buddhist (3%), none (90%)
	China	2006	1,937	Mahayana Buddhist (13%), none (80%)
	China	2008	968	Mahayana Buddhist (11%), none (82%)
	Malaysia	2003	623	Sunni Muslim (60%), Hindu (10%), Mahayana Buddhist (22%)
	Malaysia	2004	677	Sunni Muslim (62%), Hindu (8%), Mahayana Buddhist (21%)
	Malaysia	2007	850	Sunni Muslim (65%), Hindu (8%), Mahayana Buddhist (21%)
	Singapore	2004	571	other Christian (13%), Sunni Muslim (15%), Hindu (7%), Mahayana Buddhist (35%), Taoism (11%), none (13%)
	Singapore	2006	899	other Christian (12%), Sunni Muslim (22%), Hindu (9%), Mahayana Buddhist (30%), Taoism (9%), none (13%)
	total		34,031	

Source: AsiaBarometer, 2003–2008

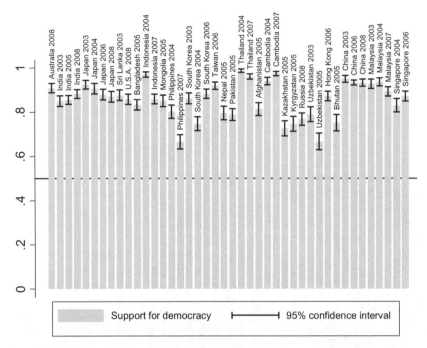

Figure 13.2 Levels of support for democracy.

Notes:
1 The levels are "very good" and "fairly good."
2 Double-sided bars represent 95% confidence interval.

newly independent authoritarian states such as Kazakhstan and Uzbekistan. Finally, stable authoritarian states are located on the far right. As expected, an overwhelming majority of people in all countries regard a democratic system as desirable, regardless of the type of political system currently in place or the past political record. If we rely exclusively on this indicator, therefore, we would come to the conclusion that existing democracies in Asia are as robust as their counterparts in the West, while surmising that democratization is imminent in most present authoritarian systems.

However, the affirmative answer to this question cannot be totally reliable because the question does not define "a democratic system" at all, which suggests the possibility that respondents approved of "a democratic system" based on their own definition or image of "democracy." As noted, given the status of the term as a golden rhetoric in real politics, it is not surprising that people tend to respond positively toward "a democratic system." Therefore, we need to test their true inclination toward democratic principles using non-democratic alternatives that contain certain elements inconsistent with democracy.

Let us next look at the proportion of respondents who rejected military rule in each survey (Figure 13.3). Perhaps due to the apparently repressive

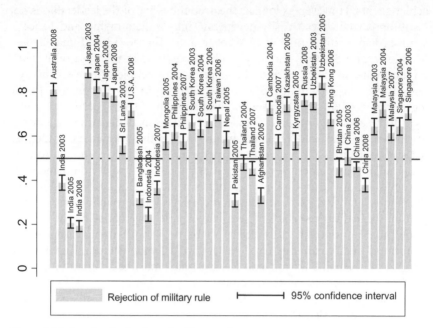

Figure 13.3 Levels of rejection of military rule.

Notes:
1 Levels of rejection: "bad" only.
2 Double-sided bars represent 95% confidence interval.

image of military government, the proportion of rejection still exceeds 50 percent in most countries. Roughly 80 percent of Japanese respondents, for instance, express abhorrence at the idea of military rule, which suggests a deep-seated distrust of the military caused by the devastating history of the first half of the twentieth century. Likewise, strong opposition to military rule seems to exist in South Korea and the Philippines, as well as in Taiwan, all of which share a memory of harsh repression by the military. In general, then, military rule as a non-democratic alternative to a democratic system does not seem to be viable in most Asian countries, although this does not hold true in countries such as India, Bangladesh, Indonesia, Pakistan, Thailand, Afghanistan, Bhutan, and China.

Turning now to the strength of support for democracy as estimated through the rejection of an unfettered leadership system, we find significantly lower levels of democratic attitudes. The system in which a powerful leader governs the state without the restriction of parliament or elections appears, at first glance, attractive, especially for countries in which the indecisiveness of the (coalition or divided) government has irritated most people during the decades of democratic experiment, because an unrestricted leader seems to guarantee a greater efficiency of governance as well as decisiveness in policy-making by reserving for him or herself some leeway to realize greater achievements. However, as long as the accountability of the leadership is not institutionalized, it can easily degenerate into a dictatorship and hence is against democratic principles. According to Figure 13.4, India, Japan, Mongolia, and South Korea seem to be susceptible to this type of authoritarianism among democracies. The percentage of people who reject this system explicitly is less than the absolute majority in these countries. In the meantime, concentrating power in the hands of a strong leader does not seem to be a viable option for would-be dictators in Bangladesh, Indonesia, Sri Lanka, Taiwan, and Thailand; incumbents in these countries would face massive opposition if they ever tried to perpetuate their hold on power. Among the present non-democracies, on the other hand, this type of non-democratic system is unpopular in Cambodia, China (including Hong Kong), Malaysia, Singapore, and Uzbekistan. This could suggest that public discontent is growing beneath the surface of seemingly stable governance by the current leadership. In contrast, there seems to be no serious opposition, for the moment at least, to an unfettered leadership system in Bhutan, Kazakhstan, Kyrgyzstan, Nepal, Pakistan, and Russia, which must be an ominous finding for democratic activists in these countries.

The final test is popular tolerance to a technocracy, in which all decision-making power is delegated to experts and electorates effectively cease to

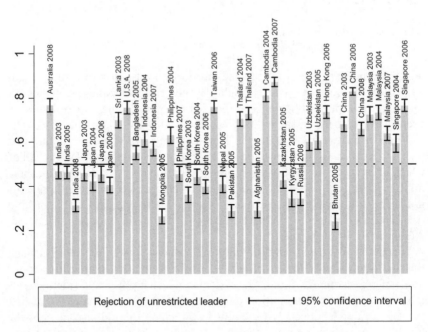

Figure 13.4 Levels of rejection of unrestricted leader system.

Notes:
1 Level of rejection: "bad" only.
2 Double-sided bars represent 95% confidence interval.

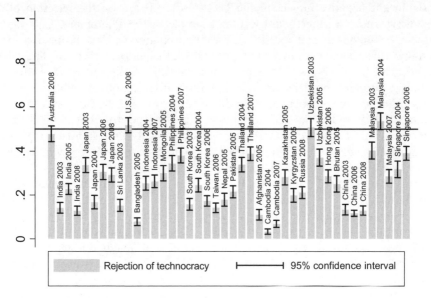

Figure 13.5 Levels of rejection of technocracy.

Notes:
1 Level of rejection "bad" only.
2 Double-sided bars represent 95% confidence interval.

participate in politics. Sadly, a majority of people in all Asian democratic countries under investigation tend to accept this type of non-democracy. Although the proportion of rejection is lower in the U.S.A. and Australia, the average level among Asian democracies is clearly even lower and vividly reveals the fragility of the support base for democracy in Asia. It seems very easy for authoritarian political leaders to transform their regimes by invoking the need for expertise. In any case, it is now evident that, in both the democratic and the non-democratic world, people tend, either consciously or unconsciously, to equate technocracy with "democracy." They seem to be unable to discern the inconsistency between the two systems.

Determinants of attitudes toward democracy

Having established the validity of measuring attitudes toward democracy through "reverse" questions, we now turn to the search for their possible determinants. Tables 13.2 to 13.13 list the estimation results of a series of logistic regressions. Beginning with the influence of religion, we note that all of the major religions for which dummy variables were inserted have an inconsistent impact on attitudes toward democracy. First, to be Catholic has a statistically significant positive effect in Australia when measured as rejection of unrestricted leadership and technocracy, but has a statistically significant negative impact in the U.S.A. when based on the rejection of military rule. In other countries, for example in the Philippines, Catholic membership has no statistically significant correlation with the propensity to support democracy in any form. Next, Greek Orthodox, which was flagged chiefly for the interview in Russia, has a statistically significant positive effect on the support for democracy in the form of rejection of military rule. Its influence on democratic attitudes measured through the rejection of unrestricted leadership and technocracy is also positive but statistically insignificant. Third, other Christian religions (chiefly Protestantism) have a statistically significant positive impact on preference for democracy in terms of rejection of unrestricted leadership and technocracy in Australia, and in terms of rejection of unrestricted leadership and military rule in Kazakhstan. In both surveys, its influence on the propensity to reject the third non-democratic alternative is positive, but not statistically significant. In South Korea 2004, however, members of other Christian religions are statistically significantly more likely to accept technocracy, although this tendency is not affirmed by the surveys conducted in 2003 and 2006. In other countries and regions, including the U.S.A. and Hong Kong, membership of other Christian religions does not have a statistically significant effect on any form of democratic attitude. Fourth, to be Sunni has a statistically significant negative impact on attitudes toward democracy in all its forms in Indonesia 2004, and in terms of rejection of technocracy and military rule in Kyrgyzstan. A negative impact is found in Kazakhstan, but only when measured as rejection of military rule. On the other hand, a statistically significant positive impact of Sunni membership is found in Singapore 2006 in terms of rejection of military rule, and in Uzbekistan 2003 in terms of rejection of technocracy. Also, the result showing that Shia Muslims in Afghanistan tend to accept technocracy implies that its reference category, Sunni Muslims, are likely to reject this form of non-democratic regime. Results in Sri Lanka show a degree of inconsistency among Sunni Muslims in that while they tend to reject military rule, they tend to accept technocracy at the same time. Sunnis in Malaysia show no systematic tendency. Fifth, Hindu membership has a statistically significant effect only in Malaysia 2003. That is, to be Hindu has a negative impact on democratic attitudes in the form of rejection of military rule. However, no other such evidence is found in surveys conducted in other years, or in other countries, including India, Nepal, and Singapore. Sixth, Mahayana Buddhism has a positive influence on democratic attitudes in terms of rejection of unrestricted leadership and military rule in Taiwan, and in terms of rejection of technocracy in Singapore 2006, but a statistically negative impact is found in China 2008, where Mahayana Buddhists systematically tend to accept technocracy. Seventh, Theravada Buddhism has a statistically positive impact on democratic attitudes measured through rejection of unrestricted leadership in Sri Lanka, through rejection of technocracy in Thailand 2004 and 2007, but has a negative impact if based on the rejection of technocracy and military rule in Cambodia

2007. Given the fact that the reference category in both Thailand and Cambodia is Mahayana Buddhism, the results in both countries indicate that the relative affinity of these sects with democratic principles depends on the context. Eighth, Taoism is found to have a statistically positive influence on democracy in Taiwan in relation to rejection of unrestricted leadership, and in Singapore 2006 in terms of rejection of technocracy and military rule. Finally, not belonging to any religious group exerts a statistically positive influence on democratic support in Australia (if based on the rejection of unrestricted leadership and technocracy), in Singapore 2006 (if based on the rejection of technocracy and military rule), and in Russia (if based on the rejection of military rule). On the other hand, non-membership of a religious group has a statistically significant negative impact on democratic support in South Korea 2003 and 2004 (in terms of rejection of unrestricted leadership and technocracy, respectively) and in Japan 2006 (in terms of rejection of military rule). China 2008 indicates some inconsistency in that technocracy is more likely to be accepted by those without any religious affiliation, whereas military rule is more likely to be rejected by people in the same category.

Let us now leave religion and turn to socioeconomic structures, which include occupation, education, and income. As noted, occupations were classified into three groups, namely, self-employed, employed, and unemployed. Using employed as baseline, we compare the effects of being self-employed and unemployed in turn. Self-employed status has a statistically significant negative effect on democratic attitudes in Japan 2003 and 2004 (when measured as rejection of military rule and unrestricted leadership, respectively), in the Philippines 2007 (when measured as rejection of unrestricted leadership), in Thailand 2007 and Russia (when measured as rejection of technocracy), and in South Korea 2004, Taiwan, Afghanistan, and Uzbekistan 2005 (when measured as rejection of military rule). But it also exerts a positive impact on the tendency to support democracy in Kazakhstan (if based on the rejection of technocracy), in Bangladesh (when measured by rejection of military rule), in Singapore 2004 (when based on the rejection of both unrestricted leadership and military rule), and in Pakistan (according to the rejection of all three non-democratic alternatives). Inconsistent effects can be found in Indonesia and China, where the self-employed systematically tend to support some non-democratic alternatives and reject others, although the types of authoritarianism favored and spurned in each country differ. On the other hand, unemployed status has a positive impact on democratic attitudes in India 2003, the Philippines 2004, and China 2008 (as indicated by the rejection of unrestricted leadership), as well as in Pakistan and China (in both 2003 and 2008) in terms of rejection of military rule. However, a negative impact of unemployed status on democratic support predominates as shown by the results in Taiwan, Malaysia 2007, Nepal, Afghanistan, and Uzbekistan 2005 (if measured through the rejection of military rule) as well as in Malaysia 2003, South Korea 2003, Thailand 2004, and Singapore 2004 (if measured through the rejection of technocracy). In Kazakhstan and Indonesia 2007, unemployed people are more susceptible than employed people to seduction by two of the non-democratic alternatives. Inconsistent (or changing) tendencies can be found in Japan, where the unemployed tended to accept unrestricted leadership in 2003 and technocracy in 2006, but rejected military rule and unrestricted leadership in other years.

Respondents' education and income level can also structure their interests, which in turn may well affect the probability of rejection of non-democratic alternatives. Most of the statistically significant effects with regard to education point to the direction of increase in the probability of rejection of some kind of non-democratic regime, whereas only a few results indicate the opposite effect, namely, those for Afghanistan, Kazakhstan, and Taiwan. China 2006, South Korea 2003, and Thailand exhibit mixed results, yet a consistency still exists whereby the more educated tend to reject military rule while tending to accept technocracy at the same time. Likewise, the effect of income is overwhelmingly positive. Only in South Korea 2003 does higher income systematically correlate with a greater probability of acceptance of technocracy. However, several inconsistencies or changing preferences are also detected. In India, while higher income promotes democratic attitudes in the form of rejection of unrestricted leadership and military rule in 2003, it facilitated the acceptance of technocracy and unrestricted leadership in 2008. In 2005, unfettered leadership was acceptable for wealthier people, but the reverse was the case for military rule. In Indonesia, the higher income segment of society in 2004 was a stronghold of democracy in the sense that unrestricted leadership and technocracy are unpopular, whereas the same tier in 2007 was willing to welcome unfettered leadership. Finally, although the Malaysian upper class in 2004 is as robust as its counterparts in the U.S.A. or in Thailand 2007 in opposing all of the three non-democratic alternatives, the 2007 cohort was more likely to succumb to technocracy.

The last causalities we examine are those emanating from a sense of political inefficacy and the untrustworthiness of incumbents acquired through the actual political process. As noted, a lower level of political efficacy should negatively correlate with the probability of rejection of non-democratic alternatives among the people in democratic systems, while the reverse sign is expected in authoritarian states. Likewise, the untrustworthiness of incumbents should have a negative influence on democratic attitudes among citizens in democracies, while among people in authoritarian states, it should enhance the probability of rejecting non-democratic systems only when the current system corresponds to the type of non-democracy asked about in the survey. The results are not as clear as our hypotheses forecast. First of all, regardless of the current type of political regime, a sense of political inefficacy tends to have a statistically significant negative impact on democratic attitudes. Although the expected positive impacts are also found in the results of surveys conducted in authoritarian regimes, it is difficult to conclude that the evidence systematically supports the hypothesis that the direction of the influence of political inefficacy depends on whether or not the current system is democratic. Second, the perceived untrustworthiness of incumbents has both positive and negative impacts on democratic attitudes, again without correlating to the type of political system currently in place. It is only in Kazakhstan, Pakistan, and Thailand 2007 that the expected effect can be found: that is, those who regard the incumbent unrestricted leaders (Kazakhstan) or military regime (Pakistan and Thailand) as untrustworthy tend to reject their respective systems.

But why did we obtain the unexpected results with respect to the influences of political inefficacy and the untrustworthiness of incumbents? One possible explanation is reverse causality: that is, those who prefer democracy and reject authoritarian systems are more likely to believe that they have political power and to subscribe to the belief that power tends to corrupt, while those who detach themselves from politics and hence are unlikely to deny the legitimacy of non-democratic systems tend to think of themselves as politically powerless and to believe groundlessly in the benevolence of power holders. Therefore, the negative impacts of political inefficacy predominate among citizens of authoritarian states, and we find evidence of both positive and negative influences of untrustworthy incumbents, especially in democracies.

However, especially for the unexpected positive influences of untrustworthiness, or the negative influences of the trustworthiness of incumbents, there is also another explanation based on the different meaning of power in the Asian context. As Lucian Pye observes, "for most Asians the acceptance of authority is not inherently bad but rather is an acceptable key to finding personal security" (Pye 1985: x). He further notes:

> In most of Asia the concept of power was exactly the opposite: to have power was to be spared the chore of decision-making. [. . .] Whereas Americans feel that it is exhilarating to make decisions and that being denied a choice is depressing, the calculus of pleasure and pain is reversed in some Asian societies. Making decisions means taking risks, while security lies in having no choices to make. It is the unfortunate weak who have to confront alternatives and make trade-offs, and thus become vulnerable to mistakes, while the [more] powerful the figure, the more constrained the life; kings and emperors were totally bound by rituals, customs, and sumptuary laws which governed every aspect of their conduct and limited their choices.
>
> (Pye 1985: 21–2)

In short, it seems that for people in Asia, as long as the authority is trustworthy, dependence on it can be legitimatized internally, whereas in the West, no matter how much one trusts the authority, it does not lead him/her to delegate his/her own rights to make decisions. Reliance goes against the concept of "having power" in the Western context, but not in Asia. Consequently, the trustworthiness of incumbents can have a different, or even an opposite effect on the rejection of authoritarianism in Asia.

Table 13.2 Determinants of rejection of military rule in stable democracies

Rejection of military rule	Australia 2000	India 2003	India 2005	India 2008	Japan 2003	Japan 2004	Japan 2006	Japan 2008	Sri Lanka 2003	U.S.A. 2008
Male	0.504** (0.216)	0.208 (0.224)	0.190 (0.194)	−0.062 (0.213)	0.122 (0.283)	0.405 (0.276)	0.571*** (0.222)	0.881*** (0.210)	0.134 (0.212)	0.276* (0.168)
Age	0.023*** (0.007)	0.035*** (0.008)	0.005 (0.006)	−0.004 (0.007)	0.026** (0.012)	0.028** (0.012)	0.018** (0.008)	0.006 (0.009)	0.026*** (0.008)	0.014** (0.006)
Self-employed	0.492 (0.560)	−0.212 (0.241)	0.136 (0.228)	0.207 (0.305)	−0.952*** (0.350)	0.643 (0.566)	−0.092 (0.307)	−0.217 (0.298)	−0.024 (0.285)	−0.184 (0.258)
Unemployed	0.147 (0.232)	−0.011 (0.230)	−0.108 (0.200)	0.127 (0.232)	−0.268 (0.315)	0.087 (0.284)	−0.154 (0.247)	0.499** (0.233)	−0.110 (0.220)	0.222 (0.203)
Education	0.281*** (0.110)	0.078 (0.054)	0.031 (0.054)	0.160* (0.085)	0.329*** (0.109)	0.177* (0.099)	0.339*** (0.091)	0.453*** (0.120)	−0.060 (0.104)	0.141 (0.092)
Income	0.041 (0.048)	0.049** (0.019)	−0.107** (0.038)	−0.081 (0.057)	0.055 (0.051)	0.045 (0.040)	−0.014 (0.030)	0.049* (0.027)	0.042** (0.017)	0.062* (0.037)
Catholic	0.393 (0.374)								−0.409 (0.330)	−0.805** (0.381)
Greek Orthodox other Christian	0.468 (0.369)									−0.425 (0.372)
Sunni Muslim									0.534* (0.325)	
Shia Muslim										
Hindu		−0.262 (0.241)	0.128 (0.267)	0.159 (0.316)						
Mahayana Buddhist					0.366 (0.528)	−0.425 (0.714)	−1.960*** (0.756)	−0.410 (0.495)		
Theravada Buddhist									−0.067 (0.218)	

Taoism

	(1)	(2)	(3)	(4)	(5)	(6)	(7)	(8)	(9)	(10)
No religion	0.287 (0.349)				-0.031 (0.365)	-0.498 (0.679)	-1.552** (0.751)	-0.337 (0.485)		-0.178 (0.423)
No power	-0.147 (0.113)	-0.220** (0.086)	-0.015 (0.066)	0.158 (0.109)	0.022 (0.159)	0.057 (0.147)	-0.069 (0.123)	-0.213* (0.113)	-0.190** (0.086)	-0.038 (0.095)
Politics complicated	0.067 (0.104)	0.052 (0.107)	-0.296*** (0.089)	-0.328*** (0.101)	0.291* (0.164)	-0.085 (0.159)	-0.268*** (0.136)	-0.012 (0.128)	-0.077 (0.091)	-0.200** (0.083)
Vote meaningless	-0.318*** (0.092)	-0.140** (0.063)	-0.160*** (0.059)	-0.126* (0.069)	-0.521*** (0.140)	-0.542*** (0.124)	-0.153 (0.103)	-0.298*** (0.092)	-0.119* (0.063)	-0.185** (0.081)
Corruption widespread	-0.219* (0.114)	-0.018 (0.109)	0.058 (0.103)	0.341*** (0.120)	0.173 (0.116)	-0.028 (0.123)	0.112 (0.117)	0.018 (0.104)	0.023 (0.101)	-0.158 (0.100)
Politicians nonresponsive	0.089 (0.130)	-0.364*** (0.111)	-0.065 (0.100)	-0.674*** (0.098)	-0.192 (0.205)	0.141 (0.191)	0.025 (0.136)	0.197 (0.131)	-0.068 (0.124)	0.005 (0.119)
Officials nonresponsive	-0.142 (0.145)	-0.043 (0.101)	-0.266*** (0.086)	-0.592*** (0.101)	0.516** (0.207)	0.284 (0.192)	0.102 (0.140)	0.041 (0.123)	0.064 (0.120)	0.002 (0.120)
Constant	0.738 (0.899)	0.647 (0.677)	1.332* (0.729)	2.393*** (0.841)	-1.852* (1.073)	-0.415 (1.224)	1.816 (1.110)	-0.417 (1.033)	0.431 (0.897)	1.611** (0.748)
Number of obs	753	782	1164	1039	747	579	680	747	681	823
LR chi²	78.36***	90.68***	47.61***	183.97***	63.88***	50.12***	56.36***	74.08***	49.61***	67.75***
df	15	13	13	13	14	14	14	14	15	15
Pseudo R²	0.108	0.087	0.040	0.181	0.123	0.094	0.083	0.096	0.053	0.069
Log likelihood	-323.924	-477.182	-569.854	-416.935	-228.637	-241.374	-312.094	-350.995	-442.400	-456.524

Source: AsiaBarometer, 2003–2008

* $p < .10$, ** $p < .05$, *** $p < .01$

Note: Dependent variable: Probability of rejection of military rule. Regression coefficients based on logistic estimation are reported. Standard errors are in parentheses. No power: "Generally speaking, people like me don't have the power to influence government policy or actions."; Politics complicated: "Politics and government are so complicated that sometimes I don't understand what's happening."; Vote meaningless: "Since so many people vote in elections, it really doesn't matter whether I vote or not."; Corruption widespread: "There is widespread corruption among those who govern the country."; Politicians nonresponsive: "Generally speaking, the people who are elected to the [NATIONAL PARLIAMENT] stop thinking about the public once they're elected."; Officials nonresponsive: "Government officials pay little attention to what citizens like me think."

Table 13.3 Determinants of rejection of military rule in new democracies

Rejection of military rule	Bangladesh 2005	Indonesia 2004	Indonesia 2007	Mongolia 2005	Philippines 2004	Philippines 2007	S. Korea 2003	S. Korea 2004	S. Korea 2006	Taiwan 2006
Male	1.078*** (0.255)	0.134 (0.215)	−0.117 (0.161)	0.460*** (0.167)	−0.011 (0.177)	0.145 (0.159)	−0.158 (0.181)	−0.125 (0.173)	−0.094 (0.156)	−0.055 (0.153)
Age	0.019** (0.008)	0.024*** (0.009)	−0.007 (0.006)	0.004 (0.007)	0.015* (0.008)	−0.003 (0.006)	−0.012 (0.009)	−0.004 (0.008)	0.002 (0.007)	0.003 (0.008)
Self-employed	0.402** (0.204)	0.021 (0.263)	−0.362* (0.189)	0.023 (0.230)	0.376 (0.265)	−0.047 (0.196)	−0.269 (0.203)	−0.534*** (0.194)	−0.171 (0.191)	−0.410** (0.203)
Unemployed	−0.015 (0.270)	−0.191 (0.233)	−0.333* (0.183)	−0.139 (0.198)	−0.114 (0.194)	0.057 (0.184)	−0.322 (0.216)	−0.206 (0.209)	0.115 (0.175)	−0.594*** (0.177)
Education	0.293*** (0.064)	0.097 (0.084)	−0.052 (0.106)	0.164*** (0.062)	0.019 (0.060)	0.047 (0.067)	0.154** (0.065)	0.103* (0.061)	0.114 (0.098)	0.130 (0.089)
Income	0.027 (0.020)	0.058 (0.045)	0.027 (0.035)	0.049 (0.071)	0.092*** (0.025)	0.023 (0.021)	0.053 (0.036)	−0.047 (0.035)	−0.003 (0.035)	0.016 (0.016)
Catholic					0.068 (0.256)	−0.236 (0.216)				
Greek Orthodox other Christian							0.010 (0.315)	0.154 (0.297)	0.366 (0.258)	
Sunni Muslim	0.275 (0.220)	−1.000*** (0.278)	−0.054 (0.258)							
Shia Muslim										
Hindu										
Mahayana Buddhist				0.186 (0.188)			0.063 (0.309)	−0.254 (0.304)	0.224 (0.260)	0.619*** (0.200)
Theravada Buddhist										
Taoism										0.111 (0.185)

	(1)	(2)	(3)	(4)	(5)	(6)	(7)	(8)	(9)	(10)
No religion							0.122 (0.298)	0.012 (0.279)	0.388 (0.243)	
No power	0.063 (0.084)	-0.182* (0.097)	0.093 (0.086)	0.041 (0.078)	-0.122 (0.095)	-0.091 (0.087)	-0.017 (0.076)	-0.117 (0.100)	0.115 (0.087)	-0.156 (0.097)
Politics complicated	0.094 (0.079)	-0.143 (0.106)	0.084 (0.091)	-0.019 (0.081)	0.164* (0.099)	0.206** (0.090)	-0.380*** (0.113)	-0.138 (0.121)	0.025 (0.101)	0.044 (0.097)
Vote meaningless	-0.306*** (0.067)	-0.230** (0.096)	-0.167** (0.082)	-0.073 (0.069)	-0.216*** (0.079)	0.067 (0.064)	-0.030 (0.072)	-0.227*** (0.067)	-0.181*** (0.065)	0.068 (0.080)
Corruption widespread	-0.149 (0.103)	0.033 (0.076)	0.237*** (0.075)	0.059 (0.090)	0.103 (0.089)	0.310*** (0.087)	0.367*** (0.127)	0.053 (0.121)	0.017 (0.110)	-0.059 (0.096)
Politicians nonresponsive	0.026 (0.097)	0.211* (0.110)	-0.046 (0.084)	0.045 (0.111)	0.047 (0.097)	0.042 (0.094)	0.121 (0.121)	0.124 (0.136)	0.134 (0.110)	0.234*** (0.086)
Officials nonresponsive	0.025 (0.106)	-0.073 (0.116)	-0.102 (0.093)	0.230** (0.102)	0.196* (0.103)	-0.101 (0.095)	0.131 (0.134)	0.109 (0.132)	-0.123 (0.111)	0.099 (0.104)
Constant	-2.949*** (0.860)	-0.468 (0.686)	-0.398 (0.621)	-2.196*** (0.673)	-2.741*** (0.715)	-1.467** (0.580)	-0.560 (0.881)	1.180 (0.822)	-0.153 (0.828)	-0.523 (0.826)
Number of obs	938	746	935	673	671	817	727	743	950	957
LR chi^2	158.13***	56.82***	26.79**	38.87***	58.4***	46.54***	45.71***	39.22***	18.87	45.88***
df	13	13	13	13	13	13	15	15	15	14
Pseudo R^2	0.135	0.068	0.022	0.042	0.066	0.042	0.049	0.040	0.016	0.039
Log likelihood	-508.819	-388.325	-600.591	-438.826	-416.395	-533.120	-441.036	-468.423	-592.679	-560.721

Source: AsiaBarometer, 2003–2008

$* p < .10, ** p < .05, *** p < .01$

Note: Dependent variable: Probability of rejection of military rule. Regression coefficients based on logistic estimation are reported. Standard errors are in parentheses. No power: "Generally speaking, people like me don't have the power to influence government policy or actions."; Politics complicated: "Politics and government are so complicated that sometimes I don't understand what's happening."; Vote meaningless: "Since so many people vote in elections, it really doesn't matter whether I vote or not."; Corruption widespread: "There is widespread corruption among those who govern the country."; Politicians nonresponsive: "Generally speaking, the people who are elected to the [NATIONAL PARLIAMENT] stop thinking about the public once they're elected."; Officials nonresponsive: "Government officials pay little attention to what citizens like me think."

Table 13.4 Determinants of rejection of military rule in unstable democracies

Rejection of military rule	Nepal 2005	Pakistan 2005	Thailand 2004	Thailand 2007	Afghanistan 2005	Cambodia 2004	Cambodia 2007	Kazakhstan 2005	Kyrgyzstan 2005	Russia 2008	Uzbekistan 2003	Uzbekistan 2005
Male	0.147 (0.178)	0.402* (0.237)	0.433*** (0.157)	0.085 (0.140)	0.502** (0.217)	0.274 (0.184)	0.028 (0.143)	0.057 (0.197)	0.184 (0.190)	-0.170 (0.170)	-0.031 (0.211)	-0.001 (0.253)
Age	0.013 (0.008)	-0.013* (0.007)	0.001 (0.007)	0.000 (0.006)	0.000 (0.007)	0.030*** (0.009)	0.023*** (0.006)	-0.007 (0.007)	0.007 (0.007)	0.005 (0.006)	-0.009 (0.009)	0.020** (0.009)
Self-employed	-0.197 (0.375)	0.551*** (0.201)	-0.263 (0.178)	0.241 (0.162)	-0.592*** (0.228)	0.393 (0.401)	-0.044 (0.232)	0.670 (0.479)	-0.192 (0.253)	-0.098 (0.332)	0.394 (0.398)	-0.921** (0.399)
Unemployed	-0.415** (0.194)	0.670*** (0.258)	-0.245 (0.214)	0.043 (0.187)	-0.514** (0.233)	-0.125 (0.187)	-0.085 (0.153)	-0.243 (0.215)	-0.246 (0.201)	-0.198 (0.199)	-0.001 (0.222)	-0.735*** (0.272)
Education	0.269*** (0.056)	-0.033 (0.062)	0.166*** (0.060)	0.037 (0.071)	-0.128** (0.063)	-0.012 (0.072)	0.159** (0.081)	-0.063 (0.076)	0.099 (0.062)	0.172** (0.084)	0.145* (0.075)	0.011 (0.091)
Income	0.048 (0.032)	0.024 (0.049)	0.056*** (0.020)	0.097*** (0.017)	0.103 (0.107)	0.032 (0.039)	0.026 (0.029)	0.072*** (0.025)	0.016 (0.017)	0.030 (0.050)	0.078*** (0.025)	0.134*** (0.044)
Catholic												
Greek Orthodox								0.817*** (0.270)		0.662** (0.272)		
other Christian									-0.129 (0.383)		-0.399 (0.352)	0.076 (0.444)
Sunni Muslim		-0.034 (0.338)						-0.538** (0.223)	-0.517* (0.311)		-0.169 (0.308)	0.168 (0.360)
Shia Muslim					-0.289 (0.269)							
Hindu	0.205 (0.293)											
Mahayana Buddhist	0.163 (0.374)											
Theravada Buddhist			-0.047 (0.156)	0.178 (0.139)		-0.606 (0.576)	-0.419** (0.188)					

	(1)	(2)	(3)	(4)	(5)	(6)	(7)	(8)	(9)	(10)	(11)	(12)
No religion									0.583* (0.344)			
No power	-0.040 (0.068)	-0.185** (0.081)	0.075 (0.083)	0.074 (0.086)	0.092 (0.095)	0.427*** (0.095)	0.070 (0.071)	0.098 (0.119)	-0.206** (0.100)	-0.039 (0.093)	0.069 (0.115)	0.183 (0.148)
Politics complicated	0.036 (0.090)	-0.153* (0.084)	-0.132 (0.089)	-0.231*** (0.089)	-0.096 (0.089)	-0.224** (0.109)	-0.061 (0.076)	-0.273** (0.116)	-0.026 (0.101)	-0.180** (0.086)	-0.151 (0.104)	-0.166 (0.136)
Vote meaningless	-0.044 (0.076)	0.016 (0.065)	-0.088 (0.087)	-0.202*** (0.061)	-0.209*** (0.070)	-0.009 (0.083)	-0.019 (0.051)	0.041 (0.087)	-0.311*** (0.070)	-0.080 (0.082)	0.078 (0.087)	-0.024 (0.108)
Corruption widespread	0.100 (0.167)	0.354*** (0.091)	-0.009 (0.078)	0.309*** (0.077)	-0.166* (0.088)	0.097 (0.071)	0.227*** (0.058)	0.036 (0.146)	-0.107 (0.109)	-0.047 (0.102)	0.169 (0.119)	-0.343** (0.168)
Politicians nonresponsive	0.274* (0.160)	-0.206** (0.096)	0.218*** (0.084)	0.136 (0.084)	0.024 (0.096)	0.129 (0.081)	0.026 (0.061)	0.001 (0.147)	-0.047 (0.112)	-0.008 (0.124)	-0.034 (0.138)	-0.166 (0.166)
Officials nonresponsive	-0.553*** (0.163)	0.134 (0.091)	-0.099 (0.088)	-0.035 (0.086)	-0.020 (0.095)	0.162* (0.090)	-0.102 (0.072)	0.129 (0.158)	-0.065 (0.122)	0.334*** (0.129)	-0.118 (0.159)	0.331* (0.184)
Constant	-0.475 (1.092)	-0.862 (0.708)	-0.877 (0.590)	-1.690*** (0.505)	0.889 (0.631)	-1.701* (0.903)	-1.161** (0.487)	1.052 (0.844)	2.592*** (0.878)	-0.214 (0.691)	-0.034 (0.913)	0.279 (1.218)
Number of obs	660	903	764	986	697	786	992	646	644	891	590	589
LR chi²	66.6***	41.91***	59.3***	100.76***	43.01***	56.71***	46.25***	53.94***	59.18***	28.6**	28.64**	31.14***
df	14	13	13	13	13	13	13	14	14	14	14	14
Pseudo R²	0.074	0.037	0.056	0.074	0.049	0.062	0.034	0.074	0.068	0.030	0.044	0.061
Log likelihood	-414.284	-538.944	-499.401	-629.128	-421.912	-430.860	-652.476	-339.021	-408.684	-471.060	-312.420	-237.954

Source: AsiaBarometer, 2003–2008

* $p < .10$, ** $p < .05$, *** $p < .01$

Note: Dependent variable: Probability of rejection of military rule. Regression coefficients based on logistic estimation are reported. Standard errors are in parentheses. No power: "Generally speaking, people like me don't have the power to influence government policy or actions."; Politics complicated: "Politics and government are so complicated that sometimes I don't understand what's happening."; Vote meaningless: "Since so many people vote in elections, it really doesn't matter whether I vote or not."; Corruption widespread: "There is widespread corruption among those who govern the country."; Politicians nonresponsive: "Generally speaking, the people who are elected to the [NATIONAL PARLIAMENT] stop thinking about the public once they're elected."; Officials nonresponsive: "Government officials pay little attention to what citizens like me think."

Table 13.5 Determinants of rejection of military rule in stable authoritarians

Rejection of military rule	Hong Kong 2006	Bhutan 2005	China 2003	China 2006	China 2008	Malaysia 2003	Malaysia 2004	Malaysia 2007	Singapore 2004	Singapore 2006
Male	0.057 (0.156)	0.015 (0.197)	0.848*** (0.161)	0.220** (0.100)	0.021 (0.138)	0.366* (0.209)	-0.033 (0.213)	0.037 (0.175)	0.060 (0.201)	0.452*** (0.164)
Age	0.007 (0.007)	0.012 (0.009)	0.005 (0.008)	0.014*** (0.004)	0.001 (0.007)	0.002 (0.009)	0.014 (0.009)	0.009 (0.007)	0.020* (0.011)	0.029*** (0.008)
Self-employed	0.513 (0.449)	0.559 (0.344)	0.185 (0.237)	-0.451*** (0.124)	0.178 (0.189)	-0.055 (0.321)	0.150 (0.338)	0.065 (0.281)	0.911* (0.498)	-0.172 (0.317)
Unemployed	-0.094 (0.172)	0.269 (0.244)	0.486** (0.192)	-0.068 (0.128)	0.408** (0.176)	0.277 (0.229)	0.021 (0.230)	-0.351* (0.190)	-0.199 (0.212)	0.187 (0.185)
Education	0.111 (0.069)	0.236*** (0.063)	0.265*** (0.065)	0.191*** (0.045)	0.137* (0.081)	0.184** (0.092)	0.133 (0.095)	0.110 (0.110)	0.105 (0.088)	0.178*** (0.071)
Income	-0.002 (0.022)	-0.001 (0.040)	0.049 (0.037)	0.080*** (0.020)	0.044** (0.021)	0.084 (0.053)	0.166*** (0.051)	-0.045 (0.046)	-0.021 (0.044)	0.049 (0.037)
Catholic										
Greek Orthodox										
other Christian	0.157 (0.251)								0.156 (0.499)	0.927*** (0.375)
Sunni Muslim						-0.405 (0.355)	-0.410 (0.367)	-0.551 (0.341)	-0.750 (0.474)	0.807*** (0.336)
Shia Muslim										
Hindu						-0.864** (0.428)	-0.578 (0.455)	0.061 (0.431)	-0.623 (0.530)	0.403 (0.373)
Mahayana Buddhist	0.151 (0.222)	-0.662* (0.372)	-0.322 (0.517)	-0.066 (0.229)	0.013 (0.346)	0.378 (0.397)	-0.221 (0.400)	-0.109 (0.363)	-0.376 (0.436)	0.371 (0.312)
Theravada Buddhist										
Taoism									-0.390 (0.496)	0.725* (0.392)

No religion	0.764**	-0.459				0.601**	0.001	-0.175	0.199**
	(0.364)	(0.489)				(0.286)	(0.195)	(0.300)	(0.099)
No power	-0.088	0.357***	0.138	-0.102	0.230**	0.077	0.042	0.108	0.088
	(0.104)	(0.125)	(0.094)	(0.105)	(0.096)	(0.090)	(0.062)	(0.100)	(0.113)
Politics complicated	-0.236**	-0.146	-0.017	-0.013	0.034	0.249**	-0.106*	0.242**	-0.004
	(0.104)	(0.128)	(0.101)	(0.114)	(0.097)	(0.101)	(0.064)	(0.108)	(0.116)
Vote meaningless	-0.039	-0.499***	-0.606***	-0.252***	-0.383***	-0.082	-0.082	-0.176**	-0.155
	(0.094)	(0.115)	(0.073)	(0.085)	(0.084)	(0.080)	(0.055)	(0.087)	(0.104)
Corruption widespread	0.018	-0.251**	0.242***	0.167	-0.104	-0.044	0.165***	0.043	0.115
	(0.093)	(0.115)	(0.092)	(0.111)	(0.098)	(0.071)	(0.046)	(0.082)	(0.128)
Politicians nonresponsive	0.023	0.028	0.220**	0.035	0.009	0.026	-0.026	-0.098	0.016
	(0.116)	(0.165)	(0.098)	(0.132)	(0.082)	(0.088)	(0.060)	(0.102)	(0.106)
Officials nonresponsive	0.337***	-0.032	0.005	0.001	0.162	-0.023	0.278***	0.227**	-0.125
	(0.121)	(0.155)	(0.109)	(0.137)	(0.099)	(0.089)	(0.063)	(0.102)	(0.099)
Constant	-2.042***	1.106	-0.139	-0.056	-0.778	-2.534***	-2.394***	-3.065***	0.614
	(0.694)	(0.942)	(0.814)	(0.864)	(0.874)	(0.646)	(0.384)	(0.711)	(0.632)
Number of obs	899	571	850	677	623	968	1937	767	916
LR chi²	60.71***	69.47***	103.35***	33.36***	59.42***	32.09***	165.77***	73.29***	26.02**
df	18	18	15	15	15	14	14	14	14
Pseudo R²	0.056	0.094	0.092	0.042	0.073	0.025	0.062	0.069	0.023
Log likelihood	-513.015	-335.665	-513.266	-382.308	-374.842	-627.334	-1254.890	-494.888	-560.354

Source: AsiaBarometer, 2003–2008

* $p < .10$, ** $p < .05$, *** $p < .01$

Note: Dependent variable: Probability of rejection of military rule. Regression coefficients based on logistic estimation are reported. Standard errors are in parentheses. No power: "Generally speaking, people like me don't have the power to influence government policy or actions."; Politics complicated: "Politics and government are so complicated that sometimes I don't understand what's happening."; Vote meaningless: "Since so many people vote in elections, it really doesn't matter whether I vote or not."; Corruption widespread: "There is widespread corruption among those who govern the country."; Politicians nonresponsive: "Generally speaking, the people who are elected to the [NATIONAL PARLIAMENT] stop thinking about the public once they're elected."; Officials nonresponsive: "Government officials pay little attention to what citizens like me think."

Table 13.6 Determinants of rejection of unrestricted leader system in stable democracies

Rejection of unrestricted leader	Australia 2008	India 2003	India 2005	India 2008	Japan 2003	Japan 2004	Japan 2006	Japan 2008	SriLanka 2003	U.S.A. 2008
Male	0.137 (0.197)	0550 ** (0.221)	0.256 (0.159)	-0.001 (0.174)	0.039 (0.172)	-0.177 (0.211)	0.056 (0.176)	0.330** (0.166)	-0.121 (0.230)	0.192 (0.179)
Age	0.012* (0.007)	0.018** (0.007)	-0.002 (0.005)	-0.005 (0.006)	0.007 (0.007)	0.017* (0.009)	-0.006 (0.007)	-0.004 (0.007)	0.016* (0.008)	0.012* (0.006)
Self-employed	-0.194 (0.426)	0.252 (0.236)	-0.232 (0.200)	-0.125 (0.248)	-0.310 (0.226)	-0.568* (0.337)	-0.171 (0.241)	-0.145 (0.245)	0.078 (0.292)	0.162 (0.293)
Unemployed	0.166 (0.223)	0.526** (0.228)	0.231 (0.165)	-0.101 (0.187)	-0.109 (0.200)	-0.459** (0.227)	-0.118 (0.203)	0.414** (0.191)	0.254 (0.238)	0.085 (0.213)
Education	0.075 (0.102)	0.129** (0.052)	-0.019 (0.044)	0.124* (0.069)	0.204*** (0.061)	0.098 (0.071)	0.077 (0.065)	0.227*** (0.088)	0.230** (0.110)	0.124 (0.098)
Income	0.089** (0.045)	0.033* (0.019)	0.063** (0.030)	-0.095** (0.048)	-0.024 (0.030)	0.058** (0.027)	0.026 (0.023)	0.020 (0.020)	-0.012 (0.018)	0.093** (0.040)
Catholic	0.660** (0.333)								0.209 (0.340)	-0.369 (0.384)
Greek Orthodox other Christian	0.786** (0.330)									-0.154 (0.372)
Sunni Muslim									0.329 (0.326)	
Shia Muslim										
Hindu		0.206 (0.237)	0.291 (0.217)	-0.179 (0.236)						
Mahayana Buddhist					-0.052 (0.300)	-0.321 (0.518)	-0.273 (0.351)	-0.249 (0.359)		
Theravada Buddhist									0.458** (0.225)	

Taoism

No religion	0.903*** (0.317)			-0.227 (0.232)	0.203 (0.491)	-0.163 (0.341)	-0.093 (0.348)			0.289 (0.436)
No power	-0.267** (0.106)	-0.219** (0.086)	-0.016 (0.055)	0.005 (0.088)	0.032 (0.088)	-0.159 (0.099)	-0.162* (0.093)	-0.005 (0.087)	0.038 (0.091)	-0.050 (0.105)
Politics complicated	-0.154 (0.100)	-0.050 (0.105)	-0.157** (0.077)	-0.143* (0.084)	0.272*** (0.100)	-0.038 (0.109)	0.083 (0.100)	0.101 (0.097)	0.049 (0.096)	0.136 (0.090)
Vote meaningless	-0.357*** (0.086)	-0.298*** (0.061)	-0.331*** (0.047)	-0.287*** (0.055)	-0.307*** (0.083)	-0.040 (0.093)	-0.300*** (0.085)	-0.093 (0.078)	-0.219*** (0.068)	-0.540*** (0.087)
Corruption widespread	-0.195* (0.107)	0.010 (0.107)	-0.077 (0.087)	0.312*** (0.098)	-0.001 (0.078)	0.135 (0.094)	0.051 (0.091)	-0.076 (0.082)	-0.175 (0.113)	-0.013 (0.106)
Politicians nonresponsive	0.076 (0.122)	-0.110 (0.109)	0.143* (0.085)	-0.241*** (0.082)	-0.125 (0.116)	-0.120 (0.138)	-0.026 (0.105)	0.065 (0.103)	0.040 (0.129)	-0.155 (0.132)
Officials nonresponsive	-0.069 (0.135)	-0.036 (0.099)	-0.212** (0.076)	-0.474*** (0.085)	0.079 (0.122)	0.207 (0.140)	0.073 (0.108)	-0.022 (0.097)	0.136 (0.126)	0.015 (0.130)
Constant	2.249*** (0.840)	0.131 (0.667)	1.361** (0.613)	2.215*** (0.680)	-1.076 (0.684)	-1.747* (0.933)	0.517 (0.737)	-1.232 (0.820)	-0.668 (0.959)	1.333* (0.779)
Number of obs	753	782	1164	1039	747	579	680	747	681	823
LR chi^2	102.62***	86.5***	89.26***	122.78***	38.29***	34.39***	27.8**	24.01**	29.74***	90.29***
df	15	13	13	13	14	14	14	14	15	15
Pseudo R^2	0.126	0.080	0.056	0.095	0.037	0.044	0.030	0.024	0.036	0.099
Log likelihood	-356.941	-497.317	-759.013	-584.166	-496.306	-376.956	-454.611	-492.389	-401.719	-412.363

Source: AsiaBarometer, 2003–2008

$* p < .10, ** p < .05, *** p < .01$

Note: Dependent variable: Probability of rejection of unrestricted leadership. Regression coefficients based on logistic estimation are reported. Standard errors are in parentheses. No power: "Generally speaking, people like me don't have the power to influence government policy or actions."; Politics complicated: "Politics and government are so complicated that sometimes I don't understand what's happening."; Vote meaningless: "Since so many people vote in elections, it really doesn't matter whether I vote or not."; Corruption widespread: "There is widespread corruption among those who govern the country."; Politicians nonresponsive: "Generally speaking, the people who are elected to the [NATIONAL PARLIAMENT] stop thinking about the public once they're elected."; Officials nonresponsive: "Government officials pay little attention to what citizens like me think."

Table 13.7 Determinants of rejection of unrestricted leader system in new democracies

Rejection of unrestricted leader	Bangladesh 2005	Indonesia 2004	Indonesia 2007	Mongolia 2005	Philippines 2004	Philippines 2007	S. Korea 2003	S. Korea 2004	S. Korea 2006	Taiwan 2006
Male	0.623*** (0.242)	0.163 (0.196)	−0.295* (0.160)	0.012 (0.186)	−0.046 (0.175)	0.069 (0.158)	0.153 (0.174)	−0.350** (0.167)	−0.192 (0.150)	−0.005 (0.164)
Age	0.004 (0.007)	0.008 (0.008)	−0.007 (0.006)	−0.009 (0.008)	0.021*** (0.008)	−0.002 (0.006)	−0.026*** (0.009)	−0.010 (0.008)	−0.002 (0.007)	0.001 (0.008)
Self-employed	−0.053 (0.199)	0.179 (0.242)	0.294 (0.187)	0.258 (0.245)	0.182 (0.255)	−0.326* (0.197)	0.026 (0.198)	0.111 (0.188)	0.073 (0.187)	0.079 (0.229)
Unemployed	0.148 (0.253)	0.070 (0.208)	−0.509*** (0.182)	−0.328 (0.224)	0.386** (0.196)	−0.172 (0.184)	−0.093 (0.212)	−0.183 (0.200)	−0.025 (0.167)	−0.266 (0.187)
Education	0.071 (0.061)	0.117 (0.083)	0.152 (0.104)	0.193*** (0.067)	0.081 (0.059)	−0.003 (0.067)	0.096 (0.061)	0.134** (0.058)	−0.071 (0.095)	0.096 (0.096)
Income	0.010 (0.018)	0.099** (0.040)	−0.062* (0.034)	0.016 (0.079)	0.036 (0.025)	0.014 (0.021)	−0.045 (0.035)	−0.026 (0.035)	−0.027 (0.034)	0.035** (0.017)
Catholic					−0.086 (0.256)	−0.204 (0.213)				
Greek Orthodox other Christian									0.379 (0.255)	
Sunni Muslim	−0.093 (0.191)	−0.930*** (0.316)	−0.294 (0.262)							
Shia Muslim										
Hindu										
Mahayana Buddhist				0.165 (0.214)			−0.314 (0.299)	−0.142 (0.294)	−0.041 (0.261)	0.406** (0.206)
Theravada Buddhist										
Taoism										0.389** (0.198)

	(1)	(2)	(3)	(4)	(5)	(6)	(7)	(8)	(9)	(10)
No religion	0.121						−0.477*	−0.163	0.194	
	(0.075)						(0.286)	(0.268)	(0.243)	
No power	0.151**	0.159*	0.027	−0.064	−0.288***		0.087	−0.170*	0.064	−0.184*
	(0.070)	(0.084)	(0.087)	(0.092)	(0.090)		(0.074)	(0.091)	(0.084)	(0.104)
Politics complicated	−0.013	−0.076	0.036	0.091	−0.040		−0.203**	0.061	−0.175*	0.061
	(0.098)	(0.089)	(0.089)	(0.098)	(0.092)		(0.101)	(0.112)	(0.097)	(0.102)
Vote meaningless	−0.295***	−0.288***	−0.085	0.024	−0.297***	−0.291***	0.012	−0.188***	−0.151**	−0.167**
	(0.054)	(0.082)	(0.081)	(0.078)	(0.078)	(0.065)	(0.071)	(0.066)	(0.063)	(0.084)
Corruption widespread	−0.239**	0.022	−0.040	0.172	0.124	0.333***	0.084	0.183	−0.037	0.075
	(0.096)	(0.069)	(0.072)	(0.107)	(0.089)	(0.089)	(0.126)	(0.120)	(0.106)	(0.101)
Politicians nonresponsive	0.060	0.300***	−0.159*	−0.356***	0.051	0.319***	−0.138	−0.089	0.089	0.300***
	(0.088)	(0.098)	(0.081)	(0.126)	(0.099)	(0.096)	(0.121)	(0.131)	(0.105)	(0.092)
Officials nonresponsive	0.140	−0.053	0.045	0.338***	−0.071	−0.174*	0.316**	0.039	−0.010	0.171
	(0.095)	(0.101)	(0.091)	(0.123)	(0.104)	(0.097)	(0.136)	(0.128)	(0.105)	(0.111)
Constant	−0.809	0.471	1.529**	−2.469***	−0.979	0.168	−0.162	0.304	0.570	−0.894
	(0.753)	(0.647)	(0.614)	(0.769)	(0.699)	(0.581)	(0.860)	(0.801)	(0.803)	(0.878)
Number of obs	938	746	935	673	671	817	727	743	950	957
LR chi²	67.42***	54.32***	41.31***	32.47***	37.88***	69.19***	32.18***	32.82***	17.79	44.89***
df	13	13	13	13	13	13	15	15	15	14
Pseudo R²	0.052	0.055	0.032	0.042	0.043	0.061	0.034	0.032	0.014	0.043
Log likelihood	−611.332	−470.846	−618.511	−371.530	−423.074	−528.438	−459.105	−493.491	−629.230	−505.307

Source: AsiaBarometer, 2003–2008

* *p* < .10, ** *p* < .05, *** *p* < .01

Note: Dependent variable: probability of rejection of unrestricted leadership. Regression coefficients based on logistic estimation are reported. Standard errors are in parentheses. No power: "Generally speaking, people like me don't have the power to influence government policy or actions."; Politics complicated: "Politics and government are so complicated that sometimes I don't understand what's happening."; Vote meaningless: "Since so many people vote in elections, it really doesn't matter whether I vote or not."; Corruption widespread: "There is widespread corruption among those who govern the country."; Politicians nonresponsive: "Generally speaking, the people who are elected to the [NATIONAL PARLIAMENT] stop thinking about the public once they're elected."; Officials nonresponsive: "Government officials pay little attention to what citizens like me think."

Table 13.8 Determinants of rejection of unrestricted leader system in unstable democracies

Rejection of unrestricted leader	Nepal 2005	Pakistan 2005	Thailand 2004	Thailand 2007	Afghanistan 2005	Cambodia 2004	Cambodia 2007	Kazakhstan 2005	Kyrgyzstan 2005	Russia 2008	Uzbekistan 2003	Uzbekistan 2005
Male	0.377** (0.183)	0.315 (0.248)	0.263 (0.171)	0.374** (0.157)	-0.200 (0.227)	-0.009 (0.206)	-0.327 (0.209)	-0.183 (0.170)	0.179 (0.192)	-0.122 (0.154)	-0.087 (0.183)	0.028 (0.183)
Age	-0.009 (0.008)	-0.026*** (0.008)	-0.013* (0.008)	-0.014** (0.006)	0.008 (0.007)	-0.006 (0.009)	0.004 (0.008)	-0.008 (0.006)	0.000 (0.007)	0.011** (0.006)	-0.001 (0.008)	-0.010 (0.007)
Self-employed	-0.396 (0.388)	0.773*** (0.210)	0.222 (0.192)	-0.048 (0.181)	0.038 (0.240)	-0.195 (0.400)	-0.068 (0.323)	0.156 (0.349)	-0.317 (0.263)	0.062 (0.277)	0.131 (0.306)	0.286 (0.323)
Unemployed	-0.275 (0.194)	0.321 (0.271)	0.008 (0.230)	0.224 (0.211)	-0.209 (0.247)	0.023 (0.217)	-0.049 (0.225)	-0.362* (0.192)	0.012 (0.202)	-0.280 (0.183)	0.048 (0.196)	0.217 (0.203)
Education	0.078 (0.056)	-0.074 (0.067)	0.062 (0.066)	-0.163** (0.081)	-0.053 (0.066)	0.195** (0.096)	0.250** (0.126)	-0.166** (0.066)	0.083 (0.063)	0.154** (0.072)	0.027 (0.066)	0.060 (0.068)
Income	0.161*** (0.033)	-0.048 (0.053)	0.019 (0.023)	0.060*** (0.020)	-0.174 (0.111)	0.077* (0.045)	0.028 (0.043)	-0.006 (0.020)	0.010 (0.018)	0.062 (0.043)	0.016 (0.021)	0.050 (0.034)
Catholic												
Greek Orthodox										0.369 (0.286)		
other Christian								0.703*** (0.216)	-0.049 (0.366)		-0.162 (0.296)	0.327 (0.333)
Sunni Muslim		0.440 (0.387)						0.329 (0.206)	-0.201 (0.294)		-0.245 (0.254)	-0.121 (0.262)
Shia Muslim					-0.038 (0.277)							
Hindu	0.475 (0.309)											
Mahayana Buddhist	0.233 (0.390)											
Theravada Buddhist			0.078 (0.168)	0.247 (0.158)		0.342 (0.496)	-0.565* (0.304)					
Taoism												

No religion

	(1)	(2)	(3)	(4)	(5)	(6)	(7)	(8)	(9)	(10)	(11)	(12)
No religion										0.474 (0.342)		
No power	0.187*** (0.070)	-0.013 (0.085)	-0.192** (0.091)	-0.193* (0.101)	-0.088 (0.096)	-0.020 (0.111)	0.045 (0.103)	0.003 (0.103)	0.005 (0.098)	0.225*** (0.081)	-0.173* (0.105)	0.133 (0.111)
Politics complicated	-0.452*** (0.091)	0.083 (0.092)	0.205** (0.095)	-0.179* (0.103)	-0.109 (0.091)	0.191 (0.117)	-0.005 (0.110)	-0.149 (0.095)	-0.336*** (0.100)	-0.145** (0.073)	0.006 (0.088)	-0.106 (0.097)
Vote meaningless	-0.162** (0.081)	-0.306*** (0.068)	-0.224*** (0.091)	-0.432*** (0.066)	-0.096 (0.073)	-0.235*** (0.088)	-0.061 (0.074)	0.147* (0.076)	-0.186** (0.073)	-0.079 (0.070)	-0.048 (0.076)	-0.186** (0.080)
Corruption widespread	0.078 (0.170)	0.375*** (0.095)	0.044 (0.083)	0.223*** (0.083)	-0.170* (0.090)	0.152*** (0.080)	0.010 (0.084)	-0.027 (0.129)	-0.002 (0.109)	0.005 (0.092)	0.016 (0.107)	-0.050 (0.116)
Politicians nonresponsive	0.020 (0.157)	0.111 (0.104)	0.254*** (0.088)	0.101 (0.093)	-0.068 (0.099)	-0.138 (0.094)	0.001 (0.089)	-0.024 (0.128)	-0.070 (0.112)	-0.160 (0.110)	0.169 (0.120)	-0.015 (0.123)
Officials nonresponsive	-0.196 (0.150)	0.329*** (0.100)	-0.038 (0.093)	0.293*** (0.095)	-0.250*** (0.097)	-0.045 (0.105)	-0.011 (0.105)	0.231* (0.138)	0.234* (0.124)	0.159 (0.117)	-0.331** (0.141)	-0.068 (0.140)
Constant	0.414 (1.076)	-3.310*** (0.795)	0.271 (0.623)	1.436*** (0.555)	2.584*** (0.663)	0.399 (0.919)	1.741** (0.719)	-0.041 (0.739)	0.037 (0.879)	-2.218*** (0.640)	1.805** (0.818)	0.842 (0.904)
Number of obs	660	903	764	986	697	786	992	646	644	891	590	589
LR chi²	93.71***	91.71***	32.37***	92.58***	48.45***	34.51***	11.45	31.51***	34.05***	31.78***	15.28	21.73*
df	14	13	13	13	13	13	13	14	14	14	14	14
Pseudo R²	0.105	0.085	0.035	0.080	0.058	0.045	0.015	0.036	0.041	0.028	0.019	0.028
Log likelihood	-399.280	-495.294	-447.773	-530.564	-395.360	-364.425	-373.827	-425.155	-397.142	-556.627	-389.437	-384.034

Source: AsiaBarometer, 2003–2008

* $p < .10$, ** $p < .05$, *** $p < .01$

Note: Dependent variable: Probability of rejection of unrestricted leadership. Regression coefficients based on logistic estimation are reported. Standard errors in parentheses. No power: "Generally speaking, people like me don't have the power to influence government policy or actions."; Politics complicated: "Politics and government are so complicated that sometimes I don't understand what's happening."; Vote meaningless: "Since so many people vote in elections, it really doesn't matter whether I vote or not."; Corruption widespread: "There is widespread corruption among those who govern the country."; Politicians nonresponsive: "Generally speaking, the people who are elected to the [NATIONAL PARLIA-MENT] stop thinking about the public once they're elected."; Officials nonresponsive: "Government officials pay little attention to what citizens like me think."

Table 13.9 Determinants of rejection of unrestricted leader system in stable authoritarian countries

Rejection of unrestricted leader	Hong Kong 2006	Bhutan 2005	China 2003	China 2006	China 2008	Malaysia 2003	Malaysia 2004	Malaysia 2007	Singapore 2004	Singapore 2006
Male	-0.140 (0.168)	0.409* (0.230)	0.343 (0.225)	0.061 (0.129)	0.020 (0.145)	0.346 (0.222)	-0.279 (0.218)	-0.109 (0.175)	0.028 (0.195)	0.565*** (0.177)
Age	0.000 (0.007)	-0.016 (0.011)	-0.021* (0.011)	0.002 (0.005)	-0.008 (0.007)	-0.016* (0.009)	0.012 (0.009)	0.018** (0.007)	0.005 (0.010)	0.010 (0.008)
Self-employed	0.212 (0.463)	0.377 (0.382)	0.528* (0.306)	-0.136 (0.159)	0.497** (0.201)	0.073 (0.354)	-0.369 (0.323)	0.186 (0.277)	0.837* (0.447)	0.353 (0.387)
Unemployed	0.036 (0.187)	-0.215 (0.304)	0.291 (0.266)	-0.096 (0.166)	0.473** (0.189)	0.226 (0.243)	-0.233 (0.235)	-0.140 (0.189)	0.061 (0.209)	0.064 (0.196)
Education	0.114 (0.074)	0.109 (0.072)	-0.114 (0.091)	0.014 (0.059)	0.172** (0.086)	0.066 (0.096)	-0.007 (0.092)	0.270** (0.111)	0.044 (0.086)	0.032 (0.075)
Income	0.010 (0.024)	-0.013 (0.046)	-0.007 (0.052)	0.003 (0.025)	0.001 (0.022)	-0.033 (0.056)	0.218*** (0.052)	-0.020 (0.046)	-0.014 (0.042)	0.052 (0.040)
Catholic										
Greek Orthodox										
other Christian	-0.225 (0.263)								0.577 (0.449)	0.191 (0.408)
Sunni Muslim						0.421 (0.359)	0.212 (0.344)	0.127 (0.319)	-0.036 (0.436)	0.330 (0.376)
Shia Muslim										
Hindu						-0.592 (0.429)	-0.002 (0.441)	0.025 (0.403)	-0.597 (0.494)	0.065 (0.415)
Mahayana Buddhist	-0.251 (0.229)		-0.824 (0.836)	0.192 (0.272)	0.485 (0.355)	0.152 (0.385)	0.242 (0.377)	0.173 (0.341)	0.237 (0.393)	0.119 (0.353)
Theravada Buddhist										
Taoism									-0.206 (0.457)	0.443 (0.442)

	(1)	(2)	(3)	(4)	(5)	(6)	(7)	(8)	(9)	(10)
No religion			-0.302 (0.392)	0.291 (0.228)	0.100 (0.284)				-0.218 (0.442)	-0.037 (0.391)
No power	0.268** (0.109)	0.221* (0.127)	-0.235* (0.135)	0.127 (0.079)	0.053 (0.096)	0.334*** (0.105)	-0.199* (0.110)	0.042 (0.094)	0.365*** (0.120)	-0.121 (0.113)
Politics complicated	0.172 (0.109)	-0.035 (0.131)	0.190 (0.155)	-0.082 (0.083)	0.384*** (0.107)	0.050 (0.105)	-0.088 (0.118)	0.029 (0.101)	0.109 (0.123)	0.091 (0.114)
Vote meaningless	-0.580*** (0.101)	-0.158 (0.118)	0.033 (0.119)	-0.203*** (0.073)	-0.386*** (0.088)	-0.495*** (0.087)	-0.365*** (0.087)	-0.494*** (0.070)	-0.392*** (0.111)	-0.477*** (0.102)
Corruption widespread	-0.312*** (0.108)	0.090 (0.147)	0.029 (0.116)	0.223*** (0.056)	-0.025 (0.077)	-0.188* (0.108)	0.207* (0.115)	0.003 (0.093)	-0.494*** (0.114)	-0.230*** (0.099)
Politicians nonresponsive	-0.096 (0.107)	-0.124 (0.123)	-0.080 (0.143)	-0.105 (0.078)	-0.304*** (0.093)	0.030 (0.090)	0.158 (0.133)	0.236** (0.098)	0.119 (0.159)	0.115 (0.126)
Officials nonresponsive	0.008 (0.107)	0.028 (0.133)	0.098 (0.144)	0.223*** (0.081)	-0.113 (0.095)	0.089 (0.106)	0.158 (0.139)	-0.098 (0.109)	-0.176 (0.149)	0.160 (0.132)
Constant	2.150*** (0.683)	-1.110 (0.873)	-0.799 (0.950)	0.471 (0.465)	1.287* (0.672)	0.975 (0.908)	-0.215 (0.865)	-0.292 (0.806)	0.797 (0.903)	0.970 (0.734)
Number of obs	916	523	767	1937	968	623	677	850	571	899
LR chi²	61.01***	26.77**	40.65***	51.29***	86.51***	61.94***	48.88***	72.92***	70.31***	61.71***
df	14	13	14	14	14	15	15	15	18	18
Pseudo R²	0.058	0.047	0.042	0.029	0.070	0.084	0.062	0.066	0.091	0.063
Log likelihood	-499.414	-274.231	-460.906	-860.110	-578.504	-336.112	-368.635	-520.085	-350.547	-459.010

Source: AsiaBarometer, 2003–2008

* $p < .10$, ** $p < .05$, *** $p < .01$

Note: Dependent variable: Probability of rejection of unrestricted leadership. Regression coefficients based on logistic estimation are reported. Standard errors are in parentheses. No power: "Generally speaking, people like me don't have the power to influence government policy or actions."; Politics complicated: "Politics and government are so complicated that sometimes I don't understand what's happening."; Vote meaningless: "Since so many people vote in elections, it really doesn't matter whether I vote or not."; Corruption widespread: "There is widespread corruption among those who govern the country."; Politicians nonresponsive: "Generally speaking, the people who are elected to the [NATIONAL PARLIAMENT] stop thinking about the public once they're elected."; Officials nonresponsive: "Government officials pay little attention to what citizens like me think."

Table 13.10 Determinants of rejection of technocracy in stable democracies

Rejection of technocracy	Australia 2008	India 2003	India 2005	India 2008	Japan 2003	Japan 2004	Japan 2006	Japan 2008	Sri Lanka 2003	U.S.A. 2008
Male	-0.141 (0.158)	0.384 (0.296)	-0.187 (0.189)	0.204 (0.231)	0.333* (0.181)	0.427 (0.283)	0.455** (0.195)	0.383*** (0.182)	0.142 (0.300)	0.058 (0.146)
Age	0.012** (0.005)	0.016 (0.010)	0.012** (0.006)	0.017** (0.008)	0.019** (0.008)	-0.009 (0.012)	0.015** (0.007)	0.019** (0.008)	0.028*** (0.010)	0.010* (0.005)
Self-employed	-0.011 (0.317)	-0.412 (0.357)	-0.053 (0.243)	-0.251 (0.330)	-0.122 (0.231)	-0.032 (0.415)	-0.227 (0.262)	0.291 (0.251)	0.312 (0.354)	-0.060 (0.222)
Unemployed	-0.053 (0.180)	0.421 (0.304)	0.115 (0.198)	-0.049 (0.246)	-0.058 (0.216)	-0.169 (0.317)	-0.423* (0.234)	0.209 (0.215)	0.187 (0.313)	0.172 (0.177)
Education	0.032 (0.082)	0.095 (0.072)	-0.063 (0.052)	0.212** (0.093)	0.100 (0.063)	0.167* (0.091)	0.138* (0.072)	0.092 (0.096)	-0.071 (0.137)	-0.058 (0.082)
Income	-0.037 (0.036)	-0.009 (0.026)	-0.027 (0.036)	-0.223*** (0.073)	-0.034 (0.031)	0.029 (0.033)	0.017 (0.025)	0.027 (0.021)	0.019 (0.022)	0.063** (0.032)
Catholic	0.618** (0.303)									-0.033 (0.299)
Greek Orthodox other Christian	0.543* (0.297)									0.236 (0.287)
Sunni Muslim									-0.739* (0.447)	
Shia Muslim										
Hindu		-0.444 (0.298)	-0.149 (0.242)	-0.151 (0.309)						
Mahayana Buddhist					0.317 (0.314)	1.292 (1.080)	-0.361 (0.378)	-0.120 (0.377)		
Theravada Buddhist									-0.335 (0.276)	

	(1)	(2)	(3)	(4)	(5)	(6)	(7)	(8)	(9)	(10)
Taoism										
No religion	0.677**				0.117	1.379	−0.372	−0.308		0.074
	(0.286)				(0.249)	(1.059)	(0.367)	(0.367)		(0.333)
No power	−0.099	−0.096	0.206***	−0.160	−0.037	−0.079	−0.269***	−0.273***	−0.082	−0.053
	(0.081)	(0.113)	(0.066)	(0.118)	(0.091)	(0.129)	(0.103)	(0.096)	(0.112)	(0.082)
Politics complicated	−0.043	−0.020	−0.300***	−0.172	−0.042	−0.132	−0.045	−0.083	0.069	−0.086
	(0.077)	(0.139)	(0.088)	(0.111)	(0.102)	(0.138)	(0.109)	(0.104)	(0.124)	(0.071)
Vote meaningless	−0.080	−0.072	−0.244***	0.026	−0.159*	−0.011	−0.140	0.007	−0.008	−0.114
	(0.076)	(0.083)	(0.055)	(0.072)	(0.086)	(0.125)	(0.094)	(0.086)	(0.084)	(0.073)
Corruption widespread	−0.258***	−0.306**	−0.038	−0.436***	0.104	0.324**	−0.220**	0.001	−0.086	0.008
	(0.086)	(0.133)	(0.103)	(0.114)	(0.083)	(0.142)	(0.101)	(0.090)	(0.131)	(0.086)
Politicians nonresponsive	−0.014	0.246	0.088	−0.076	−0.016	−0.073	0.354***	0.248**	0.096	0.118
	(0.096)	(0.158)	(0.103)	(0.114)	(0.121)	(0.180)	(0.120)	(0.114)	(0.179)	(0.104)
Officials nonresponsive	−0.034	−0.044	0.370***	0.057	0.077	0.003	0.140	0.117	0.203	−0.057
	(0.105)	(0.135)	(0.096)	(0.117)	(0.126)	(0.179)	(0.122)	(0.106)	(0.172)	(0.103)
Constant	0.599	−1.611*	−1.759**	0.518	−1.959***	−3.951***	−1.434*	−2.661***	−3.438***	−0.118
	(0.683)	(0.879)	(0.728)	(0.846)	(0.726)	(1.508)	(0.810)	(0.914)	(1.259)	(0.641)
Number of obs	753	782	1164	1039	747	579	680	747	681	823
LR chi²	43.87***	18.37	642***	52.58***	30.19***	28.43***	56.72***	49.07***	17.77	23*
df	15	13	13	13	14	14	14	14	15	15
Pseudo R²	0.042	0.029	0.052	0.066	0.032	0.054	0.068	0.055	0.031	0.020
Log likelihood	−499.284	−310.243	−591.091	−373.129	−461.757	−247.464	−389.539	−425.605	−282.167	−558.448

Source: AsiaBarometer, 2003–2008

* $p < .10$, ** $p < .05$, *** $p < .01$

Note: Dependent variable: probability of rejection of technocracy. Regression coefficients based on logistic estimation are reported. Standard errors are in parentheses. No power: "Generally speaking, people like me don't have the power to influence government policy or actions."; Politics complicated: "Politics and government are so complicated that sometimes I don't understand what's happening."; Vote meaningless: "Since so many people vote in elections, it really doesn't matter whether I vote or not."; Corruption widespread: "There is widespread corruption among those who govern the country."; Politicians nonresponsive: "Generally speaking, the people who are elected to the [NATIONAL PARLIAMENT] stop thinking about the public once they're elected."; Officials nonresponsive: "Government officials pay little attention to what citizens like me think."

Table 13.11 Determinants of rejection of technocracy in new democracies

Rejection of technocracy	Bangladesh 2005	Indonesia 2004	Indonesia 2007	Mongolia 2005	Philippines 2004	Philippines 2007	S. Korea 2003	S. Korea 2004	S. Korea 2006	Taiwan 2006
Male	0.683 (0.420)	0.377* (0.212)	-0.501*** (0.178)	0.275 (0.177)	0.285 (0.177)	0.334** (0.159)	0.102 (0.228)	-0.415** (0.190)	-0.102 (0.192)	-0.130 (0.198)
Age	-0.025* (0.013)	0.005 (0.009)	-0.002 (0.007)	-0.002 (0.007)	0.031*** (0.008)	0.007 (0.006)	-0.003 (0.011)	0.000 (0.010)	-0.007 (0.009)	-0.024** (0.011)
Self-employed	0.050 (0.322)	0.027 (0.266)	0.455** (0.207)	0.116 (0.235)	-0.001 (0.253)	-0.010 (0.198)	-0.089 (0.256)	0.208 (0.213)	0.019 (0.247)	0.223 (0.257)
Unemployed	-0.297 (0.438)	0.186 (0.227)	-0.259 (0.207)	-0.247 (0.211)	0.109 (0.198)	0.178 (0.184)	-0.484* (0.288)	-0.251 (0.232)	0.112 (0.213)	-0.112 (0.237)
Education	0.108 (0.097)	0.032 (0.083)	0.127 (0.115)	0.046 (0.064)	0.016 (0.059)	-0.038 (0.067)	-0.180** (0.085)	-0.002 (0.068)	-0.100 (0.123)	-0.239* (0.122)
Income	0.030 (0.031)	0.074* (0.044)	-0.015 (0.039)	0.055 (0.074)	-0.038 (0.025)	0.056*** (0.021)	-0.086* (0.048)	0.001 (0.039)	0.002 (0.043)	0.014 (0.021)
Catholic					0.266 (0.270)	0.093 (0.215)				
Greek Orthodox other Christian							-0.221 (0.376)	-0.510* (0.310)	0.254 (0.330)	
Sunni Muslim	0.378 (0.378)	-0.524* (0.285)	-0.180 (0.265)							
Shia Muslim										
Hindu										
Mahayana Buddhist				0.294 (0.205)			-0.739 (0.387)	-0.145 (0.315)	-0.093 (0.346)	-0.032 (0.270)
Theravada Buddhist										
Taoism										0.281 (0.247)

	(1)	(2)	(3)	(4)	(5)	(6)	(7)	(8)	(9)	(10)
No religion								−0.297 (0.352)	−0.483* (0.290)	0.122 (0.317)
No power	0.095 (0.125)	−0.220** (0.098)	−0.020 (0.096)	−0.045 (0.083)	−0.261*** (0.092)	−0.145* (0.086)	0.042 (0.097)	−0.165 (0.101)	0.099 (0.112)	−0.158 (0.119)
Politics complicated	0.061 (0.136)	−0.207** (0.104)	−0.121 (0.099)	0.069 (0.086)	0.248** (0.101)	0.143 (0.091)	0.433*** (0.149)	−0.083 (0.126)	−0.045 (0.125)	0.043 (0.128)
Vote meaningless	−0.028 (0.100)	0.111 (0.092)	−0.104 (0.092)	0.059 (0.073)	−0.035 (0.079)	−0.008 (0.064)	−0.002 (0.091)	−0.008 (0.075)	0.017 (0.080)	−0.063 (0.106)
Corruption widespread	−0.195 (0.143)	−0.056 (0.074)	0.329*** (0.085)	0.015 (0.097)	−0.086 (0.091)	0.093 (0.087)	−0.016 (0.168)	0.013 (0.135)	−0.137 (0.134)	0.016 (0.125)
Politicians nonresponsive	−0.297** (0.129)	0.305*** (0.108)	−0.166* (0.093)	0.095 (0.121)	−0.031 (0.101)	0.200** (0.095)	−0.043 (0.159)	−0.107 (0.148)	0.006 (0.135)	0.214* (0.113)
Officials nonresponsive	−0.325** (0.145)	−0.223** (0.112)	−0.264** (0.102)	0.047 (0.110)	0.145 (0.106)	−0.125 (0.095)	−0.093 (0.172)	0.089 (0.146)	−0.104 (0.134)	−0.287** (0.132)
Constant	0.206 (1.235)	−0.430 (0.671)	0.310 (0.668)	−2.300*** (0.725)	−1.609** (0.713)	−2.552*** (0.596)	−1.234 (1.143)	0.478 (0.905)	−0.353 (1.020)	0.668 (1.105)
Number of obs	938	746	935	673	671	817	727	743	950	957
LR chi²	35.99***	35.02***	47.36***	14.02	33.44***	29.96***	29.4**	18.18	8.11	24.27**
df	13	13	13	13	13	13	15	15	15	14
Pseudo R²	0.069	0.042	0.044	0.017	0.039	0.028	0.046	0.022	0.009	0.031
Log likelihood	−243.393	−404.718	−514.105	−403.338	−415.287	−527.333	−302.744	−404.555	−434.541	−379.066

Source: AsiaBarometer, 2003–2008

* p < .10, ** p < .05, *** p < .01

Note: Dependent variable: probability of rejection of technocracy. Regression coefficients based on logistic estimation are reported. Standard errors are in parentheses. No power: "Generally speaking, people like me don't have the power to influence government policy or actions."; Politics complicated: "Politics and government are so complicated that sometimes I don't understand what's happening."; Vote meaningless: "Since so many people vote in elections, it really doesn't matter whether I vote or not."; Corruption widespread: "There is widespread corruption among those who govern the country."; Politicians nonresponsive: "Generally speaking, the people who are elected to the [NATIONAL PARLIAMENT] stop thinking about the public once they're elected."; Officials nonresponsive: "Government officials pay little attention to what citizens like me think."

Table 13.12 Determinants of rejection of technocracy in unstable democracies

Rejection of technocracy	Nepal 2005	Pakistan 2005	Thailand 2004	Thailand 2007	Afghanistan 2005	Cambodia 2004	Cambodia 2007	Kazakhstan 2005	Kyrgyzstan 2005	Russia 2008	Uzbekistan 2003	Uzbekistan 2005
Male	0.507** (0.228)	-0.281 (0.268)	-0.326** (0.163)	0.155 (0.141)	0.381 (0.346)	-1.011** (0.484)	0.222 (0.275)	-0.285 (0.188)	-0.138 (0.226)	0.191 (0.178)	-0.033 (0.182)	0.223 (0.186)
Age	0.006 (0.010)	-0.003 (0.008)	-0.003 (0.008)	-0.004 (0.006)	0.008 (0.010)	0.022 (0.020)	-0.001 (0.011)	0.019*** (0.007)	0.005 (0.008)	0.010 (0.007)	0.013 (0.008)	0.002 (0.007)
Self-employed	-0.512 (0.532)	0.499** (0.236)	0.170 (0.181)	-0.366** (0.164)	-0.054 (0.323)	0.736 (0.819)	-0.398 (0.497)	0.666* (0.352)	-0.314 (0.322)	-1.250*** (0.456)	-0.056 (0.299)	0.012 (0.315)
Unemployed	0.224 (0.237)	0.310 (0.298)	-0.423* (0.232)	0.182 (0.184)	-0.298 (0.367)	0.063 (0.444)	0.054 (0.291)	-0.451** (0.219)	-0.129 (0.234)	0.029 (0.209)	-0.245 (0.194)	-0.039 (0.205)
Education	0.205*** (0.070)	0.005 (0.071)	-0.079 (0.062)	-0.137* (0.072)	-0.166* (0.098)	0.335*** (0.157)	0.075 (0.150)	0.109 (0.074)	0.118 (0.075)	-0.028 (0.085)	0.012 (0.065)	-0.085 (0.068)
Income	0.052 (0.039)	-0.086 (0.058)	0.024 (0.021)	0.037** (0.017)	-0.223 (0.157)	-0.044 (0.093)	0.029 (0.055)	0.023 (0.021)	-0.027 (0.020)	0.072 (0.051)	0.029 (0.021)	0.040 (0.035)
Catholic												
Greek Orthodox										0.439 (0.362)		
other Christian								0.046 (0.236)	-0.510 (0.397)		0.599** (0.293)	-0.447 (0.332)
Sunni Muslim		-0.111 (0.367)						-0.070 (0.224)	-0.712** (0.310)		0.469* (0.251)	-0.073 (0.261)
Shia Muslim					-0.977* (0.537)							
Hindu	-0.208 (0.359)											
Mahayana Buddhist	-0.015 (0.453)											
Theravada Buddhist			0.374** (0.162)	0.468*** (0.139)		-0.788 (0.802)	-0.832*** (0.297)					
Taoism												

	(1)	(2)	(3)	(4)	(5)	(6)	(7)	(8)	(9)	(10)	(11)	(12)
No religion										0.450 (0.423)		
No power	0.202** (0.088)	−0.124 (0.088)	−0.048 (0.085)	0.020 (0.085)	0.018 (0.136)	0.223 (0.275)	0.193 (0.133)	−0.064 (0.114)	0.175 (0.122)	−0.190** (0.090)	−0.007 (0.100)	0.170 (0.113)
Politics complicated	−0.170 (0.105)	0.148 (0.098)	−0.021 (0.091)	−0.216** (0.088)	−0.180 (0.127)	0.304 (0.318)	−0.225 (0.140)	−0.094 (0.105)	−0.132 (0.119)	−0.136 (0.083)	−0.212** (0.087)	0.011 (0.097)
Vote meaningless	0.087 (0.094)	−0.176** (0.072)	0.063 (0.088)	−0.182*** (0.061)	0.127 (0.108)	−0.213 (0.216)	−0.161 (0.103)	0.161* (0.084)	−0.076 (0.085)	0.044 (0.081)	−0.083 (0.075)	−0.135* (0.080)
Corruption widespread	−0.073 (0.198)	−0.017 (0.095)	0.044 (0.080)	0.155** (0.077)	0.024 (0.130)	0.642** (0.252)	−0.036 (0.109)	−0.107 (0.144)	−0.291** (0.123)	0.241** (0.111)	0.069 (0.106)	0.078 (0.117)
Politicians nonresponsive	−0.036 (0.185)	0.317*** (0.112)	0.008 (0.085)	0.051 (0.083)	−0.176 (0.137)	−0.047 (0.185)	−0.227** (0.114)	−0.075 (0.143)	−0.044 (0.131)	0.106 (0.132)	−0.218* (0.119)	−0.021 (0.123)
Officials nonresponsive	−0.138 (0.175)	−0.051 (0.100)	−0.028 (0.089)	0.330*** (0.089)	−0.124 (0.138)	−0.201 (0.220)	0.151 (0.136)	0.329** (0.161)	0.128 (0.145)	0.120 (0.138)	0.179 (0.136)	0.156 (0.142)
Constant	−2.049 (1.256)	−1.583* (0.810)	−0.512 (0.604)	−1.255** (0.514)	−0.229 (0.901)	−7.086*** (2.086)	−1.522* (0.887)	−2.668*** (0.838)	0.033 (1.002)	−3.153*** (0.769)	−0.246 (0.793)	−1.753* (0.923)
Number of obs	660	903	764	986	697	786	992	646	644	891	590	589
LR chi^2	34.98***	37.51***	18.07	67.27***	22.54***	28.14***	22.18*	30.43***	20.23	34.23***	24.43**	14.13
df	14	13	13	13	13	13	13	14	14	14	14	14
Pseudo R^2	0.056	0.040	0.019	0.051	0.047	0.120	0.044	0.040	0.032	0.037	0.030	0.018
Log likelihood	−292.414	−451.076	−479.538	−625.056	−230.939	−103.481	−239.381	−367.945	−311.034	−441.998	−396.687	−381.099

Source: AsiaBarometer, 2003–2008

* $p < .10$, ** $p < .05$, *** $p < .01$

Note: Dependent variable: probability of rejection of technocracy. Regression coefficients based on logistic estimation are reported. Standard errors are in parentheses. No power: "Generally speaking, people like me don't have the power to influence government policy or actions."; Politics complicated: "Politics and government are so complicated that sometimes I don't understand what's happening."; Vote meaningless: "Since so many people vote in elections, it really doesn't matter whether I vote or not."; Corruption widespread: "There is widespread corruption among those who govern the country."; Politicians nonresponsive: "Generally speaking, the people who are elected to the [NATIONAL PARLIAMENT] stop thinking about the public once they're elected."; Officials nonresponsive: "Government officials pay little attention to what citizens like me think."

Table 13.13 Determinants of rejection of technocracy in stable authoritarians

Rejection of technocracy	Hong Kong 2006	Bhutan 2005	China 2003	China 2006	China 2008	Malaysia 2003	Malaysia 2004	Malaysia 2007	Singapore 2004	Singapore 2006
Male	-0.215 (0.161)	0.116 (0.224)	0.343 (0.225)	-0.135 (0.150)	0.054 (0.197)	0.055 (0.200)	-0.082 (0.188)	-0.033 (0.182)	-0.253 (0.202)	0.336** (0.152)
Age	0.005 (0.007)	-0.028*** (0.011)	-0.021* (0.011)	-0.007 (0.006)	0.006 (0.010)	0.005 (0.008)	0.006 (0.008)	0.009 (0.007)	0.010 (0.010)	-0.007 (0.007)
Self-employed	-0.666 (0.503)	-0.102 (0.404)	0.528* (0.306)	-0.319* (0.183)	0.225 (0.252)	-0.372 (0.303)	0.161 (0.287)	0.179 (0.282)	-0.417 (0.455)	0.139 (0.289)
Unemployed	-0.049 (0.178)	0.370 (0.267)	0.291 (0.266)	-0.245 (0.194)	-0.409 (0.274)	-0.437** (0.222)	0.050 (0.204)	-0.145 (0.197)	-0.147* (0.218)	0.143 (0.173)
Education	-0.017 (0.072)	-0.031 (0.073)	-0.114 (0.091)	-0.239*** (0.071)	0.059 (0.117)	-0.053 (0.083)	0.064 (0.081)	-0.049 (0.116)	0.035 (0.089)	-0.086 (0.066)
Income	-0.012 (0.023)	0.082* (0.045)	-0.007 (0.052)	0.034 (0.027)	-0.028 (0.031)	0.053 (0.051)	0.122*** (0.046)	-0.097** (0.049)	-0.009 (0.042)	0.049 (0.033)
Catholic										
Greek Orthodox										
other Christian	-0.093 (0.252)								-0.012 (0.432)	1.227*** (0.373)
Sunni Muslim						-0.180 (0.321)	0.199 (0.295)	0.568 (0.366)	-0.237 (0.446)	0.553 (0.359)
Shia Muslim										
Hindu						-0.339 (0.407)	-0.071 (0.390)	0.655 (0.445)	-0.713 (0.544)	0.355 (0.403)
Mahayana Buddhist	-0.155 (0.232)	0.797 (0.508)	-0.824 (0.836)	-0.479 (0.321)	-0.812* (0.453)	0.063 (0.349)	-0.269 (0.321)	0.043 (0.396)	-0.025 (0.389)	0.937*** (0.339)
Theravada Buddhist										
Taoism									-0.655 (0.487)	0.681* (0.402)

	(1)	(2)	(3)	(4)	(5)	(6)	(7)	(8)	(9)	(10)
No religion	0.103 (0.101)	−0.302 (0.392)	−0.280 (0.263)	−0.629* (0.341)					−0.199 (0.446)	1.128*** (0.368)
No power		0.307** (0.131)	−0.235* (0.135)	−0.359*** (0.089)	−0.174 (0.129)	0.005 (0.092)	−0.222** (0.094)	−0.033 (0.098)	0.146 (0.119)	−0.299*** (0.097)
Politics complicated	−0.138 (0.100)	−0.150 (0.132)	0.190 (0.155)	0.035 (0.094)	−0.054 (0.144)	0.093 (0.095)	−0.123 (0.103)	0.176* (0.105)	−0.224* (0.123)	−0.093 (0.094)
Vote meaningless	−0.118 (0.093)	−0.080 (0.121)	0.033 (0.119)	0.037 (0.083)	0.311*** (0.120)	−0.376*** (0.086)	−0.183** (0.079)	−0.147** (0.073)	−0.464*** (0.117)	−0.002 (0.090)
Corruption widespread	0.329*** (0.101)	−0.209 (0.145)	0.029 (0.116)	0.111 (0.069)	0.228** (0.112)	−0.254*** (0.094)	0.101 (0.101)	−0.221** (0.095)	−0.219* (0.119)	−0.259*** (0.091)
Politicians nonresponsive	−0.068 (0.101)	−0.123 (0.120)	−0.080 (0.143)	0.170* (0.090)	−0.097 (0.124)	0.024 (0.078)	0.008 (0.122)	0.151 (0.105)	0.422*** (0.159)	−0.036 (0.108)
Officials nonresponsive	−0.164 (0.102)	−0.018 (0.131)	0.098 (0.144)	−0.044 (0.093)	0.172 (0.130)	0.023 (0.095)	0.048 (0.126)	0.086 (0.118)	−0.140 (0.148)	0.177 (0.113)
Constant	−0.647 (0.652)	−0.627 (0.916)	−0.799 (0.950)	−0.469 (0.551)	−2.948*** (0.919)	0.780 (0.823)	0.262 (0.770)	−1.356 (0.863)	0.188 (0.931)	0.432 (0.644)
Number of obs	916	523	767	1937	968	623	677	850	571	899
LR chi^2	24.34**	25.03**	13.78	37.41***	25.79**	39.93***	31.63***	38.83***	48.48***	61.64***
df	14	13	14	14	14	15	15	15	18	18
Pseudo R^2	0.022	0.043	0.023	0.027	0.034	0.048	0.034	0.038	0.068	0.051
Log likelihood	−535.190	−281.862	−295.662	−683.133	−361.432	−400.041	−451.670	−488.328	−332.394	−570.559

Source: AsiaBarometer, 2003–2008

* $p < .10$, ** $p < .05$, *** $p < .01$

Note: Dependent variable: Probability of rejection of technocracy. Regression coefficients based on logistic estimation are reported. Standard errors are in parentheses. No power: "Generally speaking, people like me don't have the power to influence government policy or actions."; Politics complicated: "Politics and government are so complicated that sometimes I don't understand what's happening."; Vote meaningless: "Since so many people vote in elections, it really doesn't matter whether I vote or not."; Corruption widespread: "There is widespread corruption among those who govern the country."; Politicians nonresponsive: "Generally speaking, the people who are elected to the [NATIONAL PARLIAMENT] stop thinking about the public once they're elected."; Officials nonresponsive: "Government officials pay little attention to what citizens like me think."

It is only when office holders are untrustworthy that people tend to become more cautious and prefer the constraints on the government that a democratic system can provide. This distinctive notion of power might also explain the unexpected positive influence of political inefficacy on democratic attitudes among citizens in democratic countries. If Asian people think of themselves as powerful, this might allow them to accept non-democratic systems that effectively delegate decision-making to office holders.

Conclusion

This chapter, using AsiaBarometer Survey data from 2003 to 2008, has explored the micro foundation of democracy in Asia, a region with a great deal of diversity in terms of the types of political systems currently in place and political history. Questions on the desirability of a democratic regime and three non-democratic alternatives revealed, first of all, that national averages of support for democracy in Asian countries, including those in non-democracies, are as high as in established Western democracies such as the U.S.A. and Australia if measured through a simple and direct way, but not if measured through a more indirect and tactical way such as denial of non-democratic alternatives. In particular, technocracy has the potential to be widely accepted throughout Asia. Second, multiple regression analyses showed that religion, socioeconomic status, and political attitudes other than regime preference respectively have independent effects on the probability of support for democracy. No simple pattern has emerged, however. Members of the same religious group were more sympathetic or hostile to democracy depending on the country to which they belong. The same was true for socioeconomic status: neither the self-employed nor the unemployed were consistently more democratic than the employed, although education and income generally correlated positively with democratic attitudes. Also, a sense of political inefficacy and the untrustworthiness of incumbents had associations with the probability of rejection of non-democratic systems, but the standard explanations based on political psychology, especially those originating in the Western literature, are of limited relevance in fully explaining the changing, if not contradictory, findings: the trustworthiness of incumbents in a democratic system, which should normally reinforce belief in the functioning of democracy, sometimes tended to cultivate authoritarian tendencies in Asia. Therefore, we referred to the distinctive notion of power, or the legitimacy of dependence in Asia as pointed out by Pye to interpret this paradoxical pattern. Asian cultures commonly tend to idealize benevolent, paternalistic leadership and to legitimate dependency. Autonomy, self-determination, and self-rule are not necessarily moral imperatives in Asia.

What then are the possible implications of our study for democracy in Asia? In the first place, we have to be careful when measuring citizens' attitudes toward democracy. It makes no sense taking at face value answers to a direct and simple question such as "Do you think a democratic system desirable?" Second, since education and income have relatively consistent influences that enhance democratic attitudes, development seems to do less harm than good anyway. Also important is the enhancement of a sense of political efficacy, because a lack thereof consistently undermines support for democracy. In the meantime, however, cultivating trustworthiness through, for example, the realization of good governance does not necessarily reinforce democratic attitudes among citizens due to the distinctive meaning of authority in Asia. Therefore, we probably need to consider Asia-specific devices for good governance and the deepening of democratization.

Notes

1 The AsiaBarometer project has been supported by various organizations: in 2003, by an assortment of business donations; in 2004, by the Ministry of Foreign Affairs of Japan; and from 2005 onwards, by the Grant-in-Aid for Scientific Research of the Japanese Ministry of Education, Culture, Sports, Science and Technology with the project identification number 17002002.
2 See the project website at https://www.asiabarometer.org/.
3 The question used in the World Values Survey is very similar to the above question: Q. I'm going to describe various types of political systems and ask what you think about each as a way of governing this country. For each one, would you say it is a very good, fairly good, fairly bad or very bad way of governing this country? Items asked about are (1) having a strong leader who does not have to bother with parliament and elections; (2) having experts, not government, make decisions according to what they think is best for the country; (3) having army rule; and (4) having a democratic political system. That is, the only notable difference is in the response categories. While the questionnaire used for the AsiaBarometer Survey adopts a three-point measure, the World Values Survey divides negative answers into two degrees. See http://www.worldvaluessurvey.org/.
4 Two samples (Maldives 2005 and Turkmenistan 2005) were dropped from the following analyses due to the unreliability of responses to these variables.
5 Due to the ambiguity or inconsistency in religious distribution, three samples (Sri Lanka 2005, Thailand 2003, and Tajikistan 2005) were dropped from the following analyses.
6 These variables are not standardized because we had no intention of conducting a pooled-sample analysis.
7 The response categories are "strongly agree," "agree," "neither agree nor disagree," "disagree," and "strongly disagree." The higher the value, the stronger the degree of agreement to the statement. "Don't know" answers were included in "neither agree nor disagree" because they effectively indicate an indecisive attitude.
8 For more details on these control variables and the demographic variables, see the fieldwork reports at https://www.asiabarometer.org/.

Bibliography

Almond, G. and Verba, S. (1963) *The Civic Culture: political attitudes and democracy in five nations*, Princeton: Princeton University Press.
Diamond, L. (1999) *Developing Democracy: toward consolidation*, Baltimore and London: Johns Hopkins University Press.

Easton, D. (1965) *A Systems Analysis of Political Life*, New York: John Wiley & Sons.

Holsti, K. J. (1996) *The State, War, and the State Of War*, Cambridge: Cambridge University Press.

Huntington, S. P. (1991) *The Third Wave: democratization in the late twentieth century*, Oklahoma: University of Oklahoma Press.

Linz, J. (1978) *The Breakdown of Democratic Regimes: crisis, breakdown, and reequilibration*, Baltimore: Johns Hopkins University Press.

Linz, J. and Stepan, A. (1996) *Problems of Democratic Transition and Consolidation: southern Europe, South America, and post-communist Europe*, Baltimore: Johns Hopkins University Press.

Mattes, R. and Bratton, M. (2007) "Learning about democracy in Africa: awareness, performance, and experience," *American Journal of Political Science*, 51: 192–217.

Mikami, S. (2008) "Popular support for democracy and democratic governance of the state: an empirical analysis based on the World Values Survey Data," in Takayuki Ito (ed.) *Between Structures and Institutions: evolving conflict over regime change*, Tokyo: Shobunsha, pp. 121–53.

Moore, B. Jr. (1966) *Social Origins of Dictatorship and Democracy*, Boston: Beacon Press.

Przeworski, A. (1986) "Some problems in the study of the transition to democracy," in G. O'Donnell, P. C. Schmitter and L. Whitehead (eds) *Transitions from Authoritarian Rule: comparative perspectives*, Baltimore: Johns Hopkins University Press, pp. 47–63.

Pye, L. (1985) *Asian Power and Politics: The cultural dimensions of authority*, Cambridge, MA: Harvard University Press.

Rueschemeyer, D., Stephens, E. H., and Stephens, J. D. (1992) *Capitalist Development and Democracy*, Chicago: University of Chicago Press.

Rustow, D. A. (1970) "Transitions to democracy: Toward a dynamic model," *Comparative Politics*, 2: 337–63.

Tessler, M. and Gao, E. (2005) "Gauging Arab support for democracy," *Journal of Democracy*, 16: 83–97.

Tsunekawa, K. and Washida, H. (2007) *"Yoron chousa de yomu raten amerika no minshuka to minshushugi" [Democratization and democracy in Latin America: an analysis based on the survey data]*, paper presented at the annual meeting of the Japanese Political Science Association, Tokyo, 9–10 June 2007.

Welzel, C. (2007) "Are levels of democracy affected by mass attitudes? Testing attainment and sustainment effects on democracy," *International Political Science Review*, 28(4): 397–424.

Welzel, C. and Inglehart, R. (2006) "Democratization as the growth of freedom: The human development perspective," *Japanese Journal of Political Science*, 6: 313–43.

Index

Please note that page references to Notes will have the letter 'n' following the note. References to Figures or Tables will be in *italic* print.

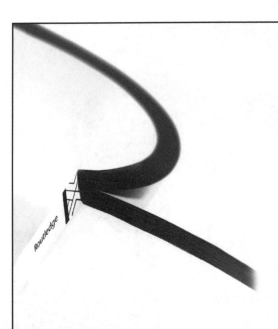